T0323375

The Collected Papers of Leonid Hurwicz

The Collected Papers of Leonid Hurwicz

Volume 1

Edited by Samiran Banerjee

Emory University
Funded in part by The Heller-Hurwicz Economics Institute
University of Minnesota

OXFORD
UNIVERSITY PRESS

OXFORD
UNIVERSITY PRESS

Oxford University Press is a department of the University of Oxford.
It furthers the University's objective of excellence in research, scholarship,
and education by publishing worldwide. Oxford is a registered trade mark of
Oxford University Press in the UK and certain other countries.

Library of Congress Cataloging-in-Publication Data

Names: Banerjee, Samiran, editor.
Title: The collected papers of Leonid Hurwicz / edited by Samiran Banerjee,
Emory University. Description: [New York] : Oxford University Press, [2022] | "Funded in
part by The Heller-Hurwicz Economics Institute, University of
Minnesota"—Title page. | Includes bibliographical references and index.
Identifiers: LCCN 2021056049 (print) | LCCN 2021056050 (ebook) |
ISBN 9780199313280 (hardback) | ISBN 9780190236328 (epub)
Subjects: LCSH: Hurwicz, Leonid. | Economics, Mathematical. | Mathematical
optimization. Classification: LCC HB135 .C6234 2022 (print) | LCC HB135 (ebook) |
DDC 330.01/51—dc23/eng/20211129
LC record available at https://lccn.loc.gov/2021056049
LC ebook record available at https://lccn.loc.gov/2021056050

1 3 5 7 9 8 6 4 2

Printed by Integrated Books International, United States of America

To my parents,
Niranjan and Ila Banerjee

Preface

This is the first of four volumes of the collected papers of Leonid Hurwicz, one of the premier mathematical economists of the twentieth century whose research spanned over six decades. A co-recipient of the 2007 Nobel Memorial Prize (with Eric Maskin and Roger Myerson) for "laying the foundations of mechanism design"—the design of decentralized institutions to bring about socially desirable outcomes when markets may fail to do so—Leo's contribution to economics has been far wider, ranging from econometrics, programming, and decision theory to microeconomic theory. It has been said that his classic 1971 paper with Hirofumi Uzawa on the integrability of demand functions alone qualified him for the Nobel.

Volume 1 is intended for an audience of non-specialist readers, a kind of a collector's edition for those of us who knew him and introducing him to those who did not. I have tried to highlight not just Leo's intellectual contribution, but also Leo the person. The book is divided into three parts. Part One is biographical, beginning with my essay on Leo's educational background in economics. This is of special interest since, remarkably, he never received a formal degree in the discipline where he left his mark. In other essays commissioned for this volume, his co-authors and long-time friends, Ken Arrow, Eric Maskin, Tom Marschak, and Roy Radner, provide their own reminiscences. A letter sent to Leo on the occasion of his ninetieth birthday celebration by Paul Samuelson is also included.

Part Two is the main collection of essays and talks that provide an overview and evolution of Leo's thinking on mechanism design over from 1969 to 1998, beginning with the ideas of centralization and decentralization, modeling economies as adjustment processes and game-forms, their incentive and informational issues, and including evolving ideas on how to model institutions. Many of these essays are scattered as chapters in books and are difficult to come by, so by presenting these in one volume, a new generation of researchers may be stimulated to pursue and develop these ideas.* Also

---

* For instance, in Chapter 15, Leo introduced the notion of an *extensive mechanism*, an extensive form game with outcomes instead of payoffs, and where outcomes could be associated with intermediate nodes, not just terminal nodes. As far as I am aware, this idea has not been pursued in the literature.

included is an early and more detailed version of what became Leo's Nobel lecture, and Roger Myerson's inaugural Hurwicz Lecture from the 2006 North American Econometric Society meetings which follows up on some of the ideas and themes in Leo's work.

Finally, Part Three is a collection of miscellanea, from book reviews of the seminal von Neumann and Morgenstern's *Games and Economic Behavior* and Debreu's classic *Theory of Value*, to expositional papers on game theory and decision theory for the uninitiated. Also included is a mimeo to the DFL party of Minnesota to ensure greater representation of the views of minority groups; it formed the basis of the "walking subcaucus" system that was adopted to elect delegates in proportion to their support. The volume ends with a complete bibliography of Leo's published works. Like the biographical essays, Chapters 12, 18, and 26 are being published for the first time.

The volumes yet to be published comprise Leo's technical papers, of interest to the specialist. Volume 2 is slated to cover his contribution to econometrics, decision theory, and programming; Volume 3 to the incentive and informational aspects of mechanism design; and Volume 4 to other papers in microeconomic theory. Each volume is slated to include previously unpublished research that was found in the Hurwicz archive at Duke University's David M. Rubenstein Special Collection.

As editor, I have taken certain liberties. First, all end-of-chapter references now follow the same format, and any original references to working papers or mimeos which were subsequently published have been tracked down and cited. Second, perhaps because he was a student of law, Leo had an inordinate love for footnotes which were frowned upon by editors of journals in the days before computerized typesetting. Consequently, it appears that he included many remarks in the body of his papers (sometimes parenthetically) that rightfully belonged in footnotes. I have accordingly relegated such remarks to footnotes, making the papers more readable. Third, I have inserted some editorial comments in footnotes ending in '—SB'. Any corrections or changes in the body of the text is included within square brackets. Fourth, I have added a postscript to some chapters to incorporate extra material that I found in the Hurwicz archive at Duke University, providing glimpses of his personality and sense of humor in some instances. Fifth, I have re-drawn all the original graphs. Finally, in what I hope is a pleasant surprise, I have interspersed a few scans of the distinctive doodles reminiscent of Kandinsky that Leo drew on the margins of his research papers as another dimension of his creativity.

This has been a daunting and gargantuan endeavor that I, as one of Leo's last doctoral students, decided to undertake only because no one else was doing so. Indeed, anyone who knew Leo encouraged me in my efforts, often adding that they were very glad *not* to be the one doing it! My sincere thanks and gratitude go to:

(a) V. V. Chari and Ellen McGrattan, the erstwhile and current Directors of the Heller-Hurwicz Economics Institute of the University of Minnesota, for underwriting this series with the generous financial support of the Institute;

(b) Terry Vaughn, my first editor at OUP, who was insistent that Leo's intellectual output not remain dispersed in the literature;

(c) the Hurwicz family, especially Ruth and David Markovitz, for the legal permission to curate these volumes and more;

(d) Will Hansen and Elizabeth Dunn, the erstwhile and current research services librarians at the David M. Rubenstein Rare Book and Manuscript Library at Duke University, who have helped with accessing items from the Hurwicz archive over the course of six visits and several requests by email; and

(e) Jeffrey Berk, Vanessa Renteria, Christiana Ting, Aditi Sarkar, and Kristi Yu, who helped to photocopy, proof-read chapters, and verify references at different times.

My deepest gratitude, however, goes to Wendy Williamson, the economics librarian at the University of Minnesota and walking economics encyclopedia. She, among other things, painstakingly put together Leo's comprehensive bibliography, chased down citations, and single-handedly did the paperwork to obtain the copyright clearances. This volume would not have been possible without her dedication, support, patience, and friendship.

This book was typeset in LaTeX using TeXShop on a MacBook Pro based on the transcriptions of the originals by Srinivasa Rao Kotte of Aditya Infotech, Hyderabad, India. All graphs were drawn using EazyDraw for Mac. I thank Everett Ayoubzadeh for the frontispiece photo; the photo on page 2 taken by David Valdez was provided by the George H. W. Bush Presidential Library. I alone am responsible for all aspects of the final product.

As with all things having to do with Leo, this volume has taken an inordinately long time to put together, about twelve years. All I can say in my defense is that it has been a single person's labor of love and I hope the final product is something that Leo himself would have approved of.

Contents

Contents

Part I
Biography and Reminiscences

Part One begins with a biography where an attempt has been made to answer a question that have intrigued many: how much formal economics was Leo exposed to as a student and who were the luminaries who likely influenced his thinking? Ken Arrow's eulogy to his lifelong friend and intellectual companion is augmented by a postscript, a tribute from 1977 when Leo was elected a Distinguished Fellow of the American Economic Association. Eric Maskin, Tom Marschak, and Roy Radner speak of their experiences in working with him. A final humorous tribute comes from Paul Samuelson, a letter he wrote on the occasion of Leo's ninetieth birthday in 2007.

Receiving the National Medal of Science in 1990, with President George H. W. Bush and First Lady Barbara Bush

1

Leo Hurwicz: A Biography

Samiran Banerjee

The Early Years

According to Leonid Hurwicz's passport, he was born on August 21, 1917,[1]
to Abraham and Zophia Hurwicz in Moscow, Russia at a time of historical
tumult, in-between the February revolution that overthrew the Romanov
dynasty and the October revolution that ushered in the Soviet Union. After
World War I ended, the family returned to Warsaw in 1919 by horse-drawn
wagon when Leo was fourteen months old.

The earliest story about Leo[2] apparently dates back to before he could
read. Somebody gave him a set of dominoes which he arrayed in increasing
order, and halfway, arrayed them in reverse order so that the sum of the dots
on any two dominoes were a constant. From that, the sum of the dots on
all dominoes could be easily calculated. This was the same idea that Gauss
discovered at the age of 8 for counting the sum of all the numbers from 1 to
100, except that Leo was much younger.

His father, who had graduated from the Faculty of Law of the Sorbonne in
Paris and Kharkhov University in Russia, was a member of the bar in Warsaw,
a social democrat, and one of "the most active members of the League of
Socialist Lawyers," one of the few political bodies which had been always

I thank Wendy Williamson and Tapen Sinha in helping me put together this biography. In
doing so, I have used documents I encountered while researching the Hurwicz archive at Duke
University's David M. Rubenstein Special Collection, including carbon copies of many letters that
Leo wrote and other memorabilia. I alone am responsible for any factual inaccuracies.

[1] Whether this date refers to the Julian calendar under which he was born, or the modern
Gregorian calendar that was adopted in Russia the following year, is unclear. It is, however, entirely
appropriate for a lover of footnotes as Leo was, that his biography begin with one!

[2] As recounted by Stanley Reiter on the occasion of Leo's ninetieth birthday celebration in
Minneapolis on April 14, 2007.

Samiran Banerjee, *Leo Hurwicz: A Biography* In: *The Collected Papers of Leonid Hurwicz Volume 1.*
Edited by Samiran Banerjee, Oxford University Press. © Oxford University Press 2022.
DOI: 10.1093/oso/9780199313280.003.0001

consistently opposed to both Nazism and Communism.[3] His mother was a school teacher who taught him and his brother, Henryk (born November 1, 1922), reading, writing, and arithmetic at home until Leo was 9, when he attended a private institution, the gimnazjum Spójnia, attended and staffed by Jews. His high school transcript reveals that he studied Polish, Latin, and German, among other subjects.

The University Years in Europe

From 1934 to 1938, Leo attended the University of Warsaw (then called Uniwersytet im. Józefa Piłsudskiego), earning an L.L.M. (Magister Utriusque Iuris), a Master of Laws degree in both civil and canon law. This was to be the only degree that he officially earned in his entire life. Additionally, over the period 1935–38, he attended the Warsaw Conservatory of Music[4] and studied the piano under M. Klimont-Jacynowa. In 1936, Leo received a French language diploma from the Warsaw extension of Université de Paris, Sorbonne; in 1937, it appears he traveled to France to obtain a Diplome de Langue Française from the Université de Poitiers.

I had once asked Leo if he faced any anti-Semitism while growing up. He told me that he was fortunate enough not to have been personally targeted, though during the time he attended university, the practice of 'ghetto benches' had been introduced in Polish universities where Jewish students were forced to sit on the left-hand side of lecture halls. At first the rector of the University of Warsaw failed to intervene, and he and other Jewish students protested by standing at the back of the class for an entire year until the practice was revoked.

According to an undated typed record, Leo wrote that even though he was studying law in Warsaw, his "chief subject of studies was political economy (i.e., economics)." Additionally, during this time, he studied experimental physics under then rector, Stefan Pieńkowski, at the Institute for Experimental Physics and acquired "a certain knowledge of mathematics and statistical methods." Leo's father, perhaps sensing potential difficulties in setting up a law practice in Poland in the changing climate of Europe, suggested that Leo apply to the London School of Economics (LSE) seeking a doctoral degree, which he did in early July 1938. His professor, Antoni Kostanecki, wrote that Leo had been attending his seminar in economics for three years. In the first

---

3 Letter dated June 7, 1941, from Cambridge, MA.
4 Now renamed the Fryderyk Chopin University of Music, after Chopin who studied there from 1826–29.

year, he presented "the general outline of the Böhm-Bawerk theory" showing "unusual and outstanding intelligence." He advised him to study the wider problem of "devaluation in the modern sense" on which he presented a series of papers in his second and third years, confirming the professor's hope that he would be able to pursue a doctoral thesis on the subject [5] In early November, Leo was interviewed by P. Barrett Whale at the LSE and admitted for a Ph. D.[6]

Over the next nine months, Leo took twelve courses: seven on money, credit, banking, and international trade, three with Nicholas Kaldor (The Theory of Production, Advanced Problems of Economic Theory—Statics and Dynamics, Public Finance and the Trade Cycle), one with R. G. D. Allen (Introduction to Mathematical Economics), and one with Lionel Robbins (Theories of Economic Policy). In addition, he was a member in two seminars with D. H. Robertson (Advanced Banking) and J. B. Condliffe (International Economic Relations). According to Leo, his English was still rudimentary, and the classes he understood best were taught by the Hungarian economist, Kaldor. "He had a worse accent than I did," Hurwicz recalled, "but I could understand it, so I took all the courses he was teaching."[7,8]

Not all of this time was spent studying, however. On February 2, 1939, Leo wrote to the secretary of LSE:

> I hereby apply for the use of the piano in Founders' Room. During the period 1935–38 I was a student if (*sic*) the State Academy of Music in Warsaw ('Coureratorium'). The most convenient time would be 3.30–5.00 p.m. but if this were impossible, I should be able to find some other time.
>
> I would play of course serious music only, e.g. Beethoven, Mozart, Haydn, Schumann, Chopin.

A week later came the reply:

> I am pleased to give permission for the remainder of this term for you to use the piano in the Founders' Room from 3.30 to 5 p.m. on Mondays and Thursdays, on the usual understanding that it may be necessary from time to time to grant other persons permission to use the room for purposes which will prevent you from playing, and on the understanding that according to the rules, serious music is played.

---

[5] Letter dated September 15, 1938, from Warsaw.

[6] Much of the following is taken from Jim Thomas's May 2009 mimeo, 'The Postgraduate File of Leonid Hurwicz at the London School of Economics 1938–1939: A Summary'.

[7] Obituary in *The Telegraph*, June 26, 2008.

[8] Although Friedrich von Hayek was on the faculty at LSE, Leo did not study with him formally. He did, however, attend his lectures.

Leo's proposed thesis under the supervision of Whale, *The currency deval-uation with further reference to the experience of the Gold Bloc countries*, was approved and he was given permission to travel to France and Switzerland at the end of July 1939 to collect data. His permission to remain in the UK expiring on August 1, Leo left on August 2 for Paris, reaching Berne on the 26th, and arriving in Geneva on September 2, 1939, the day after Germany invaded Poland in the blitzkrieg.

In the first ten weeks of the war, he had no news about his parents or younger brother, other than that the street in Warsaw where his home stood "had been almost completely destroyed by bombs."[9] Eventually, he received a letter that despite having to leave everything behind, they were all alive and in good health in Bialystok in the Russian-occupied part of Poland. Abraham Hurwicz was, however, eventually arrested by the Russians under the charge that he was "capable of intellectual leadership."[10] Later Leo found out that they were all sent to a gulag in the Arctic Circle, to Kargopolsky in Archangelsk, where they were made to fell trees in the marshy forests of the tundra.[11] He would not be reunited with them till after the war.

Not knowing how long the war might last and "in order not to lose time", he registered with the Postgraduate Institute for International Studies in Geneva and continued to work on his thesis under the supervision of Ludwig von Mises whose seminar he attended, while attempting to get an entry visa to the US. Meanwhile, he also attended two other seminars offered by William Rappard (International Contemporary Problems) and Wilhelm Röpke (Economic Stabilization and other Problems of International Economic Policy).

Obtaining an entry visa to the US at that time was not a simple task: Leo needed letters and affidavits. Earlier, he had been introduced to Oscar Lange by a mutual colleague, A. Krishnaswami, when Lange visited LSE. On November 1, 1939, Lange, who was then an associate professor at the University of Chicago, vouched for Leo saying "I know Mr. Hurwicz personally, and appreciate his intellectual and scholarly qualities very highly" and that "he would qualify as a first rate graduate student at the University of Chicago." Leo's relatives in Chicago, Helen Kotzin and her son Theodore, were willing to serve as his US sponsors.

---

9 Letter dated March 3, 1940, from Geneva, quoted in Jim Thomas's 2009 mimeo.
10 As recounted by Marcel (Ket) Richter on the occasion of Leo's ninetieth birthday celebration, "Those of us who had the privilege of knowing him, know that he was seriously guilty of the charge. And it appears to be a hereditary condition."
11 Letter dated June 7, 1941, from Cambridge, MA.

C O P Y .

Address any reply to
THE COMMISSIONER OF POLICE OF THE
METROPOLIS, NEW SCOTLAND YARD, S.W.1
quoting: -

79/H/2618 (C.2 M)

Postage must be prepaid

Your Ref. 111.G.6.1940.

NEW SCOTLAND YARD,
LONDON, S.W.1.

Telephone:
Whitehall 1212

18 March, 1940.

Sir,

      With reference to your letter of the 28th
February, 1940, respecting Mr. Leonid Hurwicz, I am directed
by the Commissioner of Police of the Metropolis to say that
this man was properly registered with the Police when resident
in this country and that nothing is known by the Police to his
detriment.

        I am, Sir,

             Your obedient Servant,

             (Signature)

             p. Assistant Commissioner

The Minister,
  Swiss Legation,
    18, Montagu Place,
      Bryanston Square,

        W.1.

Last but not least, he needed Certificates of Good Conduct from every country he had traveled to in the previous six months. He was able to obtain them from the Swiss and the French but not the British. At this point, the 22-year-old Leo asked the Swiss police to write to Scotland Yard if they had any untoward information on him while he was residing in London. The reply (see above) served as his British Certificate of Good Conduct and he was finally able to obtain his American visa at the beginning of May.

On May 22, 1940, Leo purchased a steamer ticket in Geneva on an Italian ship, *Augustus*, departing on June 4 for New York from Lisbon. A week later, he caught a Swissair flight to Barcelona, and completed his journey to Madrid and Lisbon by train only to discover that as an Axis power, Italian ships were no longer allowed to dock in the US. With difficulty, he harassed the harbormaster to recoup his money back from the Italian liner but was still short $40 for buying a ticket on a Greek vessel. While it is unclear whether he received the funds his relatives from Chicago had cabled him, he earned money tutoring the children of rich families vacationing in Estoril, a resort west of Lisbon. Eventually, he was able to buy a new ticket and board the *Nea Hellas* on July 30, 1940, to begin a new chapter of his life. Leo arrived in Hoboken, New Jersey, on August 11 and headed to Chicago to live with the Kotzins.

The University Years in the US

By mid-September, Leo was enrolled at the University of Chicago, taking one course titled International Economic Policies. Carbon copies of several typed letters to various people provide an interesting glimpse into his new world. In a letter to L. G. Robinson at LSE, he reminisces that "The year that I have spent there remains in my mind not only as very useful for my knowledge of economics (certainly more important than any other of my six years of university), but also as the most pleasant because of the 'general atmosphere' and friendliness which is so characteristic for LSE."

As regards his impressions of the University of Chicago, "[it] seems to be rather nice tho' very reactionary and orthodox", he writes in another letter. "I met Viner, Knight and other local celebrities... and didn't think much of them." Elsewhere, he says that he is "frightfully busy... writing two articles which I intend to publish. One is mainly statistical and concerns problems of what they call 'Armaments economics'. The other one is very theoretical and concerns the socialist economic theories of the last twenty years or so."[12] About a week later, he writes that "[a]t the present time I am taking advantage of free time and I am learning some mathematics, some statistics, not economics."[13]

A month later, Leo writes "At the present moment I am working with Viner which requires a good deal of patience on my part. Maybe on his too..." in one letter, and in another:

> ... [I] quarrel with Prof. Viner and Knight just as if it was another Mises or Röpke. The University is very pleasant and, as far as economics is concerned—probably the one in the US. I have reason to expect some sort of research assistanceship (sic) before long, perhaps combined with a certain amount of teaching (for the Undergraduates, of course). Strangely enough the field will be statistics, a thing that I would never have foreseen.[14]

---

[12] Letters dated September 12, 1940, from Chicago, IL. One wonders if the latter marked the beginning of his formulation of what constitutes a decentralized mechanism, an early mimeo of which appeared in 1948, and was eventually published (at Arrow's insistence) as his seminal 1960 paper.
[13] Letter dated September 18, 1940, from Chicago, IL.
[14] Letters dated October 27, 1940, from Chicago, IL.

Indeed, upon Lange's recommendation to Paul Samuelson at MIT,[15] 23-year-old Leo was given a grant from the Babson Fund and made a research assistant to 25-year-old Samuelson who was to teach a statistics class at MIT in the spring of 1941. He probably headed over to Cambridge, MA, in early 1941—incidentally, receiving an incomplete in his International Economic Policies class that remained on his transcript.

Over the period from February to June 1941, Leo enrolled at Harvard, taking two classes, Mathematical Economics with mathematician Edwin B. Wilson (who was Samuelson's mentor at Harvard), and Monopolistic Competition and Allied Problems with Edward Chamberlin, in addition to a seminar on Business Cycles and Economic Forecasting with Joseph Schumpeter and Gottfried Haberler. It was here that he met the Norwegian economist, Trygve Haavelmo, who was finishing his methodological doctoral thesis titled *On the theory and measurement of economic relations* which clarified the probability foundations of econometrics and discussed what was later to be called the 'identification problem'.[16] In the preface from the mimeo of April 1941, Haavelmo writes " . . . I am indebted to Mr. L. Hurwicz, research assistant at the Massachusetts Institute of Technology, for reading the manuscript and for valuable comments." Leo therefore was not merely present at the birth of modern econometrics, he apparently was a participant.

Leo declined a Harvard Fellowship award and chose to return to Chicago where he pursued classes (listed in the table below) over the next several years with the aim of getting his doctorate degree. In 1944, he passed language examinations in German and French, and in 1946, he filed a thesis in preparation titled *Basic postulates of the theory of economic fluctuations and their relation to empirical evidence*[17] which was never completed.

Term	Year	Course	Title
Summer	1941	MATH 1/2c. 359	Modern Theory of Integration
		MATH 1/2c. 459	Topics in the Theory of Integration
Autumn	1941	ECON 304	Economic Theory and Social Policy
Winter	1942	STAT 331	Survey of Mathematics of Statistics
Spring	1942	MATH 365	General Limits
Summer	1942	ECON 411	Statistical Economics
		MATH 322	Lattice Theory
		S.SCI 322	The US and Civilization
Spring	1945	ECON 499	Research in Statistics

[15] See Chapter 6, Samuelson's humorous letter read on the occasion of Leo's ninetieth birthday celebration in this volume.

[16] Haavelmo's thesis was subsequently published as Haavelmo (1944) and singled out for its pioneering contribution in his 1989 Nobel Prize citation.

[17] See the *American Economic Review* from 1946, 36(4) p. 748. An untitled and undated carbon copy of fifty-six typed pages that concern "the study of the nature of macro-dynamic models and their properties" and "the study of the manner in which observational data can be used to choose among the various possible models" in the Rubenstein archive is possibly a fragment of this unfinished thesis.

In addition to taking classes, this period of five years from 1941 to 1946 proved to be a time of intellectual ferment while Leo was busily employed in several parallel positions. He taught mathematics and other courses in the electronics program of the US Army Signal Corps at the Illinois Institute of Technology in 1941, followed by a stint in the Institute of Meteorology at the University of Chicago from 1942 to 1944 where he "taught prospective Army and Navy inductees statistics, mathematics and physics needed to analyze weather data"[18] and was also a research associate. Through the Cowles Commission for Research in Economics under Jacob Marschak which had recently moved to the University of Chicago in 1939, Leo served on two National Bureau of Economic Research committees in 1941–42, as executive secretary on the Committee for Price Determination where he worked with Oscar Lange, and as associate director on the Committee on Price Control and Rationing where he worked with Theodore Yntema. Leo became a Research Associate with the Cowles Commission from 1942–46 which serendipitously amassed some of the best minds in econometric research and economic theory in the subsequent years.[19] He also taught statistics in the department of economics from 1942 to 1944.

After a couple of book reviews that appeared in *American Economic Review* in 1943, 1944 marked Leo's first publication in *Econometrica*, titled 'Stochastic models of economic fluctuations' which emanated from his interest in business cycles and econometrics. This was work he had begun under the Babson Fund grant at MIT in 1941 and continued under a Social Science Research Committee grant at the University of Chicago in 1941–42.

In 1944, he was a special consultant with the Weather Division of the US Army Air Forces in Washington, DC. In the words of Ket Richter, he was "investigating statistical systems for long-range [3-day] weather forecasting when he received some upsetting news: his assistant back in Meteorology had quit. On the phone he was advised that a young economics undergraduate named Evelyn Jensen had applied for the job and that she seemed very bright. So Leo hired her sight unseen. What he didn't know was that his previous assistant had told Evelyn that it was a really great job. The only problem with it was the man she had to work for." That problem notwithstanding, Leo and Evelyn were married on July 19, 1944.

In October 1944, Leo applied for a Guggenheim Memorial Foundation Fellowship to "reexamine the basic concepts and assumptions of the theory of economic fluctuations, to facilitate the comparison of, and the choice

---

18 See Ann Bauer's 'Leonid Hurwicz's game' in *Twin Cities Business*, March 1, 2008.
19 These included several future Nobel laureates—Trygve Haavelmo, Tjalling Koopmans, Lawrence Klein, Kenneth Arrow, and Herbert Simon, joined in later years by Gérard Debreu, Harry Markowitz, Franco Modigliani, and James Tobin. Among other important figures were Theodore Anderson, Herman Rubin, Gerhard Tintner, and Abraham Wald.

between, alternative hypotheses; thereby to contribute to the unification of this branch of economics, so that foundations for empirical studies and rational policies may be laid." Not only did he receive the fellowship for the year beginning June 1, 1945, he was appointed associate professor of economics at Iowa State College with a leave of absence during the period of the fellowship. Together with work he had begun earlier at the Institute of Meteorology, this fellowship would lead to five papers in econometrics that were eventually published in Koopmans (1950). Thus began his long academic career that spanned over six decades.

The Faculty Years

Leo continued his association with the Cowles Foundation as a research consultant from 1946 onwards, coming regularly to staff meetings from Ames, Iowa, by train. He became an associate editor of the *Journal of the American Statistical Association* and was elected Fellow of the Econometric Society. He also was an intermittent consultant to the US Bureau of Standards.

Around this time, Koopmans had told Leo[20] about his work on a resource allocation problem which later became known as the 'transportation problem': given (a) a number of ports, (b) for each pair of ports the cost of shipping from one to another, and (c) a preassigned pattern of demands at some ports and supplies at others, determine the shipping plan that minimizes the total cost. A colleague at the Institute of Meteorology, an applied mathematician, had moved to the US Bureau of Standards in DC where he became aware of the linear programming formulations of activity analysis by George Dantzig and Marshall Wood[21] and had spoken to Leo about it. As recounted by Arrow, "Leo claimed he didn't fully understand either linear programming or the transportation problem, but he could recognize that the two were similar."

Earlier, during their honeymoon, Leo and Evelyn had crossed a shallow brook on foot, accomplished by stepping in zig-zag fashion on selective stones on the river bed. It had struck him that a linear programming problem could be analogously solved by moving from vertex to vertex along the edges of the polyhedron described by the constraints, and in the direction where the objective is increasing. He must have shared some ideas with Koopmans, for Koopmans arranged for Dantzig and Leo to meet in the summer of 1947. In the words of Dantzig, "Leo and I kicked around an idea we called 'climbing up the beanpole', which was a precursor of the simplex method. It assumed the variables summed to unity. Later I generalized the

---

[20] This is based on Arrow (2008).
[21] Published later as Dantzig and Wood (1951).

procedure by getting rid of the convexity constraint."[22] In his initial and classic presentation of this method, Dantzig writes that "[t]he general nature of the 'simplex' approach...was stimulated by discussions with Leonid Hurwicz" and acknowledges Koopmans "whose constructive observations regarding properties of the simplex led directly to a proof of the method in the early fall of 1947."[23,24]

During 1948, Leo was on the staff of the research division of the United Nations Economic Commission for Europe in Geneva. Upon his return in December 1948, he became associate professor in the departments of economics and sociology at Iowa State College. From Fall 1949, he joined the University of Illinois, Urbana-Champaign, as research professor of economics and mathematical statistics, part of an ambitious initiative by the then-dean of the College of Commerce and Business Administration, Howard Bowen, to make the department into one of the best in the country. But Bowen's attempt to modernize the department of economics ran against the old guard. At the height of McCarthyism in 1950, even the adoption of Samuelson's 1948 text, *Economics: An Introductory Analysis* (which was to become the most widely used textbook for beginning economics) was politicized and viewed as an infiltration of New Dealers who espoused welfare-state and deficit-spending Keynesian theories. Bowen resigned in December 1950, followed by the department chair and seven other faculty in July 1951, including Leo, who said that "the atmosphere is not favorable for a scientist who must feel free in his inquiry."[25]

Walter Heller at the University of Minnesota recruited Leo as professor of mathematics and economics in September 1951 and he remained there for the rest of his life, continuing to become chair of the statistics department in 1961 and Regents' Professor of Economics in 1969. Heller (who served as the Chair of the Council of Economic Advisers in the Kennedy and Johnson administrations) and Leo became close colleagues and were responsible for building the department of economics with spectacular hires that led to its ranking in the top 5 in the US in the 1980s. These included three future Nobel laureates: Ed Prescott (awarded in 2004), and Tom Sargent and Chris Sims (awarded in 2011).

[22] See Albers, Reid, and Dantzig (1986), p. 309.

[23] See Dantzig 1951, p. 339, n. 1.

[24] When Koopmans was subsequently awarded the Nobel Prize in 1975 along with Leonid Kantorovich of the Soviet Union for their contribution to the theory of optimal resource allocation, which included specifically their work on linear programming, he was distressed that Dantzig had not shared the Prize. Koopmans then decided to devote one-third of his Prize to the establishment of a fellowship in honor of Dantzig.

[25] Letter to the President of the University of Illinois, Dr. George D. Stoddard, dated July 24, 1951. See Solberg and Tomilson (1997) for a detailed account of the controversy.

As Leo's academic career took off, he and Evelyn began their family of what was to be four children: Sarah (Kogut, born 1946), Michael (in 1949), Ruth (Markovitz, in 1951), and Maxim (in 1953).

His professional life was punctuated by many honors and accolades, from becoming Fellow of the Econometric Society in 1949 to becoming its President in 1969, and receiving the first of his honorary doctorates from Northwestern University in 1980, followed by Universitat Autònoma de Barcelona, Spain in 1989, Keio University, Japan and the University of Chicago in 1993, Warsaw School of Economics, Poland, in 1994, and Bielefeld University, Germany, in 2004. Leo became the inaugural Curtis L. Carlson Professor of Economics at Minnesota in 1989, received the National Medal of Sciences from President George H. W. Bush in 1990, and in 2007 at 90 years of age, the Nobel Memorial Prize in Economics (along with Eric Maskin and Roger Myerson), becoming the oldest recipient of the Prize in any discipline at that time.[26,27] Too frail to travel to Stockholm to receive the award, the Swedish ambassador to the US, Jonas Hafström, presented the medal to Leo in a contemporaneous ceremony at the University of Minnesota on December 10, 2007.

Outside of his academic career, Leo was a lifelong Democrat. When Eugene McCarthy of Minnesota challenged the incumbent President Lyndon B. Johnson for the Democratic nomination in the election of 1968, he served as a McCarthy delegate from Minnesota to the Democratic Party Convention in Chicago and as a member of the Democratic Party Platform Committee. He helped design the 'walking subcaucus' method of allocating delegates among competing groups with the idea of protecting the rights of minority groups to elect delegates representing their interests (see Chapter 26 in this volume) which is still used today by the Minnesota DFL (Democratic-Farmer-Labor) Party. He remained engaged in politics, even attending a precinct caucus in February 2008 which Barack Obama won over Hillary Clinton.

At Leo's ninetieth birthday celebration in April 2007, Ken Arrow took the podium to remind the audience of what he considered to be Leo's "greatest triumph in the political sphere", his role in saving the life of an ex-colleague and co-author Andreas Papandreou, whose father, Georgios Papandreou, had been the prime minister of Greece:

> In 1967, Andreas was arrested [in] a coup led by colonels...who took over the Greek government and drove out the politicians including Andreas' father and

---

[26] His lifelong friend and co-author of many papers and two books, Ken Arrow, had been the youngest to receive the Nobel Prize in 1972.

[27] When I called to congratulate him at 6:30 in the morning as soon as the news came on the radio, Leo chuckled and said he had only received it because he was still alive, since the Nobel could not be awarded posthumously. He also said that the phone call an hour earlier from the Nobel committee came from someone who introduced himself as Adam Smith and spoke with a British accent, leading him to think that perhaps it was a prank!

arrested Andreas. We had every reason to believe that his life was in very grave danger.... Immediately, Leo got on the phone; he must have been on the phone 24 hours a day as far as I could make out! I would hear from him once or twice a day and he was calling about 50 other people at the same time. We had a telephone campaign to get the officials in every level in Washington involved. I remember some poor Assistant Secretary [of State for the Near East and North Africa]...Luke Battle...who indicated rather clearly that he had been getting lots and lots of calls, all driven by Leo who is the center of this academic network pushing for Andreas'...safety and life. In the end, we finally managed to reach the highest levels. This was...via Ken Galbraith who was a critic of the [Vietnam] war and not friendly with [Lyndon] Johnson at this point, nevertheless knew plenty of people including Joseph Califano [Special Assistant to Johnson and later Secretary of Health, Education, and Welfare]....Johnson was in Germany attending Adenauer's funeral, came back and immediately went to a diplomatic reception. Califano caught him on the floor of the reception and told him the great concern that Leo Hurwicz and the whole academic contingent were zealously worried about, Papandreou's life.

To which President Johnson famously replied, "Call up Ken Galbraith and tell him that I've told those Greek bastards to lay off that son-of-a-bitch—whoever he is." Papandreou was released shortly thereafter and allowed to leave Greece.[28]

Final Words

Leo was perennially curious about nearly everything, especially the origins and meanings of names and places, and had a prodigious memory. On his ninetieth birthday celebration in April 2007 in Minneapolis, he appeared somewhat frail as he spoke a bit haltingly, but his mind was as agile as ever. He greeted everyone in person and found something personal to say to all the people from his past who had gathered. Upon seeing me, for example, he shook my hand and said "You know, Shomu, you are the only person who published a paper with my name in the title," referring to a note I had published more than a dozen years earlier.[29] When I expressed my surprise that he remembered, he said "Oh, one does not forget something like that!"

Everybody who knew Leo, knew his inimitable sense of humor and has their own favorite anecdote. My own stems from a brown-bag lunch seminar I attended in the department of mathematics at the University of Minnesota in the late 1980s. I sat down next to Leo as he was finishing his lunch which

---

[28] See Parker (2005), p. 432.
[29] See Banerjee (1994).

consisted of a roast beef sandwich, a Tupperware of freshly sliced green and red peppers, tomato, and carrots, and a Ziploc bag of some cookies. These last he offered to me, telling me that Evelyn had made them herself. "They're very healthy you know, low in fat and sugar, and containing oat flour and raisins which are high in fiber", he said, urging me to take one. "Strictly medicinall" he added with a twinkle in his eyes.

It seems fitting to end with this quip from his ninetieth birthday celebration. Speaker after speaker had come to the podium to pay homage to Leo's 'first ninety years'. Towards the end, Leo piped up with "Can I make a brief comment?" and proceeded:

> I have one comment that occurred to me while I was listening to various words of unlimited praise. That is something that I heard from the executive secretary of the department of the Institute of Meteorology. He said that there was a group of us once and we were talking about the weather yesterday and it was a very stormy kind of summer afternoon weather and there was hail. One of the meteorologists present said "You know, I saw some pieces of hail that were one inch in diameter." And then the man sitting next to him, he said "Well, I saw something that was the size of a baseball." The third one said "Well, I saw something that looked more like a football." And there was one man left, and he only made this comment: "The first liar hasn't got a chance!"

Leo remained active in research until the end; he died of renal failure on June 24, 2008. To state that his intellectual output spanned econometrics, decision-making under ambiguity, linear and non-linear programming, consumer theory, general equilibrium, and the pioneering study of economic mechanisms in its incentive and informational aspects does not do him justice. By preserving Leo's intellectual legacy for posterity, it is hoped that this and the forthcoming volumes of his collected papers will facilitate future generations of researchers to build on his work.

References

Albers, D., C. Reid, and G. Dantzig (1986) An interview with George B. Dantzig: The father of linear programming, *The College Mathematics Journal*, 17(4): 292–314.

Arrow, K. (2008) George Dantzig in the development of economic analysis, *Discrete Optimization*, 5(2): 159–67.

Banerjee, S. (1994) An alternative proof of the Hurwicz (1972) impossibility theorem, *Economics Letters*, 44(4): 397–401.

Dantzig, G. (1951) Maximization of a linear function of a linear function of variables subject to linear inequalities, in T. Koopmans (ed.), *Activity Analysis of Production and Allocation*, 339–47. New York, NY: Wiley.

Haavelmo, T. (1944) The probability approach in econometrics, *Econometrica*, 12 (Supplement): 1–115.

Hurwicz, L. (1944) Stochastic models of economic fluctuations, *Econometrica*, 12(2): 114–24.

Koopmans, T. (1950) *Statistical Inference in Dynamic Economic Models*. New York, NY: John Wiley.

Parker, R. (2005) *John Kenneth Galbraith: His Life, His Politics, His Economics*. Chicago, IL: University of Chicago Press.

Solberg, W. and R. Tomilson (1997) Academic McCarthyism and Keynesian economics: The Bowen controversy at the University of Illinois, *History of Political Economy*, 29(1): 55–81.

Wood, M. and G. Dantzig (1951) The programming of interdependent activities: General discussion, in T. Koopmans (ed.), *Activity Analysis of Production and Allocation*, 15–18. New York, NY: Wiley.

2

Leonid Hurwicz: An Appreciation

Kenneth J. Arrow

I come to speak of that transforming figure in modern economic theory, Leonid Hurwicz. Let me first locate him in space and time. We are today accustomed to the international mobility of academics. It is hard to imagine staffing our universities, maintaining our research capabilities, even filling our graduate student ranks, without the influx of foreign scholars at all levels. Leo was also part of an international migration but under vastly different circumstances. It was not driven by voluntary decisions. It was the result of political oppression, racial discrimination, and war on a scale and with an extent that we fortunately have not approached again.

Leo and I were part of the staff of the Cowles Commission for Research in Economics during the period that it was located in Chicago. The first director, Jacob Marschak, was thrice a refugee. Tjalling Koopmans was in neutral Geneva, when his native Netherlands was invaded. Trygve Haavelmo, from Norway, was caught in the United States by the outbreak of war.

Leo's family had been caught up in the plagues of the time. Polish, they had fled from the invading German armies in both world wars. Leo was therefore born in Moscow in 1917, though the family returned to Poland at the end of World War I. Leo attended Josef Piłsudski University (now the University of Warsaw) and graduated with a law degree (in "both" the laws, i.e., civil and canon law). I have not been able to determine just how he received any kind of education in either mathematics or economics. Evidently, he was interested enough in economics to attend the London School of Economics in 1938–39. There was an outstanding group of economists there at that time, but perhaps the most intellectually influential was Friedrich von Hayek.

Written November 29, 2016, for this volume, it is a slightly revised version of a talk delivered at the American Economic Association on January 3, 2009, honoring the recipients of the Nobel Memorial Prize in Economic Science for 2007. Arrow died on February 21, 2017.

Kenneth J. Arrow, *Leonid Hurwicz: An Appreciation* In: *The Collected Papers of Leonid Hurwicz Volume 1*. Edited by Samiran Banerjee, Oxford University Press. © Oxford University Press 2022. DOI: 10.1093/oso/9780199313280.003.0002

In 1939–40, Leo attended the Postgraduate Institute of International Studies in Geneva, though already a refugee from a Poland fallen to German and Soviet invasion. Leo's parents and brother fled to the relatively more hospitable Soviet Union, where they were incarcerated in a prison labor camp. They did return to Poland in 1945 and then migrated to the United States.

Leo did manage to leave Geneva and migrated to the United States in 1940, on a ship from Lisbon. He was briefly a research assistant for Paul Samuelson and then went to Chicago, where he taught mathematics to Air Force weather trainees at the Institute of Meteorology. From 1944 on, he became associated with the Cowles Commission in Chicago. Among others, there were Marschak, Koopmans, Lawrence Klein, Haavelmo, Franco Modigliani (a visitor), and myself. From 1946 on, he had appointments at Iowa State College, the University of Illinois, and, from 1951 on, the University of Minnesota. It is noteworthy that, despite the paucity of academic credentials, Leo's ability was quickly and widely recognized. He was, for example, selected as early as 1945 to write an article-length review of von Neumann and Morgenstern's game-theoretic challenge to standard economic theory for the *American Economic Review*.[1]

There was at this point a widespread interest among economists in economic planning. A particular aspect was the "socialism controversy," kicked off by Ludwig von Mises's argument that rational calculation under socialism was impossible. Hayek put the argument in a more moderate form, that the information needed for achieving an optimum was widely dispersed and could not be assembled in one place. Since the relevant information existed somewhere, there was an implicit assumption that the transfer of information was costly.

A counter-argument was that a capitalist system also required the transfer of information, if only through market prices, and that a socialist system could achieve the same information transfer as a privately owned economy. The interest in market socialism was much more widespread in this period than anyone accustomed to current economic discourse might imagine. Fred Taylor's presidential address to the American Economic Association in 1928 dealt with it. My teacher, Harold Hotelling, belonged to this group. Although the study of the feasibility of market socialism had begun as early as 1906 and continued throughout the 1920s and early 1930s, it was given a most thorough and widely noticed statement by the Polish socialist economist, Oskar Lange, in 1938. Lange indeed accepted Hayek's argument but argued that the tâtonnements which explained how competitive markets in a private

---

[1] See Chapter 21, this volume.—SB

economy came into equilibrium could also be employed by a socialist state. Lange was a professor at the University of Chicago at this point; he was, in particular, responsible for bringing the Cowles Commission there. I can only assume that exposure to both Hayek and Lange must have sharpened Leo's interest in the question of the exchange of information needed to run the economy.

Leo brought his rigorous mind to stating the issue formally, in an unpublished paper about 1948. He laid bare what the problem was. He envisioned a number of agents (including possibly a central authority), each possessed of private information. The agents sent messages to each other, and there were conditions of equilibrium. The message space must be large enough to determine allocation. The allocation (how much each agent gets of each commodity) has to be conveyed, of course. The question is, how much larger the message space has to be than that specifying the allocation to insure optimality (in whatever sense is desired)? Economy calls for using as small a message space as possible. Leo used the dimensionality of the message space as a measure of its size. He showed that (under concavity) just $n - 1$ extra variables are needed (e.g., relative prices). To illustrate, consider two allocation methods under concavity: (1) prices, with supply and demand as responses, and equilibrium defined by equating aggregate supply to aggregate demand; (2) quantities for each agent, a response message giving all marginal rates of substitution, equilibrium when marginal rates are equal. Both methods yield Pareto optimal allocations, but, obviously, the second requires many more dimensions in the message space.

Those who know Leo know how perfectionist he was and how difficult it was for him to feel a paper was ready for publication. Some of us at Stanford (the mathematician, Sam Karlin, the philosopher, Patrick Suppes, and myself) were interested in developing the application of mathematical methods in the social sciences. We decided to have a conference, whose proceedings were to be published. I promptly invited Leo, to insure that his paper would finally see the light of day, though only in 1960.[2]

To this point, Leo had assumed that messages were truthful. The stress was on the difficulty of communication, not on incentives, and so the emphasis is quite different than in the subsequent development of mechanism design theory. His early theory has found more resonance today among some game theorists, under the name of 'algorithmic game theory.' At the time, there were alternative approaches, particularly the theory of teams, developed by Marschak and Roy Radner. Although, in my judgment, very interesting,

---

[2] See L. Hurwicz (1960) Optimality and informational efficiency in resource allocation processes, in *Mathematical Methods in the Social Sciences*, ed. K. Arrow, S. Karlin, and P. Suppes, 27–46. Stanford, CA: Stanford University Press.—SB

the theory of teams has not been taken up too much. The treatment of information costs in team theory has been rather arbitrary and less developed than Leo's dimensionality criterion.

In 1972, Leo restated the problem of choice in decentralized systems. He now added the important condition of incentive compatibility to the criteria for a suitable allocation system with decentralized information. He emphasized the game-theoretic formulation, now as a matter of design. The importance of Leo's statement and results has been emphasized in the Nobel lectures of Eric Maskin and Roger Myerson.[3]

Incentive-compatible allocation mechanisms had been studied earlier in specific fields, most notably, William Vickrey's idea of second-price auctions, where an optimal allocation is found as a Nash equilibrium (indeed, a dominant-strategy equilibrium) of a suitably designed game. But Leo was the first to give a general formulation into which all results could be fitted.

A compendium of the results in mechanism design found by Leo and his collaborators is to be found in the 2006 book by Leo and his close collaborator, Stanley Reiter. For a searching and yet spare statement of the essentials of mechanism design, please do read Leo's Nobel address, with a title which points the essential issue, 'But who will guard the guardians?'.[4]

Important as Leo's work on allocation mechanisms was, it was far from exhausting his contributions to economics. Let me list briefly a few other fields of his interest. The main research topic at the Cowles Commission during the days of Leo's participation was the development of statistical estimation of simultaneous equation systems. Hurwicz contributed several papers to aspects of this subject, several, notably a very general formulation of the concept of identification. Another area was a detailed study of the foundations of consumer demand theory, most notably in connection with the much-mooted question of integrability. The results appeared in 1971 as a volume of papers, edited by John Chipman, Leo, Ket Richter, and Hugo Sonnenschein.[5]

I had the great pleasure of working with Leo for a number of years on two topics closely related to his basic interest in decentralized allocation methods: gradient methods in concave programming, and the question of conditions under which tâtonnements converge under the usual Walrasian conditions.

Leo's breadth and strength of interests and feelings were felt not only in the world of economics. He had broad cultural interests, and, above all, his

---

3 See http://www.nobelprize.org/nobel_prizes/economic-sciences/laureates/2007.—SB
4 See *American Economic Review*, 2008, 98(3): 577–85, and Chapter 18 in this volume.—SB
5 See *Preferences, Utility, and Demand*, (1971), ed. J. Chipman, L. Hurwicz, M. Richter, and H. Sonnenschein. New York, NY: Harcourt Brace Jovanovich.—SB

political insights were deep and penetrating. He was my dear friend and intellectual companion for over sixty years. We will all miss him.

Editor's Postscript

In 1977, when Hurwicz was elected a Distinguished Fellow of the American Economic Association, Arrow presented the following citation:

> Leonid Hurwicz has brought to economics a rare combination of qualities: breadth of vision along with technical mastery, innovativeness and a sense of exploration combined with a thorough understanding and appreciation of orthodox theory, and perseverance in the pursuit of unfashionable directions of research together with leadership in laying the foundations for tomorrow's fashions.
>
> His work has encompassed statistical time series analysis and statistical decision theory—to which he contributed a generalized minimax principle; he participated in the early development of linear programming, and made numerous contributions to non-linear programming and programming in infinite-dimensional spaces; with Kenneth Arrow he developed the general-equilibrium dynamics of the tâtonnement price-adjustment process; with Hirofumi Uzawa he contributed significant conceptual clarification to the elusive integrability problem, which has applications in areas as diverse as demand theory and cost-benefit analysis; and he has pioneered a new approach to the study of decentralized resource allocation processes and comparative economic systems in which the adjustment mechanism itself is treated as a decision variable.
>
> An inspiring and witty teacher and colleague, his impatience with pomposity and obfuscation has been matched by his patient encouragement to all who would learn. By insisting that in deductive reasoning logic admits of no compromise, and by training students to think clearly and to be suspicious of unclear arguments, he has done much to enhance economics as a science.

In a letter dated January 6, 1978, he wrote:

> Dear Leo:
>
> My congratulations on your election as distinguished fellow of the American Economic Association. This citation does you less than justice. Your combination of intellectual daring and solid foundation have meant a lot to the profession and to me personally.
>
> As ever,
>
> Ken

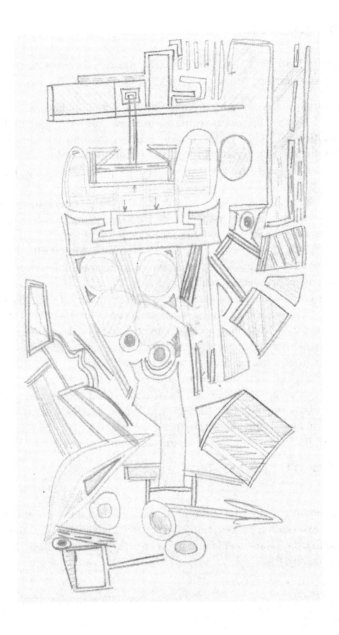

3

A Twenty-One-Year Collaboration

Eric Maskin

Leo Hurwicz quite literally changed my life. I was a math major at Harvard and had only a vague idea of what economics is all about. Then, one term I wandered almost by accident into a course on information taught by Leo's old friend, Kenneth Arrow. A major part of the course was devoted to Leo's work on mechanism design.

This was the early '70s, and mechanism design was just getting started and still on the periphery of economics. But it was soon apparent to me that this was great stuff. It had the precision and power and sometimes even the beauty of mathematics. And it could be used to answer some of the big questions of the economic world: What does decentralization mean? When does a free market perform better than a planned one? Which economic system uses information most efficiently? Leo was even able to show in a now famous theorem that in a two-person economy it is impossible to implement an efficient, individually rational allocation in dominant strategies.[1] It doesn't get better than that! So on the basis of Leo's work, I decided I would change directions and try to do mechanism design myself.

A couple of years later, Ken introduced me to Leo in person at the theory workshop then held every summer at Stanford, and I learned that mechanism design had a sense of humor—although a peculiar one. "Why do most economists prefer French fries to hash browns?", Leo asked me. It's because fries are potato optimal.

Andy Postlewaite was also at Stanford that summer, and he had discovered a puzzling phenomenon: it appeared that Walrasian outcomes on the

Written March 6, 2017, for this volume

[1] See Hurwicz (1972) On informationally decentralized systems, in *Decision and Organization: A Volume in Honor of J. Marschak*, ed. Roy Radner and Bernard McGuire, 297–336. Amsterdam: North-Holland.—SB

Eric Maskin, *A Twenty-One-Year Collaboration* In: *The Collected Papers of Leonid Hurwicz Volume 1*. Edited by Samiran Banerjee, Oxford University Press. © Oxford University Press 2022. DOI: 10.1093/oso/9780199313280.003.0003

boundary of the feasible set are not implementable in Nash equilibrium—contrary to what people had previously thought. Well, Leo, Andy, and I thought about that for a while and soon got to the bottom of it. And we wrote up a short manuscript of eight pages or so—suitable for publication as a note in the *Journal of Economic Theory*.

But would Leo actually submit the paper to the journal? "Let me put it this way," said Leo. "Wouldn't you first like to know what happens if agents can destroy their endowments?" And of course we did want to know.

So, a year later, we had answered that question and now had a manuscript of thirty pages, appropriate for a regular article in *Econometrica*. But was Leo now ready to actually send it in? "Let me put it this way," he said. "Before publishing the paper we ought to find out what happens if production can occur." And we had to admit he was right.

Six years later, when we had actually done the finding out, we had a gargantuan manuscript of eighty pages that was too long for any journal. So we thought we should turn the paper into a monograph. But was Leo prepared to do this? "Let me put it this way: No. After all, the proofs and exposition still need refinement." So over the next eleven years, at erratic intervals, Leo would send Andy and me updated versions of the manuscript in which a lemma here or a definition there would be improved.

I'm pretty sure things would have continued that way indefinitely if Stan Reiter had not been gracious enough to reach the age when it became appropriate to present him with a festschrift. And so—a full twenty-one years after we had started work on it—the paper was finally published in Stan's festschrift.[2] But Leo was able to put all this in perspective. "It just goes to show," he said, "that when writing a paper, the first twenty years are always the hardest."

[2] See L. Hurwicz, E. Maskin, and A. Postlewaite (1995) Feasible Nash implementation of social choice rules when the designer does not know endowments or production sets, in *The Economics of Informational Decentralization: Complexity, Efficiency and Stability, Essays in Honor of Stanley Reiter*, ed. J. Ledyard, 367–433. Dordrecht: Kluwer Academic Publishers.—SB

4

Some Reminiscences of Leo and His Work on Informational Requirements

Thomas Marschak

Leo Discovers "Cross-Fertilization" and Learns about Space-Filling Curves

There are several ways to state formally what Leo called a "decentralized mechanism". Here is one of them. There are n persons indexed by $i \in I = \{1, \ldots, n\}$. Each person i, and no one else, observes a changing *local environment* e_i. The set of possible local environments is E_i and E denotes the Cartesian product $E_1 \times E_2 \times \cdots \times E_n$. A *message announcer* publicly announces a *trial message* m to everyone. The set of possible messages is M, often called the *message space*. Person i says "Yes" to the announcement m if m lies in the set $\mu_i(e_i) \subseteq M$,[1] where μ_i is an *equilibrium message correspondence* from E_i to M. Suppose everyone says "Yes" to the announcement m. Then m is an *equilibrium message* for the environment vector $e = (e_1, \ldots, e_n)$. An equilibrium message leads to an *outcome* or *action* $h(m)$; h is called the *outcome function*. So a mechanism on E is a triple $(M, \{\mu_i\}_{i \in I}, h)$. The *mechanism designer* is given a *goal correspondence* G from E to the set of possible outcomes, i.e., $G(e)$ is a subset of the set of possible outcomes. The designer chooses a mechanism which *realizes* the goal correspondence G. That means that for every environment there is at least one equilibrium message, and $h(m) \in G(e)$ whenever m is an equilibrium message for e.

Here is the question Leo asks, in his work on informational requirements for decentralized resource allocation mechanisms: what's the smallest

Written August 11, 2017, for this volume.

[1] Leo called this the "verification scenario".

Thomas Marschak, *Some Reminiscences of Leo and His Work on Informational Requirements* In: *The Collected Papers of Leonid Hurwicz Volume 1*. Edited by Samiran Banerjee, Oxford University Press. © Oxford University Press 2022. DOI: 10.1093/oso/9780199313280.003.0004

message space M that allows us to realize G? In a more modest form of this question we ask: what is a lower bound to the size of the message space among all the G-realizing mechanisms? Suppose we have found a lower bound. If we are lucky, then there is an economically interesting classic mechanism—perhaps a 'price mechanism' or 'competitive mechanism'—which realizes a classic goal (e.g., Pareto efficiency) and exactly meets that lower bound. Then we have shown that this classic mechanism, long claimed to have informational merit, is indeed a winner (from the informational point of view) among all the decentralized mechanisms which achieve the classic goal.[2]

While 'size' of the message space can be given several meanings, assume that M is an open set in a (finite-dimensional) Euclidean space and let the size of M be its dimension. How can we find a lower bound to the dimension of M among all G-realizing mechanisms? Let us first select a *test class* $\bar{E} = \bar{E}_1 \times \bar{E}_2 \subseteq E$.

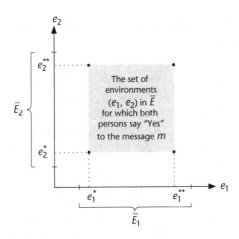

Consider the simple case of just two persons. In the figure above, the rectangle consists of all pairs (e_1, e_2) in $\bar{E}_1 \times \bar{E}_2$ such that both persons say "Yes" to the message m, i.e., m is an equilibrium message for all those pairs. The corners of the rectangle are (e_1^*, e_2^*), (e_1^{**}, e_2^{**}), (e_1^{**}, e_2^*), (e_1^*, e_2^{**}). Now suppose that m is an equilibrium message for (e_1^*, e_2^*), i.e., $m \in \mu_1(e_1^*)$, $m \in \mu_2(e_2^*)$. Suppose that m is also an equilibrium message for (e_1^{**}, e_2^{**}), i.e., $m \in \mu_1(e_1^{**})$, $m \in \mu_2(e_2^{**})$. But then m must be an equilibrium message for (e_1^{**}, e_2^*) (since $m \in \mu_1(e_1^{**})$ and $m \in \mu_2(e_2^*)$); and m must be an equilibrium message for (e_1^*, e_2^{**}) (since $m \in \mu_1(e_1^*)$ and $m \in \mu_2(e_2^{**})$). Leo called this "cross-fertilization".

---

[2] The procedure described here is sketched by Leo as a "strategy for obtaining minimality results" in Section II.3 of Hurwicz (1986).

Now suppose that the goal correspondence G has what Leo called the *uniqueness property* on the test class $\bar{E}_1 \times \bar{E}_2$. That means that *if there is an outcome that fulfills the goal G for all four corners of the rectangle, then the rectangle collapses: it must be a point.* Formally: if $G(e_1^*, e_2^*) \cap G(e_1^{**}, e_2^{**}) \cap G(e_1^{**}, e_2^*) \cap G(e_1^*, e_2^{**}) \neq \emptyset$, then $(e_1^*, e_2^*) = (e_1^{**}, e_2^{**}) = (e_1^*, e_2^{**}) = (e_1^{**}, e_2^*)$. So if G indeed has the uniqueness property on the entire test class $\bar{E}_1 \times \bar{E}_2$, then for a G-realizing mechanism and a given environment (e_1, e_2) in $\bar{E}$, there is just one message to which everyone says "Yes".

Can that message also be an equilibrium message for some other environment? Not if we further specify that for each i there is a function f_i such that $\mu_i(e_i) = \{m : f_i(m, e) = 0 \text{ for all } i\}$ and, in addition, that for all i, $f_i(m^*, e_i) = f(m^{**}, e_i) = 0$ implies $m^* = m^{**}$. Then $\mu_i(e_i)$ is a singleton. Under those conditions it is indeed the case that there is a unique equilibrium message for each environment e and that message is not an equilibrium message for any other environment.

Does that mean that the message space of a G-realizing mechanism must have at least the dimension of the test class $\bar{E}$, so that we have the lower bound that we seek? Not quite. The annoying difficulty is that one can 'smuggle' a vector of real numbers into just one real number. The pair (x, y), for example, can be smuggled into a single real number r, where x is coded as the first, third, fifth... digits of r and y is coded as the second, fourth, sixth... digits of r. Then a message space of dimension one suffices. To rule out such 'smuggling' some sort of 'smoothness' requirement has to be imposed on the μ_i.

In Leo's classic 1960 paper the sets μ_i were indeed singletons. A mechanism on E is a triple $(M, \{f_i\}_{i \in I}, h)$, where the f_i are functions, not correspondences. As just suggested, person i says "Yes" to the publicly announced message m if $f_i(m, e_i) = 0$. A mechanism's informational requirements are measured in a way that is quite different than dimension, which came well after the 1960 paper. There is only a *partial* ordering of mechanisms with respect to informational requirements.

It is based on a partitioning of the message space and refinements of the partitioning. The mechanism $(M', \{f_i'\}_{i \in I}, h')$ is *at least as informationally efficient as* the mechanism $(M, \{f_i\}_{i \in I}, h)$ if $f_i(m^*, e_i) = f_i(m^{**}, e_i)$ for all i and all $(e_1, \ldots, e_n)$ implies that $f_i'(m^*, e_i) = f_i'(m^{**}, e_i)$ for all i and all $(e_1, \ldots, e_n)$.[3]

When did Leo discover cross-fertilization and uniqueness? He may have discussed it prior to 1964 in one of the series of mathematical economics conferences organized by Stan Reiter and others at Purdue University. It certainly predated the first (February 1971) Decentralization Conference

---

[3] Leo uses slightly different notation in this definition. See Section 9 of Hurwicz (1960).

(see below). Beyond that, the dates of the discovery and its first presentation remain obscure.[4] The 'smuggling' question, on the other hand, appears in an unpublished handout which Leo and I wrote.[5] It was titled 'Informational Efficiency and Economic Organization' and we presented it on March 12, 1965, to the UCLA Colloquium on Mathematical Methods in the Behavioral Sciences (organized by Jacob Marschak). Leo's part of this paper is related to his classic 1960 paper and my part is related (but predates) my chapter in Radner and McGuire (1972).

On page 17 of this document, one finds the statement " ... disguising ... two-dimensional messages as one-dimensional ... can be ruled out by a continuity requirement". Lloyd Shapley was in the audience. He pointed out that continuity was, in fact, not enough to rule out smuggling. The Peano space-filling curve could be used. That curve is continuous and yet it allows us to map a one-dimensional set onto a higher dimensional set so that dimension one again suffices. This was new to Leo and to me. Differentiability can rule out such a mapping and so can Lipschitz-continuity.[6] Leo used a version of the latter in subsequent work.[7,8]

In the most celebrated message-space minimality result, the n persons are traders in an ℓ-commodity exchange economy, and a message is a vector of proposed prices and trades. Trader i's environment e_i consists of a utility function and an endowment. The goal is Pareto efficiency. One shows that a goal-realizing mechanism satisfying an appropriate smoothness condition must have a message-space dimension not less than $n \cdot (\ell - 1)$. But that dimension is exactly achieved by the competitive mechanism, so that

---

[4] Cross-fertilization and uniqueness appear on page 317 of Hurwicz (1972), and on page 415 of Hurwicz (1977). These papers were written before the official publication dates of those books. A systematic search of the extensive Hurwicz archive at Duke University might yield some clues as to where cross-fertilization and uniqueness were first presented.

[5] This was found in Box 131 of the Jacob Marschak Papers, Special Collections, UCLA Library.

[6] Another smoothness requirement that became widely used (by Leo and others), is *local threadedness*. That means that for every $\bar{e}$ in $\bar{E}$, there is a neighborhood $N(\bar{e})$ and a continuous function w such that $w(e^*) \in \mu_1(e_1^*) \cap \cdots \cap \mu_n(e_n^*)$ for every e^* in $N(\bar{e})$. Then the dimension of $\bar{E}$ is again a lower bound to the message-space dimension of a G-realizing mechanism.

[7] The Shapley suggestion is mentioned by Leo in footnote 9 of Hurwicz (1977). In that footnote Leo writes "The importance of smoothness considerations was first brought to my attention by Lloyd Shapley".

[8] It is interesting to note that the cross-fertilization and uniqueness ideas were developed, quite independently, by computer scientists working in the field they call "communication complexity". They consider a conversation between n persons which ends when one person has enough information to compute a *function G* of n numbers, each of them privately known to just one person. The conversation is a sequence of binary strings and it changes when the privately known numbers change. If the function G has what is called a 'fooling set', then the size of that set provides a lower bound to to the length of the worst-case conversation. In Leo's terminology, a fooling set is a set on which G has the uniqueness property.

mechanism is a winner from the informational point of view. To prove this, the utility functions in the test class take the Cobb-Douglas form, for then uniqueness can be shown to hold.

Leo Ventures into an Unexplored Terrain: Mechanisms with Finite Message Spaces

The December 1976 annual meeting of the American Economic Association and the Econometric Society took place in Atlantic City. A welfare economics session had papers by Arrow, Lerner, and Reiter. I was the discussant of Reiter's paper ('Information and Performance in the (New)^2 Welfare Economics'). In my discussion,[9] I suggested that the 'smoothness' requirements needed to rule out smuggling of many numbers into one number are somewhat artificial unless one supplies a precise model of information processing which makes non-smoothness undesirable. An alternative might be to abandon message-space dimension as the informational-cost measure and to let the message space be finite, with its size as the cost measure. This was a somewhat audacious suggestion.

Leo was spending the 1976–77 academic year at Berkeley. He and I flew back together after the conference. On scraps of paper he sketched some ideas about how the study of finite mechanisms might proceed. Back at Berkeley we had many meetings on the subject. A number of joint papers eventually grew out of the Berkeley discussions and numerous later meetings in Minneapolis. There were also several encounters at Stanford. I vividly remember one of them. Leo was attending a Stanford meeting.[10] He had rented a motel room with a small kitchen near the campus. He prepared a quite respectable meal (chicken with lemon). This was my only exposure to Leo's culinary abilities; at all the Minneapolis meetings, Evelyn did the cooking.

Suppose the designer is given a goal function and wants to construct a finite mechanism with M messages. There are non-finite mechanisms which exactly realize the goal. The designer seeks an M-message mechanism which does not exactly realize the goal but comes as close as possible. Its worst-case 'error' is as small as M messages permit. It turns out that 'dimension still matters'. Spending the M-message 'budget' on the approximation of a goal-realizing mechanism with low message-space dimension achieves lower

---

[9] See Marschak (1977).

[10] I believe his meeting was related to Leo's role as a member of the Nuclear Proliferation and Safeguards Advisory Panel of the now-vanished Congressional Office of Technology Assessment.

worst-case error than spending it on an approximation of a goal-realizing mechanism of higher dimension. Not surprisingly the cross-fertilization idea is used again in proving this proposition and related ones.

In the exchange-economy case, with n-traders and ℓ commodities and Pareto-efficiency as the goal, an approximation of the competitive mechanism turns out—as one would hope—to have lower worst-case error for a given budget M than an approximation of 'Direct Revelation'. In an approximation of Direct Revelation each trader says "Yes", in equilibrium, to an approximation of her endowment and utility function. These problems are tricky and Leo's usual tenacity was crucial.[11]

Leo Enthusiastically Responds to a Proposal for an Unusual Workshop and Becomes its Guiding Spirit

I spent the academic year 1965–66 in what was then called Yugoslavia, trying to understand the Yugoslav 'experiment', in which centrally directed planning was replaced by decentralized 'workers' self management'. Stimulated by this puzzle I wrote Leo a letter from Yugoslavia proposing a comparative-economics workshop with theorists and empiricists. Leo responded surprisingly quickly with a letter which began "Just to shock you I am replying to your letter". He enthusiastically supported the workshop idea. The result was the Workshop on Analytic Techniques for the Comparison of Economic Systems, held at Berkeley in the summer of 1967.

Leo and Stan Reiter came to Berkeley to help plan the workshop. In those days several universities had lavish Ford Foundation funds for economic research. At Berkeley the Ford funds were handled by the Institute of International Studies, chaired by Dale Jorgenson. Dale very generously awarded the Workshop a substantial sum. Participants were paid for one month at their normal summer salaries.

The empiricists included Edward Ames, Michael Montias, and Gregory Grossman. The theorists included—aside from Leo, Stan, and me—Tjalling Koopmans, Ken Arrow, Roy Radner, Ted Groves, Antonio Camacho, and C.B. (Bart) McGuire. There were at least two students, who later became prominent: John Ledyard and Martin Weitzman. The workshop was lively and innovative. It included several boisterous evening social events. As usual, Leo was the workshop's animating spirit.

---

[11] One of our papers, Hurwicz and Marschak (1985), considered 'discrete' message spaces (where every message is a countable sequence of rational numbers), as well as finite message spaces.

Leo Becomes the Heart and Soul of the Decentralization Conference

The first Decentralization Conference took place in Berkeley in February 1971. Roy Radner conceived the idea and obtained support from an NSF grant administered by the National Bureau of Economic Research. (I discussed the program of the first Conference with Roy and we roughly sketched some ideas.) In a 'decentralized' organization each person has private information, not shared by others. Each person may also have a private goal, not shared by others. Then incentives become an issue. A designer wants the organization's mechanism to perform well, in spite of the privacy.

Most papers in the first Conference dealt with the informational challenge faced by the designer. But the program lists a session called 'Incentives and Authority' in which Leo and Ted Groves talked. Leo's talk was based on what later became his chapter in *Decision and Organization*, Hurwicz (1972). Ted's talk was a preview of some of the results that later appeared in Groves (1973).[12]

In the course of many successive Decentralization Conferences Leo became the animating spirit. Everyone looked forward to his presence. In one Conference (at the University of Chicago) there was substantial electrical static at the blackboard (dry weather and carpeted floors). Without comment, Leo wore thick leather gloves in his talk. Leo would often appear somnolent during the talks of others. But that was deceptive. He suddenly sprang to life, showing that he had been following everything, and then provided sharp questions and comments, which often clarified the problem. As the Conference approaches its fiftieth meeting, Leo's impact endures.

References

Groves, T. (1973) Incentives in teams, *Econometrica*, 41(4): 617–31.

Hurwicz, L. (1960) Optimality and informational efficiency in resource allocation processes, in *Mathematical Methods in the Social Sciences*, ed. Kenneth J. Arrow, Samuel Karlin, and Patrick Suppes, 27–46. Palo Alto: Stanford University Press.

Hurwicz, L. (1972) On informationally decentralized systems, in *Decision and Organization: A Volume in Honor of J. Marschak*, ed. Roy Radner and C. B. McGuire, 297–336. Amsterdam: North-Holland.

---

[12] I'm indebted to Ted Groves for supplying this information about the session and for assembling a comprehensive collection of programs and other materials related to the Decentralization Conference, starting with the February 1971 conference. These materials will be stored in the Hurwicz archive at the Rubenstein Rare Book and Manuscript Library, Duke University.

Hurwicz, L. (1977) On the dimensional requirements of informationally decentralized Pareto-satisfactory processes, in *Studies in Resource Allocation Processes*, ed. Kenneth J. Arrow and Leonid Hurwicz, 413–24. Cambridge, MA: Cambridge University Press.

Hurwicz, L. (1986) On informational decentralization and efficiency in resource allocation mechanisms, in *Studies in Mathematical Economics*, ed. Stanley Reiter, 238–350. Washington, DC: The Mathematical Association of America.

Hurwicz, L. and T. Marschak (1985) Discrete allocation mechanisms: Dimensional requirements for resource-allocation mechanisms when desired outcomes are unbounded, *Journal of Complexity*, 1(2): 264–303.

Marschak, T. (1972) Computation in organizations: The comparison of price mechanisms and other adjustment processes, in *Decision and Organization: A Volume in Honor of J. Marschak*, ed. Roy Radner and C. B. McGuire, 237–82. Amsterdam: North-Holland.

Marschak, T. (1977) Comments, Welfare Economics session, *American Economic Review*, 67(2): 240–2.

5

Leonid Hurwicz: A Reminiscence

Roy Radner

I first met Leo Hurwicz about 1951, when Jacob Marschak hired me as a research assistant in the Cowles Commission at the University of Chicago. Leo was then a faculty member at the University of Illinois, Urbana-Champaign, and also a Research Associate in the Cowles Commission. Under the leadership of Marschak and Tjalling Koopmans, Cowles was an exciting intellectual center of new developments in economic theory and econometrics, with the participation of Kenneth Arrow, Gérard Debreu, Lawrence Klein, Clifford Hildreth, John Chipman, C. Bart McGuire, Martin Beckman, Stanley Reiter, and others.

Leo came up to Chicago from the University of Illinois regularly to attend seminars and work with other members of the group. From my vantage point as graduate student in statistics (in the committee—later department—of statistics), the Cowles seminars were one of the high points in my intellectual development. In particular, Leo invariably began the general discussion of the speaker's presentation with a brief cogent (and sometimes piercing) summary of the content of the talk, and raising relevant questions for the discussion.

Later, I had the privilege of working with Leo and Stan Reiter on a model, originally proposed by Stan and called 'Sharks and Flounders', of a market among agents with heterogeneous information. The final resulting paper described a stochastic process of repeated choices by a group of agents from a fixed set of feasible outcomes, which we called (for some obscure reason) the 'B process'.[1] We showed that—under certain conditions—the process of chosen outcomes converged to a Pareto optimal outcome in a finite number

Written January 27, 2017, for this volume.

[1] See Hurwicz, L., R. Radner, and S. Reiter (1975) A stochastic decentralized resource allocation process, *Econometrica*, 43(2): 187–221, and 43(3): 363–93.

Roy Radner, *Leonid Hurwicz: A Reminiscence* In: *The Collected Papers of Leonid Hurwicz Volume 1*. Edited by Samiran Banerjee, Oxford University Press. © Oxford University Press 2022. DOI: 10.1093/oso/9780199313280.003.0005

of stages, although the agents would never know for sure when they had reached that outcome! As others who worked with Leo have noted, Leo was a perfectionist, and writing a paper with him was sometimes frustrating. Thus the model of this paper was—in a sense—a parable of the research process itself.

The preceding anecdote might lead one to guess that Leo was a 'difficult' colleague to work with, but that was not true in my experience. His perfectionism was primarily directed at himself. He was especially warm and patient with younger colleagues. In this he was supported by his wife, Evelyn, and my family grew to appreciate the friendship of the Hurwicz family as the years went by.

6

The Hurwicz 1940–41 Year When MIT Launched Its Graduate Degree Rocket: A Letter in Honor of Leo Hurwicz's Ninetieth Birthday

Paul Samuelson

MIT's Rupert Maclaurin asked new arrival Paul Samuelson, "Who's the world's greatest economist?"

"Ragnar Frisch", I suggested.

"Okay. Let's get him here at MIT."

"No, we can't do that. He's a Norwegian patriot sequestered right now in a Nazi concentration camp, where he's reduced to studying Darwinian bee genetics."

So to speak, therefore, I had to palm off on go-getter Maclaurin 23-year-old Leo Hurwicz instead of Frisch or Tinbergen or, for that matter, Keynes.

There's a story behind this story. Whilst Harvard was keeping in its court the ball that was put there by an October 1940 MIT invite to 25-year-old Paul to levitate three miles down the Charles River, frenetic Maclaurin phoned me nightly. One warm evening he dangled before me what follows. "If you come to MIT, for your research, you will have at your disposal the Roger Babson Grant to study how Newton's Second Law of Action and Reaction applies to macroeconomics."

Babson, who personally owned only two New England colleges, won Andy Warhol celebrity fame for—now listen to my words—correctly predicting

Courtesy of the Paul A. Samuelson papers, David M. Rubenstein Rare Book and Manuscript Library, Duke University and William F. Samuelson for permission. This letter was read at Leo Hurwicz's ninetieth birthday celebration on April 14, 2007, in Minneapolis, MN, which Samuelson was unable to attend.

Paul Samuelson, *The Hurwicz 1940-41 Year When MIT Launched Its Graduate Degree Rocket: A Letter in Honor of Leo Hurwicz's Ninetieth Birthday* In: *The Collected Papers of Leonid Hurwicz Volume 1*. Edited by Samiran Banerjee, Oxford University Press. © Oxford University Press 2022. DOI: 10.1093/oso/9780199313280.003.0006

in advance the Great Wall Street Crash of October, 1929. Never mind that Babson made that prediction in 1925 when the Dow Jones Index was about one-tenth of its 1929 peak. (Maybe Newton had told him, "What goes up must fall down.")

The rest is history. I quit my late-September Harvard lecturing on Econ abruptly at the mid-hour. Arriving by Massachusetts Avenue street car, what I found awaiting me at MIT were both half a secretary and my own telephone. (Ten years later Schumpeter at Harvard still hadn't attained that affluence.) While I couldn't fetch Frisch for Maclaurin, I still could deliver to him some new star. But who? Oskar Lange—then at Chicago or Berkeley—narrowed down the field for me. He suggested two names: Hungarian Tibor de Scitovsky or a young Pole, Leonid Hurwicz, late of Warsaw, Geneva, Barcelona, and Lisbon—always one step just ahead of Hitler's mobile tanks. Tibor's work at the LSE I knew and admired. But applying Lange's needs test, Hurwicz was the one in more desperate financial need. Think of it this way. Suppose Niels Bohr could choose between say, Heisenberg or Pauli. My die was cast and MIT was the beneficiary.

Historians of stochastic intertemporal US time series, and Isaac Newton in his dissenting Anglican Valhalla, must know how we did early spectral analysis of Frickey's aggregate US output for the time slot 1865–1935. When I say "we" I do not refer to Leo and Paul only. Instead I can still see in my mind's eye Leo, whip in one hand, slide rule in the other, marshaling his crew of mostly young female National Youth Administration galley-slave computers. *Parallel* computer computation thus merits a marble marker at the northwest corner of Massachusetts Avenue and Memorial Drive. Leo began that there.

Even more melodramatic was the new Hurwicz-Samuelson grading system for my first regular statistics course. MIT engineers have always been notorious whiners. They are grade chasers beyond Philadelphia barracks lawyers anywhere. One of us—I will point no finger—said: "Let's add a hard extra credit exam question, with the proviso that it can only *raise, but not lower,* your grade." All hell broke loose when undergraduate commerce course nerds learned that their exam mark of 115 put them below the median of the class grades. It did not help when Leo explained that this was the famous Chicago grading system. Leo had little to lose. The Babson pittance was already spent. It was my tenure and future life-time career that dangled on the razor's edge. Fortunately, Japan at Pearl Harbor saved my bacon and as well that of Hitler-hating Franklin Roosevelt. Can anyone doubt creative design's superiority over atheist Darwin?

Best of all, the Leo MIT year was a fun year. You know you're a has-been when you hear yourself saying, "I gave Goethe his first job." Well, damn it, I did give Leo his.

Part II
Mechanisms and Institutions

Part Two presents Leo's legacy in the field that he pioneered, mechanism design. These dozen relatively non-technical essays, beginning in 1969 and spanning almost thirty years, originated as talks given at various forums and show the development of his ideas. Chapters 7 and 8 begin with modeling informationally decentralized resource allocation processes which provide an analytical foundation for the debates in the 1930s about the feasibility of socialism due to von Mises, Hayek, Lange, Lerner, and Taylor. Chapter 9 continues with issues of designing mechanisms when markets fail, and Chapter 10 with exploring the interaction of information and incentives within mechanisms. In Chapter 11, he goes back to his original 1960 formulation of resource allocation processes without games and ties it to his work on algorithmic mechanism design with Stanley Reiter (which culminated in a co-authored book in 2006). Chapters 12–17 provide an overview of Leo's unfinished attempt to formally model institutions and institutional change over the last twenty years of his life. Chapter 18 is a closer look at the idea of enforcement in mechanisms upon which he based his 2007 Nobel lecture. Finally, Chapter 19 is Roger Myerson's inaugural Hurwicz Lecture at the 2006 North American Econometric Society meetings which follows up on some of the ideas and themes of Chapter 18.

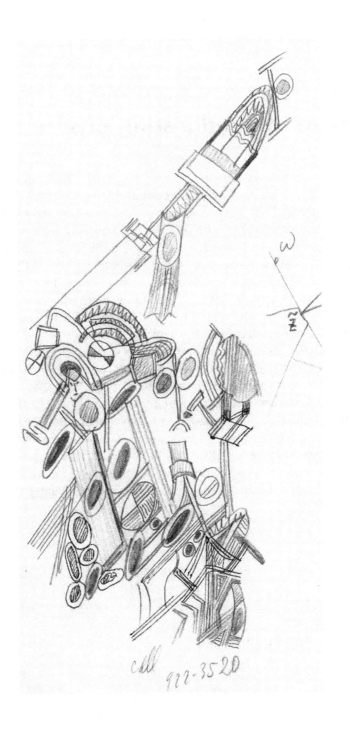

call 922-3520

7

On the Concept and Possibility
of Informational Decentralization

The economist's interest in the issue of decentralization as against central-ization is not new. It entered the eighteenth-century debate concerning laissez faire versus state-imposed restrictions, as well as the nineteenth-century controversies concerning the feasibility and desirability of socialism. Typically, however, the discussion was carried on with focus on concepts other than the degree of decentralization: ownership (private or collective), income determination, and the role of 'value.' This latter problem (see Pierson, 1935) corresponds closely to what in present-day terminology would be the issue of optimal resource allocation in a socialist economy.[1] It is not surprising that interest should subsequently have shifted to the optimality properties of (perfectly) competitive equilibrium which still constitutes a major aspect of currently taught economics of welfare.

Optimality Properties of Competitive Equilibria

Since the nature of equilibrium is regarded as an important feature of the economic process, the optimality properties of competitive equilibrium have been used as arguments in favor of the perfectly competitive mecha-nism, both in its 'free enterprise' and 'competitive socialist' (Lange-Lerner) interpretation. Not infrequently, the virtues of the perfectly competitive process have, by extension, been attributed (in an approximate sense) to the admittedly imperfect market economies of the Western European and US type. But there continued to exist expressions of dissatisfaction both with

Reprinted from *American Economic Review*, 1969, 59(2): 513–24.

[1] The notion of optimality was implicit in the discussion rather than rigorously defined but was not incompatible with the current concepts of efficiency, Pareto optimality, etc.

On the Concept and Possibility of Informational Decentralization In: *The Collected Papers of Leonid Hurwicz Volume 1*. Edited by Samiran Banerjee, Oxford University Press.

the actual workings of the market economy and even with the perfectly competitive ideal.

The limitations of the latter have been discussed in detail in the modern literature of welfare economics. It is well known by now what assumptions concerning the economic environment underlie the basic theorems relating Pareto optimality (or efficiency) and the competitive equilibrium. To guarantee that such equilibrium will be Pareto optimal, we assume absence of externalities between economic units (producers or consumers) as well as local nonsaturation (see Koopmans, 1957).[2] To guarantee the possibility of attaining every Pareto optimal allocation through the competitive mechanism, more assumptions are required, among them absence of indivisibilities and convexity both on consumption and on production sides, the latter ruling out the presence of increasing returns (Koopmans, 1957).

Nonclassical Environments

If one is unwilling to postulate that the real economic environment satisfies these 'classical' assumptions, one is naturally led to the consideration of alternatives or modifications of the perfectly competitive mechanism that would perform satisfactorily not only within the classical environments but also in the presence of such nonclassical environmental features as increasing returns, indivisibilities, etc. Both Marshall's proposal for the subsidization of increasing returns industries and the marginal cost pricing ideas of the 1930s (Hotelling, Lange, Lerner) are examples of attempts to modify the competitive mechanism to cope with nonclassical environments.[3] Similarly, there are in the economic literature suggestions for dealing with situations involving various combinations of indivisibility, externality, and public goods, by calculation techniques based on, or related to, consumers' (and producers') surplus (Dupuit, Hotelling, Lerner).

Formula versus Mechanism

But the existence of a mathematical formula characterizing (usually only implicitly) optimal solutions does not imply the existence of a mechanism for processing the relevant information to the point of obtaining even

---

[2] These are the 'direct' or, on the production side, 'technological' externalities, as distinct from what Viner and Scitovsky call 'pecuniary' externalities (Scitovsky 1954).

[3] An alternative, imperfectly competitive, mechanism to bring about optimality in the presence of increasing returns was proposed by Arrow and Hurwicz (1960).

reasonable approximations to such solutions. This was the point stressed by Robbins (1934, p. 1511) and Hayek (1935, pp. 209–12). The issues raised by them, especially those by Hayek (subsequently elaborated in 1945 and 1946), are of crucial importance in the present context, since they have to do with the centralized nature of socialism (collectivism, planning) as against the decentralized nature of the competitive market process. By analyzing these issues, we may arrive at the notions of decentralization and centralization implicit in the debate. In this writer's view these notions point to important aspects of the problem and can be built upon in considering the problem of feasibility of decentralization in the context of recent controversies.

Dispersion of Information

The fundamental point made by Hayek with regard to availability of economic information is its dispersion. A simple way of visualizing this dispersion is to assume that, at least at the beginning of the allocative process, each economic unit has perfect information concerning itself (its production function or its preference map or its resource holdings) and no information concerning the other units. During the allocative process there will be communication, then decisions, and finally their implementation. An oversimplified view of a centralized process envisions the transfer of the dispersed information to a single unit (say the central planning board) which then performs calculations yielding appropriate actions (especially in the production and input flows) to be taken by the other units. It is this transfer of dispersed information to the central unit that Hayek considered impossible.[4] And it was the need for such a transfer that was for him, implicitly, the characteristic feature of a centralized allocative process.

Transfer of Information

Now things would be easy if one could define a decentralized allocative process as one in which no information is transferred from any unit to any other unit. We would then have two polar extremes: (informational) centralization, with complete transfer of all dispersed information to a single designated unit, and (informational) decentralization, with no transfer of information as between units. Such a definition of decentralization could be adopted if there were no communication among the economic units during the allocative

---

[4] The magnitude of calculations that would have to be performed centrally was another difficulty.

process. But, unless we want to disqualify the competitive process from the decentralized class, we cannot prohibit all communication. Hayek who was perhaps the first to describe the competitive process as decentralized (see Hayek 1935, p. 211, 1945, p. 524; also 1946, pp. 48–50) stresses the need for communication among units to achieve coordination of their actions (Hayek 1945, pp. 525–27). This communication is accomplished in the competitive mechanism through bids (representing quantities supplied or demanded) and prices attached to those bids.

Communication in the Competitive Process

There is an intuitively appealing difference between the type of communication that prevails in a competitive market (where bids and prices are communicated) and the type of communication envisaged in the central planning board model (where complete descriptions of technologies or preferences or resource holdings are communicated). This difference can be used as a basis for classifying allocative mechanisms as decentralized, centralized, or in between, depending on whether their communication requirements are like those of the competitive mechanism or like those of the above central planning board model or in between. But what type of communication would we accept as being 'like that of the competitive mechanism'? If our definition is too narrow, we shall be going in the direction of almost identifying the notion of informational decentralization with that of a 'price mechanism.' Yet the intuitive concept of informational decentralization (see March and Simon 1958, p. 204) seems broader than that of a price mechanism (as yet not rigorously defined either). On the other hand, if virtually any type of communication were considered acceptable, we might find that even the central planning board model would qualify as decentralized, thus failing to express the difference between the two types of communication.

To arrive at a possible answer let us see first what kind of communication takes place in the competitive process. Geometrically, a bid is a point in the commodity space; algebraically, it is a vector with components corresponding to the goods present in the economy.[5] A price can be represented either as a half-space in the commodity space or as a point, algebraically again a vector of the dimensionality of the commodity space.[6]

---

[5] A typical bid would have most components zero, with the rest positive and negative.
[6] This point or vector representation of prices is not generally valid for infinite-dimensional commodity spaces.

A Concept of Informational Decentralization

This suggests that we accept as 'like competitive' those processes in which messages consist of vectors whose dimensionality is the same as that of the commodity space (assuming the latter to be finite). Suppose that we make this requirement a part of our definition of (informational) decentralization. Our minimum desiderata will be satisfied if the competitive process does qualify while the central planning board process does not. Now clearly, the competitive process does qualify. But have we disqualified the central planning board process?

To answer this question we must find out whether a message consisting of as many (real) numbers as there are goods can be used to transfer such information as the complete description of, say, a production function. Perhaps somewhat unexpectedly, under certain circumstances the answer may be affirmative. To begin with, and this is least surprising, the information could easily be transferred if, for instance, all production functions were in advance known to belong to a parametric family (e.g., Cobb-Douglas) with no more parameters than there are goods, since in this case the components of the transmitted vector message could be reserved (in a prearranged manner) for these parameters. But in fact it does not matter if there are more parameters to be transmitted than there are goods in the economy! The reason is the possibility of using one real number to transmit information about several (arbitrarily, but finitely, many) numbers.[7]

A Priori Admissible Environments

Hence, in an economic environment where production functions and utility functions were representable by finite-parameter families of functions, the seemingly reasonable communicational characterization of decentralization (viz., that only commodity-dimensional messages can be transmitted) turns out inadequate because it would not screen out the par excellence centralized process! Should we worry about this? Possibly not. For we may be looking for a process that would guarantee optimal resource allocation even when the variability in the economic environment exceeds any finite-parameter families of functions. For instance, suppose that a firm's production possibility set could be any subset whatsoever of the commodity space. In that

---

[7] Suppose that one decimal number, say $0.x_1x_2x_3x_4\ldots$ is to carry information about two decimal numbers, say $0.y_1y_2\ldots$ and $0.z_1z_2\ldots$; then we merely reserve the odd-place digits of x for the y digits and the even-place digits of x for the z digits: $x_1 = y_1, x_2 = z_1, x_3 = y_2, x_4 = z_2$, etc.

case the collection of all commodity-dimensional vectors is known (from set theory) to be inadequate as a representation of all such production possibility sets.[8]

Thus when the a priori admissible class of production sets (or preference maps) is sufficiently broad to be beyond finite-parameter description, the central planning board process no longer qualifies as decentralized if communication in the latter is confined to commodity-dimensional messages. Since the competitive process still does qualify, our minimum desiderata for a definition of informational decentralization are satisfied.

Let us then adopt a definition of informational decentralization which restricts communication to commodity-dimensional messages and also postulate that the only information available to any economic unit concerning the other units is derived from such communication; i.e., except for what can be inferred from such communication, every unit is assumed to be in total ignorance of other units' technologies, preferences, and resource holdings. Stated in this manner, the restrictions may appear overly severe, and certainly unrealistic as descriptions of phenomena observed in the real market place. But these restrictions are satisfied by the idealized Walrasian model of the competitive mechanism and in this sense are not too severe.

Of course, this definition would be of little interest if the competitive mechanism were the only one to qualify under it. But in fact, a number of other proposed mechanisms also qualify, especially when above communication restrictions are interpreted as permitting directed communication; i.e., communication where in each phase of the allocative process some units are permitted to send different messages to the various other units, each message still being required to be a commodity-dimensional vector.[9] In particular, "decentralized planning" procedures proposed by Malinvaud (1967, Sections III, IV, V) as well as the Kornai-Lipták process satisfy (with certain qualifications to be stated below) the requirements just formulated.[10]

---

[8] The same would hold true if we confined ourselves to a somewhat narrower class of production possibility sets satisfying certain conventional assumptions.

[9] Since the competitive process can get along without directed messages, it becomes clear that the concept of informational decentralization we are now using calls for less informational efficiency than characterizes the competitive process. A more stringent definition was used in Hurwicz (1960).

[10] In the Kornai-Lipták process there is a central body which receives from the various production units their 'local' shadow price messages and responds with proposed input-output vectors. Such a process does not satisfy the more stringent communicational requirements of self-relevance and anonymity in Hurwicz's (1960) definition.

Performance Criteria

We shall not at this point pursue the different possible variants of the decentralization concept and their respective merits. It is more interesting to see what questions can be asked given *a* (not *the*) concept of informational decentralization. In what sense is it meaningful to ask whether such decentralization is 'possible'? We have seen already that many processes satisfying the requirements of our definition can be defined.[11] Thus our use of the term possible in this context is somewhat misleading. What we want to know is not merely whether such a process can be defined, but whether it will have certain optimality properties with regard to the allocations it produces. What properties should we specify?

Pareto Satisfactoriness

Here again, we get some guidance from the situation prevailing in the 'classical' case. The economists have often been satisfied if they could prove that every equilibrium is (Pareto) optimal and every optimum capable of sustaining an equilibrium. The conjunction of these two properties (together with a sort of single valuedness which is also present in competitive equilibria) has been labeled "Pareto satisfactoriness" of a process. Thus if we want an allocative process to possess some of the important static attributes of perfect competition operating in a classical environment, we may require that it be Pareto satisfactory. With this interpretation of what we mean by the possibility of decentralization, it is evident that this possibility may depend on the (a priori admissible) class of environments the mechanism is expected to operate in. For instance, the competitive mechanism qualifies as informationally decentralized and is known to be Pareto satisfactory within the family of classical environments (no externalities, no indivisibilities, convexity). But what if our interest goes beyond these classical environments?

For instance, suppose cases of increasing returns are members of the a priori admissible class. We know that the competitive mechanism, although still decentralized, is no longer Pareto satisfactory. What about Marshall's subsidy scheme? This may conceivably be Pareto satisfactory, but appears to violate the communicational requirements of decentralization, since the subsidy level decisions might require detailed knowledge of the production functions on the part of the subsidy granting body.[12]

It is seen that the possibility of a decentralized mechanism outside the classical environment sphere is by no means obvious. To expect that there

---

[11] This remains true even for more stringent variants of the concept.

[12] The preceding statement is merely a conjecture. A rigorous study remains to be carried out.

would exist mechanisms both decentralized and Pareto satisfactory for all conceivable environments does not seem reasonable. But what about the class of all environments that are free of externalities? This class contains some of the most troublesome cases (increasing returns, indivisibilities, discontinuities of preferences). Hence, it is perhaps somewhat surprising that decentralization within this broad class of environments is possible.[13]

Malinvaud's Criteria

If one thinks of actually using a given allocative process to arrive at a decision, one is no longer satisfied by Pareto satisfactoriness, even if accompanied by convergence (stability of equilibrium). In fact, one may be willing to sacrifice the good static features of equilibria and convergence (as the number of iterations tends to infinity) in exchange for some needed features obtainable after a finite number of iterations. Malinvaud (1967) has focused his attention on requirements of this type. Thus, for instance, he requires that the solution obtained after a finite number of iterations be feasible in terms of the available resources and technology. Malinvaud points out that certain Walrasian tâtonnement procedures related to gradient processes need not yield feasible plans if interrupted after a finite number of iterations.[14]

Thus, it is not obvious that informational decentralization is possible (in the sense of Malinvaud's performance requirements) even for all classical environments. Malinvaud's paper shows that two processes satisfy his performance requirements for certain narrower classes of environments. The Taylor process (Malinvaud 1967, Section IV) satisfies Malinvaud's performance requirements for the class of the Leontief-Samuelson environments. His other process (Malinvaud 1967, Section V]) satisfies his performance requirements when certain conditions of convexity, closedness, and boundedness are

---

13 The latter statement requires qualification. Two processes have been designed to cope with the class of all environments that are free of externalities. The earlier of the two is presented under the name of "greed process" in Hurwicz (1960). This process is Pareto satisfactory in the sense of the preceding definition but qualifies as informationally decentralized if a message is permitted to contain not merely a single commodity-dimensional vector but also a set of such vectors; i.e., in this respect the Hurwicz (1960) definition is less stringent than the present one, although it is more stringent in other respects: anonymity and self-relevance. The more recent process, to be published in a paper by Hurwicz, Radner, and Reiter [see Hurwicz et al. (1975)], satisfies the more stringent informational requirements—in particular, messages are single vectors, and anonymity and self-relevance hold—but it excludes discontinuous divisible environments, while permitting indivisibilities and nonconvexities, and is probabilistic in nature. Hence, so is its Pareto satisfactoriness. On the other hand, it has, unlike the greed process, good convergence properties as well.

14 These are procedures based on the work of Arrow, Hurwicz, and Uzawa [see Arrow and Hurwicz (1977)].

satisfied by the environment.[15] Unfortunately, Malinvaud is 'buying' the performance properties he is interested in (in particular, the feasibility of the final plan) by a weakening of the informational decentralization aspect; viz., by his assumption that the planning bureau has initial knowledge of a feasible plan. This assumption violates one aspect of our definition of informational decentralization. If one were to abandon Malinvaud's assumption that the planning bureau has such initial knowledge, his processes (Malinvaud 1967, Section IV, V) will qualify as informationally decentralized under our definition but may no longer satisfy Malinvaud's performance criteria.

If we insist on our definition of decentralization, it is still not obvious whether decentralization is possible in terms of Malinvaud's performance criteria even for, say, a class as narrow as that of Leontief-Samuelson environments.[16]

Decentralizability of Non-Pecuniary Externalities

Let us now return to (static) Pareto satisfactoriness as our performance criterion. Subject to this criterion, what are the limits of informational decentralizability; i.e., for how broad a class of environments could there be an allocative mechanism that is both informationally decentralized and Pareto satisfactory? We have seen already that the class of all or most environments that are free of externalities can be taken care of either by the (set-valued) greed process or by its stochastic (point-valued) counterpart. But what about environments that do have externalities?

In the last decade there have been several important contributions that have bearing on this issue. The most interesting from our point of view is the exchange between Wellisz (1964) and Davis and Whinston (1966). A central issue in the debate was the feasibility of the Pigou system of taxes and subsidies to supplement the workings of the market so as to produce optimality. In their earlier paper, Davis and Whinston (1962) pointed out some of the difficulties of treating the problem of externalities in the Pigovian fashion, specifically when these externalities are of the bilateral nonseparable type. Wellisz, in addition to questioning some of their arguments, proposed what he called a "Pigovian solution to the problem of externalities." Denoting by $C_i(q_i, q_j)$, $j \neq i$, the total cost function of the ith firm, $i = 1, 2$, with the

---

[15] The class of environments covered is not much narrower than the classical. However, the informational requirements of this process are much more stringent than those of the competitive process in that cumulative 'memory' is postulated for the planning bureau.

[16] We have not as yet examined the Kornai-Lipták process from this point of view.

presence of q_j indicating the externality, the Wellisz approach consists in finding two functional relations g_i, $i = 1, 2$, with whose help he constructs the modified ("internalized") cost functions $C_i'(q_i) = C_i(q_i, g_i(q_i))$.[17]

The basic Davis-Whinston objection to the Wellisz solution is that the calculation of each of the two 'response functions' g_i requires the knowledge of both cost functions C_1 and C_2. Thus if the ith firm were to compute its g_i, it would also have to know the other firm's cost function C_j, $j \neq i$. If one assumes that initially information is "dispersed," so that each firm only knows its own cost function, the calculation required by the Wellisz proposal could only be carried out if the relevant information about the other firm's [cost] were transferred through appropriate communication; clearly, this does not seem to be in the spirit of informational decentralization as defined in the present paper. Davis and Whinston (1966), in fact, claim that "the informational requirements of the Wellisz proposal are just as stringent as those of a centralized scheme" (p. 310) or "of a (partially) centralized scheme" (p. 312). However, their attempt to establish this claim is vitiated by the absence of a rigorous definition of what type of communication they regard as corresponding to either (informationally) centralized or "partially centralized" or decentralized schemes.[18] According to Davis and Whinston, it is "in general" necessary to find the optimizing values of the respective outputs q_1 and q_2 in order to calculate the 'response functions' g_i. If this is so, they say, one might as well have a central authority dictating these outputs to the two firms rather than helping them "internalize" their cost functions. However, their example (aside from the above weakness) only shows that the calculation of optimal outputs is sufficient to obtain the response functions; the necessity is not rigorously established. Since there is a variety of possible "adjustment processes" (Hurwicz, 1960) corresponding to the Wellisz scheme, one would, presumably, have to show that none of those can satisfy the requirements of a specific definition of informational decentralization, e.g., of that given in the present paper, or some other which may have been implicit in the Davis and Whinston arguments. This has not as yet been done.

[17] Although Wellisz refers to g_i as the "Pigovian taxes," a better interpretation would seem to be that of 'conjectured response functions.' I.e., $g_i(q_i)$ would yield the value of q_j conjectured by unit i to be j's response to i's choosing quantity level q_i. The difficulty with the tax interpretation can be seen in the separable case where, say, $C_1(q_1, q_2) = C_{11}(q_1) + C_{12}(q_2)$. The modified cost function is here given by $C_1' = C_{11}(q_1) + C_{12}(g_1(q_1))$. Hence the amount of tax paid would seem to be $C_{12}(g_1(q_1))$ rather than $g_1(q_1)$. It is also worth noting that g_1 and g_2 are mutually inverse.

[18] A further weakness of their exposition is due to the fact that an example designed to show the difficulties of the Wellisz proposal does not possess a joint optimum. In fact, the joint profit function given in their equation (19), p. 311, as $P = 3q_1 + 4q_2 - (q_1 + q_2) - q_1q_2$ can be made arbitrarily large by setting $q_1 = 0$ and letting q_2 tend to infinity. However, the phenomenon which the example is meant to illustrate could probably be exhibited in the context of another similar example possessing a finite optimum.

Whinston's Scheme

Having adopted the (admittedly plausible) conclusion that the Wellisz scheme does not qualify as informationally decentralized, Davis and Whinston propose a very interesting alternative (originally due to Whinston 1964) which in their view does qualify. Their scheme is valuable on its own merits, but is of particular interest here as throwing light on what one may mean by informational decentralization. The basic idea of the proposal is to give each firm two decision variables: the ith firm chooses not only its own output q_i but also the output x_j it proposes for the other firm. A third party ('the authority') sets unit charges to be paid by one firm to the other (in the sense of tâtonnement, with payments only at the end of iteration or in equilibrium). These charges are proportionate to the discrepancy between q_i and x_i, with the level of charges set by the authority according to a formula also involving the size of the discrepancy. This process appears to have satisfactory static properties, although its stability properties are not clear to this writer. But our main interest here is in its informational features. The authors state that "it does not require that information concerning cost functions be communicated to any party (including the government). In this respect it is informationally decentralized. All that is required (aside from the requirements that firms know their own cost functions, etc.) is that the existence of externalities be recognized" (Davis and Whinston 1966, p. 312). "Similarly, the governmental authority does not need to have a knowledge of the cost curves of the two firms. It simply adjusts the per unit charges according to the stated rules" (Davis and Whinston 1966, pp. 315–16).

The notion of informational decentralization implicit in these statements is in accord with that of our earlier discussion: in a decentralized allocative process there should not be transmission of detailed information concerning one unit (cost functions, production functions) from that unit to another unit, whether the latter be a firm or some third party (in this case a government authority). Since it is recognized, however, that some communication must take place between units to ensure optimality (or even feasibility) and that such communication is bound, indirectly at least, to convey some information about the unit, we are again faced with the problem of what kind of communication will qualify as still informationally decentralized.

The characteristic feature of the Davis-Whinston proposal is that each firm has two decision variables (its own output and the output it proposes for the other firm) rather than merely one. In addition, the third party (the government authority) is endowed with new variables under its control; viz., the two discrepancy charges. One is entitled to ask whether there is no limit on the proliferation of the number of variables before we conclude that the mechanism no longer qualifies as informationally decentralized.

The terminological label is not the important thing, however. It may seem artificial to decide precisely where the boundary is drawn. The significant aspect of the example is that the (Davis-Whinston) scheme proposed does have higher communicational requirements than the corresponding environment would have had if the external effects had been eliminated. From this point of view the interesting question to ask is whether this increase in communicational requirements is unavoidable, and if so, to what extent.

That the presence of externalities would call for more communication is intuitively clear, since the same action by a given unit may or may not be optimal (or even feasible) depending on the other unit's behavior. But care must be exercised in formalizing the nature of this concept of 'more information.' Mere counting of the number of transmitted variables (or messages) is inadequate for reasons indicated earlier in this paper; viz., that it is possible to have one number serve as a vehicle for transmitting several. It would appear that the proper way to rule out such seeming paradoxes is to impose restrictions on the continuity (or smoothness) of the functions representing the responses (decision-making) of the participants in the allocative process.[19] While such mathematical restrictions may at first lack intuitive appeal, they result, in the writer's opinion, in a closer approximation to the intuitive notion of the dimensionality of the message than mere counting of numbers contained in it. Along these lines, the two questions would be whether the Davis-Whinston scheme calls for more information transfer than would have been required in the absence of externalities and, assuming the answer to be in the affirmative, whether one could not get by with less.

Commodity Interpretation

As to the latter question, it should first be noted that the additionally introduced variables of the Davis-Whinston scheme are quite natural if one views the phenomenon of externality as the presence of an additional commodity which is being ignored by the usual market mechanism. For instance, if the externality is due to smoke being blown from factory 1 to factory 2, we may think of this (in the absence of zoning prohibitions) as a commodity (smoke) being 'sold' by factory 1 to factory 2 without the latter's consent. If smoke were declared a commodity like any other, factory 1 could not be forced to "buy" smoke without its consent; presumably it might do so at some negative price. Thus, by declaring smoke to be a commodity, we

---

[19] Results along these lines were presented in Hurwicz (1966) on the decentralizability of externalities [subsequently incorporated in Hurwicz (1977)].

would be introducing two more variables into the system; viz., the price of smoke and the quantity of smoke demanded by the second factory. This agrees with the two extra variables per externality in the Davis-Whinston scheme.

The smoke example points, however, to a possible improvement of the Davis-Whinston scheme in the sense that the variable 'quantity of smoke demanded by 2' has lesser informational requirements than the Davis-Whinston variable 'level of output in 1 proposed by 2.' For when 2 talks only about the amount of smoke it will receive, it is up to factory 1 to determine the relationship between its level of output and the amount of smoke emitted.[20]

An Alternative Scheme

While it is thus seen that the Davis-Whinston scheme is consistent with a traditional view of externalities as involving commodities that bypass the market process, it is still legitimate to ask whether a mechanism could not be devised involving fewer variables. To explore this in the spirit of the example considered by Davis and Whinston and in much of the other literature, and without claiming generality, we consider two firms with total net profit functions $f^i(q_1, q_2), i = 1, 2$, the functions being assumed differentiable and concave so that joint profit (i.e., the maximum of $f^1 + f^2$) is obtained by setting the sum of appropriate partial derivatives equal to zero. I.e., the optimality conditions are

$$f_1^1(q_1, q_2) + f_1^2(q_1, q_2) = 0$$
$$f_2^1(q_1, q_2) + f_2^2(q_1, q_2) = 0,$$

where the subscript j denotes the partial differentiation with respect to q_j.

We shall now consider a communication scheme in which the ith firm communicates f_j^i, for $i \neq j$, to the other firm through a message denoted by m_j^i.[21] Its own proposed level of output is denoted by m_i^i. With t as the variable of iteration ("time") we consider the following adjustment process: the equation

$$f_1^1(m_1^1(t), m_1^2(t-1)) + m_1^2(t-1) = 0 \qquad (1.1)$$

---

[20] The formal model underlying this remark is one in which the cost function of the second factory is, say, $F_2(s_1, q_2)$ while $s_1 = \phi_1(q_1)$, where s_1 represents the amount of smoke sent from 1 to 2, and we assume that factory 2 only knows F_2 while factory 1 knows the technological relation ϕ_1.

[21] This message is a single number.

is solved by firm 1 to determine $m_1^1(t)$; the equation

$$m_2^1(t) = f_2^1\big(m_1^1(t), m_2^2(t-1)\big) \tag{1.2}$$

is used by firm 1 to determine $m_2^1(t)$.

Similarly, for firm 2, the message $m_2^2(t)$ is obtained by solving equation

$$m_2^1(t-1) + f_2^2\big(m_1^1(t-1), m_2^2(t)\big) = 0; \tag{2.1}$$

and the equation

$$m_1^2(t) = f_1^2\big(m_1^1(t-1), m_2^2(t)\big) \tag{2.2}$$

is used to obtain $m_1^2(t)$.[22]

A modification along the lines of the smoke example above could be carried out as follows. Assume that, say, $f^2(q_1, q_2)$ can be expressed as $F^2(s_1, q_2)$ where $s_1 = \phi^1(q_1)$, with similar relations in the other direction. Then the relations (2.1)–(2.2) would respectively be replaced by the following:

$$m_2^1(t-1)\phi_2^2\big(m_2^2(t-1)\big) + F_2^2\big(s_1(t-1), m_2^2(t)\big) = 0, \tag{2.1$'$}$$
$$m_1^2(t) = F_1^2\big(s_1(t-1), m_2^2(t)\big). \tag{2.2$'$}$$

Equations (1.1)–(1.2) would be replaced by analogous (1.1$'$)–(1.2$'$).

Not surprisingly, it is seen that the terms involving m_j^i, $i \neq j$, reflect the marginal externalities (marginal external costs or marginal productivity of the 'input' smoke). An interpretation in terms of 'demand price' for smoke etc., seems possible.

It should be noted that neither system involves an outside authority. Furthermore, while the 'smoke model' (with primes) involves six variables (the m_j^i's and the s_i's), only four of these are involved in outside communication (the s_i's and the m_j^i's with $i \neq j$). Hence the communication requirements would in both schemes be lower than in the Davis-Whinston proposal. It should be made clear, however, that this does not necessarily imply an overall superiority of the former over the latter because of possible increase in computational complexity. The purpose of our construction is merely to push somewhat further the exploration of the possibilities of saving on the extent of communication between the economic units in the presence of externalities and also to see to what extent one can get by without introducing third parties.[23]

---

[22] In the right members of (1.2) and (2.2), $m_i^j(t)$ could be replaced by $m_i^j(t-1)$.

[23] But let us remember that this paper ignores issues of motivation and enforcement which might require the intervention of third parties for reasons other than communication.

The alternative schemes just proposed still fail to answer the question of how much 'better' one could do in economizing on the number of messages to be transmitted. Always bearing in mind that the message number counting must be done subject to 'smoothness assumptions,' a partial answer is provided in [Hurwicz (1966, 1977)] where it is shown that even for quadratic profit functions two messages would, in general, be insufficient when bilateral externalities are present.[24]

A reference should be made to the existence of other proposals in the direction of informational decentralization in situations involving externalities. In particular, an ingenious extension of the greed process is contained in [Camacho (1970)]. Its communicational requirements, however, go beyond what would qualify as informationally decentralized both under the standards of the present paper (because set-valued messages are used, as in the greed process) and under those of [Hurwicz (1960)] (because self-relevance of messages appears to be violated). It is nevertheless conceivable that the Camacho scheme ('D-process') is close to being maximally informationally efficient for the class of environments it deals with. Additional research is needed in this direction.

Pecuniary Externalities

A discussion of the issue of decentralization in the presence of externalities would be incomplete without at least a brief consideration of the problem of the 'pecuniary' externalities. In fact, a perusal of the existing literature (Rosenstein-Rodan, 1943; Scitovsky, 1954; Sirkin, 1968) shows that the pecuniary externalities are a major reason given for considering planning as superior to the market mechanism in certain situations, especially in underdeveloped economies. A detailed analysis of the problem would exceed the scope of this paper, and we shall confine ourselves to a few comments.

Since a great many different phenomena are lumped under the pecuniary externalities label, let us limit ourselves to the case [attributed to Allyn Young in Rosenstein-Rodan (1943)] of the problem where two capital goods (a subway—'tube'—and a housing development) whose services (transportation, shelter) are complementary. The claim made in favor of 'planning' (or merger)—i.e., against decentralization of the investment decisions—is that there is uncertainty on each side as to the decision of the other. Since our focus is on the possibility of informational decentralization, it is natural to ask first whether the competitive model (as distinct from the actual

---

[24] The smoothness requirements can be taken to mean the Lipschitzian property of the decision rules; mere continuity is not enough.

market structure) could be used here. The answer is in the affirmative if the complementarity of the services is the only 'troublesome' aspect of the situation. What is then needed, however, is the existence of a market for such services, so that at the time investment (construction) decisions are made there exist prices equilibrating the market for such services, to be taken into account in the investment decisions. But the services are in the future. Hence a market for future goods would have to be created, possibly in a 'simulated' or 'shadow' form.[25] From the informational point of view this would be acceptable as a decentralized solution.[26]

The preceding paragraph was addressed to the case where complementarity of services was the only 'trouble.' In fact, investment decisions may also involve indivisibilities or increasing returns. Here we are back to the difficulties of nonclassical environments discussed earlier.

References

Arrow, K. and L. Hurwicz (1960) Decentralization and computation in resource allocation, in *Essays in Economics and Econometrics*, ed. R. Pfouts, 34–104. Chapel Hill, NC: University of North Carolina Press.

Arrow, K. and L. Hurwicz (1977) *Studies in Resource Allocation Processes*. Cambridge, MA: Cambridge University Press.

Camacho, A. (1970) Externalities, optimality and informationally decentralized resource allocation processes, *International Economic Review*, 11(2): 318–27.

Davis, O. and A. Whinston (1962) Externalities, welfare, and the theory of games, *Journal of Political Economy*, 70(3): 241–62.

Davis, O. and A. Whinston (1966) On externalities, information and the government-assisted invisible hand, *Economica*, 33(131): 303–18.

Hayek, F. (1935) *Collectivist Economic Planning*. London: Routledge.

Hayek, F. (1945) The use of knowledge in society, *American Economic Review*, 35(4): 519–30.

Hayek, F. (1946) *The Road to Serfdom*. London: Routledge.

Hurwicz, L. (1960) Optimality and informational efficiency in resource allocation processes, in *Mathematical Methods in the Social Sciences*, ed. K. Arrow, S. Karlin, and P. Suppes, 27–46. Stanford, CA: Stanford University Press.

[25] A suggestion to this effect by K. J. Arrow is quoted in Hayek (1935, p. 306).

[26] The objections (see Stockfisch, 1955; Wellisz, 1964) to the centralized planning solution for such situations point out the possibility that economic units might have information concerning the units which might undertake construction resulting in satisfying the requirements of complementarity, thus reducing uncertainty. This is not to be denied as an empirical fact, but it should be noted that the availability of such information violates the postulate of dispersion of information and thus that of informational decentralization. As to models involving expected prices of future goods, the difficulty is that (a) not all market participants would necessarily have the same expectations, and (b) even if their expectations were unanimous, the outputs decided on the basis of such expectations might fail to equate future demand and supply. In any case, one should keep in mind the fact that optimality here must be defined as ex ante, not ex post.

Hurwicz, L. (1966) On decentralizability in the presence of externalities, University of Minnesota mimeo.

Hurwicz, L. (1977) On the dimensional requirements of informationally decentralized Pareto-satisfactory processes, in *Studies in Resource Allocation Processes*, ed. K. Arrow and L. Hurwicz, 413–24. Cambridge, MA: Cambridge University Press.

Hurwicz, L., R. Radner, and S. Reiter (1975) A stochastic decentralized resource allocation process, *Econometrica*, 43(2): 187–221, and 43(3): 363–93.

Koopmans, T. (1957) *Three Essays on the State of Economic Science*. New York, NY: McGraw-Hill.

Malinvaud, E. (1967) Decentralized procedures for planning, in *Activity Analysis in the Theory of Growth and Planning*, ed. E. Malinvaud and M. Bacharach, 170–208. London: Macmillan.

March, J. and H. Simon (1958) *Organizations*. New York, NY: Wiley.

Pierson, N. (1935) The problem of value in the socialist society, in *Collectivist Economic Planning* ed. F. Hayek, 42–85. London: Routledge.

Robbins, L. (1934) *The Great Depression*. New York, NY: Macmillan.

Rosenstein-Rodan, P. (1943) Problems of industrialization of Eastern and South-Eastern Europe, *Economic Journal*, 53(210/11): 202–11.

Scitovsky, T. (1954) Two concepts of external economies, *Journal of Political Economy*, 62(2): 143–451.

Sirkin, G. (1968) *The Visible Hand: The Fundamentals of Economic Planning*. New York, NY: McGraw-Hill.

Stockfisch, J. (1955) External economies, investment, and foresight, *Journal of Political Economy*, 63(5): 446–49.

Wellisz, S. (1964) On external diseconomies and the government-assisted invisible hand, *Economica*, 31(124): 345–62.

Whinston, A. (1964) Price guides in decentralized organization, in *New Perspectives in Organization Research*, ed. W. Cooper, H. Leavitt, and M. Shelley II, 405–48. New York, NY: Wiley.

8

Centralization and Decentralization in Economic Processes

Background

Interest in alternative economic structures can be traced to antiquity: Plato's *Republic* illustrates the possibilities of state planning, while Aristotle points out the disadvantages of collective ownership. Over centuries, humanity has resorted to a variety of institutional settings serving as background for the economic process. These settings, sometimes idealized into 'economic systems,' have been a subject of systematic comparative study, until recently primarily descriptive in nature.

Philosophers and scholars, however, have not had the field all to themselves. Those dissatisfied with their economic environment have often felt that the system itself is to be blamed and that it should be replaced by a different structure. Such views were implicit in the various 'Utopias,' of which Plato's *Republic* is a forerunner. In addition to Mora's imaginary island community which is responsible for the term, these included Bacon's *New Atlantis* and Campanella's *Civitas Solis*. But it is only in the early nineteenth century that the idea of replacing the existing economic system by a new one comes into full view in the writings, as well as actual experimentation, of the early socialists (Owen, Saint-Simon, Fourier). While some, at least, of the socialist schemes called for a measure of centralized control of the economic activities, an alternative direction of structural change—away from governmental power and toward voluntary association of independent units—was envisaged by Proudhon and his anarchist successors.

From *Comparison of Economic Systems: Theoretical and Methodological Approaches*, ed. A. Eckstein, 79–102. ©1971 University of California Press: Berkeley. Reprinted by permission of University of California Press.

Centralization and Decentralization in Economic Processes In: *The Collected Papers of Leonid Hurwicz Volume 1*. Edited by Samiran Banerjee, Oxford University Press. © Oxford University Press 2022. DOI: 10.1093/oso/9780199313280.003.0008

In a less radical form, the debate concerning the role of the government in relation to the economic process has been among the most striking features of the development of economic thought. This discussion occurred, for instance, during the transition from mercantilism in the direction of laissez-faire during the eighteenth century, with Adam Smith as one of the famous protagonists, and again, over a century and a half later, in the context of controlling, or at least moderating, the fluctuations in employment and prices.

The Issue

The early developments just sketched have in common two features of importance in the present context. First, they are largely normative in that they look toward a better economic system than that which prevails. In this respect, they are to be classified with modern welfare economics. True, much welfare economics deals with evaluation of alternative resource allocations or distributions, but—directly or indirectly—there is implied an assessment of alternative economic structures (e.g., perfect competition versus monopoly or oligopoly).

Second, a common dichotomy is at issue. The comparative merits of alternative systems are typically being debated under such labels as centralization against decentralization, social control or planning against free markets, or in similar terms. This dichotomy was present in the famous Mises-Hayek-Lange-Lerner controversy concerning the feasibility of socialism, and it persists today even in the distinction between two 'socialist' economies, that of the USSR (the 'command economy') and of Yugoslavia (the 'socialist market economy').

A survey of the literature will show that issues concerning the proper internal structure of business and other large organizations involves similar dichotomies. Decentralization is a fashionable slogan in many corporations. Decentralization is a popular idea among advocates of 'participatory democracy' as well as critics of present-day industrial society. Decentralization is also part of the cure proposed for the ills that plague our universities, witness recent events on many campuses.[1]

The current (though by no means universal) predilection for decentralization contrasts somewhat with the emphasis a few decades ago on the merits of (central) planning as against the dangers of (decentralized) chaos of 'free' markets.

---

[1] Paul Goodman's (1968) discussion is perhaps symptomatic.

Analytical Approach

Even if one were tempted to conclude that the issue of economic centralization is subject to cyclical swings of fashion much like the length of feminine garments, clarification would be needed of the basic terms used in the debate. Contrary to a superficial impression, it is far from obvious what is meant by the statement that "the free market with free individual enterprises offers the well-known example of a complete decentralization of production decisions..." (Tinbergen 1964, pp. 84–5). Certain iterative procedures involving information feedback between a planning agency and producing units may be regarded as decentralized by some and as centralized by others.

Similarly, the terms planning and markets, so central in certain debates, have contradictory uses. Galbraith (1967) in *The New Industrial State* speaks of industrial "planning" in describing phenomena (price formations) which other economists might classify under market system, but which Galbraith regards as eliminating market influences.

While there is leeway in the nature of definitions that one may wish to adopt, orderly discussion, and even description, is impossible without some definitions. It is perhaps characteristic of the state of the literature in this field that we may be provided with a definition of what it means to have a more or less centralized (decentralized) market economy and another definition of what it means to have a more or less centralized command economy, but no definition of "decentralization" to clarify the meaning of the statement that a market economy is decentralized in comparison with a command economy (Grossman 1967, p. 21).

But the need for conceptual clarification goes beyond a scholar's natural desire to bring verbal order into classical controversy. A discussion, conducted at least to some extent in a normative spirit, concerning both historically observed and non-existent idealized economic structures must have an important analytical element. To make such analysis possible, we shall construct a model of rather general nature, so that a variety of economic structures can be regarded as its special cases. Once the model has been constructed, such concepts as centralization, decentralization, command, or planning can be defined in terms of the properties of the model. It then becomes possible to proceed with analysis and to try to answer, within the framework of the model, questions about the feasibility of certain organizational structures in relation to assumptions concerning the economic environment. An example of such a question is whether decentralization without loss of optimal properties is possible in the presence of externalities.

A General Model of the Economic Process

We picture the economic process as consisting of two *phases*. In the first phase, the economic agents (producers, consumers, resource holders, government agencies) exchange 'messages' (proposals, bids, plans, information about technology or preferences). In the second phase, these messages are translated into plans of action (production, exchange) for the various units and ultimately into decisions to be actually implemented.

For such a process to be well-defined, we must first specify the nature of the first phase. To begin with, we must specify the *language* in which communication takes place. For instance, in the conventional model of a (perfect) market, messages specify either points (vectors) in the commodity space (input-output vectors or commodity bundles being exchanged) or price vectors. But this type of language is inadequate for the sort of communication involved in planning. On the one hand, a planning agency may be specifying not just one input-output vector (as would be the case for an individual firm), but many—one for each sector or enterprise under its supervision; similarly it may specify not just one trade vector (as would be the case for an individual engaged in barter), but many—one for each entity under it. Messages of such multiple type can be regarded as special cases of *resource flow matrices*, which I have defined elsewhere (see Hurwicz 1960a).

But even the language of resource flow matrices is insufficient to cover messages whose content describes the economic environment (technology, preferences, resource endowment). Yet in a planning system where individual producing units communicate their technologies to a central planning agency these more complex messages must be available. We see that the specification of the language to be used is a very important feature of model construction and may have decisive influence on the possibility of centralization within the given organizational structure.[2]

The first phase, in general, is thought of as iterative in nature, i.e., it consists of a sequence of *stages*. A given stage is characterized by the messages emitted by various economic agents. The message emitted by agent i in stage s will be denoted by the symbol m_s^i. By definition, every message is an element of the language M. If the agents are labeled $1, 2, \ldots, n$, there is produced in each stage a message n-tuple $(m_s^1, \ldots, m_s^n)$, written briefly as m_s. The iteration starts with an initial message n-tuple m_0, to be followed by $m_1, m_2, \ldots, m_{T-1}$, and the terminal message n-tuple m_T.[3]

---

[2] The language will be denoted by M.

[3] This notation is related to that in Malinvaud (1967). In particular, m_T does not correspond to Malinvaud's 'plan' P^s, since in our model the 'plan' is formulated in the second phase of the process.

For the process to be well-defined, it is essential to specify how the message n-tuple of a given stage is formulated in relation to the messages of the preceding phases; also, there must be a rule to determine the initial messages.[4] The rule relating messages of a given stage to their predecessors are called *response functions*, the response function of the i-th unit at stage s being denoted by f_s^i. In general, the response depends not only on earlier messages but also on the unit's information concerning the *environment* (technology, preferences, resource endowment); our symbol for a complete specification of the environment is e. When the description of the environment can be split into separate descriptions e^i, pertaining respectively to the economic units, we may think of e as an n-tuple of the *individual environmental components e^i*, so that $e = (e^1, \ldots, e^n)$.

In the literature of the decentralization problem much emphasis has been placed on cases in which the i-th economic unit can only be presumed to know its own environmental component e^i (its own technology, preferences, resource endowment), at least in the initial phase (*dispersion* of information). Of course, the messages received in the course of phase one may provide at least partial information about environmental components of other units. This may be incidental to the nature of the process or it may be the purpose of certain stages of communication as in a planned economy where the central agency is assumed to collect technological information from units under its supervision.

The dependence of response on the preceding messages and the knowledge of the environment may be expressed by the equation system

$$m_s^i = f_s^i(m_{s-1}, m_{s-2}, \ldots, m_0; e) \quad i = 1, 2, \ldots, n, \quad s = 1, 2, \ldots, T.$$

The determination of the initial messages can similarly be written as

$$m_0^i = f_0^i(e) \quad i = 1, 2, \ldots, n.[5]$$

Two features of the response relations deserve comment. First, we have allowed for the possibility that the response at every stage may be based on information (messages) from *all* previous stages all the way back to the initial one. Malinvaud's model (1967, Ch. V) calls for such accumulation of information obtained by the central planning agency from the various producing units concerning feasible input-output vectors. On the other hand, many processes, as for instance the Walrasian competitive market

---

4 These rules and relations may be probabilistic in nature.
5 Although stochastic f's can and have been used, we shall primarily discuss the problem with reference to non-probabilistic response rules.

process, can be formulated as first-order difference equations, so that the response function depends on the immediately preceding message but not on earlier ones. This type of a *first-order* process can be written as

$$m_s^i = f_s^i(m_{s-1}; e) \quad i = 1, 2, \ldots, n \quad s = 1, 2, \ldots, T.$$

The distinction between processes of finite order (such as first-order processes) and those that accumulate past information indefinitely is of considerable importance. We shall see that informational decentralization requires that the information available to any one participant in the process be limited. This limitation may be achieved with the help of restrictions on the nature of the message language M. Such restrictions, intended to preclude the possibility of a given unit completely communicating its environmental component (e.g., its preferences or technology) to a central agency, may however be rendered ineffective when indefinite accumulation of past messages is permitted. It is therefore essential to formulate simultaneous restrictions on the process both with regard to its language and its order (as a difference equation).

Second, we have also allowed for the possibility of varying the response rule as between stages; this is indicated by the subscript s (denoting the stage) attached to the response function symbol f_s^i. Processes free of such variability (i.e., where f_s^i is the same for all $s = 1,\ldots, T$), which may be called temporally homogeneous, are of particular interest.[6] Again, the Walrasian process does possess this special property. However, certain formalizations of the market process, in particular those involving a 'referee,' as in T. Marschak's (1959) model, lack this homogeneity. They resemble the type of dialogue envisaged by Malinvaud between the central planning agency and the individual producing entities. These dialogue processes exhibit a sort of cyclical homogeneity, in the sense that $f_s^i = f_{s-2}^i$. Basically, there are two fixed response patterns respectively for even-numbered and odd-numbered stages. Similarly, there may be two languages. In Malinvaud's terminology, one is called prospective indices and the second proposals.

The centralized process described by T. Marschak, on the other hand, lacks temporal homogeneity, because its early stages involve collecting environmental information by the center from other units to be processes by the center during the intermediate stages, with action commands to be transmitted from the center in the terminal stages through m_T.

The message n-tuple m_T produced in the terminal stage serves as the basis for decisions as to actions to be taken. The language of the terminal messages

---

6 Temporal homogeneity does not require that all the functions f_0^i be the same.

may or may not be that of possible actions. If not, one must, as it were, decode the terminal messages. Ideally, the decoded terminal message should provide for a feasible action plan. But in many cases it may turn out to be a set of mutually inconsistent action proposals, which we may call the *paper plan*.[7] For instance, the paper plan may specify the quantities demanded and supplied by the various units, although excess demand may not be equal to zero. It would then be necessary to make a transition from such a paper plan to a (by definition feasible) *real plan*.[8] The transition from the paper plan to the real plan might also be iterative in nature, but we shall ignore this possibility. Our real plan corresponds to Malinvaud's 'plan' P^S, which he explicitly requires to be feasible, as is true of the real plan in this paper.[9]

The operation that transforms the terminal message into a (paper) plan is defined by what we may call the *decoding* function d; we thus have a relation

$$b = d(m_T)$$

where b denotes the paper plan. In turn, a transition must be made from the paper plan b to the real plan a, written as

$$a = r(b)$$

where the functional symbol r represents the realization function to remind us that a is to be a real (i.e., feasible) plan.[10]

Since m_T indirectly determines a, we may also write

$$a = \phi(m_T)$$

with ϕ called the *outcome* function.[11]

A plan specifies the prospective actions of all units and we may show this by writing

$$b = (b^1, \ldots, b^n), \quad a = (a^1, \ldots, a^n),$$

---

[7] What is here for the sake of brevity called a 'paper plan' may actually be an unreconciled complex of individual plans.

[8] This could, for instance, be done by scaling down (or up) all (paper plan) demands proportionately until they equal the supply available under the paper plan, if we assume that the only feasibility difficulty lies in the inconsistency of the plans (i.e., that all aspects of the paper plan are *individually* feasible) and that the scaling down or up does not destroy individual feasibility.

[9] He does not introduce the paper plan concept, but we have found it useful in discussing problems of planning. In fact, some sceptics may claim that the paper plan is a realistic concept, while the concept of a necessarily feasible real plan often has no empirical counterpart.

[10] Note that neither $d(\cdot)$ nor $r(\cdot)$ involves knowledge of the environment e.

[11] [Here] $\phi = r \circ d$ is a composite function.

just as

$$m_T = (m_T^1, \ldots, m_T^n).$$

A plan (whether 'paper' or 'real') may be thought of as a resource flow matrix, the i-th component of the plan being the i-th row of such a matrix. In a more complete treatment, one might want to allow for certain indeterminacies, and thus a plan might correspond to a set of resource flow matrices. In the terminology I have used, the choice of the language M, of the response functions f_s^i, and of the outcome function ϕ (involving the specification of the decoding and realization functions d and r) specifies an adjustment process, to be denoted by π (see Hurwicz, 1960a). To a considerable extent, the study of organizational structures involves the analysis of special properties of adjustment processes. This is true of the studies of the competitive mechanism, as well as of the contributions of Malinvaud, Kornai and Lipták, T. Marschak, J. Marschak, Reiter, Radner, and others.

On Choosing the Adjustment Process

Some of the historically important controversies involve not the analysis of a particular adjustment process but of the institutional framework that determines how the process itself is chosen.

Thinking now of the adjustment process π as a variable, one may consider that it will be chosen from some 'natural' domain Π. To facilitate understanding, let us focus on the response function aspect of the adjustment process π while ignoring the outcome function. The responses of the i-th economic unit are governed by the $(T+1)$-tuple of the response functions f_s^i, $s = 0, 1, \ldots, T$, to be denoted by $f^i = (f_0^i, f_1^i, \ldots, f_T^i)$. For the sake of brevity, we shall call f^i the i-th *behavior rule*. A domain from which f^i could conceivably be chosen will be denoted by $\mathcal{F}^i$.

It is often said that certain behavior rules would not be compatible with individual incentives. Since the notion of incentives is of fundamental importance in discussions concerning the possibility of a planned, centralized, or socialist economic system, it is advantageous to formalize it. This formalization can be accomplished, for instance, by using the concept of Nash equilibrium in non-cooperative games of strategy. We may think of f^i as the strategy employed by the i-th unit, with $\mathcal{F}^i$ as the domain from which the strategy could be chosen. It is further necessary to introduce some payoff (utility) function that represents the individual's motivation in choosing his strategy. We shall denote it by u^i.[12]

---

[12] The environment e will affect this utility, but we shall not go into the details of this admittedly important aspect of the problem. The effect of e, aside from the preferences of the

The Nash-optimal n-tuple of behavior rules $\bar{f}^i = (\bar{f}^1, \ldots, \bar{f}^n)$ would be determined by the relations

$$\bar{f}^i = \operatorname*{argmax}_{f^i \in \mathcal{F}^i} u^i(f^i, \bar{f}^{-i}) \quad i = 1, \ldots, n$$

where f^{-i} contains the $n-1$ components f^j other than f^i.[13] An n-tuple $\bar{f}$ may be called (individually) *incentive-compatible* if it is Nash-optimal.

Similarly *group incentive-compatibility* may be defined in terms analogous to the concept of the core. More specifically one might introduce the concept of *admissible coalitions* (somewhat as in Luce-Raiffa ψ-stability;[see Luce and Raiffa 1957, ch. 10]) and define group incentive-compatibility as non-existence of admissible blocking coalitions. According to this definition, individual incentive-compatibility is a special case of group incentive-compatibility with the admissible groups each consisting of one individual.

A good deal of so-called positive economics attempts to see which behavior rules are and which are not compatible with individual or group incentives. The proposition that economic units will treat prices parametrically when these units are very small in comparison with the total market—but not otherwise—belongs to this category.[14]

On the other hand, the theory of government intervention in economic activities, whether in the form of zoning regulations, tariffs, or socialism, deals with restrictions on the choice of behavior rules by individuals.[15] The totality of these restrictions may be referred to as the prevailing *economic regime*.[16] Formally, the regime defines a *permissible domain* F^i from which the i-th unit is entitled to choose its behavior rule. The permissible domain F^i is a subset of the natural domain $\mathcal{F}^i$. The regime may be identified with the n-tuple $(F^1, \ldots, F^n)$. Two polar cases suggest themselves: The permissible domain F^i may equal the 'natural' domain $\mathcal{F}^i$ for all units. One is tempted to call this condition the 'true laissez-faire' regime; but of course no advocate of laissez-faire would have advocated such an extreme solution. At the other extreme, each unit's permissible domain might contain a single behavior rule

*i*th unit, might be treated probabilistically and integrated out through the computation of an expected value.

[13] It should be noted that the preceding discussion sidesteps the problem of coalition formation which might occur when participants are free to determine their behavior rules.

[14] However, economics often chooses to focus on how a given process, e.g., the Walrasian mechanism, would work if its rules were followed, regardless of whether these rules are incentive compatible.

[15] Restrictions on behavior constitute a special case of restrictions on behavior rules.

[16] Frisch (1959) has used this term in a related but different sense, while J. Marschak (1954) speaks of a *constitution*.

(F^i a singleton set). Here the individual has no freedom of choice left, and the regime might be called 'completely programmed' or automatized.[17]

If the permissible domains F^i are broad enough to contain the respective Nash-optimal behavior rules $\bar{f}^i$, the regime itself may be called incentive-compatible. The critique of certain 'decentralized socialism' proposals has focused on their failure to be incentive compatible. Similar observations apply to perfect competition when individual units are not sufficiently small.

The concept of permissible domains may deserve some attention as providing a tool for the formalization of the institutional framework of the economic system, including, in particular, the legal framework. It can also be applied to interpret two possible usages of the term 'centralization,' viz., as (a) a situation in which a decision-maker determines the permissible domains for the other units, (b) a situation in which all but one decision-maker has one-element (singleton F^i) permissible domains. In both cases the exceptional decision-maker is the 'center.'

Structure of Authority

From now on we shall be studying situations in which a particular adjustment process has been chosen, and we shall explore those of its attributes that would suggest labeling it centralized or decentralized. In this section we shall deal with aspects of an adjustment process corresponding to structure of authority.

In defining centralization we want to cover a broader class of processes than (but including) that introduced by T. Marschak (1959, pp. 411–12). In particular, we want to accommodate the typical hierarchical decision structures observed in bureaucracies and certain planned economies. Marschak's case involves a one-person center which in the last stage tells everyone else what to do. This can be formally expressed as a property of the decoding function, viz., that

$$b^j = d^j(m_T^i) \quad \text{for all } j. \tag{1}$$

Here i is the (*one-person*) *center*, the other units j, $j \neq i$, are the *subordinates*. Thus (1) expresses a crucial aspect of one-person centralization.[18] In contradistinction, we will say that the *j*th *unit* has *autonomy* if

$$b^j = d^j(m_T^j). \tag{2}$$

---

[17] The reader should recall that, although the exposition is in terms of the f's, the concepts are meant to apply to other components of the adjustment process as well, viz., the outcome functions and language.

[18] 'Person' may stand for an agency.

In either definition we want to exclude the *trivial* case where

$$b^j = \text{const.,} \text{ (independent of } m_T) \quad \text{for all } j = 1, 2, \ldots, n. \tag{3}$$

But the conditions (1) and (2) are not sufficient to provide correspondence of terminology with the intent of usage. In particular, we want to exclude from the definition of centralization the case in which m_T^i (which other units must obey) was 'dictated' to unit i by the other units at the preceding stage of the iterative process. Formally, this is expressed by the requirement that

$$f_T^i(m_{T-1}; e) \text{ be 'sensitive to' } e^i, \tag{4}$$

where $e = (e^1, \ldots, e^n)$. With

$$e^{-i} = (e^1, \ldots, e^{i-1}, e^{i+1}, \ldots, e^n),$$

the statement in equation (4) means that, for a certain selection of the argument m_{T-1}, two distinct values of e^i (while e^{-i} remains the same) produce different values of m_T^i. Thus, by definition, *unit i is a one-person center when* (1) *and* (4) *hold and* (3) *does not.*

Similarly, to make autonomy of j meaningful, we wish to rule out the case where m_T^j was dictated to j by one of the other units. Formally, we require that

$$f_T^j(m_{T-1}; e) \text{ be 'sensitive to' } e^j \tag{5}$$

in the previously defined sense. Thus, by definition, *unit j is autonomous when* (2) *and* (5) *hold and b^j is 'sensitive to' m_T^j.*

It will be noted that there can be no one-person center when more than one unit is autonomous.

We may wish to use the term 'decentralized' (with regard to authority) when some autonomy prevails, so that there could be different degrees of decentralization (of authority).

The concepts of center and of autonomy can be generalized in several respects. For instance, to define the i-th unit as a (one-person) center we may replace (1) and (4) by the following requirements: that there exist some stage s' (possibly, but not necessarily, equal to T) such that, (1) for all j, $b^j = g^j(m_{s'}^i)$, and (2) there does not exist a subset K of units not including i for which $b^j = h^j(m_{s'-1}^K, m_{s'-2}^K, \ldots)$ for all j.[19]

The concept of autonomy can be generalized in a similar manner.

---

[19] In the earlier definition, for the special case $s' = T$, condition (2) of the generalized definition is satisfied by virtue of equation (4), but it could be satisfied in other ways as well.

Another direction of generalization allows for the existence of a *directing group* instead of a one-person center. We shall only sketch this concept here. The actions of all units are determined by the messages of members of the directing group K; i.e.,

$$b^j = g^j(m^K) \quad \text{for all } j, \tag{6}$$

where m^K is the matrix of all m_s^k, k in K and $s = 0, 1, \ldots, T$. Furthermore group K is minimal in the sense that (6) is not true for any proper subset of K.[20]

For some purposes one may wish to look at the hierarchical structure of the directing group. Unit 1, for instance, would be *directly under orders of* unit 2 *in stage s* if the following were true: $m_s^1 = f_s^1(m_{s-1}; e)$ is equivalent to $m_s^1 = g_s^1(m_{s-1}^2; e)$ where the range of g_s^1 is a subset of M ('the language') determined by m_{s-1}^2. The interpretation of this requirement is that unit 2 issues to unit 1 (at stage s) an order which specifies a restricted range of messages, say M_s^{12}, from which unit 1 must choose; the choice will be determined, according to a rule g_s^1, by the information unit 1 has about the environment e. In the limiting case where the set M_s^{12} is a singleton, there is, of course, no latitude left to unit 1. It is easy to see bow a tree type diagram of hierarchical structure could be constructed depicting the relation of directly taking orders when certain assumptions (e.g., asymmetry) are made.

These concepts could be used to represent a planning hierarchy of the following (one-step) type. For each economic sector (group of, say, producing units) there is a 'sector supervisor,' and he in turn directly takes orders from the 'chief supervisor.' In the initial stage of the process, the producing units convey their production functions to the respective sector supervisors who aggregate them and inform the chief supervisor of the aggregate production functions of their respective sectors. The chief supervisor makes certain decisions in terms of these aggregates and other information available to him (say aggregate resource endowment) and sends to the sector supervisors messages in terms of sector aggregates. Finally, the sector supervisors determine the input-output vectors for their respective producing units. Here the directing group consists of the sector supervisors, but the hierarchy also includes the chief supervisor from whom they take (aggregate) orders. These orders can be interpreted as restrictive M-sets. The orders given by the sector supervisors to the producing units are singletons, i.e., the producing units lack autonomy. In fact, they have no influence on the choice of their input-output vectors, in the sense that, for a producing unit j, b^j not only is not determined by m_T^j but in fact does not even depend on m_T^j.

---

[20] Under suitable assumptions K will be unique, although this is not obvious from the preceding definition. More generally, the set of all units $\{1, 2, \ldots, n\}$ might be partitioned into subsets each having its directing group.

It might seem appropriate to couch a definition of command economy in terms of the authority concepts just developed (see Grossman 1967, p. 15). Such an economy prevails when there exists a set of units constituting the hierarchy (the directing group being a subset of the hierarchy, and the units outside the hierarchy lacking autonomy or even influence on their own actions). The one-person center economy described earlier is, therefore a special case of a command economy, whose hierarchy and directing group are collapsed into one unit—the center.

The exchange of information in a command economy need not be of the one-step variety sketched in the preceding paragraphs.[21] The producing unit, instead of conveying all (or, at least, all relevant) information in one iteration stage, may take part in repeated iterations between itself and members of the hierarchy. Malinvaud's (1967, Ch. IV) formalization of Taylor's procedure belongs to this type, with the hierarchy being of the one-person (planning bureau) type.[22] It is perhaps characteristic of the present state of terminology that while the term 'command' seems appropriate as a description of such a process and has been so used by some workers in the field (e.g., Marglin [1969]), Malinvaud himself discusses the process as an example of a "decentralized procedure for planning."[23]

In a hierarchical structure it is possible to introduce concepts of centralization. In particular, a hierarchy is centralized when all of its members are under the orders of one member, either directly or indirectly.[24] It is obvious that a 'one-person-center' hierarchy is centralized, hence the present usage is consistent with that developed earlier. It should be noted that the command economy, as here defined, may but need not be centralized. On the other

---

[21] T. Marschak's (1959) centralized process is of the one-step (no feedback) variety, with a one-person center.

[22] Of course, the planning bureau might have an internal hierarchical structure of the type described above, but Malinvaud ignores this aspect.

[23] It may be natural to inquire about the meaning attributed by Malinvaud to the term "decentralized" in this context. In the absence of an explicit statement, the following elements seem to enter: the information concerning production functions is initially available only to the respective producing units (dispersion of information); the language of messages between the producing units and the planning bureau is of a simple nature, typically a vector of the dimensionality of the commodity space (or less); not all calculations are carried out by the planning bureau—some are done by the producing units. As noted above, one of Malinvaud's examples involves the accumulation of all the past messages, i.e., is not a difference equation system of finite order.

The fact that a given adjustment process may qualify both as command (in fact, of the centralized variety) and, at the same time, as a decentralized planning procedure points up the importance of the distinction between the authority aspects and informational aspects in classifying centralization phenomena. Malinvaud's procedures may be centralized with regard to authority structure but largely decentralized with regard to informational aspects.

[24] Unit 1 is (indirectly) under orders of unit 2 if there exists a sequence of units, say $i_1, \ldots, i_p$, ($p \geqq 1$), such that 1 is directly under orders of i_1, which is directly under orders of i_2, and so forth, up to i_p, directly under orders of unit 2. The term 'directly under orders' was rigorously defined above.

hand, a centralized economy is necessarily a command economy. It should be clear that a Walrasian price adjustment economy is not of the command type, hence not centralized. In fact, in such an economy there is no directing group (hence no hierarchy) and all units are autonomous; thus the process is decentralized with regard to authority.[25]

Structure of Information

The now classic von Mises-Lange-Hayek controversy did not focus on the structure of authority in resource allocating mechanisms but rather on the informational aspects. In extolling the virtues of the market mechanism, Hayek (1945) stressed that its communication requirements, although minimal, were sufficient to provide the needed coordination between economic units. By contrast, a (one-step) command economy would presumably require tremendous transfers of information from the individual units to the planning authorities as well as huge calculations to be performed by the latter, if efficient resource allocation were to be attained.

The need for calculation is obvious and its difficulties received particular attention in the early stages of the discussion when, following Barone, the planning authority was thought of as solving the Walrasian general-equilibrium equation system for the whole economy (see Hayek, 1935, p. 208). The Taylor-Lange remedy prescribed that the calculations be carried out by an iterative dialogue between the planning authority and the individual (producer) economic units, in a manner analogous to the operation of the market. In this fashion the calculating capacity of these units is enlisted to supplement that of the planning authority. If calculation is regarded as a sort of production process, this amounts to using several workers to accomplish a task that is excessive for one. The use of the calculating capacities of the individual economic units is an important aspect of the notion of decentralization of the resource-allocating mechanism in the context of this debate.[26] In the light of recent developments in the field of giant high-speed electronic computers the merits of decentralizing calculations would deserve systematic consideration.

The problem of calculating solutions given the availability of relevant information is only one of the computational difficulties. Generally speaking,

---

[25] I have formalized an adjustment process closely related to the Walrasian under the label of the quasi-competitive process (see Hurwicz 1960a, footnote 5). To relate the treatment there to the present work, certain details must be modified, since in the earlier paper the role of terminal messages m_T was not made explicit and there is no distinction between a paper plan and a real plan.

[26] It also seems implicit in Malinvaud's (1967) usage.

extensive calculations (in addition to experimentation, and so forth) would be required for an individual unit to estimate, say, its complete production function as called for under a one-step centralized procedure. In the 'iterative dialogue' approach involving the individual units this burden is avoided by requiring the producing units to obtain (and transmit) at any given stage of iteration information concerning only a limited region of the production set.

Underlying the Hayek type of argument is the basic assumption that the information concerning a given unit's environmental component e^i (its production set, resources, tastes) can be obtained more easily and more accurately by that unit than by anyone else. In idealized form, this assumption can be expressed by postulating that at the initial stage of the adjustment process each unit has complete knowledge of its own environmental component and no knowledge at all of other units' environmental components (dispersion of information).

This postulate can be formalized by specifying that, for a given set of incoming messages, a given unit's response function depends only on its own environmental component, but not on those of other units; i.e., we have

$$\begin{cases} m_s^i = f_s^i(m_{s-1}; e^i) & i = 1, 2, \ldots, n \quad s = 1, 2, \ldots, T \\ m_0^i = f_0^i(e^i) \end{cases} \tag{7}$$

where e^i has replaced the symbol $e = (e^1, \ldots, e^{i-1}, e^i, e^{i+1}, \ldots, e^n)$ found in the general adjustment process formula.[27] The term *privacy* has been suggested to label processes of the type formalized by [equation (7)].[28]

One implication of [equation (7)] is that no one has (or can use) any information about other units at the initial stage ($s = 0$). Subsequently he only has such information as may have been conveyed to him through the messages. Thus, for instance, at stage $s = 1$, unit 2 only knows about unit 1 as much as was conveyed through the message m_0^2.[29]

In a first-order process with privacy (as in [equation (7)]), [a] given unit's knowledge of other environmental components is confined to that contained in their messages from the immediately preceding stage. More generally, one may consider a process

---

[27] For the sake of simplicity, we are confining ourselves here to a first-order process.

[28] The term I originally proposed in Hurwicz (1960) footnote 5 'externality,' turned out to be confusing by association with such phenomena as external diseconomies of scale.

[29] In the present exposition we have ignored the possibility of using 'addressed' messages, i.e., messages that are received only by some of the units. To some extent, the equivalent effect can be introduced by making, say f_s^3 insensitive to m_{s-1}^4; this could be interpreted as meaning that, in stage s, the message from unit 4 was not addressed to unit 3.

$$\begin{cases} m_s^i = f_s^i(m_{s-1}, \ldots, m_0; e^i) & i = 1, 2, \ldots, n \\ m_0^i = f_0^i(e^i) \end{cases} \tag{8}$$

in which information obtained from earlier messages can also be retained.

It is at this point that the nature of the permissible messages becomes crucial. If there were no difficulty in transferring complex messages, we might postulate that each m_0^i contains complete relevant information about e^i. Hence it could be assumed that one of the units, say unit 2, could become a one-person center in stage $s = 1$, because at this time $f_1^2(m_0^1, \ldots, m_0^n; e^2) = f_1^2(e^1, \ldots, e^n; e^2)$. Thus one-stage centralization becomes easy.[30] The classic (Hayek-type) objections to such a procedure must be interpreted as implying difficulties in effecting such information transfers, at least in a single stage (one-step) of the process.

To formalize such difficulties one may proceed by imposing restrictions on the language M of the process, i.e., on the nature of permissible messages. It is natural, in the context of the present discussion, to make these restrictions severe enough to prohibit the transmission of complete information about production sets, indifference maps, and resource endowments, while still permitting messages of complexity comparable to those occurring in a Walrasian market process. To satisfy the latter requirement, one must permit the transmission of proposed input-output vectors as well as price vectors. As it happens, when the number of commodities is assumed finite, the dimensionality of the commodity and price vectors is the same, equal to the number of commodities (say m) in the economy. Hence, at the very least, the language M must be rich enough to contain messages specifying arbitrary points of an m-dimensional space. Formally, this could be accomplished by setting M equal to such a space. This would mean that a message is always an ordered m-tuple of real numbers.

In certain situations, it seems preferable to consider the effects of having a language M that is restricted, but not quite as severely. In particular, one may wish to permit messages specifying subsets, rather than merely points, of the commodity space. Such a language may appear overly rich since it makes possible the transmission of complete information concerning production sets. Nevertheless, this milder restriction on language would still make it impossible to operate a command-type process of first order (as in [equation (7)]) in an economy with more than one producing unit. The difficulty here would be not so much in transmitting technological information about the individual units to the center as transmitting the individualized commands

---

[30] Commands would still have to be sent back to the individual units from unit 2, but that information transfer is simpler than the transfer of the environmental information.

from the center to the separate units. For instance, let the center be unit 1, the producing units 2 and 3. Suppose the center has selected the respective input-output vectors, say x^2 and x^3, for the two producing units. Obviously these could not be transmitted under the assumption that the message emitted by unit 1 must be a single point of the commodity space. But even if the center can transmit the set consisting of x^2 and x^3, this ability would not resolve the difficulty as long as the set transmitted was an unordered set, i.e., the two producing units would not, in general, know which vector pertains to which producing unit.[31]

An important relationship exists between the restrictions imposed on the language of the messages and the number of lagged message n-tuples permitted in the difference equations of ([8]) above. When more than one lagged value of m_s is permitted, the effect is somewhat equivalent to permitting a less restrictive language. Thus if m_{s-1} and m_{s-2} are permitted as arguments of f_s^i for $s = 2, 3, \ldots, T$, and a message is restricted to a point in the commodity space, the i-th unit can hold in its "memory" two such points (from the two lagged messages); the result is similar to what might have happened if there was only a single lag but it was permitted to use two-point messages. The problem of issuing differentiated commands discussed in the preceding paragraph, for instance, could be handled in a two-lag (second-order difference equation) system by having, say, f_T^2 responsive to m_T^1 while f_T^3 is responsive to m_{T-1}^1. In particular, in systems with unlimited memory, i.e., with f_s^i containing as arguments all the past messages back to the initial stage, we come very close to obviating any restrictions imposed on the language. It is therefore somewhat questionable whether such processes constitute satisfactory formalizations of the difficulties postulated in the informational decentralization debate.

Among other requirements to be considered in the present context is that of 'anonymity.'[32] I shall not present it here in detail.[33] Suffice it to say that this requirement is satisfied by the Walrasian process where price adjustments depend on aggregate excess demand rather than on the individual bids. On the other hand, the requirement is violated in a command economy where it is essential to know the origin of a message.

---

[31] In Hurwicz (1960a), I restricted messages to arbitrary subsets of the commodity space. In joint work with Radner and Reiter (see Hurwicz et al. 1975) a stochastic adjustment process is used in which the language is restricted to single points of the commodity space.

[32] Under 'anonymity' the response to a message does not depend on its origin.

[33] See Hurwicz (1960a) and also (1960b).

Informational Efficiency and Decentralization

Intuitively, an adjustment process is *informationally centralized* if, at some stage of the process, at least one of the participants comes into possession of all relevant information concerning everyone's environment and everyone's prospective actions. A process is informationally *non-centralized* if such concentration of information in one agent's hands cannot occur.

To rule out such concentration at all stages of the process, one must rule it out for the beginning and for the later stages of the process. To rule it out at the beginning, one can postulate initial dispersion of information; this dispersion is reflected in the requirement of *privacy*[34] imposed on the response functions [equation (7)].

But even with initial dispersion, information might concentrate in one hand in the course of the adjustment process if there are no limitations on how much information is transferred and retained, at each stage. Such limitations are inherent in the attributes of *anonymity* and *self-relevance*,[35] as well as from the assumption that the process is (a difference equation system) of finite order.[36]

In my earlier work, I assumed the process to be of finite (first) order and defined *informational decentralization* in terms of privacy, anonymity, and self-relevance. Thus defined, informational decentralization constitutes a subcategory with respect to informational non-centralization. At present, partly under the influence of work done by Camacho, Radner, Reiter, and the Marschaks (J. and T.), I would be inclined to regard the concept of non-centralization as perhaps the more fundamental. However, the attributes of privacy, anonymity, and self-relevance, together with finite-order assumption, remain of particular interest. For on the one hand, they are all present in the Walrasian competitive process which has served as the economist's inspiration for the notion of informational decentralization; on the other hand, they cannot all be present in the 'command' economy, the economist's standard example of informational centralization. If one thinks of different economic systems (adjustment processes) as points on a map, the aim in providing a definition was to draw a boundary line so as to divide the map into two regions, with the competitive mechanism situated in the 'informationally decentralized' region and the command economy outside of it. Clearly, there are many ways of drawing such a line. Some writers have had a tendency to shrink the 'informationally decentralized' region almost

---

34 Previously called 'externality.'
35 'Self-relevance' permits an entity to specify what would happen to itself only.
36 The finite-order assumption limits the 'memory' of participants.

to the point of containing nothing but the competitive mechanism, others have been more broad-minded.[37]

Why is it of importance how the line is drawn? One answer lies in the use to which the definitions are put. In the present case, the choice of definition affects the answer to the question as to how wide a class of environments is capable of (informational) decentralization without sacrificing the allocative efficiency ('performance') properties characteristic of the competitive mechanism. These properties may be formulated in terms of technological efficiency, or—somewhat more ambitiously—in terms of Pareto optimality, or even in terms of social welfare functions. Elsewhere (see Hurwicz 1960a, footnote 5), we settled on the complex of optimality properties arising naturally in the context of welfare-economics theorems concerning competitive equilibrium. We defined a process as Pareto-satisfactory if its equilibria were Pareto optimal and certain other properties were also present. Without going into formal definitions, suffice it to say that these are almost exactly the properties established by Arrow, Debreu, and Koopmans for the competitive mechanism when the environment satisfies, among others, the well-known conditions of absence of external (dis-)economies, absence of indivisibilities, convexity of production sets and of the preference functions.[38]

It is well known that equilibria may be non-optimal or even fail to exist when some of these environmental conditions are violated. It then becomes natural to ask whether one can conceive of a system that would have the desired properties (Pareto-satisfactoriness) on the performance side. Now if the competitive mechanism will not do, what is the class of mechanisms that would be considered acceptable? If no restrictions were imposed on the informational nature of the mechanism, the problem could be solved by postulating an omniscient planner with infinite capacity to carry out computations within arbitrarily short time periods. To make the problem nontrivial, one must take into account some of the difficulties of handling information outlined in the preceding section.

Perhaps the simplest approach is to specify some of these restrictions under the label of informational decentralization (e.g., as at the beginning of this section) and ask whether it is possible to devise processes that are both informationally decentralized and Pareto-satisfactory (or, more generally, *performance-satisfactory*) in environments that violate some of the classical assumptions (e.g., where external (dis-)economies or indivisibilities are present). When the concepts used are rigorously defined, it is possible to answer such questions in certain cases. It turns out, for instance, that

---

[37] Typically, these concepts are only implicit in a writer's discussion rather than expressed through a formal definition or model.

[38] We call these the 'classical environments'.

presence of indivisibilities can be overcome, but external (dis-) economies may not be capable of informational decentralization without sacrificing performance-satisfactoriness.

At this point we become aware of the implications of adopting definitions of informational decentralization that are either too narrow or too wide. If the definition is very narrow (e.g., almost equivalent to that of the price mechanism), it will appear that environments other than the classical one are not (in the sense of such a definition) capable of decentralization without sacrificing performance. If the definition is extremely 'lenient,' practically every environment is formally decentralizable, but one may feel that such 'decentralized' mechanisms are actually infeasible or excessively costly due to the difficulties stressed by Hayek and others.

At this stage of the discussion, it is possible to take two alternative, though not incompatible, routes. First, one may introduce the concept of *informational efficiency*. A process is said to be informationally more efficient than another if it requires, in some sense, less information for its operation. Properties such as 'privacy,' 'anonymity,' and so forth, may be regarded as specifying a certain minimum of information efficiency. Thus it may be interesting to know whether an adjustment process is performance-satisfactory (e.g., in the Pareto sense) without requiring more information than permitted by such restrictions as privacy or anonymity. This approach was explored by the writer and by others in a number of recent contributions.[39]

The alternative approach, whose merits have been stressed by both [Jacob] Marschak and [Thomas] Marschak in different contexts, takes explicit account of the technology, costs, and risks, of information processing that goes on when the economic mechanism (adjustment process) operates. A mechanism can then be defined as optimal if it is feasible (in terms of information processing technology) and provides the maximum value of outcomes, net of the costs of operating the system. For instance, one could determine, in principle at least, whether under specified circumstances a command or autonomous structure of authority would come closer to such 'net' informational optimality.[40]

In what follows, we sketch briefly a model that could serve as a common base for both approaches. This model makes explicit that there are *error components* both in the perception and transmission of information pertaining to the environment and to messages received and that these errors are more

---

[39] See Camacho (1970), Kanemitsu (1966, 1971), and Ledyard (1968).

[40] Here, as elsewhere in this paper, we abstract from the difficulties in enforcing the mechanism and also from values, such as freedom of decision, which are not explicitly included in the Pareto ordering of outcomes, since they involve a valuation of the mechanism as such.

or less serious and costly depending on the information-processing activities used.[41]

We shall start with a very simple case. Perception errors will be denoted by generic symbols v, w, with a prescript denoting the perceiving unit. Thus $^iv^j$ will denote the error in perception by the i-th unit of the environmental component e^j; similarly, $^iw^j_s$ will denote the error in the perception by the i-th unit of the message m^j_s.[42] The adjustment process can now be written as

$$m^i_s = f^i_s(m^1_{s-1} + {}^iw^1_{s-1}, \dots, m^n_{s-1} + {}^iw^n_{s-1}; e^1 + {}^iv^1, \dots, e^n + {}^iv^n) \qquad (9)$$

for all i, and $s = 1, \dots, n$, with an analogous formula for $s = 0$.[43]

Now the requirement of privacy can be justified, for instance, by specifying that the variance of $^iv^j$ is very large whenever $i \neq j$ and zero for $i = j$. A more realistic picture is obtained by introducing an informational activity variable x which describes the techniques involved in producing the perceptions used in the adjustment process. The information technology can then be described by specifying (a) the set X of feasible values of x, and (b) two groups of functional relations, associating respectively the error variances and costs with the values of x. Thus for instance, denoting the error variances by $\sigma^2(^iw^j_s)$ and $\sigma^2(^iv^j)$, we may write functional relations of the first group as

$$\sigma^2(^iw^j_s) = \beta_{w,i,j,s}(x),$$
$$\sigma^2(^iv^j) = \beta_{v,i,j}(x).$$

Covariances could also be assumed to depend on x in an analogous manner. Similarly, one might postulate informational cost functions written as

$$c = \gamma(x)$$

where c could be a resource vector, rather than monetary cost.

In such a model of informational technology we need no longer postulate that the error components have fixed variances. Instead, it might be postulated that one must use very costly technologies x to produce low variance values for $^iv^i$, $i \neq j$, while the cost of a technology x' that can produce a low variance $^iv^i$ is negligible in comparison.

---

[41] A similar approach can be employed with regard to calculations, but we shall not introduce it here.

[42] If the errors are thought of as random variables (obviously only a very special case), their variances indicate the obtainable accuracy.

[43] The m's and e's are the true values, $m + w$ and $e + v$ the perceived values.

Similarly, restrictions on the language M used in communication can be rationalized in terms of either feasibility or costs. Thus the variances of the w's may be relatively low when the message is simple (e.g., a single point of the commodity space) but high otherwise, unless, perhaps, one resorts to very costly methods of transmission of the messages. Certain correlations between the errors ${}^i w_s^1, \ldots, {}^i w_s^n$ may be used to explain the requirement of anonymity or aggregativeness of the process.

Clearly, the additive error model is very crude. More generally, one could define multi-dimensional random mappings from the spaces of true variables and [to] account for various limitations of perception in a more natural manner. The mapping representing i's perception of received messages will be denoted by ${}^i \mu_s$, that representing i's perceptions of the environment by ${}^i \varepsilon_s$.[44] The adjustment process can now be written as

$$m_s^i = f_s^i [{}^i \mu_s(m_{s-1}); {}^i \varepsilon_s(e)] \tag{10}$$

where $m_{s-1} = (m_{s-1}^1, \ldots, m_{s-1}^n)$ and $e = (e^1, \ldots, e^n)$. In relation to the 'mapping model' of (10), formula (9) represents a special case in which the range of the mapping has the same dimension as its domain, so that the dimensionality of the 'true values' and of the 'perceived values' is the same. More generally, however, these dimensionalities need not be the same: when we perceive only the sum or average value of the components of a vector, the true values are multi-dimensional, but the perceived values one-dimensional. A phenomenon of this type may occur with regard to the (message perception) mapping ${}^i \mu_s$, thus again justifying anonymity or aggregativeness.

As in the simpler error model, the nature of the mapping may be determined by the value of the informational activity variable x chosen from its domain X; variances and costs are again determined by functions defined on this domain.

Extreme assumptions (zero or infinite variances, costs, or both) lead to an analysis of a restricted class of adjustment processes (e.g., informationally decentralized) whose members are equally acceptable, while those outside the class are totally unacceptable. When knowledge about intermediate values of variances and costs becomes available, a more sophisticated analysis will be possible.

---

[44] The subscript s in ${}^i \varepsilon_s$ allows for informational activities, e.g., market research that would increase the i-th entity's knowledge of the environment through channels other than formal messages. (This generalizes the concept of the adjustment process beyond its formalization elsewhere in the paper.)

Open Issues

In the light of the preceding discussion, is there a meaningful problem of centralization versus decentralization of the economic system? Are we condemned to perpetual arguments about definitions, or are there substantive empirical or theoretical issues involved?

Perhaps not surprisingly, the writer feels that there are genuine problems, but also that these problems can be successfully tackled only within the framework of a formal model and with the help of rigorous definitions. One way of summarizing the complex of issues under discussion is in terms of the relationship between the structure of authority and the structure of information, taking into account performance-satisfactoriness on the one hand and the class of environments to be served by the system on the other. Figuratively, we may think of four variables ('axes') representing the structure of authority (command, autonomy), structure of information (privacy, anonymity), an indicator of performance-satisfactoriness (e.g., Pareto-satisfactoriness), environment class (e.g., free or not free of external diseconomies, indivisibilities, convex, continuous, etc.). Many of the questions raised can be expressed in the following manner: Which points (i.e., combinations of the values of variables) of this four-variable space are feasible, and among feasible ones which are preferable in terms of net performance (net in the sense that informational costs have been deducted)?

As an example, the market corresponds to a point in this space characterized by autonomy on the structure of authority axis, by privacy (and other components of what the writer has called informational decentralization) on the information structure axis, and by Pareto-satisfactoriness on the performance axis when the environment axis is chosen with the classical characteristics of divisibility, convexity, absence of externalities, and so forth. One hopes to establish impossibility theorems showing that certain points of the space are unoccupied, for instance combinations calling for informational decentralization, Pareto-satisfactoriness, and certain types of external diseconomies. When performance criteria are of the type specified by Malinvaud (1967), it seems possible to devise command economies with partial informational decentralization, but so far for rather narrow classes of environments (e.g., Leontief-Samuelson economies).

Another important 'axis' is that corresponding to individual or group incentive-compatibility. It may be conjectured that, in general, one cannot hope to achieve Pareto-satisfactoriness, informational decentralization, and individual incentive-compatibility even when externalities are absent.[45]

---

[45] If the conjecture is true in the form stated, it would a fortiori be true with group incentive-compatibility replacing individual incentive-compatibility, since the former implies the latter, an individual being regarded as a special type of group.

When performance-satisfactoriness is required and the environment class is reasonably broad, there may be general relationships to be discovered between the structure of authority and the structure of information. Thus requirements such as privacy or anonymity might rule out command structure of authority, because privacy would make it impossible for the center to acquire enough information for optimal, or even feasible, decisions.

Among the so far unresolved controversial issues would be: What type of mechanism is appropriate for environmental conditions involving sharp transitions (e.g., war mobilization)? Traditionally it has been argued that conditions of this type require a command structure of authority.

Another important problem deserving investigation is the type of mechanism suitable, in the absence of operating markets for future goods, for investment decisions in economies where a great deal of complementarity results from separate investment decisions. Assuming that it is not feasible to create a market for the relevant future goods (which might conceivably take care of the difficulties), one may ask what combination of authority and information structure would provide performance-satisfactory results. Are some of the traditional arguments in favor of a command economy justified for such situations within the framework of the present analysis?

References

Camacho, A. (1970) Externalities, optimality and informationally decentralized resource allocation processes, *International Economic Review*, 11(2): 318–27.

Frisch, R. (1959) On welfare theory and Pareto regions, in *International Economic Papers, No. 9*, ed. A. Peacock et al., 39–92. New York, NY: Macmillan.

Galbraith, J. (1967) *The New Industrial State*. Boston, MA: Houghton Mifflin.

Goodman, P. (1968) *People or Personnel: Decentralizing and the Mixed System*. New York, NY: Random House.

Grossman, G. (1967) *Economic Systems*. Englewood Cliffs, NJ: Prentice-Hall.

Hayek, F. (1935) *Collectivist Economic Planning*. London: Routledge.

Hayek, F. (1945) The use of knowledge in society, *American Economic Review*, 35(4): 519–30.

Hurwicz, L. (1960a) Optimality and informational efficiency in resource allocation processes, in *Mathematical Methods in the Social Sciences*, ed. K. Arrow, S. Karlin, and P. Suppes, 27–46. Palo Alto, CA: Stanford University Press.

Hurwicz, L. (1960b) Conditions for economic efficiency of centralized and decentralized structures, in *Value and Plan*, ed. G. Grossman, 162–83. Berkeley, CA: University of California Press.

Hurwicz, L., R. Radner, and S. Reiter (1975) A stochastic decentralized resource allocation process, *Econometrica*, 43(2): 187–221, and 43(3): 363–93.

Kanemitsu, H. (1966) Informational efficiency and decentralization in optimal resource allocation, *The Economic Studies Quarterly*, 16(3): 22–40.

Kanemitsu, H. (1971) On the stability of an adjustment process in non-classical environments, mimeo (revised 1975). Abstract in *Econometrica* 1971, 39(4): 132–35.

Ledyard, J. (1968) Resource allocation in unselfish environments, *American Economic Review*, 58(2): 227–37.

Luce, D. and H. Raiffa (1957) *Games and Decisions*. New York, NY: Wiley.

Malinvaud, F. (1967) Decentralized procedures for planning, in *Activity Analysis in the Theory of Growth and Planning*, ed. E. Malinvaud and M. Bacharach, 170–208. London: Macmillan.

Marglin, S. (1969) Information in price and command systems of planning, in *Public Economics: An Analysis of the Public Production and Consumption and their Relation to the Private Sector*, ed. J. Margolis and H. Guitton, 54–76. London: Macmillan.

Marschak, J. (1954) Towards an economic theory of organization and information, in *Decision Processes*, ed. R. Thrall, C. Coombs, and R. Davis, 187–220. New York, NY: Wiley.

Marschak, T. (1959) Centralization and decentralization in economic organizations, *Econometrica*, 27(3): 399–430.

Tinbergen, J. (1964) *Central Planning*. New Haven, CT: Yale University Press.

9

The Design of Mechanisms for Resource Allocation

Traditionally, economic analysis treats the economic system as one of the givens. The term 'design' in the title is meant to stress that the structure of the economic system is to be regarded as an unknown. An unknown in what problem? Typically, that of finding a system that would be, in a sense to be specified, superior to the existing one. The idea of searching for a better system is at least as ancient as Plato's *Republic*, but it is only recently that tools have become available for a systematic, analytical approach to such search procedures. This new approach refuses to accept the institutional status quo of a particular time and place as the only legitimate object of interest and yet recognizes constraints that disqualify naive utopias.

A wealth of ideas, originating in disciplines as diverse as computer theory, public administration, games, and control sciences, has, in my view, opened up an exciting new frontier of economic analysis. It is the purpose of this paper to survey some of the accomplishments and to consider outstanding unsolved problems and desirable directions for future efforts.

It is not by accident that the terms 'analytical' and 'institutional' were only a few words apart in the preceding statement of scientific goals of our inquiry. In the past, especially in the nineteenth century, cleavage developed between analysts who tended to focus on the competitive and monopolistic market models, and institutionalists who, either as historians or as reformers, felt the need for a broader framework, but found the existing analytical tools inadequate for their purposes. It is perhaps symbolic that a lecture named after "the father of institutional economics in the United States" (see H. C. Taylor, 1944) should provide a forum for a step toward synthesis of the two approaches.

American Economic Association's Richard T. Ely lecture, reprinted from *American Economic Review*, 1973, 63(2): 1–30.

The Design of Mechanisms for Resource Allocation In: *The Collected Papers of Leonid Hurwicz Volume 1*. Edited by Samiran Banerjee, Oxford University Press. © Oxford University Press 2022. DOI: 10.1093/oso/9780199313280.003.0009

I should make clear that I do not regard Richard T. Ely as a hundred percent kindred spirit. One reason for this may be seen from the following quotation of his views (1884, p. 601) on mathematical economics:

> No mention has been made of the younger 'mathematical school' of political economists, of whom the chief representatives are Stanley Jevons...and Léon Walras..., because it is difficult to see in their mathematico-economical works anything more than a not very successful attempt to develop further the older abstract political economy. Any advance of the science due to the mathematical character of their method has certainly not yet become widely known, and the writer is much inclined to believe that the works which have advocated the application of mathematics to economics form no essential part of the development of economic literature. Certain unreal conceptions and a few definitions are used as bases for mathematical deductions.

Yet I find much to agree with Ely in his broader scientific objectives. However, I shall not go so far as to propose reinstatement into the bylaws of the American Economic Association the platform provisions which he proposed (1886, pp. 6–7) when the Association was being formed:

> 1. We regard the state as an educational and ethical agency whose positive aid is an indispensable condition of human progress. While we recognize the necessity of individual initiative in industrial life, we hold that the doctrine of laissez-faire is unsafe in politics and unsound in morals; and that it suggests an inadequate explanation of the relations between the state and the citizens.

What I do sympathize with in Ely's attitude is the desire to view the economic system as a variable and to go beyond analytical frameworks that were unable to cope with this problem. A sharp statement illustrative of the 'activist' point of view of that era (quoted by Ely who, however, characterizes it as too narrow) is the following definition, due to the Belgian Émile de Laveleye, dating from 1882: "Political economy may...be defined as the science which determines what laws men ought to adopt in order that they may, with the least possible exertion, procure the greatest abundance of things useful for the satisfaction of their wants, may distribute them justly and consume them rationally." I do feel that Ely underestimated the potential of development of theory (and of mathematical theory in particular) to help in this endeavor; but given the lag of a better part of a century in this development, perhaps he can be forgiven.

In what follows, I want to focus on developments that are relatively recent, primarily those of the last two decades, and characterized by at least an attempt at rigorous mathematical formulation. First, however, I want to acknowledge the value of work that preceded the recent period.

In spirit, I regard the Utopians, and Utopian socialists in particular, as the initiators of what one might call an 'activist' (as well as critical) attitude toward the social system in general, and the economic system in particular. They were, in a sense, the first systems designers in the social sphere. Marx, Engels, and their followers broke with the Utopian socialists. An unfortunate byproduct was the neglect of problems of resource allocation in the ("historically inevitable") socialist economy of the future, with Kautsky something of an exception. In the late nineteenth century there were, however, nonsocialist (and even antisocialist) economists who tackled the problem in a remarkably objective spirit, among them Pareto, Böhm-Bawerk, and von Wieser.[1] Barone's now famous 1908 paper [reprinted 1935] was at least partly stimulated by Pareto's earlier analysis.

A 'second round' of discussion was largely provoked by von Mises' skepticism as to even a theoretical feasibility of rational allocation under socialism. Oskar Lange's contribution to the debate in the 1930s [Lange and Taylor (1938)] is well known, but there was a remarkable earlier reply by Jacob Marschak in 1924.

While Lange's line was to be that socialism is as capable of playing the perfectly competitive game as is capitalism, Marschak took the opposite view: capitalism is a world not of perfect competition but of monopolies and cartels, which (in a Schumpeterian spirit) has its good points, especially in the realm of dynamics. Marschak expected similar phenomena under the brand of democratic 'socialism' he had in mind and was not depressed by the prospect. He felt that the advantages of imperfect competition would carry over into collectivism. The real issues would be not rational economic calculation, but motivation, stimulation of initiative, and intensity of effort—under an egalitarian system where managers would be democratically elected.[2]

In the 1930s, two major lines of development are relevant. One line was the work of Lange, Lerner, and others on resource allocation in a socialist economy, the slightly earlier (1929) paper by F. M. Taylor on trial and error methods, Hotelling's contribution on marginal cost pricing and consumer-producer surplus, and the 'new welfare economics' of Hicks, Kaldor, Scitovsky, and others. The other line of development, started in the 1940s, was the mathematization of 'classical welfare economics' by Lange (1942), Allais

---

[1] It is striking that Pareto (1896–97, p. 58), in addition to pointing out the theoretical feasibility of rational allocation in what he called a collectivist regime (it would have the same coefficients of production as free competition), also dealt with costs of operating the system: "A second approximation will take account of the expense of putting the mechanism of free competition in full play, and will compare this expense with that necessary for establishing some other new mechanism which society may wish to test." Similarly, in the *Manuel* (p. 364), Pareto points out the need to compare the expense on the entrepreneurs and proprietors under the system of private property with that of state employees under collectivism. But, he says, "pure economics does not give us a truly decisive basis for choosing between organization based on private property and a socialist organization."

[2] Still, he regarded these problems as less severe than those of 'centralistic' socialism.

(1943, 1945), Debreu (1951), and Koopmans (1957), with the Arrow–Hahn (1971) book a recent entry in this series.

I have so far been stressing the ideas oriented toward redesigning the economy of a nation or similar collectivity. But with the enormous growth of private enterprises and governmental bodies, similar issues arise in determining the relationships between the headquarters of a firm and its divisions, or a ministry (department) and its components. Most of the proposed mechanisms are highly relevant in such circumstances, but the team theory model may be particularly appropriate.

There is also a close relationship with information theory and with problems of administrative organization. For linking up resource allocation with information processing and organization, major credit must go to Marschak's development of economic theory of information and to Herbert Simon for his work on organization and economic behavior [(as in Simon, 1951)].

Also one should not forget a pioneering effort toward an abstract formalization undertaken by J. B. Kruskal, Jr., and Allen Newell in 'A Model for Organization Theory', circulated at Rand Corporation in 1950 but, I believe, never published.

It has been said, only half in jest, that the theory of organization is a field rich in definitions, but short on results in the form of theorems. This is no longer true. There are two categories of results. On the one hand, quite a few specific allocation mechanisms have been invented and their properties, such as feasibility, optimality, and convergence, rigorously established. On the other hand, there are also some more general results, dealing with the possibility or impossibility of various types of decentralized mechanisms, depending on the environments with which they must cope. We shall mention a few of these results, following the sampling of the specific mechanisms and the discussion of a framework required for formulating the more general questions.

Specific Mechanisms Whose Properties Have Been Investigated

As promised, we shall now sample, although very incompletely, some of the wealth of specific mechanisms that have been formulated in a rigorous way, mostly during the last two decades—but without forgetting the crucial influences of their less formal predecessors.

We shall confine ourselves to procedures that have been formulated with sufficient precision to avoid ambiguity as to which economic agent says what to whom and when. This makes it possible to determine the informational requirements, as well as convergence and optimality properties.

A major impetus was given to the design of such mechanisms by these developments of the 1940s:

(1) activity analysis and linear programming (including the simplex method)—Dantzig, Kantorovitch, Koopmans;

(2) game theory, including the iterative solution procedures—von Neumann and Morgenstern, George Brown, Julia Robinson;

(3) discoveries concerning the relationships connecting programming (linear or non-linear), two-person zero-sum games, and the long-known Lagrange multipliers—Gale, Kuhn, Tucker.

While in economics one deals with goal conflicts due to multiplicity of consumers, linear and non-linear programming models usually presuppose a single well-defined objective function to be, say, maximized, i.e., a situation corresponding to an economy with a single consumer. So it is not surprising that the mechanisms designed under the influence of programming theory dealt to a large extent with one-objective function problems and thus failed to face the crucial issue of goal conflict. Nevertheless, one should not underrate their usefulness as a necessary step on the road to the harder multi-objective problem, since the difficulties of the simpler situations do not disappear when goal conflicts are introduced.

We can distinguish two strands here: one, a rather close relative of the programming approach; the other, 'team theory' (J. Marschak, Radner, Groves), more closely related to the theory of statistical inference and decision-making. We shall concentrate on the former.

We thus have a situation where there is only one consumer (individual, firm, or even nation) and, hence, only a single utility function to be maximized, but a multiplicity of producers and resource holders. The technological relations (production functions) and limits of resource availability constitute the constraints subject to which maximization must be carried out.

Two difficulties make the problem non-trivial: calculation and information transfer. First, consider the calculation of the maximizing values for the variables of the problem. Assuming even that all the relevant information concerning the parameters of the problem is in the hands of a computing agency, this agency needs a well-defined computational procedure (algorithm) to find solutions.

For linear economies, the simplex method is such an algorithm. For 'smooth' (non-linear) unconstrained maximization problems resembling the task of groping one's way in the dark to the top of a hill, the obvious idea of moving uphill is embodied in the notion of gradient (or 'steepest ascent') processes. Equally evident is the fact that a valley between the spot one is at and the peak of the hill would cause trouble; hence, the success of gradient procedures depends on the curvature characteristics of the terrain, a natural requirement being that the hill be dome-like (technically, a strictly concave function).

A natural extension of the gradient process idea was suggested by the famous Kuhn-Tucker theorem associating with a constrained maximum a saddle point, i.e., a maximum-minimum point of the so-called Lagrangean expression; thus the search for a maximum with respect to certain decision variables was converted into a mixture of maximizing and minimizing tasks to each of which one could apply the gradient idea (groping upward in terms of the decision variables and downward with respect to certain auxiliary variables—Lagrange multipliers to the mathematician, shadow prices to the economist). *Statically*, the Kuhn-Tucker result required little more than the concavity (not necessarily strict) of the relevant functions and, hence, was applicable to linear problems as well as the typical smoothly curved pictures of classical economics (Pareto, Hicks). But we shall see that dynamics was more troublesome.

Even when there is an algorithm suitable for calculations by an agency to whom all the data are available, it may be that the information processing capacity of any one such agency is inadequate because of the size of the problem (the number and complexity of constraints, objectives, and variables). If there are several potential information-processing agencies (and here every human brain qualifies to some extent), we may be saved by devising computing procedures which parcel out the work among them; these are called decomposition algorithms.[3]

It should be recalled that one of Hayek's (1935, p. 212) chief points in summing up the state of the debate concerning the feasibility of a centralized socialist solution was that the number of variables and equations would be "at least in the hundreds of thousands" and the required equation solving "a task which, with any of the means known at present, could not be carried out in a lifetime. And yet these decisions would... have to be made continuously". The market-simulation procedure developed by Lange and Lerner may be viewed as an early example of a decomposition algorithm.

From the point of view of the economics of information processing it is clear that a parceling out of the task may be advantageous even if single agency capacity constraints have not been reached; this may well lower the resource cost and cut down the time required for the completion of the computing process.

---

[3] In recent years, related problems have been studied in connection with the design of electronic computer utilization under the label of multi-processing.

But another informational consideration, stressed by Hayek (1935, 1945) has gained special prominence: the difficulty of placing all the relevant information in the hands of a single agency because information is dispersed throughout the economy. A natural assumption is that, initially, each economic unit has information about itself only: consumers about their respective preferences, producers about their technologies, and resource holders about the resources. An attempt to transfer all this information to a single agency before it starts its calculations is regarded as either impossible (in the sense that much information would be lost) or too costly in relation to the existing accuracy requirements.[4]

If the economic units which initially are the only ones with information about themselves are also capable of carrying out calculations, it is natural to seek computing procedures that would both minimize the need for information transfers and also parcel out the tasks of calculation. This is what informationally decentralized procedures are meant to accomplish.

In the 1930s it would have been most natural to start with 'smooth' strictly concave economies (diminishing marginal utilities and returns), without kinks or corner solutions. But around 1950, linear models were in fashion. Furthermore, the simplex method was available and proved to be convergent. Since the simplex method, applied to the economy as a whole, lacked informational decentralization, a search for an alternative was bound to occur. For the economist, an obvious candidate was a simulated (perfectly competitive) market process à la Lange, Lerner, and (specifically in the context of a linear economy) the Koopmans model with a helmsman representing the consumer, production managers maximizing profits, and resource custodians adjusting prices according to excess demand.

From a static point of view, the equilibrium of such a process would be optimal. But if the initially proposed process and quantities were 'wrong', would there be convergence to equilibrium? To make this question meaningful, one must specify the dynamics of the adjustment process, e.g., by how much prices are to be raised per unit of time given the magnitude of excess demand, etc. A pioneering model of this type is due to Samuelson (1949) who postulated a system of differential equations in which prices vary proportionately to excess demand, and resource use rises when low resource prices yield positive profits. He immediately noted that this dynamic system would behave like a frictionless pendulum, i.e., would not converge

---

[4] One reason for this difficulty is that even the individual units have the required information only in potential form, except for situations corresponding to their past experience: e.g., firms know only certain parts of their production functions. It is easier to use 'localized' procedures which require an exploration only of the relevant parts of the individual units' maps; but such localization is impossible if whole maps are to be conveyed to the single computing agency at the beginning of the computing process.

to an equilibrium position. Whether we are thinking of computations or of designing an economy, we must look further.[5]

Samuelson's discovery posed a challenge: can an informationally decentralized convergent allocation process be designed for linear economies?[6] One line of attack involves the replacement of the fixed (that is, parametric) price idea by that of a price *schedule* and is applicable not only in the linear (constant returns) case but also under increasing returns.[7] Another approach, to be discussed first, retains the parametric prices; it grew out of linear programming techniques, with the Dantzig-Wolfe (1961) decomposition method its earliest example.

The Dantzig-Wolfe economy has special features which provide scope for the decomposition approach. These are the usual features of a resource allocation model without technological externalities, in which the objective function is a sum of the contributions of the individual units and in which certain resources must be utilized by all units.[8] The mechanism may be viewed as a dialogue between the producing units (who know their technologies and contributions to the objective function) and a 'center' which knows the total resources available. One aspect of the dialogue is that the center proposes tentative resource prices and the producing units develop corresponding profit-maximizing production programs (with prices treated parametrically). In the light of these programs, the center revises the proposed prices. Because of the linear character of the economy, both the center and the producing units can use linear-programming (primal and dual) techniques, and an equilibrium is reached in a finite number of steps. So far, we may regard the algorithm as a variety of the market (parametric price) process. But there is a difference. The final allocation will not necessarily correspond to the final production programs of the producing units. Rather,

---

5 Samuelson himself suggested "a little intelligent speculation or foresight." (Interestingly enough, a 1972 contribution by Groves to dynamic team theory exploits a similar idea to increase the average performance of a 'truncated' Lange-Lerner process.) In addition to this dynamic defect of the competitive mechanism in a linear economy, several recent papers have also studied what is perceived to be a static defect: even when the prices are correct (i.e., at their competitive equilibrium values), the producer will typically be indifferent between 'socially correct' and 'incorrect' actions because both types of actions may be on the same iso-profit line. Bessière and Sautter (1968) speak of absence of 'separability' and Jennergren (1971) makes a similar finding. However, with 'incorrect' individual actions there would not be equilibrium; this would become evident to the price setters, because excess demand would be different from zero. Since excess demand must be checked to know whether the price is 'correct', the requirement of 'separability' in the above sense seems too strong. Nevertheless, it is of some interest to note that where individual profit optima are unique (e.g., with strictly concave production functions), 'separability' is present.

6 Of course, there is also the problem of designing such processes for economies with increasing returns. But here the difficulties are bound to be serious, since the competitive mechanism lacks even the usual static properties.

7 See the modified Lagrangean Arrow-Hurwicz (1958, [ch. 8]) approach below.

8 Both the objective function and the overall constraints are 'additively separable.'

the center will 'order' each producing unit to undertake a program which 'mixes' (averages) the final proposal with several previous ones.[9]

As pointed out by Baumol and Fabian (1964), the procedure can be extended to situations where constraints pertaining to single producing units are non-linear, while the overall constraints pertaining to resources needed by all units remain linear. In this case, however, the units must have a computational algorithm for their non-linear problem since the simplex method can no longer be used. For other non-linear economies, and especially those with increasing returns, different processes had to be sought.

Before we look at those, however, let us examine a mechanism designed specifically to guide a *linear* economy but in a manner that partly reverses the roles played by the 'center' and the 'periphery' (the producing units), the process due to Kornai and Lipták (1965). The assumption concerning the economy, as in the Dantzig-Wolfe model, is that of 'block angularity', i.e., there are subsets of constraints each pertaining to a given sector and also resource constraints affecting the whole economy. In the dialogue, the center proposes allotments of scarce resources to the various sectors; then each sector responds with shadow prices (marginal rates of substitution) minimizing the value of the allotment subject to sectoral dual constraints (non-profit condition for every sectoral activity). The center's aim, on the other hand, is to maximize the contributions of the sectors to the objective function, i.e., to maximize the value of the allocated resources at the shadow prices received from the sectors, subject to the limitation of available resource totals.

Taking advantage of the equivalence of linear-programming programs and games, Kornai and Lipták, by structuring the dialogue as a fictitious game, are able to establish convergence to an equilibrium with any desired degree of accuracy, though (unlike in the Dantzig-Wolfe procedure) without reaching the equilibrium in a finite number of steps. In addition to the latter disadvantage, it has also been pointed out (by Jennergren, 1971) that the Kornai-Lipták procedure is not completely informationally decentralized, since each sector's resource sectoral allotments must be large enough ('evaluable') to assure the existence of a feasible solution for that sector.

One advantage claimed for the Kornai-Lipták procedure is that it may be computationally manageable where alternative decomposition algorithms are not. I regret that I have not had an opportunity to look into this question. But another feature of this process is of great interest to the economist.

---

[9] The need for such averaging is due to the fact that a firm's final program in the Dantzig-Wolfe procedure can be a profit-maximizing 'corner', while 'social optimality' may require the utilization of a 'non-corner' profit-maximizing production program. In effect, by considering the various averages of the producing unit's programs, the center determines the whole set of profit-maximizing programs and, from among those, picks out the socially optimal one. (See Baumol and Fabian, 1964.)

This is the fact that the center, instead of simulating the market as does the Taylor-Lange-Lerner mechanism, specifies quantitative input and output targets or restrictions, while the sectors supply the center with productivity information in the form of shadow prices. This appears more in line with many observed planning practices and thus may provide a useful descriptive model.

There are several other mechanisms, in general designed for non-linear economies, which are also of the 'quantity-guided' type (as distinct from the 'price-guided' type), that is, where the center sends out messages concerning quantities (e.g., targets) and the periphery (the producing units, sectors) responds with marginal entities or shadow prices. Informationally, since the center is sending different quantity messages to different sectors, its total signals are of higher dimensionality than in price-guided systems where the same message (price vector) goes out to all sectors.[10] Whether this difference is significant is somewhat controversial; the negative has been strongly expressed by Marglin (1969) who has constructed quantity-guided (called by him 'command') counterparts of certain price-guided processes. One of Marglin's mechanisms requires the center to allocate the scarce inputs on the basis of information obtained from the producing units concerning their marginal productivities and their excess demands. Adjustment ceases when aggregate excess demand is zero and the marginal productivities of producers are equalized.[11]

A process, characterized by a mixture of price- and quantity-guided elements and also due to Heal (1971), is particularly interesting because (with some qualifications) it converges to optima even for non-convex economies, in particular for increasing returns. An essential informational feature is that certain functions of each producing unit's marginal productivities (roughly, its shadow prices for particular resources) must be conveyed to the center. The center can then calculate improved resource allotments, or else it may calculate and send to the units a resource price (the same for all units) and so enable them to determine their respective resource requirements. The latter option is, of course, informationally more decentralized: it requires fewer message transfers from the center to the periphery, and fewer computations are carried out at the center.[12]

Heal's process has the further merit that if the initial allocation is feasible, so are all the later ones, thus satisfying a Malinvaud postulate.[13]

---

[10] We must bear in mind that each quantity vector has the same dimension as the price vector.

[11] A similar process was proposed by Heal in 1969.

[12] Marglin had a similar process for a more restricted class of economies. It is not clear whether his process could be adapted to corner maxima in nonconvex cases.

[13] The same seems true of Marglin's process, although, unlike Heal, he does not assume the initial position to be feasible.

The maintenance of feasibility is simple in models without intermediate goods because the procedure always allocates all available resources and producers are required to stay on their efficient frontiers. The matter gets more complicated when intermediate goods are introduced and only special cases appear to have been dealt with so far by this approach.

Processes in which the center specifies quantities and the peripheral units convey their individual marginal rates have also been used in models where public goods are among those to be allocated. I shall mention three treatments of this case, due to Drèze and de la Vallée Poussin (1971), Malinvaud (1970), and Aoki (1971). In the versions known to me, each is somewhat specialized: Malinvaud and Drèze-Poussin have only one producer but many consumers, Aoki only one consumer; also, Drèze-Poussin deal primarily with the case of only one private good, although they indicate how the results may be generalized to more. Aoki's economy is closest to those we have been considering so far because it has only one consumer (the center), hence, no income distribution problems; it also has many producers. His mechanism uses price-guidance for private goods and quantity-guidance for public goods. A producer develops production plans that maximize net revenue given the central 'guidelines' (prices for the private goods, quantities for the public goods), and conveys to the center his demands for private goods and marginal evaluations, including marginal cost, for public goods. The center, in turn, adjusts the price of each private good according to the difference between its marginal utility and price (as in the Arrow-Hurwicz 1958 gradient process); the targets for public goods are increased in proportion to the net aggregate of marginal valuations (users' minus producers'); thus the center combines the functions of the helmsman and resource custodian of the Koopmans model for private goods with target setting for public goods. The other two processes have the same adjustment rule for public goods targets, but differ in other respects. In particular, they specify the rules of income distribution.

All three processes converge (at least locally) under suitable convexity assumptions concerning the environment. Somewhat paradoxically, Malinvaud's process does not seem to satisfy his desiderata of feasibility maintenance and monotonicity, while the other two do.

I shall now go back to the price-guided processes, but more briefly because they came earlier and are better known. Here again, I shall focus on the one consumer case. For a linear economy, Koopmans (1951) described the functioning of such a mechanism in the spirit of the Taylor-Lange-Lerner rules by setting up an 'allocation game' to be played, in an informationally decentralized manner, by a helmsman (setting the prices of final goods and thus representing consumer preferences), commodity custodians (adjusting the prices of resources according to excess demand), and activity managers who determine the production programs. Koopmans's adjustment rule (similar to Samuelson's) is that managers expand profitable activities and curtail those bringing losses; in a constant returns economy this is equivalent to profit maximization. Koopmans stressed that "the dynamic aspects of these rules have on purpose been left vague." We know that Samuelson's experiment in this direction yielded non-convergent oscillations.

On the other hand, in an economy where all functions (including the utility indicator) are strictly concave (i.e., we have diminishing returns) similar rules produce a process with the desired stability properties. Utilizing the notion of gradient approach to the saddle point of the Lagrangean expression, Arrow and Hurwicz (1960) used the following rules: the helmsman, taking the prices of desired commodities as given, changes each final demand at a rate equal to the difference between its marginal utility and price; each manager, again taking prices as given, changes the scale of his process in proportion to its marginal profitability; each commodity custodian varies the price of his commodity in proportion to excess demand.[14] A limiting form of such a process is the price-adjustment method in which prices are varied as before, but both the helmsman and each manager reach (as against merely moving toward) the values of their decision variables which maximize their respective objective functions: for the helmsman, the difference between utility and price; for the manager, the level of profit. The familiar Walrasian competitive process is a variant of such price-adjustment in which the demand for final goods is determined by utility maximization subject to a budget constraint with specified income or wealth.

Although the gradient process is informationally decentralized and converges to an optimum under strict concavity assumptions, it has certain disadvantages. To begin with, it is formulated in continuous time, while realistic mechanisms operate more naturally by iterations, i.e., with a discrete time parameter.

But it is possible to construct a discrete time parameter counterpart of the gradient process. In fact, this was done by Uzawa (1958) and further elaborated by Malinvaud (1967) who, however, pointed out another undesirable feature of the gradient process: although it converges to a feasible solution, its 'interim' proposals are, in general, not feasible. In other words, while the process pushes the participants toward compatibility in their claims on resources, they may be demanding either more or less than the total available while the process is going on. Thus if the gradient process were to be interrupted at a finite time, there might be a problem of reconciling incompatible claims.

---

14 I am omitting modifications pertaining to corners and zero prices.

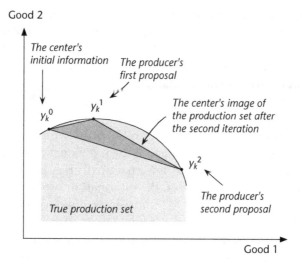

Fig. 1.

Malinvaud then formulated a desideratum, viz., that (discrete time parameter) adjustment processes yield feasible solutions after a finite number of iterations. He then proceeded to construct two processes (for different environments) which satisfied this desideratum. In both cases he assumed that the initial proposal, serving as the point of departure for the iterations, was feasible. In effect, he was paying a 'price' for the feasibility of all his interim proposals—namely, he assumed that the center had an additional piece of information: a feasible point of departure; the Arrow-Hurwicz gradient process, on the other hand, was designed for situations where this information was not available to the center.

It is worthwhile to become acquainted with Malinvaud's second procedure. The center proposes prices to the producing units which, in turn, determine production plans maximizing the value of the firm's output in terms of those prices. The center then builds up its picture of each unit's production set (see Fig. 1) by taking all convex mixtures of its previous proposed input-output vectors, together with the initial feasible vector, assumed known to the center.[15] Treating its pictures of the production sets as if they were the actual sets, the center then maximizes its utility function subject to the resource availability constraint and proposes a new set of prices corresponding to the relevant marginal rates of substitution.

---

[15] Since the production sets are assumed convex, this yields an increasing subset of the unit's true production set. But, again, there is an informational price to be paid: the center must accumulate, on a disaggregated basis, all past proposals from the units.

It could perhaps happen that, even after several iterations, the only production program compatible with resource constraints is the one originally assumed known to the center; or that, even if new feasible programs are generated, their utility is no higher than that of the original known feasible allocation. But it was shown by Malinvaud that, as the number of iterations goes to infinity, the utility associated with the corresponding plans tends to the upper bound of its feasible values.

Roughly speaking, the center constructs plans which would be nearly optimal for the economy if its images of the individual production sets were sufficiently close to correct. The informational price paid is the need for building up these images; in effect, the information concerning the production functions is being transferred to the center, although on an installment plan. This differs from the usual informationally decentralized procedures where the center does not accumulate such information and never knows more than the structure of the production set in the neighborhood of the current proposal.

The process also illustrates another desideratum formulated by Malinvaud: that the utility of successive proposals should not decrease as iterations progress ('monotonicity'). The preceding process obviously satisfies this requirement because earlier proposals are always among the available alternatives during the utility maximization phase of the center's calculations.[16]

A procedure, which is a sort of dual to that of Malinvaud, has been proposed by Weitzman (1970). While Malinvaud's center is rather timid and only considers plans known to be feasible for the units, Weitzman's central planning agency constructs imaginary production sets it knows to be too ambitious, formulates targets that are, in general, infeasible and then lets the units scale down the proposals to feasible levels (see Fig. 2). Also, the units provide the center with respective marginal rates (shadow prices) as a basis for subsequent central targets. Here again, the center must accumulate all previous information concerning the structure of the individual production sets. Convergence is assured (even in a finite number of steps when the production sets are polyhedral). But the center's proposals will, in general, be infeasible for the units, and the units' counterproposals may not be compatible with resource availabilities. Hence, termination after a finite number of iterations may give rise to the same problems of feasibility brought out by Malinvaud with reference to gradient processes.

Perhaps a less ambitious form of the Malinvaud feasibility postulate would be acceptable: that the process should not depart from feasibility once it has encountered a feasible point in the process of iterations and that, in

---

[16] Heal's process also has the monotonicity property when the initial proposals are feasible.

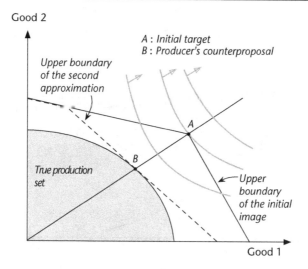

Good 2

A : *Initial target*
B : *Producer's counterproposal*

*Upper boundary
of the second
approximation*

*True production
set*

B

A

*Upper
boundary
of the initial
image*

Good 1

Fig. 2.

any case, it should converge to optimality, hence, to a feasible point. I have not explored Malinvaud's processes in the light of this modified postulate. It seems, however, that the following procedure would satisfy the modified postulate: use the gradient process when starting from an infeasible set of proposals, but switch to a Malinvaud type mechanism as soon as a feasible point is reached.

We may note that the feasibility problem arises for any Walrasian tâtonnement process which is terminated at a finite time. Typically, supply will not equal demand for all goods and, if actual allocation is to be made at the termination time, one must have a way of resolving conflicts. When demand exceeds supply, one can think of prorating the available goods or using the first come first served principle. However, this will not, in general, yield a feasible solution. Even for a pure exchange economy some individuals might be getting less than subsistence requirements; with production involving intermediate goods the situation would be all the more difficult.

Informational considerations aside, both cumulative procedures (Malinvaud's and Weitzman's) rely on the convexity of production sets. Malinvaud's other price-guided process (related to Taylor's suggestions) assumes a Leontief-Samuelson constant returns economy. What about decentralized resource allocation in *non-convex* environments?

We have already seen one procedure designed to cope with such situations, that of Heal (1971). This process is shown to converge to a 'critical point' of the optimization problem, i.e., a point where first-order conditions for maximization are satisfied. Under conditions of convexity, such points will, of course, be (at least local) maxima. But without convexity, they no longer

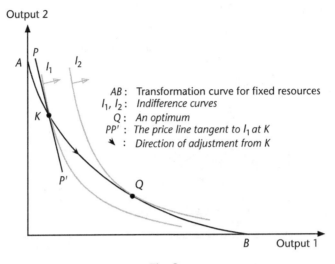

Output 2

AB : Transformation curve for fixed resources
I_1, I_2 : Indifference curves
Q : An optimum
PP' : The price line tangent to I_1 at K
➤ : Direction of adjustment from K

Fig. 3.

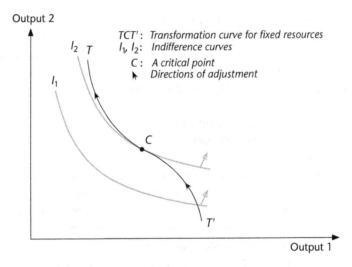

Output 2

TCT' : Transformation curve for fixed resources
I_1, I_2 : Indifference curves
C : A critical point
➤ Directions of adjustment

Fig. 4.

need be even local maxima. Now in Heal's process, if one starts from a feasible point which is not a critical point, the subsequent points will also be feasible and have a rising utility; hence, the point to which the process converges cannot be a local minimum, but it need not be a maximum (see Figs. 3 and 4). However, if the starting point happened to be a local minimum, it seems that the rules of the process would generate an equilibrium there. It may be that this difficulty could be avoided by some modification of Heal's rules (e.g., by tâtonnement in the neighborhood of any critical point).

An alternative was proposed by Arrow and Hurwicz (1956, 1958, 1960). Mathematically, it amounts to rewriting the nonconcave constraints in such a manner that the *modified Lagrangean* expression becomes locally strictly concave in the activity variables so that a local saddle point is created and the gradient method can be used, at least locally.[17] Hence, we then have available to us a gradient process which is guaranteed to converge to a local optimum, not merely to a local critical point. Admittedly, convergence to a global optimum would be preferable. However, in the absence of concavity properties, one cannot hope to guarantee convergence to a global optimum on the basis of local first-order properties only! The modification just described can also be applied to produce *strict* concavity in linear situations. We thus have a solution of the dilemma of non-convergent oscillations encountered by Samuelson in the linear case.

It should be admitted that computational experiments along these lines (T. Marschak, 1958) did not turn out encouraging. Nevertheless, the economic interpretation of the modified Lagrangean (Arrow-Hurwicz) process seems of interest. Here the Lagrange multipliers are no longer interpreted as prices. In fact, the custodian announces a *price schedule* (of which the Lagrange multiplier is a parameter) with the price depending on the quantity purchased. The helmsman and the managers must perform their marginal calculations on the basis of such schedules. The custodians adjust the schedules by varying the Lagrangean parameters according to supply and demand conditions. Thus optimal allocation is achieved through monopolistic practices and imperfect competition.[18]

It is not surprising that monopolistic elements should appear in a process that simulates market phenomena, since we know that perfectly competitive equilibrium need not exist in nonconvex situations and even where it exists in linear cases it has certain undesirable indeterminacies. It should be noted that the modified approach just described is informationally less decentralized than was the case in a world of concave functions without the monopolistic modification. It is a major problem of the general theory to what extent such informational losses are unavoidable.

A very different price-guided process was suggested by Radner and developed by Groves (1969, 1972). Their framework is that of team theory, with a simple common goal (total output maximization) and randomly fluctuating productivity parameters. The production functions are classical (differentiable and concave, or even quadratic). One of the adjustment processes considered is in the spirit of Lange-Lerner procedures. Others have

---

[17] There are many ways of bringing about this modification.

[18] Jennergren recently explored the use of price schedules in allocative processes for concave, including linear, environments. Heal made a related suggestion.

information structures ranging from complete communication to absence of communication.

The distinguishing feature of the model is that allocative decisions are made without waiting for equilibrium to be reached, hence usually on the basis of only partial information. Also, there is a departure from the Lange-Lerner rules in that the production manager's decisions do not maximize profits, although profit figures are used for informational purposes.

Among the remarkable findings is the fact that the asymptotic value of communication per enterprise (as the number of enterprises increases) is as good under Radner's 'One-Stage-Lange-Lerner' process as it would have been under complete communication.

Although the results so far obtained are valid only for rather specialized models, they show how to go beyond traditional equilibrium analysis, while exploiting ideas developed in equilibrium-oriented models.

Basic Concepts

We may think of economists as taking part in a contest to design a 'superior' mechanism, with some submitting entries before it has been clarified what would qualify as a mechanism and which mechanisms would be considered 'superior', or even feasible.

It is fortunate that our predecessors did not wait for such definitions. In the process of submitting their entries, they have provided examples of mechanisms, the foremost among them competitive and marginal cost pricing, and, by now, many others which can be used as guides in constructing a definition. Similarly, theorems concerning the efficiency and optimality properties of these mechanisms suggest possible classification criteria.

One could, of course, get by without formalizing what one means by a resource allocation mechanism. But it is then impossible to determine to what extent the various desiderata implicit in the past debates are compatible with one another, or what the 'tradeoffs' are among them. Also, in searching for alternatives to known mechanisms for nonclassical situations (indivisibilities, increasing returns, externalities, public goods), it helps to have a rigorous formulation of what a resource allocation mechanism is and which of its features are desirable. Notions of a mechanism different from that given below may well have greater merit. Our picture of a mechanism will in fact sacrifice possible greater generality to gain definiteness and simplicity.[19]

---

[19] This section is largely based on Hurwicz (1960).—SB

Nevertheless, it will be general enough to embrace (as it stands or with minor modifications) most of the economic systems we wish to study.

It is the function of a resource allocation mechanism to guide the economic agents (producers, consumers, bankers, and others) in decisions that determine the flow of resources. Simplifying to the utmost, we may imagine each agent having in front of him a console with one or more dials to set; the selection of dial settings by all agents determines uniquely the flow of goods and services (trade vector) between every pair of agents and also each agent's production (input-output vector), his 'trade with nature.' Not all dial settings are possible and some are possible only in conjunction with other dial settings. Thus the feasibility of a complex of actions (a specified combination of dial settings for all agents) can be split into individual feasibility and compatibility.[20]

It is natural to demand that the mechanism should guide the agents toward actions which are at least feasible, and even that can be difficult. Yet in classical welfare economics we require more than feasibility, viz., such attributes as efficiency or optimality. After decades of meanderings, we are fairly clear on our options—from efficiency in production (as defined by Koopmans), through optimality (introduced by Pareto under the label of maximum ophelimity), to the maximization of a social welfare function (as defined by Bergson, Samuelson, or Arrow). From our point of view, these different attributes have an important feature in common: they are defined independently of the mechanism. An optimality criterion which presupposes a particular mechanism cannot serve as a legitimate criterion for comparison with other mechanisms.

Specifically, whether an allocation is or is not optimal depends on its feasibility and on the individual preferences, with feasibility determined by the individual endowments and the technology. The individual endowments, the technology, and preferences, taken together, are referred to as the *environment*. More generally, the environment is defined as the set of circumstances that cannot be changed either by the designer of the mechanism or by the agents (participants).[21]

---

[20] In our standard models, any point on a given agent's production function is individually feasible for this agent, but two individually feasible input-output vectors of two firms may be incompatible if one calls for an input which the other does not propose to supply.

[21] For instance, in a multi-period model, where inventive activity is a controllable factor of production, the environment is given not by the existing technology, but rather by the relationship between inventive activity and the resulting production function in later periods. This interpretation fits the more general definition of environment if the latter relationship cannot be altered by the decision-makers. Similarly, the existing preferences do not constitute the environment in its generalized sense when tastes are malleable, e.g., on grounds adduced by Galbraith. But if the responsiveness of tastes to influences such as advertising cannot be influenced by decision-makers, it should be regarded as part of the environment. (To make meaningful welfare judgments possible, some underlying values or 'true preferences' would have to be postulated.)

To simplify matters, we shall confine ourselves to mechanisms analogous to the tâtonnement process where a period of dialogue without action is followed by decisions as to resource flow (production and exchange). Ultimately, we shall need a more general theory in which dialogue, decisions, and actions overlap in time, as in the non-tâtonnement processes.

The participants in the dialogue constitute a broader group than the 'doers' (consumers, producers, etc.), since they may include governments, planning agencies, central banks, or unions. If we excluded such participants, we should obviously be unable to develop a theory general enough to encompass centrally planned or even mixed economies. The dialogue is an exchange of messages between the participants. The nature and contents of the messages vary from mechanism to mechanism. They may be proposals of actions, bids, offers, plans of resource flow for the whole economy, or they may contain information about the environment (preferences, technology, resource endowments). The totality of messages permissible under a given mechanism constitute its *language*.

The mechanism specifies rules according to which, given the information available to him at a given time, a participant sends messages to others. The information consists of messages previously received, as well as some (direct) knowledge of environment, and are called *response rules* because they govern the message response to messages previously received.[22] To provide for a transition from dialogue to decisions and actions, the mechanism must also have an *outcome rule* which specifies what actions are to be taken given the course of the dialogue. The rules may be deterministic or probabilistic; mathematically they are expressed as functions.

Both market phenomena and command systems can be fitted into this schema. Thus, in the Walrasian tâtonnement process, the language consists of prices and quantities demanded or supplied by the various agents. If the model contains an 'auctioneer', his response function calls for price changes proportional to aggregate excess demand, while the response functions of others require them to convey their excess demands given the prices called out by the auctioneer. In an extreme version of a 'pure command' system, the dialogue starts with the peripheral agents sending to the center messages describing their respective components of the environment (e.g., their resource holdings and production functions), whereupon the center, after suitable data processing and calculations, sends to the peripheral agents the orders for action. In this command system, the outcome rule is clear: to carry out the orders received. In the Walrasian tâtonnement process, the matter is a bit more complicated. One must wait until equilibrium is

---

[22] By 'direct' is meant knowledge of the environment derived from sources other than messages previously received.

somehow established, i.e., everyone is repeating his previous message. Then the outcome rule is to carry out exchanges according to the equilibrium bids made.

The languages of the two mechanisms are also different. In the Walrasian process, messages are the proposed prices and commodity bundles. Namely, a message can be regarded as an ordered sequence of numbers, as many as there are goods in the system, i.e., as a vector whose dimension is that of the commodity space. In the 'pure command' system, a message may contain the description of a production function or of a preference map. Since it may take arbitrarily many parameters to specify a production function, no a priori upper bound can be imposed here on how many numbers might have to be transmitted in such a process. The language of the command process is much larger than that of the Walrasian process. We must remember, however, that the pure command process is finished after only two exchanges of information while the tâtonnement may go on a long time.

The purpose of the two examples has been not to compare their merits, but to illustrate the meaning of the terms used in describing the resource allocation mechanisms we shall be dealing with. We shall call such mechanisms *adjustment processes*. Thus, an adjustment process is specified by its language, response rules, and the outcome rule.[23]

With this formulation, given a class of environments which the designer must cover, there is a well-defined family of adjustment processes that can at all be constructed with any specified language. This is so because, mathematically speaking, the class of environments and the language delimit the domains and ranges of the response and outcome functions (rules), and the class of functions with any given domain and range is well-defined. This opens the door to impossibility or possibility theorems concerning the family of adjustment processes that use specified languages and cover a given class of environments.[24]

We have already mentioned one natural desideratum for adjustment processes—that they yield feasible outcomes. More ambitiously, one may ask that the outcomes be optimal. A process whose outcomes are optimal for a given class of environments will be called *nonwasteful over that class*.[25] But it is crucial to realize that nonwastefulness, although appealing, is not enough. After all, a process lacking any positions of equilibrium would have to be

---

[23] As we shall see later, 'distributional parameter settings' also enter the picture.

[24] The resemblance to Arrow's social welfare function problem is purely formal: in both cases one is investigating the family of functional relations with specified domains and ranges. However, the functions—rules—defining an adjustment process bear no direct relationship to the social welfare functions.

[25] For instance, a competitive process is nonwasteful, in a Pareto optimality sense, over environments that are free of externalities and of locally saturated preferences.

classified as (vacuously) nonwasteful. So, we would wish to require that the process possess *some* equilibrium position for every environment of the class it is designed to cover.

Yet even this is insufficient. What if the equilibria of the process always tend to favor one group of participants at the expense of another? The victims would hardly be comforted by the fact that the outcomes are always Pareto optimal.

Here again the experience of classical welfare economics points the way. Whether we study Arrow (1951), Debreu (1959), or Koopmans (1957), we find not one but two basic theorems. One establishes nonwastefulness. The other asserts that any Pareto optimum can be attained as a competitive equilibrium. A precise statement of the latter property turns out to be complicated, however. For we know that, given the option—always available to resource owners—of not trading and not producing, ordinary competitive equilibrium cannot yield levels of satisfaction below the original ones. Hence, inferior optima could never be reached and the second theorem might seem false. But the theorem refers not merely to a market process. When interpreted within the framework of a private ownership system, it envisages a market process preceded by transfers of resource holdings and (in a production economy) of claims to profits (Allais, Debreu, Arrow, Arrow and Hahn). It is these transfers that can lead to optima that are inferior for some of the participants.

Perhaps the most important point here is that the mechanism can no longer be viewed as accepting as given the distributional aspects of the system. Rather, it consists of two parts: a setting of what we may call the *distributional parameters* (resource holdings, profit shares), followed by a tâtonnement procedure. The property of the competitive mechanism expressed by the second classical welfare economics theorem, which we shall call *unbiasedness*, amounts to this: given any conceivable Pareto optimal position of the economy, there exists a setting of the distributional parameters which would make that position an equilibrium of the process.[26] Thus if there is an optimal allocation that cannot be made into equilibrium by any setting of the distributional parameters, the process fails the test of unbiasedness.

In a pure exchange economy there is no difficulty in interpreting the meaning of setting distributional parameters: it is merely a matter of reshuffling the initial endowment. But in the presence of production, the matter is more complicated. In a private ownership economy, profit shares can be shifted. But in searching for alternative systems of different institutional nature, we do not want to commit ourselves to considering profits or incomes as well-defined concepts, since both involve prices, and prices may not be defined in

---

26 Again this property holds *over some* specified *class of environments*.

certain institutional structures.[27] Yet it is possible to provide a definition free of institutional limitations by interpreting the distributional parameters as guaranteeing to each participant a minimum level of satisfaction corresponding to a particular resource allocation. The manner in which this guarantee is implemented does involve institutional arrangements.

One more requirement. Ideally, we might demand that the rules of the process send the economy to a uniquely determined allocation. But this turns out to be difficult to accomplish and even the competitive mechanism may yield multiple equilibrium allocations compatible with a *particular* equilibrium price. Since, however, all these allocations happen to have the same utility for all participants, the indeterminacy is acceptable. We shall call a process *essentially single-valued* if any equilibrium indeterminacies are of this trivial nature.[28]

We are now ready to formulate the basic set of performance requirements for processes to be considered: that they be nonwasteful, unbiased, and essentially single-valued. This trio of requirements will be, for short, referred to as (*Pareto-*) *satisfactoriness*. Whether the requirements are or are not met by a given process depends on the environments in which it is asked to operate. The environments which have the properties stated in the classical welfare economics theorems are, naturally, called classical. Thus *classical environments* are free from externalities or indivisibilities, their sets are convex, etc. In particular, increasing returns are not classical!

With this long introduction, the two great welfare economics propositions may briefly be stated thus: the competitive process is Pareto-satisfactory over classical environments.

This statement immediately provokes the question: what about the non-classical environments? Can we find Pareto-satisfactory processes for them too? For all environments, or just some?

These questions would be meaningless if some restrictions were not imposed on the information (or incentive) structure of the processes to be considered. The explicit recognition of the role played by the information structure is one of the major accomplishments of Jacob Marschak and Roy Radner[29] in their work on the theory of teams. An analysis of informational issues, with emphasis on feasibility, timing, and costs, with particular reference to the issue of decentralization, is due to Thomas Marschak (1959).

---

[27] This, incidentally, shows some of the difficulties of even formulating the problem without implicitly presupposing market like conditions.

[28] Note that this does not require that allocations corresponding to *different* equilibrium prices, when there are multiple equilibria, yield the same satisfactions to all participants. Ruled out is only a situation in which, corresponding to a particular equilibrium price, there would be alternative allocations yielding different levels of satisfaction.

[29] See Marschak (1955); Radner (1972a, 1972b); and Marschak and Radner (1972).—SB

Oniki (1974) has pioneered in comparisons of numbers of messages that flow in different processes.

The formulation I have adopted here is conceptually much less satisfactory. I consider certain specific restrictions on the informational aspects of the process and then, as a first step, I ask whether for a given class of environments (wider than classical) one can design Pareto-satisfactory processes.[30]

As a second step, adjustment processes can be compared with respect to the required "size" of the language (e.g., the cardinality or dimensionality of the message space), or according to the fineness of the perceptions they call for (informational efficiency), and other aspects of information processing effort or expense. These concepts and their relationships have been studied by Kanemitsu (1966) and by Reiter (1974a, 1974b).

But back to the 'first step', the formulation of requirements. To express them, it is necessary to distinguish between information obtained directly (say, by one's own observation) and through messages received. My first postulate is that participants have direct information only about themselves, not about others. I have never found a good term for this property, but currently I refer to it as *privacy* (of the adjustment process).

It is clear that the restriction on direct information would be virtually meaningless if arbitrary messages were permitted, for then 'in one move' any information not available directly could be obtained through a message. Thus the *language* (the set of permissible messages) must somehow be restricted. It turns out from mathematical considerations (something I had not been fully aware of in my original work) that restrictions on the language may also turn out to be ineffective unless certain conditions (akin to but stronger than continuity) are imposed on the response and outcome functions.

The totality of these and certain other conditions (including some pertaining to the language) I have labeled *informational decentralization*. There is, of course, some arbitrariness in such a definition, but it enables us to formulate a simple 'yes or no' question: how broad is the class of environments for which Pareto-satisfactory, informationally-decentralized processes can be designed? In particular, can informationally-decentralized processes be designed for the class of all environments free of externalities (*decomposable environments*)?

---

[30] These restrictions are satisfied by the competitive process, so there is no problem with regard to classical environments. But it is proper to ask whether there could be processes that are informationally 'even better' than the competitive process. In terms of certain criteria of dimensionality of messages, the answer obtained independently by Hurwicz (1977), by Mount and Reiter (1974), and—from a somewhat different point of view—by Sonnenschein (1974) is in the negative: in a specified sense, one cannot do 'better.'

Some Results

With all this machinery, we have finally managed to ask a question. Are there answers? Indeed there are, some positive, some negative.

To begin with, it is possible to construct processes that are informationally decentralized for all decomposable environments. As for nondecomposable environments, it seems that one would have to say "no", but this has not as yet been rigorously established. It can be shown that informational requirements increase when nondecomposability (externalities) enters. While this is hardly surprising, the fact that informational decentralization is possible for the class of all decomposable environments, was, to me at least, a surprise, particularly because of the well-known difficulties that arise in the presence of indivisibilities. Indivisibilities do make trouble, but not to the point of making informational decentralization impossible.

To show this, it is sufficient to exhibit an informationally-decentralized process which is Pareto-satisfactory for all decomposable environments. In fact, there exists at least one, although with certain limitations and defects. The process works roughly as follows. A message is a listing (or description) of trades (with others or with nature) that a participant is prepared to engage in. The response is a counterproposal listing all those trades that are better, or at least as good, from the respondent's point of view.[31] The process does qualify as informationally decentralized because the privacy requirement is satisfied, since the participant needs to know only his own characteristics; and the language, that of trade sets, also fits the definition.[32]

Furthermore, it is simple to show that this process (which is only defined for decomposable environments) yields optimal equilibria and any optimum can be reached by it. It is Pareto-satisfactory. But this is only a static property. Dynamically, the greed process is terrible. Unless we start it from an optimal position, it oscillates indefinitely with constant amplitude. So we get more ambitious and look for a *convergent* Pareto-satisfactory process.

It is possible to 'fix up' the greed process by building into it a certain amount of 'inertia', i.e., dependence on earlier values. Kanemitsu (1971) showed that such a greed-inertia combination does result in convergence in *continuous* decomposable environments. This is quite a broad class (including increasing returns and other nonconvexities), but it rules out indivisibilities. Whether one can generalize this to discrete (indivisible) economies is, I believe, an open question. So, we have not yet exhibited a *convergent* informationally-decentralized process that is Pareto-satisfactory for *all* decomposable environments!

---

[31] You can see why this has been called the *greed process*.
[32] There is no denying, of course, that the messages used are very 'heavy' and complex.

At this point, the idea of randomness, not a stranger to search procedures, comes to the rescue. By introducing an element of randomness, we can obtain convergence (although, I must admit, in a probabilistic sense only) and also simplify the structure of messages. This process, developed by Hurwicz, Radner, and Reiter (1975), is particularly simple when all goods are *indivisible*. Let me describe it for the two-trader Edgeworth Box case.

At each time point, each participant picks at random (but according to a fixed probability distribution) a trade that will leave him at least as well off as he is at present. If the two trade proposals happen to be compatible, the bargain is sealed, and the traders start all over again from the newly reached point. It is clear that the process has the privacy property: one needs to know only one's preferences and subsistence requirements; in fact, the process, even in the more general situations (with any number of traders and production) is informationally decentralized. Unbiasedness is also intuitively clear: one can pick any optimal allocation as a point of departure and the rules make it impossible to get away; thus there is a (probabilistic) equilibrium. It is not obvious that the traders won't 'get stuck' at some non-optimal position, in which case the process would be wasteful. But a certain amount of mathematics leads to the conclusion that we are protected from such a fate with probability one.[33]

So, the indivisible case turns out to be relatively simple, although one cannot make any practical claims until the speed of convergence has been investigated. But the usually well-behaved, continuous, *divisible* environment makes trouble here, since under the just-stated rules the probability of encounter would be zero: the proverbial needle in the proverbial haystack. So[34] there has to be a modification: when commodities are perfectly divisible, a proposal will consist of not only the point picked at random but also a certain neighborhood of it (say, a square or a cube), with the further unattractive proviso that any part of the neighborhood whose utility is below that of the original endowment is cut off by the participant before the proposal is sent out. Now if the two (neighborhood) proposals fail to meet, one must try again; if they do meet, a point is chosen at random from the intersection area and the game goes on. Under rather mild assumptions of topological nature, probabilistic convergence can again be proved and the process is Pareto-satisfactory. It also qualifies as informationally decentralized, but it is clear that the informational burden is much greater than in the indivisible case, since the cut off neighborhoods might be very irregular in shape.

---

33 [N]ote that in the indivisible goods case, the messages here are not sets but single trade proposals, [which are definitely] very superior to the greed process.

34 For the case of one private good, Drèze-Poussin find correct revelation the only good strategy in the minimax (as distinct from Nash) sense.

Facing such complexities of the process, it is natural to ask whether these are merely due to lack of cleverness on our part. Can we hope to design a process with all the nice properties of this one but with a smaller informational burden? A. P. Lerner (1944) raised this point in his *Economics of Control* after he proposed dealing with indivisibilities by a consumer-producer surplus type of criterion. His answer was that "the necessity of making unreliable estimates is in the nature of the problem and not in the method of solving it. . . . The same estimates and guesses must be made in *any* economy where knowledge is imperfect and where large decisions have to be made" (p. 198).

I believe that Lerner was right, but even now, almost thirty years later, we do not have a rigorous proof of this contention. The main difficulty is conceptual. We must define precisely what would be considered informationally less burdensome. Namely, we need a concept of informational efficiency, somewhat similar to production efficiency—a partial ordering criterion. Once the informational efficiency ordering is available, we can interpret Lerner's question (although he stated it as an assertion) as follows: is a given proposed process (e.g., that embodying his criterion) informationally *maximally* efficient among, say, informationally-decentralized processes that are Pareto-satisfactory for all decomposable environments? Although some informational-efficiency criteria have been suggested, we do not as yet have a definitive answer to Lerner's question.

But there are partial answers based on the criterion of message space size which is related to informational efficiency (see Reiter 1974a). In particular, it has been shown that, in the absence of convexity or monotonicity restrictions on the environment, there is no upper bound to the number of auxiliary parameters that must be used in a privacy-preserving Pareto-satisfactory process (Hurwicz, 1977). This comes close to confirming Lerner's view. Note the contrast with classical environments where the number of auxiliary parameters need only be as high as the number of commodities— as when prices are such parameters.[35]

When the assumption of decomposability of the environment is abandoned (i.e., externalities are permitted), the preceding processes are not even defined. But when they are redefined so as to cover non-decomposabilities (Ledyard, 1968), they may lose their informationally-decentralized character.

For a particular class of non-decomposable situations, however, an interesting possibility emerges. It is well known that it may be possible formally to eliminate externalities by enlarging the commodity space (although this is based on implicit observability assumptions). Now Starrett (1972) has

---

[35] As already mentioned, fewer auxiliary parameters would not work; the competitive mechanism is 'dimensionally efficient.'

pointed out that such enlargement may introduce non-convexities in a previously convex world. Namely, we have either fewer goods and convexity but with externalities, or more goods and no externalities, but no convexity. Thus the competitive mechanism fails either way, because of externalities or because of non-convexities. Still, not all is lost. If continuity is not impaired, a probabilistic process such as that outlined above might provide a decentralized Pareto-satisfactory and convergent solution.

Incentive Compatibility

So far we have been asking whether it is possible to design process rules which, if followed, would have certain desirable consequences. Where the answer is in the negative, we at least know our limitations. But if a process with the desired properties is found, the question arises whether one could expect the participants to follow the rules, since there is a possibility of collusions or of individual departures from the prescribed norms. We shall consider only the latter.

Whether a certain configuration of behavior patterns is compatible with the participants' 'natural inclinations' is a problem in the theory of games, in this case noncooperative games without side payments. There are differences of opinion as to what constitutes a reasonable concept of solution for such games. For the sake of definiteness we shall adopt that of a Nash equilibrium which seems to be a good formalization of many intuitive ideas prevailing among economists. A configuration of behavior patterns constituting a Nash equilibrium will be referred to as (individual-) *incentive-compatible*. Such a configuration is present if no participant finds it advantageous to depart from his behavior pattern so long as the others do not. For instance, in a bilateral monopoly situation, competitive behavior is not (usually) incentive-compatible because when one participant is a price-taker, it would be to the other's advantage to be a price-setter (monopolist) rather than a price-taker.

One might, however, assume that there exists an enforcement system (carrots or sticks) which makes it unattractive for the participants openly to defy the prescribed rules. But suppose that the enforcing agency has no knowledge of the characteristics of the individual participants (their preferences, technologies, or endowments). It is then conceivable that the participants would 'cheat' without openly violating the rules. A participant could try to 'cheat' by doing what the rules would have required him to do had his characteristics been different from what they are—i.e., he could 'pretend' to be poorer than he is, or less efficient, or less eager for certain goods.[36]

Economists have long been alerted to this issue by Samuelson (1954) in the context of the allocation problem for public goods. But, in fact, a similar problem arises in a 'non-atomistic' world of pure exchange of exclusively private goods. Consider, for instance, an economy consisting of two traders, as conventionally represented by an Edgeworth Box, with classical strictly convex indifference curves and a positive non-optimal initial endowment of both goods for both traders. We already noted that if they were both told to behave as price-takers it would pay one of them to violate this rule if he could get away with it. Now we assume that he cannot violate the rule openly, but he can 'pretend' to have preferences different from his true ones. The question is whether he could think up for himself a false (but convex and monotone) preference map which would be more advantageous for him than his true one, assuming that he will follow the rules of price-taking according to the false map while the other trader plays the game honestly. It is easily shown that the answer is in the affirmative. Thus, in such a situation, the rules of perfect competition are not incentive-compatible.

It follows that the enforcing authority could not hope to maintain competitive (price-taking) behavior without directly checking up on the participants' characteristics, thus transgressing the requirements of informational decentralization. Perfect competition is not incentive-compatible.

But might there not exist some other set of rules to generate a process avoiding this difficulty? We have so far seen only that the conventional parametric price mechanism will not do the job, and there are many alternative mechanisms one could experiment with. But the same trouble will be present in *any* process yielding Pareto optimal outcomes and giving the participants the option of remaining at their initial endowments if they so desire (the 'no-trade option'). For it turns out that, given any such process, the non-law-abiding trader can profit by behaving in a way that successfully misrepresents his true characteristics (Hurwicz, 1972). Thus, in a non-atomistic exchange economy, there can be no incentive-compatible mechanism with optimal equilibria and the no-trade option even though there are no public goods![37]

These results show that the difficulty is due not to our lack of inventiveness, but to a fundamental conflict among such mechanism attributes as the optimality of equilibria, incentive-compatibility of the rules, and the

---

[36] It is important to understand that he would not be doing this directly by uttering false statements, but indirectly by behaving inappropriately according to the rules for his true characteristics.
[37] See also Ledyard (1972).

requirements of informational decentralization. Concessions must be made in at least one of these directions.

The possibility of successful false revelation of individual characteristics is particularly important in an economy with production. The issue has come up in many contexts. It has been raised as an objection to the Lange-Lerner mechanism. It has also been recognized in connection with situations where targets and norms are set, whether for enterprise managers in a Soviet-type economy or for workers on a piece rate under capitalism. In all of these cases there is a 'superior' and a 'subordinate', and the latter has an incentive to depress the norms when the penalty for failure to reach a target is severe.

In analyzing the situation, one should distinguish cases in which the subordinate's reward depends only on activities observed by the superior from those where, as in Leibenstein's X-efficiency model, the subordinate's satisfaction is affected by factors under his control which cannot be observed by the superior. More realistically, one may assume that the superior can observe more or less, but only at a cost. Furthermore, if we think of the superior as a central authority and the subordinate as a manager of a plant, it is reasonable to suppose that the subordinate possesses technological knowledge while the superior knows the (social) objective function and, perhaps, resource availabilities.

Under such circumstances the superior faces a dilemma. If he gives his subordinate a great deal of autonomy and does not make an effort at observation, the subordinate will maximize his own rather than the superior's objective function. If the superior makes the costly effort at observation and deprives the subordinate of autonomy, he is likely to give wrong orders because of his technological ignorance. A possible solution is a reward structure which brings the objectives of the two parties closer together (e.g., output sharing); this may give the subordinate a motivation consonant with the superior's and would make him use his technological knowledge to maximize the superior's objective function if he were given sufficient freedom to select the correct actions. The loss to the superior from sharing may in some cases exceed the gains in efficiency. But we can see that it is meaningful to seek an optimum combination of observation effort, delegation of authority (grant of autonomy), and reward structure.

The example is instructive because it shows the difference in the conceptual structure needed for the investigation of the interplay of authority, incentive, information, and performance issues. Where only performance and information were being investigated, the object of study was the mechanism or adjustment process. But from the viewpoint of incentive and authority structure, it is helpful to note (as does Camacho, 1972) that the actual responses of the participants may be regarded as the resultant of two factors: the official rules ('the regime') and the behavioral characteristics of the participants. In general, the rules limit the responses of the participants, but do not prescribe them uniquely. Given the rules, together with the punishment and reward structure for transgressions, the actual responses are determined by the participants' behavioral characteristics. Laissez-faire may be defined as a regime granting the participants maximal leeway; at the other extreme (and equally unrealistic) would be an economy in which the rules make all participants into pre-programmed automata.

Aside from value judgments and preferences for freedom of decision-making, one can regard the degree of restrictiveness of the regime, together with the reward structure and informational activities (insofar as these can be varied by the designer) as unknowns of the problem. The objective is to attain optimal performance. The behavioral characteristics of the participants and the class of environments for which the system is being designed are the givens.[38]

Let us go back to consider the incentive-compatibility issue in a production economy, assuming complete observability of all activities.[39] A very simple example involves two persons: a farmer producing wheat, and a laborer.[40] The farmer wants to maximize the amount of wheat after paying off the laborer (in wheat); the laborer's net satisfaction is measured by the difference between the amount of wheat received and an index of disutility of labor. If the production function and the disutility curve have their classical shapes, there will be a unique Pareto optimum at a point where the marginal disutility of labor equals its marginal productivity. Perfect competition would produce this resource allocation. But it will be found that the farmer can get more wheat by misrepresenting his production function, namely, by underestimating the marginal productivity at a point below the optimum output level.[41]

Thus again perfect competition is not incentive-compatible. However, unlike under pure exchange, it *is* possible here to devise a reward scheme that would eliminate the incentive toward misrepresentation on the part of one participant. For in this simple farmer-laborer example, it so happens that Pareto optimality is equivalent to the maximization of the difference between the total output and the total disutility of labor.[42] Thus if the two participants, the farmer and the laborer, are promised fixed shares of this difference (say, one-third for the farmer, two-thirds for the laborer), with the laborer in addition getting an amount of wheat just sufficient to compensate

---

[38] Examples of this type, but with information structure regarded as given, were worked out by Camacho (1972).

[39] But not necessarily of all characteristics!

[40] See the postscript.—SB

[41] It is assumed that the laborer remains a wage-taker.

[42] This disutility, under the assumptions made, can be considered cardinally measurable.

him for the disutility of labor, the farmer will have an interest in reaching the Pareto optimum. Thus one could ask them to play the market game, but only for the purpose of determining the proper labor input level, following which a non-competitive 'surplus-sharing' rule would be implemented.

Here the manager (farmer) would have an incentive to be truthful. Thus we have a situation where perfect competition is not incentive-compatible for either party, but for the manager, another process, departing from perfect competition in its distributive aspects, is. However, I rather doubt that this is typical. In more elaborate situations, with the managers' utilities depending on the product mix of the economy, informationally-decentralized mechanisms that are incentive-compatible on management side may well fail to exist. But in "team"-type situations (with scalar additive outputs) sharing formulas will be safe against misrepresentation, while competitive price mechanisms in general will not.[43]

The incentives for truthful revelation of [preferences] when public goods are being allocated were examined by Drèze and de la Vallée Poussin. Unfortunately, their conclusions are not directly comparable with those we have reached for the world of private goods. They do find that, in terms of their criterion, at an equilibrium of the process, all consumers have an incentive to reveal their preferences correctly. However, their criterion is an *instantaneous* change in utility, while the criterion used here (and, it seems, that implicit in Samuelson's argument) refers to the utility of the *final* outcome.

Heal points out that an incentive-compatible reward structure (on the output side) can be obtained for his (1971) process in the case of one producer when the center's utility function is positively homogeneous. The producer would not pay for the centrally allocated resources, but would get paid for the outputs, with prices equal to the marginal utilities of the outputs. In this case the utility is a strictly increasing function of the value of output; hence, if the producer were rewarded, say, by a fixed share of the value of output, he would find it to his advantage to maximize the center's utility. Unfortunately, where there are several firms, the one-to-one relationship is between utility and the value of outputs *aggregated* over all producing units; this does not imply *individual* incentive-compatibility.

Jennergren shows the incentive for misrepresentation in the Dantzig-Wolfe decomposition procedure, specifically an incentive to 'hide' a part of the (feasible) production set. Both Marglin and Jennergren stress the incentive toward 'cheating' under the (parametric) price mechanism in the case of small numbers of producing units. For the 'atomistic case', Marglin suggests

---

[43] Related questions of incentive-compatibility were examined by Groves (1969).

a combination of a 'command' (quantity-guided) system in the search for an optimum with a profit-maximization motive to provide suitable incentives. This is, in a sense, the reverse of the system considered above for the farmer-laborer example.

From the preceding discussion it is evident that the incentive structure is largely determined by what the participants can achieve for themselves by their free actions; this in turn depends on such institutional phenomena as private property, rules for the distribution of profits, or the freedom not to trade. A tool appropriate for the analysis of such phenomena is the characteristic function of a game defined by von Neumann and Morgenstern. Shapley and Shubik (1967) carried out a study of different institutional property arrangements, including feudalism, sharecropping, and the village commune, by constructing the corresponding characteristic functions and exploring the different versions of game solutions (von Neumann-Morgenstern solutions, the core, the Shapley value). Thus a significant step is taken toward a formalization of the distributional aspects of the economic system.[44]

In the context of distributional issues, the conflict between informational decentralization and incentival considerations is illustrated by a model due to Pazner and Schmeidler (1972). Their objective is to show that preassigned income distribution can be attained without sacrificing either Pareto optimality or informational decentralization. To accomplish this, they postulate a central agency distributing money (purchasing power) to individuals in accordance with the desired income distribution. Also, there are central agencies in charge of allocation of manpower. These custodians of labor operate as if they owned it. The workers can buy their leisure back from the manpower agency, but they have no freedom of choice where to work. The total supply of labor is assumed fixed and independent of the rewards. In the absence of individual checking procedures and given ordinary human motivations, such an assumption may be difficult to maintain.

Conclusion

The proper integration of the information and incentive aspects of resource allocation models is perhaps the major unsolved problem in the theory of mechanism design. Many other questions also remain unanswered. Nevertheless, I think this survey shows that economic analysis has broken out of its traditional limits in at least two important ways: (1) devising specific new

---

[44] See also Shubik (1962) and Shapley (1970). The distributional parameters introduced above, as well as the no-trade option, may be regarded as special cases of a similar approach.

mechanisms; and (2) exploring the constraints and tradeoffs to which the design of mechanisms is subject.

The new mechanisms are somewhat like synthetic chemicals: even if not usable for practical purposes, they can be studied in a pure form and so contribute to our understanding of the difficulties and potentialities of design. The design point of view enlarges our field of vision and helps economics avoid a narrow focus on the status quo, whether East or West.

We have made significant progress in understanding the problems of designing resource allocation mechanisms. But the field is still in its infancy because these are hard problems.

References

Allais, M. (1943) *A la Recherche d'une Discipline Économique, I.* Paris: Atelier Industria.

Allais, M. (1945) *Économie Pure et Rendement Social.* Paris: Sirey.

Aoki, M. (1971) Two planning processes for an economy with production externalities, *International Economic Review*, 12(3): 403–14.

Arrow, K. (1951) An extension of the basic theorems of classical welfare economics, in *Proceedings of the Second Berkeley Symposium*, ed. J. Neyman, 507–32. Berkeley, CA: University of California Press.

Arrow, K., and F. Hahn (1971) *General Competitive Analysis.* San Francisco, CA: Holden-Day.

Arrow, K., and L. Hurwicz (1956) Reduction of constrained maxima to saddlepoint problems, in *Proceedings of the Third Berkeley Symposium*, ed. J. Neyman, 1–20. Berkeley, CA: University of California Press.

Arrow, K. and L. Hurwicz (1958) Gradient method for concave programming, in *Studies in Linear and Non-Linear Programming*, ed. K. Arrow, L. Hurwicz, and H. Uzawa, chs. 6, 8. Palo Alto, CA: Stanford University Press.

Arrow, K. and L. Hurwicz (1960) Decentralization and computation in resource allocation, in *Essays in Economics and Econometrics*, ed. R. Pfouts, 34–104. Chapel Hill, NC: University of North Carolina Press.

Barone, E. (1935) The Ministry of production in the collectivist state, in *Collectivist Economic Planning*, ed. F. Hayek, 245–90. London: Routledge. (Reprinted from Giornale degli Economisti, 1908.)

Baumol, W. and T. Fabian (1964) Decomposition, pricing for decentralization and external economies, *Management Science*, 11(1): 1–32.

Bessière, F. and E. Sautter (1968) Optimization and suboptimization: The method of extended models in the non-linear case, *Management Science*, 15(1): 1–11.

Camacho, A. (1972) Centralization and decentralization of decision-making mechanisms: A general model, in *Jahrbuch der Wirtschaft Osteuropas No. 3*, 45–66. Munich: Günther Olzog Verlag.

Dantzig, G. and P. Wolfe (1961) The decomposition algorithm for linear programs, *Econometrica*, 29(4): 767–78.

De Laveleye, É. (1882) *Éléments D'Économie Politique.* Paris: Librairie Hachette.

Debreu, G. (1951) Coefficient of resource utilization, *Econometrica*, 19(3): 273–92.

Debreu, G. (1959) *Theory of Value*. New Haven, CT: Yale University Press.

Drèze, J. and D. de la Vallée Poussin (1971) A tâtonnement process for public goods, *Review of Economic Studies*, 38(2): 133–45.

Ely, R. (1884) *The Past and the Present of Political Economy*. Baltimore, MD; Johns Hopkins University Studies, Second Series, III.

Ely, R. (1886) *Publications of the American Economic Association, I*. Baltimore, MD: J. Murphy & Co.

Groves, T. (1969) The allocation of resources under uncertainty: The informational and incentive roles of prices and demands in a team, Center for Research in Management Science, University of California, Berkeley, Technical Report No. 1. Published as Groves, T. and R. Radner (1972) Allocation of resources in a team, *Journal of Economic Theory*, 4(3): 415–41.

Groves, T. (1972) Market information and the allocation of resources in a dynamic team model, *Joint Automatic Control Conference of the AACC*, Stanford 1972, 8–17. Published as Groves, T. (1983) The usefulness of demand forecasts for team resource allocation in a stochastic environment, *Review of Economic Studies*, 50(3): 555–71.

Hayek, F. (1935) The present state of the debate, in *Collectivist Economic Planning*, ed. F. Hayek, 201–43. London: Routledge.

Hayek, F. (1945) The use of knowledge in society, *American Economic Review*, 35(4): 519–30.

Heal, G. (1969) Planning without prices, *Review of Economic Studies*, 36(3): 346–62.

Heal, G. (1971) Planning, prices, and increasing returns, *Review of Economic Studies*, 38(3): 281–94.

Hurwicz, L. (1960) Optimality and informational efficiency in resource allocation processes, in *Mathematical Methods in the Social Sciences*, ed. K. Arrow, S. Karlin, and P. Suppes, 27–46. Palo Alto, CA: Stanford University Press.

Hurwicz, L. (1972) On informationally decentralized systems, in *Decision and Organization*, ed. C. McGuire and R. Radner. Amsterdam: North-Holland. Second edition, 1986, 297–336. Minneapolis, MN: University of Minnesota Press.

Hurwicz, L. (1977) On the dimensional requirements of informationally decentralized Pareto-satisfactory processes, in *Studies in Resource Allocation Processes*, ed. K. Arrow and L. Hurwicz, 413–24. Cambridge, MA: Cambridge University Press.

Hurwicz, L., R. Radner, and S. Reiter (1975) A stochastic decentralized resource allocation process, *Econometrica*, 43(2): 187–221, and 43(3): 363–93.

Jennergren, L. (1971) *Studies in the Mathematical Theory of Decentralized Resource-Allocation*, Ph.D. dissertation, Stanford University.

Kanemitsu, H. (1966) Informational efficiency and decentralization in optimal resource allocation, *The Economic Studies Quarterly*, 16(3): 22–40.

Kanemitsu, H. (1971) On the stability of an adjustment process in non-classical environments, mimeo (revised 1975). Abstract in *Econometrica* 1971, 39(4): 132–35.

Koopmans, T. (1951) Analysis of production as an efficient combination of activities, in *Activity Analysis of Production and Allocation*, ed. T. Koopmans, 33–97. New York, NY: Wiley.

Koopmans, T. (1957) *Three Essays on the State of Economic Science*. New York, NY: McGraw-Hill.

Kornai, J. and T. Lipták (1965) Two-level planning, *Econometrica*, 33(1): 141–69.

Kruskal, Jr., J. and A. Newell (1950) *A model for organization theory*, Technical Report LOGS-103. Santa Monica, CA: Rand Corporation.

Lange, O. (1942) The foundations of welfare economics, *Econometrica*, 10(3/4), 215–28.

Lange, O. and F. Taylor (1938) *On the Economic Theory of Socialism*, ed. B. Lippincott. Minneapolis, MN: University of Minnesota Press.

Ledyard, J. (1968) Resource allocation in unselfish environments, *American Economic Review*, 58(2): 227–37.

Ledyard, J. (1972) A characterization of organizations and environments which are consistent with preference revelation, Discussion Paper 5, Center for Mathematical Studies in Economics and Management Sciences, Northwestern University. Published as Ledyard, J. (1977) Incentive compatible behavior in core-selecting organizations, *Econometrica*, 45(7): 1607–23.

Lerner, A. (1944) *The Economics of Control*. New York, NY: Macmillan.

Malinvaud, E. (1967) Decentralized procedures for planning, in *Activity Analysis in the Theory of Growth and Planning*, ed. E. Malinvaud and M. Bacharach, 170–208. London: Macmillan.

Malinvaud, E. (1970) The theory of planning for individual and collective consumption, presented at the symposium on the problem of modeling the national economy, Novosibirsk. Published as Malinvaud, E. (1972) Prices for individual consumption, quantity indicators for collective consumption, *Review of Economic Studies* 39(4): 385–405.

Marglin, S. (1969) Information in price and command systems of planning, in *Public Economics: An Analysis of the Public Production and Consumption and their Relation to the Private Sector*, ed. J. Margolis and H. Guitton, 54–76. London: Macmillan.

Marschak, J. (1924) Wirtschaftsrechnung und Gemeinwirtschaft, *Archiv für Sozialwissenschaft und Sozialpolitik*, Tübingen, 51(2): 501–20.

Marschak, J. (1955) Elements for a theory of teams, *Management Science*, 1(2): 127–37.

Marschak, J. and R. Radner (1972) *Economic Theory of Teams*. New Haven, CT: Yale University Press.

Marschak, T. (1958) An example of a modified gradient method for linear programming, in *Studies in Linear and Non-Linear Programming*, ed. K. Arrow, L. Hurwicz, and H. Uzawa, 146–53 Palo Alto, CA: Stanford University Press.

Marschak, T. (1959) Centralization and decentralization in economic organizations, *Econometrica*, 27(3): 399–430.

Mount, K. and S. Reiter (1974) On the informational size of message spaces, *Journal of Economic Theory*, 8(2): 161–92.

Oniki, H. (1974) The cost of communication in economic organizations, *Quarterly Journal of Economics*, 88(4): 529–50.

Pareto, V. (1896–97) The new theories of economics, *Journal of Political Economy*, 5(4): 485–502.

Pareto, V. (1963) *Manuel d'Économie Politique, II*. Paris: Giard et Brière.

Pazner, E. and D. Schmeidler (1972) Decentralization, income distribution, and the role of money in socialist economies, private circulation. Published as Pazner, E. and D. Schmeidler (1978) Decentralization and income distribution in socialist economies, *Economic Inquiry*, 16(2): 257–64.

Radner, R. (1972a) Teams, in *Decision and Organization*, ed. C. McGuire and R. Radner. Amsterdam: North-Holland. Second edition, 1986, Minneapolis, MN: University of Minnesota Press, 187–215.

Radner, R. (1972b) Allocation of a scarce resource under uncertainty: An example of a team, in *Decision and Organization*, ed. C. McGuire and R. Radner. Amsterdam: North-Holland. Second edition, 1986, Minneapolis, MN: University of Minnesota Press, 217–36.

Reiter, S. (1974a) Informational efficiency of iterative processes and the size of message spaces, *Journal of Economic Theory*, 8(2): 193–205.

Reiter, S. (1974b) The knowledge revealed by an allocation process and the informational size of the message space, *Journal of Economic Theory*, 8(3): 389–96.

Samuelson, P. (1949) Market mechanisms and maximization. Santa Monica, CA: The Rand Corporation. Reprinted in *Collected Scientific Papers of Paul A. Samuelson, I* 1966, ed. J. Stiglitz, 425–92. Cambridge, MA: MIT Press.

Samuelson, P. (1954) The pure theory of public expenditure, *Review of Economics and Statistics*, 36(4): 387–89.

Shapley, L. (1970) Simple games: Application to organization theory, presented at the Second World Congress of the Econometric Society, Cambridge, UK. Abstract printed as Shapley, L. (1971) A game-theoretic model for organizations, *Econometrica* 39(4): 98.

Shapley, L. and M. Shubik (1967) Ownership and the Production Function, *Quarterly Journal of Economics*, 81(1): 88–111.

Shubik, M. (1962) Incentives, decentralized control, the assignment of joint costs, and internal pricing, *Management Science*, 8(3): 325–43.

Simon, H. (1951) A formal theory of the employment relationship, *Econometrica*, 19(3): 293–305.

Sonnenschein, H. (1974) An axiomatic characterization of the competitive mechanism, *Econometrica*, 42(3): 425–34.

Starrett, D. (1972) Fundamental nonconvexities in the theory of externalities, *Journal of Economic Theory*, 4(2): 180–99.

Taylor, F. (1929) The guidance of production in a socialist state, *American Economic Review*, 19(1): 1–8.

Taylor, H. (1944) Obituary: Richard Theodore Ely, *Economic Journal*, 54(2/3): 132–38.

Uzawa, H. (1958) Iterative methods for concave programming, in *Studies in Linear and Non-Linear Programming*, ed. K. Arrow, L. Hurwicz, and H. Uzawa, 154–65. Palo Alto, CA: Stanford University Press.

Weitzman, M. (1970) Iterative multi-level planning with production targets, *Econometrica*, 38(1): 50–65.

Editor's Postscript

The farmer-laborer model corresponding to footnote 40 is based on some handwritten derivations written in Lafayette, Indiana, dated May 3, 1973, found in the Hurwicz archive. The following reconstruction is presented to clarify the argument. An explicit numerical example in these notes has been omitted.

Part I: Competitive equilibrium

Suppose a farmer produces wheat q with a production function $q = f(n)$ using labor n provided by the laborer, where $f' > 0$ and $f'' < 0$. Denoting the farmer's share of the output by q^* and the laborer's share by q^{**}, we have $q = q^* + q^{**}$. Suppose the wage rate for labor (in terms of wheat) is w per unit, so $q^{**} = wn$. Then the farmer maximizes $q^* = \pi = f(n) - wn$, where π denotes the farmer's profit. Suppose $\phi(n)$ is the laborer's disutility from labor, where $\phi' > 0$ and $\phi'' > 0$. Then the laborer maximizes his utility $u = wn - \phi(n)$.

Under perfect competition, the farmer maximizes π by setting

$$\frac{d\pi}{dq} = f'(n) - w = 0,$$

while the laborer maximizes u by setting

$$\frac{du}{dn} = w - \phi'(n) = 0.$$

Then at a competitive equilibrium, $f'(\tilde{n}) = \phi'(\tilde{n}) = w$.

Part II: Pareto optimality

Let the farmer's utility function be $\psi(q^*)$ with $\psi' > 0$ and $\psi'' < 0$. Then Pareto optimality requires that we maximize $\psi(q^*)$ subject to $q^{**} - \phi(n) \geq \alpha$ and $q^* + q^{**} - f(n) = 0$, where α is the fixed utility level of the laborer. Maximizing the Lagrangian

$$\mathcal{L} = \psi(q^*) + \lambda(q^{**} - \phi(n) - \alpha) + \mu(q^* + q^{**} - f(n))$$

for an interior solution, we obtain

$$\frac{\mathcal{L}}{\partial q^*} = \psi'(q^*) + \mu = 0, \tag{1}$$

$$\frac{\mathcal{L}}{\partial q^{**}} = \lambda + \mu = 0, \tag{2}$$

$$\frac{\mathcal{L}}{\partial n} = -\lambda \phi'(n) - \mu f'(n) = 0. \tag{3}$$

From (1), $\mu \neq 0$; from (2), $\lambda = -\mu \neq 0$. Therefore, from (3), $\phi'(\hat{n}) = f'(\hat{n})$, so the competitive equilibrium is Pareto optimal.

Part III: Monopoly

Suppose the laborer treats w parametrically while the farmer behaves as a monopoly. The former implies that $w = \phi'(n)$ while the latter implies that the farmer maximizes $\pi = f(n) - \phi'(n)n$. At a maximum,

$$\frac{d\pi}{dn} = f'(n^M) - \phi'(n^M) - \phi''(n^M)n^M = 0.$$

Then

$$f'(n^M) - \phi'(n^M) = \phi''(n^M)n^M > 0$$

because $\phi'' > 0$. Hence, $f'(n^M) > \phi'(n^M)$ and $n^M < \hat{n}$ as seen in the graph below.

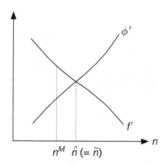

Part IV: 'Cheating' by farmer

In the figure below, let $\mathring{f}$ (shown by the solid curve) represent the true production function and $\tilde{f}$ (shown by the dashed curve) the misrepresented one, where the farmer underestimates the laborer's marginal productivity at n^M, below the marginal productivity at the optimum labor level, $\hat{n}$. If the laborer remains a wage-taker, the farmer can therefore obtain more wheat, showing that perfect competition is not incentive-compatible.[45]

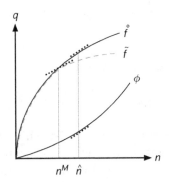

Part V: Incentive-compatibility under sharecropping

The farmer's reward is now $r \equiv \theta(f(n) - \phi(n))$, where $0 < \theta < 1$. Suppose that the laborer does not cheat. Then the farmer will maximize $f(n) - \phi(n)$ and set $f'(n) = \phi'(n)$, i.e., $n = \hat{n}$. So in equilibrium, $\tilde{f}(n) = \mathring{f}(n)$ and sharecropping is incentive-compatible for the farmer.[46]

---

[45] Note that the vertical distance between $\mathring{f}$ and ϕ is not π! With price of wheat set at unity, total revenue equals f, and total cost is $wn = \phi(n)n$.

[46] An unstated presumption appears to be that the farmer can only under-represent the false production function.—SB

10

On the Interaction between Information and Incentives in Organizations

Although the title of my paper refers to organizations in general, the reader should be warned that my thinking has evolved primarily in the context of economic organizations—be they whole nations or individual firms. I do believe that my framework, even though developed for dealing with economies, is also relevant to other types of organizations. It is, however, a framework quite distinct from that familiar from control theory. Since the term 'control' appears in the title of this conference, as well as of this session, I shall start by showing how I see the relationship of my framework, to be called *structural change framework,* to the *control theory framework.* I shall follow this up by formulating first the informational and then the incentival aspects of structural change in organizations, and then look at the problem of choosing organizational structure given the interactions between these two aspects.

Control Theory versus Structural Change Framework

To begin with, there are important features common to the two approaches. Both are *normative* in spirit. That is, they do not accept the status quo, but rather look for modes of intervention that would bring the system as close to optimality as possible. Thus the mode of intervention is the unknown of the problem. But while rejecting a purely passive attitude toward the workings of the system, they also try to avoid the danger of Utopianism by taking into account the constraints to which intervention and its effects are subject.

From *Communication and Control in Society*, edited by K. Krippendorff, 123–47. ©1979 Gordon and Breach Science Publishers: New York. Reproduced by permission of Taylor & Francis Books UK.

On the Interaction between Information and Incentives in Organizations In: *The Collected Papers of Leonid Hurwicz Volume 1*. Edited by Samiran Banerjee, Oxford University Press.
© Oxford University Press 2022. DOI: 10.1093/oso/9780199313280.003.0010

The two approaches differ, however, with respect to the form of intervention they envisage. This can be seen against the background of a simple dynamic model governing the behavior of some *state variable*, to be denoted by x, usually a vector. Since the model is dynamic, the state variable is a function of time, say $x(t)$. The laws according to which it varies can be formulated as systems of differential equations, as is customary in much of control theory, or systems of difference equations, as is often convenient in economics. At this point of our presentation, in order to facilitate comparison, we shall use the differential equation formulation.

Using a dot over a symbol to denote the derivative with respect to time, we can represent a purely autonomous dynamic system by the (vectorial) equation

$$\dot{x} = f(x). \tag{1}$$

Assuming $x = (x_1, \ldots, x_n)$, this is equivalent to the system

$$\frac{dx_i}{dt} = f^i(x_1, \ldots, x_n) \quad i = 1, \ldots, n. \tag{1'}$$

Now the control theory model introduces another (vectorial) variable, the *control variable*, denoted by u, assumed to be subject to our manipulation. Since the control variable influences the behavior of the state variable, the dynamic system represented by (1) above is replaced by

$$\dot{x} = g(x, u). \tag{2}$$

If we think of nonintervention as corresponding to setting the control variable at zero, we may consider (1) to be a special case of (2), with

$$f(x) = g(x, 0). \tag{3}$$

Given a criterion of optimality, the problem is that of finding the appropriate time pattern $u(t)$ to be followed by the control variable. But reality is usually complicated by various perturbations, so that instead of dealing with a system governed by (2), we have

$$\dot{x} = h(x, u, y), \tag{4}$$

where y represents the disturbance. Again, (2) may be regarded as a special case of (4) with $y = 0$, so that

$$g(x, u) = h(x, u, 0). \tag{5}$$

Typically, the perturbation y can be neither predicted in advance nor even observed after the event, although we may assume it to be a random variable with known probability distribution. It is clear that in such circumstances it would be inadvisable to choose the time pattern $u(t)$ before observing the impact of the disturbance on the state variable. It is possible, however, to determine the optimal *policy* concerning the selection of control variable level as a function of the state variable that will be observed as the process develops. Denoting this function (sometimes called *feedback* controller *synthesis* function) by ψ, we can express the dependence of the control variable on the state variable by

$$u(t) = \psi(x(t)). \tag{6}$$

If this feedback synthesis is adopted as the rule governing the control of the system, the behavior of the system is described by substituting (6) into (4), i.e., by

$$\dot{x} = h(x, \psi(x), y). \tag{7}$$

Thus, although the direct instrument of control is the variable u, the unknown of the problem becomes the synthesis function ψ, since—by hypothesis underlying the control theory model—we cannot modify the laws governing the system as expressed by the function h and by the probability distribution of the perturbation y. It is in this latter respect that the structural change framework is different.

It is, of course, natural to regard the *structure function h* in (4) as immutable if it represents a law of nature, say the Newtonian laws of mechanics. But if (4) represents a human system, some of the components h^i of the structure function $h = (h^1, \ldots, h^n)$ represent the behavior patterns and decision rules that are being followed by those operating the system, and these are far from immutable. They can be changed or influenced by laws, regulations, reward and punishment structures, etc. Hence, it is possible to consider the function h itself as an unknown of the problem, to be selected in an optimal manner. It would, of course, be unrealistic to suppose that behavior can be imposed in any desired manner; hence the unknown function h will be assumed to be selected from some family H of a priori admissible functions, with H representing the known invariants of human behavior and other constraints. This formulation, involving optimization with respect to the structure function h over the a priori admissible family H is characteristic of what we have called the structural change framework.

Let h_0 denote the structure function in the absence of any intervention and h_* the changed structure. It is possible to think of the control theory model as a special case of the structural change model in which

$$h_*(x, u, y) = h_0(x, \psi(x), y), \tag{8}$$

i.e., where the change in the structure function is effected by feedback synthesis. An important example arises in connection with influencing an economic system through properly designed reward formulas. To see this we only need to regard, the reward, say allocation of goods, as a control variable, with output as a state variable and the reward formula as the feedback synthesis relating the reward to output. If u_i and x_i denote respectively the reward to and the output produced by the i-th individual, the reward (synthesis) formula can be written as

$$u_i = \psi^i(x_i).$$

In economics one often thinks of the component structure functions h^i as expressing either natural or imposed rules of behavior. An example of such a rule is a firm's decision-making behavior based on profit maximization with prices treated parametrically, i.e., regarded as uninfluenced by the firm's decision. Such behavior would be natural for a very small firm in a very large economy. On the other hand, such behavior could be imposed by law in an economy with only a few large firms. Indeed, the Lange-Lerner model of a socialist price-guided economy postulated the imposition of this rule in the absence of increasing returns to scale. It is simple to interpret such a proposal within the structural change framework, with h_0 corresponding to natural behavior of large firms (presumably oligopolistic or monopolistic—which involves non-parametric treatment of prices) and h_* corresponding to the imposed rule of profit maximization with parametrically treated prices. This interpretation disregards the question of enforcement of the imposed rule. If the enforcement is explicitly built into the model, the laws governing the penalties for disobeying the imposed rules could be interpreted along the lines of the control theory framework, with penalties as control variables and the laws as feedback synthesis functions.

We see, therefore, that there is no conflict between the two frameworks and the choice between them is to a large extent a matter of convenience in the context of a particular problem. Although we shall from now on work within the structural change framework, there would be little difficulty in translating the discussion into control theory language.

Structural Change in an Economic Adjustment Model

In this section we shall consider problems of structural change against the background of an economic adjustment process model which has certain affinities with the simplest of the above models, viz., that of equation (1), in that it lacks both control variables and perturbation factors, although it differs from (1) in that it uses difference rather than differential equations. The basic state variables of the adjustment process model are *messages* transmitted between participants. For the sake of simplicity we treat messages as if they were broadcast to all participants so that only the sender but not an addressee need be specified. We denote by $m^i(t)$ the message sent out by participant i at time t. In order to make the model applicable to a variety of organizational (in particular, economic) structures, we do not restrict the nature of messages; they can be verbal or numerical (scalar or vectorial) and even pictorial (graphs of functions, etc.). The set of signals eligible to be used as messages is called a *language* and is denoted by M. Corresponding to the structure functions f^i in equation (1') above, we encounter in an adjustment process *response functions* (also denoted by f^i) which determine the messages emitted by participants at a point in time, given earlier messages and information acquired by the participants independently of the message exchange process. Assuming we denote the information acquired independently of the message process by the i-th participant to be constant over time and denoting it by z^i, we represent the adjustment process by the difference equation system

$$m^i(t+1) = f^i(m(t); z^i) \quad t = 1, 2, \ldots; i = 1, 2, \ldots, N, \tag{9}$$

where N is the number of participants and $m(t) = (m^i(t), \ldots m^N(t))$. We shall further suppose that the process possesses a unique *equilibrium* (stationary) message N-tuple, $\bar{m} = (\bar{m}_1, \ldots, \bar{m}_N)$, defined by

$$\bar{m}^i = f^i(\bar{m}; z^i) \quad i = 1, 2, \ldots N. \tag{10}$$

Furthermore, as is often true in economics, we shall focus on the system's performance at this equilibrium position.[1] Now equation (10) only specifies the equilibrium position of the message exchange process; a transition must be made to events in the sphere of real phenomena. For the economist, these phenomena are the resource flows between participants (exchange) and other economic actions, including consumption and production. Thus the economic process is not specified until a rule is present determining the resource flows given the outcome of the message exchange process. We therefore complete our model by introducing the *outcome function* ϕ which determines the equilibrium resource flow $\bar{a}$ resulting when the equilibrium message N-tuple is $\bar{m}$, i.e.,[2]

$$\bar{a} = \phi(\bar{m}). \tag{11}$$

---

[1] This can in some cases be justified by postulating rapid convergence of the system to its equilibrium values, but such an assumption should be regarded as only one of methodological convenience; it shows how much work still remains to be done in this area.

[2] For instance, in the case of pure exchange, the outcome $\bar{a}$ can be thought of as a $N \times N$ matrix whose (i, j)-entry is $a_{ij} = (a_{ij1}, \ldots, a_{ijL})$, with a_{ijk} denoting the net flow of commodity k from participant i to participant j in a world with L commodities.

Adopting the point of view of the structural change framework, we now consider the problem of the designer of the system. The designer is assumed to have an evaluation criterion which he applies to the outcome $\bar{a}$ of the process. For instance, economists often use the criterion of Pareto optimality of the outcome.[3] Noting that optimality is relative to the environment, one may ask whether a given 'economic mechanism' (defined by the language M, the response function $f = (f^i, \ldots, f^N)$ and the outcome function ϕ) guarantees the optimality (here and below this term is understood in the Pareto-sense) of outcomes relative to all environments e belonging to a specified class E. For instance, the so-called perfectly competitive mechanism has been shown to yield optimal outcomes for what are sometimes referred to as "classical" environments, where the sets and functions characterizing the environment have certain convexity and continuity properties and where externalities and public goods are absent. On the other hand, for nonclassical environments the perfectly competitive mechanism may fail to have equilibrium positions altogether (e.g., due to increasing returns, i.e., to non-convexity) or may produce non-optimal equilibrium outcomes (e.g., in the presence of externalities such as pollution).

Within the structural change framework let us look at the problem of a system designer whose evaluation criterion is the Pareto optimality of equilibria. His situation is very different depending on whether the mechanism is being designed for operation in classical environments only—or for some broader category of environments. When the mechanism is being designed for operation in classical environments only, there is an obvious candidate for a mechanism to be adopted, viz., the perfectly competitive mechanism, since in classical environments equilibrium positions exist and yield optimal outcomes. But we do not know as yet whether this candidate is eligible in the sense of belonging to the family of feasible mechanisms (the a priori admissible family of structure); in fact, we have not as yet formulated any criteria for eligibility for membership in the family of feasible mechanisms (admissible structures). Although one obviously cannot hope for an exhaustive listing, we distinguish two important categories of requirements: informational and incentive. In the following section we focus on the informational requirements, to the exclusion of incentive considerations.

---

[3] An outcome is defined as Pareto optimal relative to the possibilities and preferences characterizing an economy if there is no other possible outcome more attractive for some participants and equally attractive for others. A complete specification of possibilities and preferences *is* called *environment* and denoted by *e*; a class of environments is denoted by *E*. [Note: In later years—see, for example, Hurwicz (1985)—this terminology was modified: *e* is called an *economy*, and a class of economies denoted by *E* is called an *environment*.—SB]

Informational Properties of Adjustment Models

As just indicated, the discussion of this section is focused on the problem of designing a mechanism (i.e., finding a language M and functions f and ϕ) guaranteeing the existence and optimality of equilibria for a specified class E of environments (whether restricted to classical ones or broader). Since we are at this stage disregarding the issue of incentives, we shall not ask whether the participants would be inclined to obey the rules of the prescribed mechanism, but only whether rules can be found that would—if obeyed—yield optimal outcomes. However, we shall be concerned about the informational characteristics of the rules.

This concern is primarily related to the fact that, typically, no single participant has—at least at the beginning of the adjustment process—the information required to determine which resource flows would be optimal. As we have seen above, optimality depends on possibilities and preferences. In turn, the possibilities of the economy depend on the availability and distribution of productive resources among the participants, to be represented by the *initial endowment* N-tuple $w = (w^1, \ldots, w^N)$, where w^i denotes the resource endowment of the i-th participant, as well as on the *technologies* of the society's producers, to be represented by the technology N-tuple $Y = (Y^1, \ldots, Y^N)$, with Y^i denoting the technology of the i-th producer. Similarly, preferences are represented by the N-tuple $R = (R^1, \ldots, R^N)$, with R^i representing the preference relation (map, pattern) of the i-th participant. Merely to determine whether a given resource flow is possible, one would have to know something about each of the initial endowments and technologies; to answer questions of optimality, one would also need to know the various preferences. In practice, different decision-makers are likely to have only partial information about these matters. One simple, although extreme, assumption is that each participant knows his own components of the three N-tuples w, Y, and R, but no one else's, i.e., that the i-th participant knows his characteristic $e^i = (w^i, Y^i, R^i)$ of the environment but is completely ignorant of all the other characteristics e^j (j different from i). We shall refer to such a situation as *initial dispersion* of information.

Assuming such initial dispersion of information and (for the sake of analytical simplicity) absence of memory or learning, we may replace in equations (9) and (10) the symbol z^i (representing the information acquired by participant i independently of message exchange) by his characteristic e^i. For this is now the only information—other than messages just received—he is assumed to have available in arriving at the message $m^i(t+1)$ to be emitted during the given time interval. Such a process, written as

$$m^i(t+1) = f^i(m(t), e^i) \qquad\qquad (9')$$
$$\bar{m}^i = f^i(\bar{m}, e^i), \qquad\qquad (10')$$

is called *privacy-preserving*.

The property of being privacy-preserving partly captures the notion of *informational decentralization* underlying much of the thinking in this area. However, the initial dispersion of information would not be much of an obstacle to the determination of optimality if it was easy to transmit the individual characteristics e^i and other information from one participant to another. For in that case, each participant could send, at time $t=0$, a message $m^i(0)$ containing the complete description of his e^i to (say) the first participant; aside from problems of computational capacity, the first participant could then determine an optimal resource flow pattern and, in turn, inform all participants of appropriate actions to take. Thus to supply an essential element of informational decentralization, we must express analytically the limitations on the capacity to transmit and/or process information. A natural first step is to assume limits to the complexity of the messages to be transmitted and to the complexity of algorithms implicit in calculating the values of the response functions. We shall concentrate on the messages.

A clue as to these limits is obtained from a study of known mechanisms, in particular the perfectly competitive. So far we had been considering the messages as elements of some arbitrary abstract set M called the *language*. To transmit complete information as to a producer's technology, the language would have to contain as elements, sets of a variety of shapes in the L-dimensional space, where L is the number of commodities. The transmittal of preferences might require even a richer language. In any case, even for classical environments, the language M would be larger (in the sense of cardinality) than any finite-dimensional space. I.e., even for a classical economy with specified numbers of participants N and commodities L, there is no finite integer K such that complete information about individual characteristics could be conveyed by messages consisting of K-dimensional vectors. Yet the competitive process provides an algorithm which is privacy-preserving and yields optimal equilibria with a language of dimension $K = N \cdot (L-1)$. It is also important to note that this is accomplished by the competitive process with smooth (e.g., continuously differentiable) response and outcome functions.[4]

The foregoing discussion suggests that without some restriction on the dimensionality of the message space (language M) used, the notion of informational decentralization loses much of its interest. For this reason we shall

---

[4] The dimensionality of the message space is not invariant and hence not meaningful without some smoothness restrictions on the functions used by the mechanism; hence a smoothness restriction will be implicit in subsequent references to the dimensionality of the message space.

call a mechanism *informationally decentralized for a given class E of environments* if its language M is of finite dimension (given N and L), the response functions are privacy preserving, and both the response and outcome functions are smooth. Of course, there is nothing sacred about this definition and, indeed, I have used alternative concepts on other occasions. What seems to me important is that if we at all use the notion of informational decentralization, we should make it rigorous enough to give precision to the question of decentralizability of various classes of environments. We shall be calling a class E of environments informationally decentralizable if it is possible to design a mechanism that is informationally decentralized for this class and where equilibria exist and are optimal. Thus, for instance, the class of 'classical' environments is informationally decentralizable because the competitive mechanism is privacy preserving, smooth, and—for a given N and L—only requires a language of dimension $N \cdot (L - 1)$ to guarantee the optimality of equilibria.

The situation is much less clear with regard to environments that are not 'classical', e.g., environments characterized by increasing returns, indivisibilities, and various other non-convexities or discontinuities. Already in the 1930s, Lerner, Hotelling, and Lange developed the marginal cost pricing principle which, under certain assumptions can be viewed as a necessary first-order condition for optimality. Under somewhat stronger assumptions one can also design a mechanism whose equilibria are characterized by the equality of marginal costs and prices, with prices treated parametrically, and optimality is likely to result, at least for initial positions close to such an equilibrium. However, from recent research work it appears that even relatively mild departures from the 'classical' domain may be sufficient to kill decentralizability.[5] Under such circumstances one will have to settle for something less than decentralization—or something less than full optimality.

Incentive Properties of Adjustment Models

We have just seen that there are no informationally decentralized mechanisms guaranteeing optimality for nonclassical as well as classical environments, except in certain narrow categories of cases. On the other hand, no such informational difficulties arise when we confine ourselves to classical

---

[5] Note that informationally decentralized mechanisms form a much wider category than the class of mechanisms (of which marginal cost pricing system is a member) that guide decision-making through prices. Hence the claim that a class of environments is not informationally decentralizable is significantly stronger than an assertion that no price mechanism can be used to guarantee the optimality of outcomes.

environments. However, even classical environments lack immunity with regard to incentive problems, unless we restrict ourselves to 'atomistic' environments—those where every economic unit (firm, household) can be regarded as infinitesimal in relation to the market in which it operates.[6] To understand the issue we shall first introduce the concept of *incentive compatibility*. Although this concept can be formulated in a very general manner, we shall consider it only in a very simplified setting. We shall suppose that a central authority can impose (and enforce) an outcome function ϕ^* of its choosing and that it also, in addition, attempts to prescribe the response functions to be used by the participants in the process. We shall denote the prescribed response function for the i-th participant by f^{i*}. There would, of course, be no problem of incentives if the prescribed response functions could also be enforced without difficulty. We shall assume, however, that each participant is able to depart from the prescribed behavior, although within certain limits. We shall denote by F^i the class of response functions (called *enforceable domain*) the i-th participant can choose from; naturally this class ordinarily contains the prescribed behavior f^{i*}.

Each participant now must decide whether to follow prescribed behavior or whether to choose one of the alternatives available within F^i, and if so, which one. Given the behavior of others, and assuming he knows the outcome function, he can calculate the consequences of the alternative behaviors open to him and hence find that behavior which would maximize his level of satisfaction. But since others are facing the same decision problem, it is far from obvious that he can take the behavior of others as given. We recognize the dilemma as that typical of a noncooperative game, and hence we approach it in the spirit of the theory of such games. More specifically, we shall use the concept of *Nash equilibrium*.

To do so, we shall find it convenient initially to define *behavior functions g^i* by the relations

$$g^i(m^1, \ldots, m^N) = f^i(m^1, \ldots, m^N, e^i) \quad i = 1, \ldots, N. \tag{12}$$

That is, a behavior function incorporates both the response function and the characteristic and simply describes what message the i-th participant will emit given the messages he has just received. Now, the stationary (equilibrium), message N-tuple $\bar{m} = (\bar{m}^1, \ldots, \bar{m}^N)$ is given by the relations

$$\bar{m}^i = g^i(\bar{m}) \quad i = 1, \ldots, N$$

---

[6] There is need here for a terminological warning: recent measure-theoretic mathematical economics literature uses the term 'non-atomic' to describe what we are calling, in line with more traditional usage, 'atomistic'.

or, in vector notation,

$$\bar{m} = g(\bar{m}), \quad g = (g^1, \ldots, g^N). \tag{13}$$

We see that the stationary message N-tuple $\bar{m}$ is a fixed point of the behavior function g. Assuming this fixed point to be unique, we see that it is determined by the behavior function g. We may write this as

$$\bar{m} = \lambda(g). \tag{14}$$

Given the outcome function ϕ^*, we can use equation (14) to express the outcome a as a function of g, viz.,

$$a = \phi^*[\lambda(g)], \tag{15}$$

and, finally, the satisfaction derived by the i-th participant—measured through a utility indicator u^i— as

$$u^i(\phi^*[\lambda(g)]) = P^i(g). \tag{16}$$

The composite function $P^i(g) = P^i(g^i, \ldots, g^N)$ may be regarded as the payoff function in a noncooperative game in which the behavior functions constitute strategy variables. Each participant has available to him as strategy domain G^i, the set of all behavior functions obtainable according to (12) with e^i fixed and f^i roaming over the enforceable domain F^i. Having defined the payoff functions and strategy domains for the game, we now apply the definition of a Nash equilibrium as a strategy N-tuple $g^\# = (g^{1\#}, \ldots, g^{N\#})$ at which every player is satisfied with his strategy choice provided that others do not abandon theirs. Formally, $g^\#$ is a *Nash equilibrium* for the above game if, for every $i = 1, \ldots, N$, the behavior function $g^{i\#}$ belongs to the domain G^i and

$$P^i(g^\#) \geq P^i(g^{1\#}, \ldots, g^{i-1,\#}, g^i, g^{i+1,\#}, \ldots, g^{N\#}) \quad \text{for all } g^i \text{ in } G^i. \tag{17}$$

Although there are well-known controversies in game theory concerning the merits and weaknesses of this solution concept, we shall take it as representing the natural spontaneous behavior of the participants, i.e., the direction in which the incentives draw them. In the light of this interpretation, it is clear what one means by saying that a given prescription for behavior is compatible with incentives: a situation in which the Nash equilibrium coincides with the prescription. Formally, let g^{i*} denote the behavior functions obtained from (12) by using on the right-hand side the prescribed f^{i*} response functions (and the true characteristics e^i). We define a prescribed mechanism (M, f^*, ϕ^*) as *incentive-compatible* (with regard to the domains F^i) if the Nash equilibrium behavior is the same as the prescribed behavior, i.e., if

$$g^\# = g^*. \tag{18}$$

A justification of this terminology lies in the fact that, provided we accept the hypothesis of 'Nash-like' spontaneous behavior, an incentive-compatible mechanism would be self-enforcing.[7]

In economics, the issue of incentive compatibility became prominent in connection with the search for an allocation mechanism that would generate optimal resource allocation of public as well as private goods, since the competitive process was clearly inadequate for the task. An alternative mechanism proposed by Lindahl satisfied the requirements of informational decentralization and would yield optimal allocations provided that the participants would act on the basis of truthful information about their respective preferences. The difficulty, stressed by Samuelson, was that in an informationally decentralized system one could not enforce truthful behavior and, unfortunately, participants could profit by departing from truth. To use our present terminology, the Lindahl mechanism was not incentive-compatible. Samuelson's conjecture (formulated in the mid-1950s) was that we were facing a fundamental difficulty—that one could not design an incentive-compatible mechanism guaranteeing optimality for economies with public goods. It is only recently that his conjecture has been shown correct. Indeed, it has also been shown that a similar difficulty arises in 'classical' environment economies lacking public goods unless we are in the 'atomistic' case.[8]

To understand these results we relate them to the preceding formal framework. We may suppose that the central authority has no knowledge of the *true* characteristic, now to be denoted by $\mathring{e}^i$. Hence it is possible for the participant to adopt as his behavior function any g^i satisfying (12) with the prescribed f^{i*} but using some 'strategic' (true or false) characteristics, to be denoted by $\tilde{e}^i$.[9]

---

[7] Also, our definition of incentive compatibility ignores the possibility of collusions, i.e., it would be more accurate to use the term *individual* incentive compatibility. The theory can be extended to cover collusions and coalitions as well.

One could extend the theory by postulating that the central authority, instead of prescribing specific behavior, merely confines the participants to a set of prescribed behaviors, i.e., imposes certain limitations. We could then define incentive compatibility as being present if the Nash equilibrium behavior $g^\#$ was an element of the set G^* of permissible behaviors.

[8] See Hurwicz (1972).

[9] The assumption that the participants abide by the prescribed response function f^{i*}, although possibly using a false characteristic $\tilde{e}^i$, can be motivated as follows. We can imagine that there is an enforcement-inspection system which would require that a participant be able to justify his behavior as compatible with his claimed characteristic. Were he to use some 'illegal' adjustment function (whether with true or false characteristic), he might generate (through (12)) a behavior function (assumed observed by the inspector) that could not be explained as 'legal'.

Since under these circumstances, with f^{i*} kept constant, variations in g^i can only be achieved by manipulating $\tilde{e}^i$, we may consider the $\tilde{e}^i$ to be the strategic variables (with some domains corresponding to 'plausible' even though false values). The utilities can now be regarded as functions of the strategic characteristics and a Nash equilibrium is defined in the spaces of the characteristics. Proceeding as above, let $\tilde{e}^\#$ denote the Nash equilibrium N-tuple of strategic values of the characteristics; we shall call this equilibrium the *Manipulative Nash Equilibrium*. A prescribed mechanism will be called *incentive-compatible over E in the narrow sense* if the Manipulative Nash Equilibrium strategic N-tuple of characteristics $\tilde{e}^\#$ is the same as the true one $\mathring{e}$, i.e., if

$$\tilde{e}^\# = \mathring{e} \quad \text{for all } \mathring{e} \text{ in } E. \tag{19}$$

Under our hypothesis of spontaneous Nash-like behavior, the interpretation is that in such a mechanism truthfulness is self-enforcing. Samuelson's assertions can be translated into this framework as stating that no mechanism guaranteeing optimality can also guarantee[10] the self-enforcing truthfulness of (19); in particular it follows that the Lindahl mechanism lacks the property of (19).

So far we have followed the tradition of our subject by focusing on the relationship of the equilibria to truth, or, more generally, of spontaneous self-interested behavior to prescribed behavior. But it is possible to take a broader view and simply ask whether spontaneous behavior will lead to an optimum, without raising the question whether spontaneous behavior obeys the edicts of the center. In fact, it has been shown that in certain environments involving public goods,[11] it is possible to design mechanisms whose Manipulative Nash Equilibria do generate optimal allocations, even though the strategic equilibrium characteristics are not, in general truthful, i.e., where $\tilde{e}^\# \neq \mathring{e}$.[12]

Unfortunately, the environments in which such optimal allocations are self-enforcing (in the sense of being Manipulative Nash Equilibria) constitute a small class.[13] For broader classes, the situation changes for the worse, so that, in general, one cannot hope for self-enforcing optima (see Hurwicz 1975), even if we abandon our insistence on truthfulness and obedience to prescribed behavior rules. However, we must remind ourselves that these negative results are obtained subject to the requirement of informational decentralization. When this requirement is abandoned, we can imagine

---

[10] For all $\mathring{e}$ in E.

[11] Those where preferences can be represented by utility functions linear in the private goods.

[12] The fact that such equilibria involve behavior departing from that prescribed may imply that the distributive aspects of the resource allocation are different from those intended by the designers of the system.

[13] See footnote 11.

inspection systems that, by violating the privacy postulate, might make departures from prescribed behavior impossible. Again, we seem to run into the dilemma of having to sacrifice either optimality or the self-enforcement feature, or informational decentralization.[14]

It should be stressed that the phenomenon of non-optimality of manipulative equilibria arises even in the economist's standard model of pure exchange (Edgeworth Box) and not merely when there are public goods present. It is useful to consider the classroom example where the environment is represented by the Edgeworth Box with two goods and two traders, and the prescribed mechanism is that of perfect competition. We know that if the environment is classical (i.e., preferences convex, etc.) and the participants follow the prescribed rules, the system does possess positions of equilibrium (the competitive equilibrium) and these positions are optimal. But suppose that the participants' behavior is manipulative. What allocations will be generated by the Manipulative Nash Equilibria? It turns out that there is an infinity of such allocations (indeed a continuum) and that they fill the interior of the set bounded by the so-called offer curves[15] of the two traders. We may note that none of these allocations is optimal, although some of them are arbitrarily close to an optimum. Unfortunately, others are arbitrarily close to the initial allocation, i.e., as far away from an optimum as one can get under a non-coercive mechanism (see Fig. 1).

There does not as yet exist an approach that would narrow down a range or indeterminacy in such situations, nor is there an agreed upon way of arriving at some average or minimax measure of inefficiency of such a mechanism. Yet there is an urgent need for progress in this direction since our general theorems tell us that any alternative mechanism will have some of the same problems.

Up to this point we have been dealing with situations in which the participants could manipulate the preference components of their characteristics, i.e., "misrepresent" their preferences through strategic behavior. However, one could imagine an economy in which preferences are centrally known with sufficient accuracy, but there is no central knowledge as to productivity.

---

14 A note of warning. The notion of optimality or efficiency implicit in this discussion ignores the resources used to operate the mechanism; it only looks at resources used for production and consumption. We may term this notion 'gross' optimality (or efficiency), while the corresponding 'net' notion would take into account the resources used to operate the system. Now suppose that, in order to reach 'gross' optimality, we decide to sacrifice self-enforcement or informational decentralization. There will then arise a need for additional resource use in enforcement or inspection and it is conceivable that the resulting allocation will be further away from 'net' optimality than the original one. (In addition, of course, there is also the 'non-economic' loss due to added restrictions on individual freedom.)

15 An offer curve of the i-participant is the locus of points he would choose when maximizing utility subject to the budget constraint with the price ratio of the two goods ranging over all positive numbers while his initial endowment and preferences remain fixed.

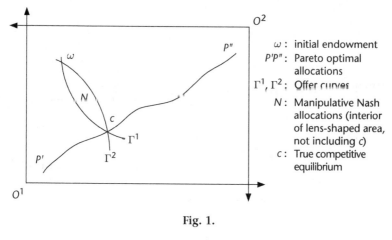

Fig. 1.

ω : initial endowment
P'P" : Pareto optimal allocations
Γ^1, Γ^2 : Offer curves

N : Manipulative Nash allocations (interior of lens-shaped area, not including c)
c : True competitive equilibrium

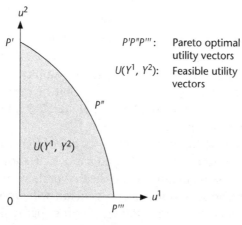

Fig. 2.

$P'P''P'''$: Pareto optimal utility vectors
$U(Y^1, Y^2)$: Feasible utility vectors

The problem then arises as to whether such partial central knowledge is sufficient to install a self-enforcing mechanism with optimal equilibria. It turns out, for a change, that the answer is in the affirmative. To indicate the nature of the solution, with its strengths and weaknesses, we shall outline it briefly in the context of two participants, each of whom has preferences and is also a producer. Since preferences are assumed known, the center can adopt a standard procedure for representing these preferences by utility indicators ('canonical' utilities). Let the utilities be denoted by u^i and the production possibility sets by $Y^i, i = 1, 2$. Given these, there is a set of feasible aggregate productions and distributions and, consequently, a set—to be denoted by $U(Y^1, Y^2)$—of the feasible utility vectors (u^1, u^2). The usual diagrammatic representation is in the form of a curvilinear triangle in the (u^1, u^2)-space (see Fig. 2). Its 'hypotenuse' $P'P''P'''$ represents the various optimal utility combinations.

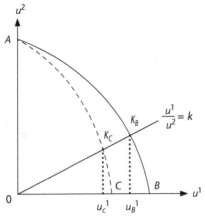

$u_B{}^1 - u_C{}^1$: The measure of utility loss by participant 1 due to misrepresentation

$\triangle OAB$: $U(\overset{\circ}{Y}{}^1, \overset{\circ}{Y}{}^2)$

$\triangle OAC$: $U(\tilde{Y}{}^1, \overset{\circ}{Y}{}^2)$

K_B: Utility generated by $U(\overset{\circ}{Y}{}^1, \overset{\circ}{Y}{}^2)$

K_C: Utility generated by $U(\tilde{Y}{}^1, \overset{\circ}{Y}{}^2)$

Fig. 3.

Now let the allocation rule be formulated as follows. The center fixes the ratio of utilities it regards as desirable, say $u^1 : u^2 = k$.[16] Suppose that the first participant misrepresents his production possibility set and claims some false $\tilde{Y}^1$ instead of the true $\overset{\circ}{Y}{}^1$. We postulate that he cannot with impunity exaggerate the size of his set, so $\tilde{Y}^1 \subset \overset{\circ}{Y}{}^1$. Hence $U(\tilde{Y}^1, \overset{\circ}{Y}{}^2)$ is bound to be smaller than (contained in) $U(\overset{\circ}{Y}{}^1, \overset{\circ}{Y}{}^2)$.

Now the procedure for allocation is to pick out of $U(Y^1, Y^2)$ the best point on the ray corresponding to the desired ratio k. It should be clear from Figure 3 that under such circumstances, the first participant cannot improve his utility by misrepresentation and, in general, will worsen it.[17] Furthermore, the situation is the same whether the other participant is truthful or not. Thus 'truth is the dominant strategy'. But truth generates optimality, since the point chosen is at the intersection of the ray corresponding to k with the 'hypotenuse', and all points of the 'hypotenuse' are optimal.

The preceding example illustrates the interaction, referred to in the title of this paper, between incentives and information. We had seen earlier that there is no self-enforcing mechanism guaranteeing optimality when preferences are unknown to the center (and so preference-manipulation is possible). In the example with production, we see that the situation changes drastically when preferences are assumed known to the center, even though production sets are still unknown: here we do have a self-enforcing mechanism guaranteeing optimality at the Nash equilibrium. Suppose, however, that preferences, instead of being centrally known, can become known with

16 The desired ratio k can, but need not, equal one.

17 The implicit assumptions are such as to make the 'hypotenuse' of the curvilinear triangle downward sloping; this is implied by the continuity and monotonicity of preferences.

a certain expenditure of resources on inspection, etc. Would it be worth acquiring such information? The answer depends on a comparison of the loss of efficiency in the absence of such information (a loss to be expected from our general theorems) with the cost of acquiring the information.

'Synthetic' Mechanisms for Non-manipulative Behavior

There are differences of opinion as to the likelihood of manipulative behavior postulated in the preceding section. Although my own inclination is to regard such behavior as very likely under many circumstances, there are situations where non-manipulative behavior may well prevail. It is therefore of considerable interest to investigate the possibility of designing self-enforcing allocation systems in the absence of manipulation. Here the model is somewhat simpler. We still have the outcome function ϕ which is assumed imposed and enforceable; they constitute the incentive structures. Let the utility function of the i-th individual be written as $u^i(a)$ where a is the resource flow. Since the outcome function makes the resource flow a function of the message N-tuple, the utility becomes a composite function of this N-tuple; we shall denote this composite function by v^i. That is,

$$v^i(m) = u^i(a) = u^i[\phi(m)] \quad m = (m^1, \ldots, m^N), \; i = 1, \ldots, N. \tag{20}$$

Now in a world of nonmanipulative behavior, each participant uses his true preferences and the i-th message component m^i becomes his strategy variable. Again treating this as a Nash noncooperative game, we regard v^i as the i-th payoff function. Thus an N-tuple m^* is defined as a *Nonmanipulative Nash Equilibrium* if, for every $i = 1, \ldots, N$, and m^{i*} in M,

$$v^i(m^*) \geq v^i(m^{1*}, \ldots, m^{i-1,*}, m^i, m^{i+1,*}, \ldots, m^{N*}) \quad \text{for all } m^i \text{ in } M. \tag{21}$$

Now it turns out that, under certain assumptions of convexity and differentiability, it is not difficult to find outcome functions that guarantee the optimality of resource flows at equilibrium.[18] What is perhaps particularly interesting is that one can obtain (necessary) conditions in the form of differential equations defining rather large classes of such outcome functions and then, as it were, manufacture a variety of allocation systems possessing the desired properties by finding functions satisfying these differential equations. We shall illustrate this by the pure exchange (Edgeworth Box) example, partly

---

[18] A trailblazing example is due to Groves and Ledyard (1977) for the case of public goods.

because of its simplicity—but also to show a "synthetic" alternative to the conventional competitive system.

Let there be two goods x and y and three traders. The outcome functions (components of ϕ) will be denoted by X^i and Y^i. Thus X^i determines the net trade (increment) in terms of good x going to the i-th trader, and similarly for Y^i. We assume the language M to be the real axis, i.e., every message m^i is a real number. We do not provide any interpretation for the possible meanings of these messages. Then $X^i(m^l, m^2, m^3)$ is the net increment in holdings by i of good x when the respective messages emitted by the three participants are m^1, m^2, m^3; similarly for $Y^i(m^1, m^2, m^3)$. Now a necessary condition for the optimality of equilibria[19] turns out to be

$$X_1^1(m^*)/Y_1^1(m^*) = X_2^2(m^*)/Y_2^2(m^*) = X_3^3(m^*)/Y_3^3(m^*), \qquad (22)$$

where the subscript i indicates partial differentiation with respect to m^i and all derivatives are evaluated at the equilibrium point, $m^* = (m^{1*}, m^{2*}, m^{3*})$.

In addition, since we are assuming pure exchange, at equilibrium the (net) trades must add up to zero, i.e.,

$$X^1(m^*) + X^2(m^*) + X^3(m^*) = Y^1(m^*) + Y^2(m^*) + Y^3(m^*) = 0. \qquad (23)$$

While these conditions are only necessary, they turn out to be sufficient when second-order derivatives have appropriate signs. Also, although conditions (22) and (23) are only required to hold at an equilibrium, it does not hurt if they hold for all values of m, and it turns out easy to find such functions, even among quadratics. As an example of such a 'synthetic' system we may give the following

$$\left. \begin{array}{l} Y^i(m) = m_i - (\frac{1}{2})(m_j + m_k) \\ X^i(m) = -m_i(\frac{1}{2}m_1 + m_2 + m_2) + (\frac{1}{4})(m_j^2 + m_k^2) + 2m_j m_k \end{array} \right\} \qquad (24)$$

where $i, j, k = 1, 2, 3$ and $i \neq j \neq k \neq i$.[20] It is easily verified that equations (23) are identically[21] satisfied. Also,

$$Y_i^i(m) = 1 \text{ and } X_i^i(m) = -(m_1 + m_2 + m_3) \quad \text{for all } m \text{ and } i = 1, 2, 3. \qquad (25)$$

Hence equation (22) are also identically satisfied. Finally, second-order conditions can be shown to hold also. Therefore, the incentive structure (outcome

---

[19] I.e., the Nonmanipulative Nash Equilibria.
[20] Here we use subscripts on the m's to avoid confusion with algebraic exponents.
[21] Not only at equilibrium.

function) specified by equation (24) guarantees the optimality of Non-manipulative Nash Equilibria defined in (21).

A warning is in order. We do not claim that the above allocation system has all the properties that one might wish for. However, it is interesting to compare it with the competitive system. They both guarantee optimality of equilibria. The 'synthetic' system in (24) is probably inferior with regard to the domain[22] of existence of equilibria. Also, unlike the competitive system, the 'synthetic' system can place participants at utility levels inferior to initial ones. On the other hand, it happens (although this cannot be regarded as crucial) that the 'synthetic' system sometimes uses a message space of lower dimensionality (its dimension is three) than that version of the competitive system whose equilibria can be regarded as Nash equilibria (the dimension there being four, three quantities and a price). What does seem important is our ability to manufacture such synthetic systems from purely mathematical considerations rather than having to rely on precedents of observed economies.

Incentive Structures for Unilateral Maximization

In the preceding sections we have used as our optimality concept the Pareto definition which treats all participants' welfare symmetrically. We sometimes encounter problems, however, in which the incentive structure is set up in such a manner as to maximize the degree of attainment of objectives for one of the participants through incentives designed to intensify the efforts of others. We shall illustrate this by two examples, one from the private sector and one involving public welfare.

The private sector example[23] in a very simplified form, deals with the problem of a landowner whose land is being worked by a sharecropper. Ignoring inputs other than the laborer's effort z, we postulate that his output y is a strictly increasing function f of effort; his utility function u is assumed to decrease with the amount of effort he expends but increase with the reward r (his share[24] of output). The owner wishes to maximize his share of output π. Informational assumptions made are the following: the owner can only observe the output y but not the effort z; the laborer observes both y and z; also, the functions f and u are known to the laborer but not to the owner. The owner's only control 'variable' is the reward formula ρ, specifying the laborer's reward r as a function of his output y. Thus the model can be written as

---

[22] In the space of environments.

[23] See Hurwicz and Shapiro (1978).—SB

[24] Here the term 'share' means the absolute amount of the good produced given to a participant rather than the fraction of the total.

$$\left.\begin{array}{l} y = f(z) \\ U = u(r, z) \\ y = r + \pi \\ r = \rho(y), \end{array}\right\} \tag{26}$$

and the owner's problem is to find a reward formula ρ to maximize π.

To solve the problem, one must make some assumptions about the laborer's behavior. We shall postulate that he behaves in a non-manipulative manner and seeks to maximize his utility level U given the functions f, u, and ρ. Because of the structure of the model, the laborer's utility can be expressed as a function of effort, viz.,

$$V = u[\rho(f(z)), z], \tag{27}$$

or, since the production function is invertible, as a function of output, viz.,

$$U = u[\rho(y), f^{-1}(y)]. \tag{28}$$

Making the appropriate regularity assumptions, we shall find that there is a unique output level $\bar{y}$ maximizing U for a given reward formula ρ, and a corresponding $\bar{z} = f^{-1}(\bar{y})$. We shall write $\bar{y} = Y[\rho; f, u]$ to indicate the dependence of on the functions in brackets. Now the owner's problem is to maximize his share, i.e., to maximize the expression

$$\pi = Y[\rho; f, u] - \rho(Y[\rho; f, u]) \tag{29}$$

with regard to the reward formula ρ which he is free to choose. The difficulty is, of course, that the solution to this maximization problem depends on the functions f and u which are unknown to the owner. Hence, he is faced with a problem in choice (decision-making) under uncertainty.

To cope with this problem in its full generality one would have to select one's preferred principle of decision-making under uncertainty, be it minimax or Bayesian. In the latter case, a prior distribution on the space of function pairs (f, u)—representing the landowner's ideas about the likely forms and parameters of production and utility functions—would also have to be supplied; thus we would be postulating partial, although subjective, information concerning these functions. On the other hand, if the minimax approach is adopted, we could stay with the assumption of complete ignorance (within specified function classes) on the part of the landlord.

We shall not attempt here to deal with the general problem. Instead, we shall consider a very special case where production is characterized by constant returns, so that

$$f(z) = cz, \quad c > 0, \tag{30}$$

and the sharecropper's utility function is linear in the reward and quadratic in effort:

$$u(r, z) = r - (\tfrac{1}{2})bz^2, \quad b > 0. \tag{31}$$

We may assume that the landlord knows the functional forms (30)–(31), but not the values of the parameters b, c.

Furthermore, instead of permitting the landlord to choose any arbitrary reward formula ρ, we shall confine him to fixed share ratios, so that

$$\rho(y) = \alpha y \quad 0 \leq \alpha \leq 1. \tag{32}$$

Thus, the landlord's problem boils down to finding the best (from his point of view) value of the parameter α. Now it turns out that for any given value of α, treated parametrically by the sharecropper, the corresponding level of output maximizing the sharecropper's utility will be

$$y = \alpha \hat{y}, \tag{33}$$

where

$$\hat{y} = c^2 / b \tag{34}$$

is the Pareto optimal level of output for this economy. Therefore, the landlord's share is

$$\bar{\pi} = \bar{y} - \bar{r} = (1 - \alpha)\bar{y} = (1 - \alpha)\alpha\hat{y}. \tag{35}$$

Hence, regardless of the (to the landlord unknown) parameter values, b, c, the landlord's best strategy is to set $\alpha = \tfrac{1}{2}$. We note that this choice results in a level of output that is only one-half of optimal output.

Now there arises the question whether the landlord could increase his gain if he were to abandon the fixed share ratio formulas (32) and consider other functions ρ of output. This problem has not as yet been completely solved, but we have examined it when the criterion used is that of maximizing the minimum (with respect to the unknown $\hat{y}$) level of $\pi / \hat{y}$. It appears that from this point of view, the landlord cannot do better (get a higher minimum guarantee regardless of the parameter values) than by offering the sharecropper the fixed share ratio arrangement with $\alpha = \tfrac{1}{2}$ as above, with the guaranteed ratio $\pi / \hat{y} = (1 - \alpha) = \tfrac{1}{4}$.[25]

We have so far been assuming that the landlord has no information concerning the values of the parameters b, c, and, in particular, does not know $\hat{y}$. As before, we are particularly interested in the changes that occur

---

[25] Here we continue to assume that equations (30)–(31) hold.

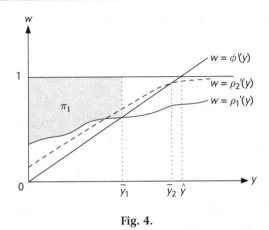

Fig. 4.

when the information structure is altered. Now it is not too difficult to see that there exist reward functions that would induce the laborer to select an output level arbitrarily close to the optimal y and with the ratio $\pi/\hat{y}$ arbitrarily near (and above) $\frac{1}{2}$. This can be seen as follows. For a continuously differentiable reward function ρ, the laborer's (interior) first-order utility maximization condition is

$$\rho'(\bar{y}) = \bar{y}/\hat{y}. \tag{36}$$

Hence (see Fig. 4), for the reward function ρ_1 (whose derivative ρ'_1 is indicated by the solid line), the equilibrium output would be $\bar{y}_1$. The corresponding share π_1 of landlord's output is measured by the area above ρ'_1, to the left of $\bar{y}_1$ below the line[26] $w = 1$, and to the right of the vertical axis. Now the limiting position of ρ' would make it coincide with the ray[27] ϕ', and in this case the ratio $\pi/\hat{y}$ would equal $\frac{1}{2}$. By choosing a reward function ρ_2 whose derivative ρ'_2 is indicated by the broken line in Figure 4, the landlord would induce the output $\bar{y}_2$ very near $\hat{y}$ and his ratio $\pi_2/\hat{y}$ would be very near $\frac{1}{2}$. Thus he would be getting arbitrarily close to his maximum, but he could do this only if he knew the value of $\hat{y}$, which implies (partial) information concerning the parameters b, c. Otherwise the reward function of the type ρ_2 would be very good for some values of the parameters and very bad for others.

Thus we have another illustration of the extent to which the possibility of designing an effective reward structure depends on the state of information available to the designer, in this case the landowner.

---

[26] In Fig. 4, w is the symbol for the ordinate.

[27] Here $\phi(y) = y^2/2\hat{y}$ is the disutility of effort expressed as a function of output. Hence, $\phi'(y) = y/\hat{y}$ is represented by a ray from the origin, with $\phi'(\hat{y}) = 1$.

At this point we shall redeem an earlier promise to provide another illustration characterized by a similar relationship between information and incentives, but involving issues of public interest. We can think of a community threatened by an outside danger. The community's total output of goods and services y (which we shall treat as if it were one-dimensional) must be divided between the defense of the community's existence, to be denoted by π, and its consumption r. As individual workers, the members of this community maximize their utility which depends positively on the consumption r and negatively on the effort z. But as voters, these citizens give priority to the community's survival. Hence they want to design an incentive structure that would maximize the community's survival probability, i.e., maximize π—without regard to the effort involved, but taking into account the utility maximizing behavior of individual workers. Clearly, the mathematical structure of this problem is equivalent to that of the landowner-laborer example above. In particular, therefore, it is clear that more effort for defense could be extracted through a properly constructed reward structure from the citizenry—if additional information were available with regard to production functions and preferences. Alternatively, given additional information, with the same level of defense, more would be available for consumption r.[28]

Information Cost and Performance of Systems

In the course of the above analysis, we have come across instances of 'trade-offs' between expenditure of resources on the improvement of the designer's (or the participants') state of information on the one hand, and the attainable level of the system's performance on the other. I have occasionally found it helpful to think of this relationship abstractly in terms of the following diagram (Fig. 5). As our abscissa, we use something to be called cost of information acquisition, it being assumed that the resources used to acquire information are deployed in an efficient manner. It should be understood that such costs are in fact multi-dimensional and include not only the various resources utilized but also certain intangibles, e.g., loss of privacy. As our ordinate, we use some measure of performance of the system, e.g., the maximum attainable level of defense effort in our last example, or (say) a constant plus the negative of the distance from Pareto optimality in the earlier examples. Denote the abscissa (cost of information) by c and the ordinate (maximum attainable performance) by p. Now any organizational

[28] This is so because total output y would be closer to Pareto optimality.

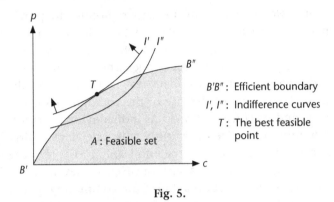

Fig. 5.

structure or mechanism, to be denoted by μ, determines a point in the (c, p) space; denoting this point by (c_μ, p_μ), we interpret c_μ as the (minimal) informational cost associated with the mechanism μ and p_μ, as the (maximal) performance attainable with this mechanism. A mechanism μ' can be called *more efficient than* μ'' if it has either lower informational cost or higher performance or both; a mechanism can be called *efficient* if no other feasible mechanism is more efficient.

Now let us also suppose that the society's values imply a preference in the (c, p) space, with more p and less c naturally being preferred. In Figure 5, we have drawn a conventional map of this sort and also indicated by shading the set A of (c, p) points corresponding to *feasible* mechanisms. The North-West boundary $B'B''$ of this set contains the points corresponding to *efficient* mechanisms. Among points of this boundary there is one, labeled T (for tangency) which is *best* among the feasible ones in terms of the preference map.

Given the assumptions made, one would want to choose as the mechanism to be used that which generates the combination (c_T, p_T) corresponding to the point T. If we did not have the preference map, we could not select the point T, but would presumably want to avoid points that are not on the (efficient) boundary $B'B''$. The shape of this boundary represents the nature of the unavoidable tradeoffs between information cost and performance.

Of course, this way of looking at our problems is only schematic. For applications, one must go back to detailed formulations describing the mechanism in terms of language, response, and outcome functions, and commit oneself to a specific performance criterion (optimality concept). In addition, a model must be constructed relating the informational costs to the structure of the mechanism and other data. We have made no more than a start by distinguishing such informational properties as privacy-preserving features and the dimension of the message space. We are still far from being able to use the construction of Figure 5 in a concrete way.

References

Groves, T. and J. Ledyard (1974) An incentive mechanism for efficient resource allocation in general equilibrium with public goods, Center for Mathematical Studies in Economics and Management Science, Northwestern University Discussion Paper No. 119. Published as Groves, T. and J. Ledyard (1977) Optimal allocation of public goods. A solution to the 'free rider' problem, *Econometrica*, 45: 783–809.

Hurwicz, L. (1972) On informationally decentralized systems, in *Decision and Organization*, ed. C. McGuire and R. Radner. Amsterdam: North-Holland. Second edition, 1986, 297–336. Minneapolis, MN: University of Minnesota Press.

Hurwicz, L. (1975) On the Pareto-optimality of manipulative Nash equilibria, presented at the International Econometric Society, World Congress, Toronto. Published as Hurwicz (1981) On incentive problems in the design of non-wasteful resource allocation systems, in *Studies in Economic Theory and Practice: Essays in Honor of Edward Lipinski*, ed. N. Assorodobraj-Kula, et al., 93–106. Amsterdam: North-Holland.

Hurwicz, L. and L. Shapiro (1978) Incentive structures maximizing residual gain under incomplete information, *The Bell Journal of Economics*, 9(1): 180–91.

Hurwicz, L. (1985) Incentive aspects of decentralization, in *Handbook of Mathematical Economics*, vol. 3, ed. K. Arrow and M. Intriligator, 1441–82. Amsterdam: North-Holland.

Editor's Postscript

This paper is a more detailed version of a talk given at a 1974 conference on 'Communication and Control in Society' sponsored by the American Society for Cybernetics in Philadelphia. A transcript of the talk begins as follows.

"When I heard reference to my grandfatherhood,[*] I had a feeling this is the first time that I've been involved in a paternity suit. I think that past experience shows that the person who has been charged in such a suit has very little chance to disprove the claim, however false it may be, so I won't try to argue!

Beyond this, I perhaps might say that I had some hesitation, as the organizers of this meeting will admit, about accepting this invitation, partly because my association with the term "Keynote Speech" usually is a memory of rather long-winded talks at various national conventions, and also because I felt that perhaps I would be operating under false pretenses in a meeting of cyberneticists. But from talking to a number of people, I find that quite a few of them here I think, perhaps, can be described as being on the border of the field. In fact, I'm beginning to develop the feeling that cybernetics is a field with a very thick boundary, but fortunately a non-empty interior." (Laughter)

---

[*] Most likely a reference to being introduced as a pioneer in the field of information and incentives in organizations.—SB

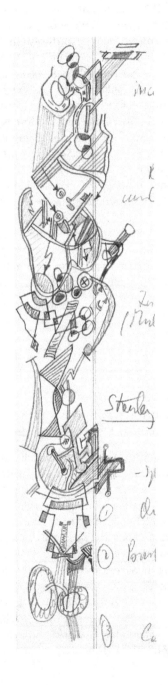

11

Mechanism Design without Games

The concept of an economics mechanism has many origins. My own think-ing was greatly influenced by welfare economics, activity analysis (especially Koopmans's formulation), the Hayek-Mises-Lange debate, the team theory of Jacob Marschak and Roy Radner, and, very importantly, the collaborations with Kenneth Arrow, Thomas Marschak, and Stanley Reiter. And just as there are many origins, there are also different approaches to the study of economic mechanisms. Those using a game-theoretic framework are at present particularly popular, but others focus on informational issues without using the tools of game theory. Some integrate the two approaches. Hence the title of this note.

The two fundamental theorems of welfare economics are the central achievements of general equilibrium theory in its normative aspects. They specify the (Pareto) optimality properties of competitive equilibria in 'classical'[1] economic environments. These results may be viewed as answers, but to what questions? A comparison with alternative economic structures is implied. To make comparisons it seems necessary to define an umbrella concept covering perfect competition as well as other systems with which we might want to compare it.

Traditional economic analysis was largely devoted to perfect competition but it also dealt with monopoly and oligopoly, and studied the effects of government intervention through taxes and regulation. Indeed, comparisons were the essence of 'comparative systems' studies. However the needed umbrella concept was not formalized. 'Mechanism' was intended to fill that gap.

The Hayek-Mises-Lange debate, as well as Hayek's 1945 paper, did involve comparison of systems; however, they were focussed on their informational

From *Advances in Economic Theory*, ed. M. Sertel and S. Koray, 429–37. ©2003 Springer-Verlag: Berlin.

[1] I.e., environments satisfying such conditions as convexity, non-satiation, etc.

(rather than incentive) aspects.[2] The need for an umbrella concept covering different economic systems became particularly obvious when one attempted to provide a rigorous definition of decentralization. Since it was an attribute of the economic mechanism or system, it required a prior definition of the latter. Hence, especially, there was need for a general concept meaningful for a broad class of economic institutions—not just those defined in game-theoretic terms. And, influenced by the Hayek-Lange focus on information, it was natural to treat decentralization as a property of the informational aspects of economic mechanisms—as distinct from, for instance, as an attribute based on the structure of authority. Hence the notion of *informational decentralization*.

But back to the needed umbrella mechanism concept. The Walrasian *tâtonnement* process seemed a natural point of departure. Its usual form,

$$\frac{dp_i}{dt} = h_i(f_i(p)), \quad i = 1, \ldots, L, \tag{1}$$

dealing with the adjustment of prices of various commodities, and the f_i's their excess demands, it can be generalized by substituting for prices messages, say, m_i, of arbitrary form, with the subscript referring to the agent sending out the message. Furthermore, messages need not be numerical or even vectorial, and the adjustment functions need not be differentiable. Hence a further step toward generalization leads to the following discrete time form:

$$m_{i,t+1} = f^i(m_t, e), \quad i = 1, \ldots, n. \tag{2}$$

Here again i refers to the agent sending out the message, n denotes the number of agents, $m_t = (m_{1t}, \ldots, m_{nt})$, $e = (e_1, \ldots, e_n)$, and e_i is the *characteristic* of the i-th agent (e.g., his/her endowment and preference relation).

The function f^i is called the i-th *response function*. Note that in this formulation, messages need not be numerical, nor even members of an additive group. However, if the messages do belong to an Abelian (additive commutative) group (e.g., they are integers) then a special case could have the form

$$m_{i,t+1} = m_{it} + \phi^i(m_t, e), \quad i = 1, \ldots, n \tag{3}$$

which is closer to a discrete analogue af the price tâtonnement equation system.

---

[2] In retrospect it may seem surprising that incentive aspects of nationalized enterprises were not made a central issue by critics of socialism. However, to the extent that Lange's model of 'market socialism' required profit maximization (with parametric treatment of prices), it took care of the problem.

The response equation system, like its tâtonnement forebear, is a *dynamic* system, although the time variable may represent not 'real' time in which economic actions (exchanges, consumption, production) occur but rather time for a sequence of proposals to be exchanged by the agents, prior to actions taking place.

Our theoretical structure, like much economic theory, will be confined to the *static* aspects of the process. In the present context, the relevant equilibrium concept is therefore that of stationarity. By definition, $m = (m_1, \ldots, m_n)$ is a *stationary* message n-tuple if it satisfies the equation system (2) with $m = m_{t+1} = m_t$, i.e., when

$$m_i = f^{*i}(m, e), \quad i = 1, \ldots, n. \tag{4}$$

The function f^{*i} is called the *stationary response function*. Note that in the special case of Walrasian tâtonnement (1), with the price as message n-tuple, the stationary value of p is the Walrasian equilibrium price.

When the message space is Abelian, the stationarity equation system can be written in the implicit form

$$g^{*i}(m, e) = 0, \quad i = 1, \ldots, n, \tag{5}$$

with the function g^{*i} called the *i-th equilibrium function*.

As indicated above, this abstract formulation covers the special Walrasian equilibrium case, but also many other types of economic situations, including imperfect competition and certain forms of centralized planning.[3] What is particularly of importance, it also covers a class of Nash equilibria.[4] Consider, for instance, a class of games whose payoff function $\pi^i(s_i, s_{-i})$ of each player is concave and differentiable in that player's own strategy s_i. Then a Nash equilibrium is determined by the system of equations

$$\frac{\partial \pi^i}{\partial s_i}(s_i, s_{-i}) = 0, \tag{6}$$

which is of the form of (5) with $m_i = s_i$ and $g^i = \partial \pi^i / \partial s_i$.

To make the description of (5) complete, we must specify the set from which the message n-tuples may be drawn. We call this set the *message space* and denote it by M.

---

[3] See Hurwicz (1960) where the concepts of adjustment process and informational decentralization were introduced; also Hurwicz (1971).

[4] See Hurwicz (1981).

Next, we return to our objective of defining *informational decentralization*. For purposes of the present paper, we confine ourselves to what elsewhere has been called the *privacy preserving property* of the response and equilibrium functions: in both cases, the *i*-th function is independent of characteristics other than the *i*-th characteristic e_i. Hence the response function can be written as $f^i(m, e_i)$ and the equilibrium function as $g^i(m, e_i)$.

The system is *informationally decentralized* if and only if, there exists for each agent *i* and equilibrium function, say g^{*i} such that the systems (4) and (5) can respectively written as

$$m_i = f^i(m, e_i), \quad i = 1, \ldots, n, \tag{7.1}$$

and

$$g^i(m, e_i) = 0, \quad i = 1, \ldots, n. \tag{7.2}$$

While either of these equation systems defines the stationary (equilibrium) position of the system, it does not specify the actions agents are supposed to take. This information is provided by the *outcome function* $h : M \to Z$ where Z is the *outcome space* and provides information as to actions to be undertaken. For example, in a typical microeconomic model, Z specifies the net trades among agents, consumption levels, as well as inputs and outputs of firms.

An *adjustment process*[5] is defined by the triple (M, f^*, h) or (M, g^*, h) where $f^* = (f^{*1}, \ldots, f^{*n})$ and $g^* = (g^{*1}, \ldots, g^{*n})$, and each f^{*i} and g^{*i} may depend on all agents' characteristics, as in (4). It is *informationally decentralized* or *privacy preserving* when represented by the triple (M, f, h) or (M, g, h), where $f = (f^1, \ldots, f^n)$ and $g = (g^1, \ldots, g^n)$ and each f^i (resp. g^i) depends only on the *i*-th agent's own characteristic e_i. Each agent is assumed to know his/her own characteristic and equilibrium function (resp. response function), but not know those of others.

The operation of the mechanism can be visualized as follows. A screen, seen by all agents, is programmed to display elements of the message space M. When the screen displays a give message m, agent *i* responds with a "yes" if $g^i(m, e_i) = 0$, otherwise with a "no". (Since, by privacy preserving, g^i does not depend on characteristics other than e_i, agent *i* has all the information

---

[5] These days it is customary to call an adjustment process as here defined a *mechanism*, and we sometimes follow this custom in the present paper. This usage of the term 'mechanism' must, of course, be distinguished from the usage in game-theoretic literature where a mechanism is synonymous with a game-form, i.e., the strategy domain and the outcome function. However, associated with a game-form (S, h) is an adjustment process (S, g, h), where $S = M$, g is the equilibrium function derived from the game-form and the players' utility functions using the Nash solution concept. (See equation (6) above.)

required for an appropriate response.[6]) In joint work with Professors Marschak and Reiter, this phase of the process is called the *verification scenario*.

The process is in equilibrium if and only if all agents reply with a "yes", and the value of m to which the unanimous response was "yes" is called an equilibrium message. When the process is in equilibrium, the equilibrium message m is used as an input into a computer, programmed to calculate the outcome value $z = h(m)$, the output of the process.

If we were dealing with the problem of searching for equilibrium, we would have to answer the question what happens when there is no unanimous "yes". But, like much economics, we are limiting ourselves here to the study of a system in equilibrium, i.e., to the static aspects of the problem, and so the question of appropriate steps to be taken at disequilibrium will remain unanswered.

Nor are we concerned with the possibility that the agents would fail to provide truthful answers, the problem of incentive-compatibility that plays a central role in the game-theoretic models of mechanism design, especially implementation. The reason for this is that our model gives rise to results of sufficient generality to apply to mechanisms based on game-theoretic principles that take incentives into account as well as those that do not. The results provide upper bounds (sometimes maxima) for informational efficiency (lower bounds for message space size or other measures).

Upper Bounds for Informational Efficiency

Our central interest here is centered on an important aspect of the informational efficiency of mechanisms, namely the *efficiency of communication* used by the mechanism.[7] For instance, the 'size' of the message space M is a rough measure of the resource cost involved in communication required by the mechanism. When the message space is Euclidean of finite dimension, that cost is viewed (other things being equal) as an increasing function of the dimension of M, i.e., the number of numerical variables the mechanism is required to handle.

Of course, more complex tasks may unavoidably call for a message of higher dimension. We may think of the purpose of the adjustment process

---

[6] This applies to the response form of the adjustment process. In that case, when the response equations define a Nash equilibrium (as in (6)), the response functions may be thought of as representing the best reply. Even in the case of incomplete information, the i-th player can form his/her best reply without knowing the other players' payoff functions or characteristics since the verification scenario only requires the knowledge of one's own equilibrium function and characteristic.

[7] Another aspect, not discussed here, is that of the *complexity of computations* involved in the operation of communications. These problems have been studied by Mount and Reiter (2002).

as that of determining action z (in the outcome space Z) that is considered desirable as a function P of the characteristic n-tuple $e = (e_1, \ldots, e_n)$, i.e., $z = P(e)$, where P is called the *goal function*. (For instance, P might be a social welfare function.) But no one knows the whole n-tuple e; only its individual components (characteristics) are known to individual agents. The designer's task then is to construct equilibrium functions g^i and an outcome function h such that (i) for each a priori admissible n-tuple e, there exists an equilibrium message m in M for e, i.e., there exists m in M such that $g^i(m(e_i)) = 0$ for all i; and (ii) if m is an equilibrium message for e, then $h(m) = P(e)$; i.e., the outcome $h(m)$ produced by the equilibrium message m for e is the goal outcome $P(e)$ associated with the characteristics n-tuple e. A mechanism satisfying the latter two requirements is said to *realize the goal function P*.

The designer will try to find among decentralized mechanisms realizing the given goal function one maximizing informational efficiency. For instance, this may involve the minimization of the size (cardinality or dimension) of the message space. There are now available in the literature several results providing lower bounds (sometimes minima) on the dimension of the message space. These results apply to mechanisms whose equilibrium functions (or correspondences) satisfy certain regularity (e.g., Lipschitz continuity), conditions stronger than mere continuity. Without some such conditions the concept of dimension becomes meaningless.

Different Message Space Situations Depending on Convexity Properties of the Economic Environments

Convex economic environments, indirect mechanisms (Walrasian, Lindahl)

In particular, it has been shown that in convex exchange economies, the Walrasian mechanism, as usually defined in microeconomics, has the lowest dimension among decentralized mechanisms satisfying the regularity requirements and realizing the Walrasian goal correspondence, or more generally, guaranteeing the Pareto optimality of equilibrium outcomes in *classical* (convex, externality-free) *economic environments*. In pure exchange economies, this minimal dimension of M is equal to $n(L - 1)$, where n is the number of agents and L the number of goods. It is important to note that this minimal dimension does not depend on the number of parameters entering the trader's utility function. An analogous result exists for Lindahl mechanism in economies with produced public goods.

The results for both Walrasian and Lindahl mechanism provide minimal dimensions, not just lower bounds. As noted above, these minimality results apply in particular to game theoretic mechanisms (see equation (6) above).

The results for indirect mechanisms such as Walrasian or Lindahl available in convex economies contrast with the situation with the same economies when *direct revelation* mechanisms are used. With direct revelation mechanisms, the dimensionality of the message space grows with the number of parameters entering the utility functions.

Non-classical (non-convex) economic environments

By contrast, it turns out that in certain *non-classical* (non-convex) *environments* (increasing returns to scale or severe externalities), there exist no decentralized mechanisms with message space of *finite* dimension that satisfy the continuity conditions and realize the Pareto correspondence, i.e., guarantee Pareto optimal equilibrium outcomes.[8]

Observe that in both cases, the term 'equilibrium' is used in the sense of stationary position of the system as defined above. It applies in particular to Nash equilibrium outcomes, as well as Walrasian equilibria as defined in standard microeconomics textbooks.[9]

The negative results cited above imply that marginal cost pricing cannot guarantee Pareto optimality, and also that in economies where externalities result in non-convexity of the transformation set, Pigovian taxes cannot guarantee Pareto optimality.

Idealized Mechanism Construction

An alternate approach[10] to study the limits (or upper bounds) to which informational efficiency can be pushed is by considering mechanisms that maximize some index of informational efficiency without taking into account the possibly conflicting interests of the agents, i.e., by assuming that the agents can be programmed to follow prescribed rules of procedure.[11]

So far, this program has only been carried out for economies where the individual characteristics and goal functions are specified by a finite number of real-valued parameters. A major objective of the author's joint work with Reiter[12] has been to develop systematic procedures ('algorithms')

---

[8] See Calsamiglia (1977), Hurwicz (1999).

[9] In the non-classical (non-convex) economies mentioned above, Walrasian equilibria would, in general, not exist.

[10] This section reports on joint work with Stan Reiter. The framework is related to joint work by Reiter, or the author with Tom Marschak, Don Saari, Leonard Shapiro, and Steve Williams.

[11] The goal function (e.g., a social welfare function) may, of course, take into account the agents' possibly conflicting preferences. Furthermore, it is assumed that, in their behavior, the agents will follow the rules specified by the mechanism regardless of their individual preferences.

[12] See Hurwicz and Reiter (2006).—SB

for designing informationally efficient decentralized mechanisms when the designer has only the following data: (1) the finite-dimensional factored parameter space $\Theta = \Theta^1 \times \ldots \times \Theta^n$ and, when the components are Euclidean, their dimensions; (2) the outcome space Z; (3) the goal function $F : \Theta \to Z$ (more generally, goal correspondence) to be realized. The designer does not know the prevailing values of the parameters. Decentralization means that after the mechanism is designed and becomes public knowledge, each agent will know his/her own parameter vector but not those of others.

For a variety of reasons, but in particular because the parameter spaces may be either Euclidean or finite sets, it turns out natural to use a concept of informational efficiency that differs from (although is related to) the size of the message space.[13] The concept used in the recent joint work by Hurwicz and Reiter involves looking at the 'coarseness' (opposite of fineness) of the covering generated by the mechanism.[14] The coarser the covering, the more informationally efficient the mechanism. Hence we aim at maximal coarseness (our concept of informational efficiency). Minimal message space size usually implies maximal coarsening but maximal coarseness does not imply minimum message space size.

It has turned out possible to formulate systematic procedures ('algorithms'[15]) that, given the above listed data available to the designer, produce maximally coarse informationally decentralized mechanisms. The procedures consist of two phases. In the first phase, we use the 'Method of Rectangles' to obtain a covering indexed by points of the parameter space.[16] The second phase uses either the Method of Transversals[17] or what we call Condensation[18] to provide more economical indexing by what becomes the message space. That final covering is decentralized and maximally coarse, hence in our sense informationally efficient.

The mechanisms so obtained only show how much informational efficiency can be attained when, in the spirit of theory of teams of Jacob Marschak and Roy Radner, agents are assumed to obey the rules of the mechanism regardless of their individual preferences. It seems of interest to know

---

[13] When the message space is finite-dimensional Euclidean, its size is usually taken to be its dimension; when it is a finite set, its size is its cardinality.

[14] By definition, covering C of Θ is a collection of subsets k of Θ such that every point θ of Θ belongs to some k in C. (The sets k are called members of C.) A partition is a covering without overlaps of its member sets. The covering C' is said to be coarser than the covering C'' if every member k'' of C'' is a subset of some k' of C'. The coarsening is proper if for some k'' in C'' there is k' in C' such that k'' is a proper subset of k'. A covering C of Θ is maximally coarse if there is no covering that is properly coarser than C.

[15] We use quotation marks because the procedure may require the solution of a system of non-linear equations.

[16] Hurwicz and Reiter (1990, 2001).

[17] Using Leonard Shapiro's 'flagpole' suggestion.

[18] Utilizing a result in Mount and Reiter (1996).

how the designer, who is given only the goal function and the parameter spaces, can devise systematic procedures for designing an informationally efficient decentralized mechanism that realizes that goal. This avoids having to guess or to limit oneself to mechanisms already known.

One may hope that it will be possible to develop systematic procedures for devising informationally efficient mechanisms in situations where conflicting objectives and incentives are present.[19]

References

Calsamiglia, X. (1977) Decentralized resource allocation and increasing returns, *Journal of Economic Theory*, 14(2): 263–83.

Hurwicz, L. (1960) Optimality and informational efficiency in resource allocation processes, in *Mathematical Methods in the Social Sciences*, ed. K. Arrow, S. Karlin, and P. Suppes, 27–46. Stanford, CA: Stanford University Press.

Hurwicz, L. (1971) Centralization and decentralization in economic processes, in *Comparison of Economic Systems*, ed. A. Eckstein, 79–102. Berkeley, CA: University of California Press.

Hurwicz, L. (1981) On incentive problems in the design of non-wasteful resource allocation systems, in *Studies in Economic Theory and Practice: Essays in Honor of Edward Lipinski*, ed. N. Assorodobraj-Kula et al., 93–106. Amsterdam: North-Holland.

Hurwicz, L. (1999) Revisiting externalities, *Journal of Public Economic Theory*, 1(2): 225–45.

Hurwicz, L. and S. Reiter (1990) Constructing decentralized mechanisms by the method of rectangles, presented at the NBER-NSF Decentralization Conference, April 27, 1990, Northwestern University, Evanston, IL.

Hurwicz, L. and S. Reiter (1991) Transversals, systems of distinct representatives, mechanism design, and matching, *Review of Economic Design*, 6(2): 289–304.

Hurwicz, L. and S. Reiter (2006) *Designing Economic Mechanisms*. Cambridge, MA: Cambridge University Press.

Mount, K. and S. Reiter (1996) A lower bound on computational complexity given by revelation mechanisms, *Journal of Economic Theory*, 7(2): 237–66.

Mount, K. and S. Reiter (2002) *Computation and Complexity in Economic Behavior and Organization*. Cambridge, MA: Cambridge University Press.

Osana, H. (1978) On the informational size of message spaces for resource allocation processes, *Journal of Economic Theory*, 17(1): 66–78.

Reichelstein, S. and S. Reiter (1988) Game forms with minimal message spaces, *Econometrica*, 56(3): 661–92.

Sato, F. (1981) On the informational size of message spaces for resource allocation processes in economies with public goods, *Journal of Economic Theory*, 24(1): 48–69.

---

[19] Reichelstein and Reiter (1988) constitutes a step in this direction.

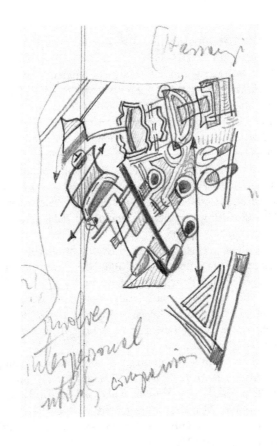

12

On Modeling Institutions

In contrast to the 1930s when there seemed to be a gulf between economic theory and a recognition of the role of institutions in economic phenomena, much of the recent literature represents an effort to synthesize the two.

At least two streams of thought are involved. One of these has been focused either on specific institutions such as forms of land tenure (renting, sharecropping, wage labor), capitalism, socialism, or on problems such as vertical integration where institutional factors (e.g., property rights) play a crucial role. The contributions of Williamson, Stiglitz, Grossman, Hart, Holmström, Eliason, Kornai, and others are among the outstanding examples, illustrating the diversity of issues studied. The other approach has aimed at developing a framework of sufficient generality to accommodate a wide spectrum of institutional arrangements and so to facilitate comparative as well as normative analytical work. The paper by Shapley and Shubik (1967) on ownership and the production function as well as much of the theory of economic mechanisms may qualify in this category. A major contribution in this area is Schotter's (1981) study of social institutions.

The present paper must be classified as a further effort in developing a general framework but one having enough structure to provide a bridge to contributions of the first category.[1] In particular, my aim is to suggest possible approaches to the modeling of institutions in a manner that is closely related to the theory of mechanisms. As the title indicates, my concern is with the appropriate structure of models to be used in the study of institutions, and the paper contains no new results. Furthermore, although I am primarily interested in economic institutions and mechanisms, some of

This paper (transcribed by Xavier Calsamiglia and printed with his permission) was presented on June 14, 1989, at the Universitat Autònoma de Barcelona on the occasion of receiving an honorary doctorate. An earlier version was presented at the 1988 American Economic Association meetings in New York.

[1] A bridge between two streams is, of course, a metaphor of doubtful merit!

On Modeling Institutions In: *The Collected Papers of Leonid Hurwicz Volume 1.*
Edited by Samiran Banerjee, Oxford University Press. © Oxford University Press 2022.
DOI: 10.1093/oso/9780199313280.003.0012

the considerations are of a more general nature and may be relevant outside of economics.

My basic objective, in a language that can be viewed as either figurative or mathematical, but which in any case oversimplifies matters, is to define a 'space' whose various 'points' (or subsets) are distinct institutions. If one thinks of this space as characterized by many dimensions ('axes'), an institution is defined by specifying the values of various 'coordinates'. Of course, these coordinates may well involve non-quantitative attributes; indeed, that may be the typical situation.

The term 'institution' has two rather different meanings: (a) a set of rules or arrangements such as property rights, and (b) an entity such as an organization or office. Although some of the literature uses definitions broad enough to cover both, I prefer to maintain the distinction and to reserve the term 'institution' (sometimes 'institutional arrangement') for sense (a). Not surprisingly, however, we shall see that entities corresponding to sense (b) of the term play a very important role in the description of institutional arrangements.

Another distinction may be noted. One may be interested in institutions in the spirit of either positive or normative science. The positive science approach deals with explanations of the effects of institutions on various economic (and other social) phenomena and also with processes that result in the (endogenous) formation of institutions. But unless one were to deny the possibility of conscious acts and decisions that result in institutional change, there is also room for a normative or design point of view. Either of the two approaches can benefit from the availability of a rigorous framework in which to analyze institutional change, whether endogenous or designed.

No uniqueness or originality is claimed for the framework to be proposed in this paper. At best, I regard it only as a first step. It is not difficult to think of alternatives that have at least equal merit. For me, however, a natural point of departure is the theory of mechanisms. In fact, to indicate the direction in which I am going, I shall regard an institution as a class of mechanisms[2] (with particular characteristics)—but with mechanisms conceived somewhat more broadly and endowed with more structure than has been customary.

In view of what has just been said, it is natural to start by devoting some attention to the concept and certain structural aspects of mechanisms. And this, in turn, may be introduced by the historical background. One source

---

[2] An alternative approach is adopted by Schotter (1981, p. 29) who views social institutions "...not [as] part of the rules but part of the solutions to iterated games of strategy." Let us note, however, that the concept proposed in the present paper views an institution not as a set of rules of a game to be played but rather as a set of restrictions on what rules are admissible. The latter distinction could perhaps be avoided (by redefining the nature of the game to be played), but at the cost of losing some transparency in the phenomena being studied.

of interest in mechanisms is the standard 'neoclassical' microeconomics with its emphasis on market processes, especially those in perfectly competitive markets. The perfectly competitive market becomes the archetype of a mechanism. But since such a market cannot always exist (e.g., under increasing returns) or may be inefficient (e.g., in the presence of externalities), efficient alternatives are considered—for instance, marginal cost pricing with subsidies when increasing returns prevail, Pigovian taxes and subsidies for externalities, Lindahl solutions for public goods, etc. The search for such alternatives is motivated, in part at least, by the analysis of the mechanisms more likely to be encountered in such situations—monopoly, oligopoly, regulation, or a command economy—with their various undesirable characteristics.

Mechanisms

Particular mechanisms have, of course, a long history of formalization—a century and a half for oligopoly. But the formulation of a general theory of mechanisms, of which the above examples could be regarded as special cases, is more recent.

There are in fact two notions of a mechanism, interrelated but distinct. One of these, the *message model ('adjustment process')*, views a mechanism as the exchange of information over time, followed (at the terminal period or after equilibrium has been established) by the outcome specified by a rule called the 'outcome function'; the other, the *game model*, as a 'game-form', that is a specification of actions available to the economic agents (called strategy or action spaces) and a rule specifying the consequences of actions (again called the outcome function). The particular game models used may cooperative or non-cooperative; the latter may be in normal or extensive form. Extensive form models do pay attention to informational aspects and hence have points of contact with the message models.

Message Model or Adjustment Process

The message model specifies the signals (*languages* or individual *message spaces*, with the i-th agent's language denoted by M^i) that can be emitted by the agents as well as rules (called *response functions*) which specify the signals to be emitted by an agent given messages previously received and the information concerning both own and the others' *characteristics*. An agent's characteristic, denoted e^i, specifies such data as the agent's preferences, endowment, and production possibilities. If the number of agents is n, the n-tuple of characteristics is called the *environment* and is denoted by e. So $e = (e^1, \ldots, e^n)$.

161

An adjustment process is called *privacy preserving* if an agent's response cannot directly utilize any information concerning the other agents' characteristics. Formally, with the i-th agent's response function denoted by f^i, the subscript representing points in time and the superscript referring to the agent, a privacy preserving process is governed by equations of the form

$$m^i_{t+1} = f^i(m^1_t, \ldots, m^n_t, e^i) \quad i = 1, \ldots, n; \quad t = 1, 2, \ldots$$

while in general (when the process is not privacy preserving) the right hand side could contain any of the components of the environment, hence any e^j with $j \neq i$. The privacy preserving property of the response functions is intended to express part of the notion of informational decentralization of the adjustment process. In particular, perfectly competitive markets can be modeled as having privacy preserving response functions.

An adjustment process is completely specified by the choice of the individual languages, response functions, and the outcome functions, written as $(M^1, \ldots, M^n; f^1, \ldots, f^n; h)$ where h denotes the outcome function. The response functions may be imposed from outside or may have behavioral interpretations, but the message model does not analyze their origin—it takes them as given. Furthermore, once initial message values have been chosen, the adjustment process completely determines the final outcome.[3]

Game Model

The situation is quite different in the game model. Here the model prescribes only the individual strategy domains S^i (counterparts of the individual languages in the message model) and the outcome function. There is no exact counterpart of the response functions. Instead, the behavior of agents is postulated to be based on certain strategic calculations. If the game is non-cooperative, the most widely used assumption is that of Nash equilibrium where each agent maximizes his/her satisfaction given the others' strategy choices. However, alternative behavioral postulates are also often used such as 'refinements' of Nash equilibrium (subgame perfect, undominated, etc.) as well as non-Nash solutions such as maximin. Thus the game model mechanism specified by the strategy domains S^i and the outcome function h (i.e., the game-form $(S^1, \ldots, S^n; h)$) is not sufficient to determine the outcome; one must also specify the behavioral postulate implicit in the choice of the game solution concept.

---

[3] A variant of this model uses multi-valued outcome functions; in that case there is an element of indeterminacy.

In fact, the behavioral postulates determining the choice of strategies by the agents need not be confined to game theoretic solution concepts. One could, for instance, postulate instead that this choice is determined by such (non-strategic) factors as tradition, law, moral precepts, etc. It is important, therefore, to note that what we call the game model is of greater generality than the term seems to imply.

Tâtonnement and Non-Tâtonnement. One feature that the usual message models and extensive form game models have in common is that there are essentially two phases: (1) exchange of messages, resp. a sequence of moves, and (2) the realization of outcomes, resp. payoffs, following the last message (or the equilibrium message), resp. the last move. This two-phase structure corresponds to what in economics is called the Walrasian tâtonnement. Whatever its merits as an idealization of certain market phenomena, it is obviously too narrow as a description of how markets work. Indeed, there have been constructed non-tâtonnement models of pure exchange in which goods change hands at each bargaining step. For our purposes, however, we shall need a structure encompassing both polar cases, but also permitting mixtures.

Expanded Adjustment Process. While in the earlier adjustment process with each time point t is associated the n-tuple

$$m_t = (m_t^1, \ldots, m_t^n),$$

we shall now associate with each time point a triple (m_t, a_t, z_t); here a_t represents actions at time t, and z_t represents the outcomes materializing at time t. A similar generalization will be introduced into the extensive game, so that outcomes affecting preferences or utilities materialize before the final moves.[4] We shall refer to the first two components of the above triple simply as behavior at time t and denote it by b_t.[5] A reason for the generalization is to accommodate commitments (including contracts) and their fulfillment. Thus undertaking a commitment may be modeled as a message at time t', while its fulfillment may be an action at a later time t''. If the commitment at time t' is made by agent i, it will constitute a part of the content of m_t^i. Hence, at a minimum, the language M^i will have to be rich enough to specify an appropriate element of the action space as well as the timing of fulfillment. In this context, identifying actions and messages (as is often done) conceals

---

[4] This is particularly appropriate, indeed seemingly unavoidable, in infinite horizon extensive form games. I am indebted to Ehud Kalai for enlightenment on this point.

[5] In an extensive game messages and actions may be regarded as components of moves. A generalization of this type, with an element of 'on line' operations was suggested by Thomas Marschak several years ago in a paper presented at a decentralization conference.

the structure of commitment and fulfillment, matters of particular interest in the study of institutions.

A further enrichment of the structure is desirable in order that we should be able to refer to commitments or actions by groups (coalitions), i.e., various subsets of the set $\{1, \ldots, n\}$ of all players, as distinct form individual agents. Similary, commitments may be made by groups. An action by group J taken at time t will be denoted by $a(J, t)$.[6] In addition to this role of groups, we shall also allow for the creation of, and participation by, artificial persons such as states, firms, labor unions, churches, etc.[7]

I shall defer until later the details that are necessary to represent specific features of the phenomena of commitment and fulfillment (or the consequences of non-fulfillment).

Institutions as Classes of Mechanisms

Recent literature has many examples of modeling economic phenomena within the framework of standard ('un-enriched') versions of either of the two models, game or message exchange, and with institutional factors taken into account. Why then should there be a need for a change in modeling? Basically because we want to be able to treat institutions as variables and need to define a space over which they can vary. Thus, for instance, the Arrow-Debreu model of a perfectly competitive market does not provide us with a natural way of considering other types of markets, and much less other economic systems such as command economies. By contrast, Stiglitz's (1974) paper on sharecropping defines a family of outcome functions with the worker's reward r given by the formula

$$r = ay + b$$

where y is the worker's product (e.g., income generated by the worker) while a and b are numerical parameters. Various institutional arrangements can be defined by subsets of the two-dimensional parameter space (a, b). Thus when $a = 1$ and $b < 0$ the worker is a renter; when $a = 0$ and $b > 0$, he/she is

---

6 Hence $a(i, t)$, where we write i instead of $\{i\}$, is the same as a_t^i. Similarly for messages and outcomes.

7 The distinction between actions by groups and by artificial persons may seem unnecessary. but I regard it as useful when trying to relate, on the one hand, to structures of game theory (especially cooperative games), and those of law with its ways of treating certain entities as if they were persons. The role of action by collective bodies was among the main points stressed by Commons (1924, 1934, 1951).

a wage-earner; ('pure') sharecropping is defined by $0 < a < 1$ and $b = 0$.[8] While the Stiglitz model treats many institutional aspects of the situation as constant, it provides a most helpful illustration of the notion of a space of institutions.

In particular, we see that every point of the (a, h)-plane can be viewed as representing a conceivable mechanism. Thus, a particular sharecropping mechanism is defined by a pair such as $(1/3, 0)$ which specifies that the worker's share is $1/3$).[9] Since each of the institutions under consideration is represented by a subset of the plane, it becomes natural to consider an *institution* as a *class of mechanisms*.[10] This idea is a point of departure for attempting a working definition of what we here mean by an institution and also for modeling institutions. Recalling that a (game model) mechanism is defined (in normal form) by a list of strategies and the outcome function, an institution is then specified by a set whose elements are the $(n + 1)$-tuples $(S^1, \ldots, S^n; h)$.

Restrictions on Outcome Functions and Strategy Domains. The land tenure example distinguished institutions by varying the class of admissible outcome functions. Thus the institution of sharecropping is defined by all outcome functions of the form

$$r = ay,$$

with a ranging between zero and one. Regulation (e.g., price control) illustrates the institutions defined by restrictions on the agents' strategy spaces rather than on the outcome functions. For instance, let S^i represent the price to be set by agent i (the seller). In the absence of regulation, S^i is the whole

---

[8] To use an analogy, suppose we have a macroeconomic model in which the rate of interest r plays a role. One might use a particular value of the rate of interest, say 7%, and analyze the workings of such a model. This would not be ignoring the role of the rate of interest, but it would not enable us to analyze the consequences of its changes. Moreover, if we just inserted .07 wherever the rate appeared without indicating that it is a particular value of a variable r, the user would have no way of knowing how to use such a model to consider alternative values of the variable r. This may seem belaboring the obvious, but the distinction between introducing into the model a particular institution as a 'constant' on the one hand, and treating it as a particular value of a variable is crucial; the analogy may help make the point clearer.

[9] Alternatively, when agents are free to choose such parameters as wage rates by voluntary agreement, it is more natural to view the whole set of points $W = \{(a, b): a = 0, b > 0\}$ as corresponding to the wage earning mechanism. However, the full description of the arrangement would require the specification of various legal or customary rules governing the non-monetary aspects of the wage contract, rules not subject to modification by the contracting parties. One may think of such rules as points on a third (non-numerical) axis, the z-axis. Rules compatible with the notion of a wage contract constitute a subset Z' on this axis. A particular wage mechanism is defined by a pair (W, z^*) where z^* is a particular point belonging to z'. The institution of wage earning is then defined as the collection of all such pairs, i.e., by the set $\{(W, z): z \in Z'\}$. (I am indebted to Stanley Reiter for enlightening comments concerning these issues.)

[10] Another reason for thinking of an institution as a class of mechanisms is that a mechanism typically refers to only some aspects of people's activities (e.g., work and rewards) while other aspects (say leisure activities) remain outside the mechanism model.

real axis, since the seller can sell at any price (positive, negative, or zero). On the other hand, when (maximum) price controls are introduced, a specific price ceiling prevails, say $8/item; hence the *mechanism* prescribes S^i as the set of all real numbers not exceeding 8. But the price control *institution* is defined by class of S^i's each of which is an interval of real numbers of the form $(-\infty, k]$ where k ranges over positive numbers.

Additional Requirements. While we view an institution as a class of mechanisms, it is of course not the case that every class of mechanisms is an institution. There are at least three additional aspects that must be introduced: (a) enforcement, (b) prior human actions, and (c) what I shall call 'universality'. By 'universality' I here mean that the rules are meant to apply not just to a particular person or group of persons at a particular point in time, but rather to a category of situations and persons, thus applying to all persons and situations qualifying in such categories, with the rules intended to remain valid over an extended (often not limited in advance) period of time.[11]

Enforcement

Usual Implicit Assumption: Game-Form Prevails. The issue of enforcement raises analytical problems that can be only mentioned here. Looking first at standard mechanism theory, it is implicit in the usual interpretations that a given game-form prevails. That means that the players will not use strategies outside of the prescribed domains S^i and that, once the strategies have been chosen, the consequences will be those specified by the outcome function. Now given the assumption that the prescribed game-form will prevail, and if one regards Nash equilibrium (possibly in 'refined' form) or some other non-cooperative game solution as behaviorally realistic, it is possible to regard the equilibrium configuration (n-tuple) of the players' strategies as self-enforcing.

The assumption that a particular game-form prevails (i.e., is abided by the players) may be plausible if the strategy domains are only limited by physical (or similarly unavoidable) factors, and where the outcome function represents laws of nature. But that is far from being the case in game-forms that have been designed to implement certain social goals, as for instance in the mechanism for allocation of public goods due to Groves and Ledyard (1977), Hurwicz (1979b, 1979c), and Walker (1981), or in the mechanisms for the implementation of the Walrasian correspondence (i.e., the attainment of perfectly competitive equilibrium allocations) proposed by

---

11 The definition given by Schotter (1981, p. 11) as well by Lewis (quoted in Schotter, p. 9), refers to behavior 'in recurrent situations'. It would seem that universality with respect to persons affected is also a significant feature.

Schmeidler (1980), Maskin (1977), Postlewaite and Wettstein (1983), and others, including myself (Hurwicz 1979a). In such models we, for instance, limit the participants to proposing prices and quantities or numerical messages, while (as in Schmeidler's mechanism) the actual flow of goods may involve a specified form of rationing when proposed demand exceeds supply. One must ask why the players would voluntarily abide by the requirements of the game-form or how they could be induced to do so. A similar question arises with regard to the Groves and Ledyard mechanism, especially because it is not individually rational (i.e., unlike in a mechanism implementing the Lindahl correspondence, an individual might be worse off at the end than he/she was before the game). Unless forced to, some individuals might prefer not to participate, especially if they had enough information to anticipate that they would be the losers in equilibrium. But even when individual rationality is satisfied, e.g., when the game-form implements the Lindahl correspondence, some players might prefer not to abide by the rules of the game-form.

Augmented vs. Primary Game. It is then natural to think of introducing an element of enforcement into the situation. This can be viewed as creating an *augmented game* consisting of the *primary game* (say the game-form defined by Groves and Ledyard) plus a policing system specifying penalties for transgressions and providing incentives to a set of additional[12] players (policemen, judges, etc.) to prevent or punish transgressions.[13] Of course, the same questions that were raised with regard to the primary game can also be raised with regard to the augmented game. It would be fortunate (although very unlikely) if the (say, Nash) equilibrium of the augmented game were such that it succeeded in inducing the primary game agents to obey its rules. Even then, the augmented game would no longer be implementing the ('original') social choice (goal) correspondence because the enforcement apparatus costs resources. In practice, one typically settles for a trade-off between the degree of imperfection in the enforcement of the primary games rules (say, of tax law) and the cost (or even feasibility) of enforcement. One can also consider an augmentation of the augmented game (a second-order augmented game) which would provide for the policing of the enforcers of the primary game, and so on. But the problem would reappear at the next stage. Thus any proposal to redesign ('reform') a social institution (say, an

---

[12] It is not necessary to have additional players as enforcers. The primary players may be motivated to play that role themselves. Honor codes are one example; societies where citizens are encouraged to spy on and denounce one another also illustrate the fact that the primary players can have a role in the process of enforcement, activity that was completely carried out by the primary players without any outside enforcers. The incentive structure required to induce such behavior would ordinarily imply that the goal function of the primary game would no longer be implemented.

[13] I have benefitted from a conversation with Andrew Postlewaite concerning problems of modeling enforcement.

economic system)—which in our interpretation involves changing the class of admissible game-forms—raises questions of enforcement, its feasibility, cost, as well as 'side-effects' involving various societal values.[14]

Enforcement in 'Organically Emerging' Institutions. The apparent need to introduce an enforcement system is by no means confined to artificially designed mechanisms. In fact, the point is emphasized by Schotter (1981, p. 11) in his informal definition which characterizes a social institution as 'a regularity in social behavior that is agreed by all members of society, specifies behavior in recurrent situations, and is either self-policed or policed by some external authority'. He illustrates the need for an external enforcing authority (here the state) by the system of property rights, a social institution. The importance of the example lies in the fact that it is regarded as one of the institutions 'that emerge organically by human action but not by human design...' (Schotter 1981, p. 28). Indeed, both the emergence of a system of property rights and of the enforcing state are viewed as due to such an 'organic' process.

Artificial (Juristic) Persons

One byproduct of the preceding discussion is the emergence of the role of the state or other bodies whose function is to enforce or police the rules. The phenomenon is of importance not only in the context of the enforcement process but also because it introduces a potential new participant in the social processes—an *artificial person* of which a 'juristic person' is a special case. Of course, this concept is much broader than that of a state or enforcement agencies; corporations and labor unions are among instances of particular interest to the economist. Although there are obvious distinctions to be drawn between natural and artificial persons, it is important to recognize that the latter should for many purposes be regarded as separate players. That is the case even for situations where there is an office (say, that of the President of the United States) occupied by a single (natural) person; indeed there may be a conflict between the two. Actions taken in the name of the office (even though carried out by the occupant) are distinct from those taken

---

[14] This does not mean that analysis ignoring enforcement problems is without value. In particular, various impossibility theorems based on the implicit assumption that the game-forms can be costlessly enforced are likely to be a fortiori valid when the enforcement issues are raised. Also, there may be situations where there are obvious reasons to expect that the participants will abide by the rules of the game-form without any additional enforcement apparatus. Finally, it may sometimes be adequate to recognize the cost imposed by the need for enforcement without having to consider explicitly the way in which the augmented game differs from the primary game.

in the name of the occupant as a natural person. As this example illustrates, one should not identify the notion of an artificial person with that of an organization, although usually an organization is an artificial person.

Mission and Agency. An important characteristic of such bodies as enforcement entities or ombudsmen is that they have a role or *mission* in the institutional design: to make the system implement (or at least come closer to implementing) some social goals. It would be convenient to have a special term for such entities, perhaps *agencies*.[15] When new institutional arrangements are introduced it is usual that an agency is at the same time created to help implement[16] these arrangements. The role of the agency is often to specify the 'parameters' that would (in the terminology of this paper) convert an institution (i.e., a class of game-forms) into a mechanism (i.e., a game-form), as well as to help enforce the rules of the mechanism. Examples, especially from the regulatory field, abound. Price controls and anti-trust are among the obvious ones.

Once the role of artificial persons and agencies is recognized, the internal structure of the game-form must be sufficiently enriched to accommodate the formation, activities, and even demise of these entitles. In particular, the message space must be rich enough to accommodate a variety of individual and group commitments, with or without built-in contingencies.

Formation through Prior (Human) Action or Behavior

A second essential feature in the concept of an institution as a class of admissible mechanisms (game-forms) is that it comes into existence through prior (usually collective) human action or behavior. Since some moves or behaviors are physically or psychologically ruled out, this means that not all restrictions on admissibility of mechanisms are institutional in nature. Descriptively, these prior actions may take the form of legislation or the adoption of customs or ethical norms. Within the framework of game theory there are various possibilities of formalizing the process of institution formation.

Reiter-Hughes Two-Game Model. The route chosen by Reiter and Hughes (1981) in modeling regulation was to postulate a sequence of two games. The first one is a cooperative game representing the political process

---

[15] I am not sure how close this notion of an agency is to the second meaning (listed as (b) in the introductory section above) of the term 'institution', as applied for instance to an entity such as a university (rather than to a phenomenon such as the system of property rights).

[16] This use of the term 'implement' is closer to the usual meaning than that introduced by Maskin.

(say, congressional legislation) which formulates the rules of the regulatory process. The second is a non-cooperative game of incomplete information (with economic agents and regulators as players) in which the specific regulations are arrived at. An alternative might have been to combine the two games of the Reiter and Hughes model into a single one, presumably a non-cooperative game in extensive form, with the earlier moves corresponding to their first game.[17] Reiter and Hughes also consider the dynamic aspects of regulatory phenomena taking into account the effects of changes in the (economic) environment (e.g., capital formation, technology), both exogenous and those due to the regulation. Hence, except initially, both games are being replayed.

Supergame. This suggests modeling the process as a supergame, of which institution formation and the actual regulatory process operate at all points of time. A possible difficulty with the supergame approach lies in the fact that the cast of players changes over time, so that there is imperfection of memory and some of the customary threat/reward strategies are not applicable.

Sequences of Games. It therefore seems not without interest to consider a compromise in which there is enough myopia so that the dynamics is in the nature of a sequence of games, though possibly with some memory from (say) one game to the next. Hence both game and adjustment process elements are present. Certain elements of such a model were described in Hurwicz (1987) and will be briefly sketched in what follows.

We consider an infinite sequence of time intervals (perhaps in some respects reminiscent of Hicksian weeks). During each week an extensive form incomplete information game is played with a finite number of moves, say $t = 0, 1, \ldots, T$.[18] There may be some memory from one week to another which might, for instance, be used to affect a player's conjectures about the other players' characteristics but still each period is viewed as a separate game.[19] However, the dynamic phenomena recognized by Reiter and Hughes would be present, and—in principle—the model could lend itself to a study of convergence, trends, cyclicities, etc.

Commitments. A week is viewed as long enough so that any commitments (including contracts) made during a week are (or at least supposed to be) carried out during the same week.[20] Let $N = \{1, \ldots, n\}$ denote the set of players.[21] Denote by K any non-empty subset of N, i.e., a group or a coalition.

---

[17] But in a multi-period world, institutions last over many periods!

[18] A more complete notation would use a pair, say (t, τ), where τ is the week and t the move number during that week.

[19] In particular, institutions persist from week to week.

[20] Hence a year or a decade might have been a better label for this time period!

[21] To simplify notation we shall ignore the fact that artificial persons may be created during the week, so that the set of players will, in fact, vary from move [to move] within the week.

The behavior of the group K at t-th move is denoted by $b(K, t)$; it has two components: the message $m(K, t)$ and the action $a(K, t)$; the outcome (say resource allocation)[22] for the group K at the t-th move is $z(K, t)$. These outcomes may generate utilities at every move—not merely at the end. Hence this is not in general a tâtonnement process, although tâtonnement is a legitimate special case.

Enforceability. To make matters easier, we initially avoid the consideration of an augmented game (with an enforcement sector), but in order to permit moderately realistic treatment of commitments (again including contracts), we classify actions according to whether they are enforceable. For each (move) t, we define the set $A(t)$ of mutually compatible actions, with

$$A(t) = \{a(K', t), a(K'', t), \ldots : \}$$

as the set of mutually compatible actions by the various groups. In the above notation, we assume a complete listing of all the subsets of N, with K' the first element of that list, K'' the second, and so on; the empty space after the colon would have to be filled with a specification of the spaces over which these mutually compatible actions can range. We would then postulate set of actions $L(K, t)$ enforceable on K at move t (within $A(t)$).

'Bounded Rationality' Modeling. In models dealing with the institution of ownership, complexity (or other aspects of 'bounded rationality') is invoked to explained the incompleteness of contracts, and it is desirable to model this explicitly. A crude way of doing this starts with a set $C(t)$ of contingencies that can be envisaged at t. The idea that there are limits on how much detail concerning contingencies can be built into a contract is expressed by postulating a partitioning $\Gamma(t')$ [at time t'] of the set $C(t)$. Two contingencies belonging to the same set of this partition are considered formally (say, for purposes of legal proof) indistinguishable.[23] Similarly, we postulate a partitioning $\Sigma(K, t)$ of the set of enforceable actions, with the interpretation that two actions belonging to the same set of the partition are considered as formally equivalent. These phenomena of indistinguishability or equivalence may mean that one of the parties has a choice of interpretation as to which contingency or enforcement action is appropriate. The equivalences thus permit certain agents to acquire residual powers of the sort that Grossman and Hart (1986) associate with ownership, but which also characterize the

---

[22] Taking account of operating (hence transaction) costs.

[23] This may correspond to some of the considerations in Williamson (1975, 1985) as well as in Grossman and Hart (1986).

discretionary powers of bureaucrats or party organizations in countries such as the People's Republic of China or the Soviet Union.

Commitment: Consistency Requirements. A commitment (in particular a contract) is viewed as a part of a message consisting of a 'flag' (signaling formal commitment) and a functional relation whose argument is a contingency and whose value is a set of (presumably) feasible actions. A commitment (contract) entered into by group K at move t is a part of the message $m(K, t)$. In principle, this function should be constant on the (indistinguishable) elements of the partition $\Gamma(t')$, where t' is the time at which the commitment is to be carried out. Let this function be written as $\varphi_K(c, t, t')$ where t is the time the commitment is made, t' when it is to be carried out, and c is a contingency. Let its value, i.e., the set of actions from which fulfillment must be selected at time t' by the group K, be denoted by $D(K, t')$. To be properly enforceable, this set should be the intersection of the feasible set $A(K, t')$ with a set of the partition $\Sigma(K, t')$. However, in fact, the function may not satisfy the preceding consistency requirements, and so leave ambiguities to be resolved either by legal procedures or by the residual power of certain participants.

Residual Power. The specification of such residual powers is an essential element distinguishing the institutional structures of various societies. There is an interesting parallelism between the role played in institutional structure by such power residuals and the role played in institutional structures by the location of residual risks (as in the land tenure example). In fact, these examples suggest a possible further narrowing down of the definition of an institution to express the qualitative differences that make one label two situations as being [two] different institutional arrangements. It is as if institutions corresponded to subspaces being defined by fixing the values of a (typically finite) number of coordinates.[24] The fixed values would typically be zeros or ones.

My Motivation. It should be clear that the sort of model suggested in the preceding paragraphs would not displace the more specific models present in the literature of which some examples have been cited above. The aim is, rather, to provide a framework in which such models could be embedded, so as to facilitate comparative or normative approaches. In particular, a target is to develop an implementation[25] theory whose product (proposed institutions or mechanisms) would be framed within the same universe of discourse, and took into account the limitations that are encountered in

---

[24] Hence, even if the space of mechanism were infinite-dimensional, an institution would correspond to a subplace (more generally, subset) of finite codimension.

[25] In the usual (non-Maskin) sense.

actual efforts toward institutional change currently observed in many countries, both capitalist and communist, such as measures toward deregulation, privatization, and the substitution of markets for bureaucratic procedures. In the normative sphere, such a development would presumably be of the 'second best' type,[26] less satisfying, but more realistic. It could also be helpful in the realm of positive theory aimed at explaining current and past observed phenomena.

References

*Atkins, W., et al. (1931) *Economic Behavior: An Institutional Approach*, vol. 1. Boston, MA: Houghton Mifflin Co.

Commons, J. (1924) *Legal Foundations of Capitalism*. New York, NY: Macmillan.

Commons, J. (1934) *Institutional Economics*. New York, NY: Macmillan.

Commons, J. (1951) *The Economics of Collective Action*. New York, NY: Macmillan.

*Eliason, G. ed. (1986) *The Economics of Institutions and Markets: IUI Yearbook 1986–1987*. Stockholm: Industrial Institute for Economic and Social Research.

Grossman, S. and O. Hart (1986) The costs and benefits of ownership: A theory of vertical and lateral integration, *Journal of Political Economy*, 94(4): 691–719.

Groves, T., and J. Ledyard (1977) Optimal allocation of public goods: A solution to the 'free rider' problem, *Econometrica*, 45(4): 783–809.

*Hart, O. and B. Holmström (1987) The theory of contracts, in *Advances in Economic Theory, Fifth World Congress*, ed. T. Bewley, 71–156. Cambridge, MA: Cambridge University Press.

*Hart, O. and J. Moore (1990) Property rights and the nature of the firm, *Journal of Political Economy*, 98(6): 1119–58.

*Hicks, J. (1939) *Value and Capital*. Oxford: Clarendon Press.

*Holmström, B. and R. Myerson (1983) Efficient and durable decision rules with incomplete information, *Econometrica*, 51(6): 1799–1819.

*Hurwicz, L. (1960) Optimality and informational efficiency in resource allocation processes, in *Mathematical Methods in the Social Sciences*, ed. K. Arrow, S. Karlin, and P. Suppes, 27–46. Palo Alto, CA: Stanford University Press.

*Hurwicz, L. (1972) Organizational structures for joint decision-making: A designer's point of view, in *Interorganizational Decision-Making*, ed. M. Tuite, R. Chisholm, and M. Radnor, 37–44. Chicago, IL: Aldine Publishing Co.

Hurwicz, L. (1979a) On allocations attainable through Nash equilibria, *Journal of Economic Theory*, 21(1): 140–65.

Hurwicz, L. (1979b) Outcome functions yielding Walrasian and Lindahl allocations at Nash equilibrium points, *Review of Economic Studies*, 46(2): 217–25.

Hurwicz, L. (1979c) Balanced outcome functions yielding Walrasian and Lindahl allocations at Nash equilibrium points for two or more agents, in *General Equilibrium, Growth, and Trade*, ed. J. Green and J. Scheinkman, 126–36. New York, NY: Academic Press.

---

[26] In particular because of operating costs.

Hurwicz, L. (1987) Inventing new institutions: The design perspective, *American Journal of Agricultural Economics*, 69(2): 395–402.

*Hurwicz, L. (1989) Mechanisms and institutions, in *Economic Institutions in a Dynamic Society: Search for a New Frontier*, ed. T. Shiraishi and S. Tsuru, 87–104. New York, NY: St. Martin's Press.

*Knight, F. (1952) Institutionalism and empiricism in economics, *American Economic Review*, Papers and Proceedings Supplement 42: 45–55.

*Kornai, J. (1986a) The Hungarian reform process: Visions, hopes, and reality, *Journal of Economic Literature*, 24(4): 1687–1737.

*Kornai, J. (1986b) *Contradictions and Dilemmas: Studies on the Socialist Economy and Society*. Cambridge, MA: MIT Press.

*Lagunoff, R. (1988) Fully endogenous mechanism selection and the Coase theorem, mimeo, University of Minnesota. Published as Lagunoff, R. (1992) Fully endogenous mechanism selection on finite outcome sets, *Economic Theory*, 2(4): 465–80.

Maskin, E. (1977) Nash equilibrium and welfare optimality, MIT mimeo. Published as Maskin, E. (1999) Nash equilibrium and welfare optimality, *Review of Economic Studies*, 66(1): 23–38.

Postlewaite, A. and D. Wettstein (1989) Feasible and continuous implementation, *Review of Economic Studies*, 56(4): 603–11.

Reiter, S. and J. Hughes (1981) A preface on modeling the regulated U.S. economy, *Hofstra Law Review*, 9(5): 1381–1421.

*Reiter, S. (1977) Information and performance in the (new) welfare economics, *American Economic Review*, 67(1): 226–34.

*Ruttan, V. (1978) Induced institutional change, in *Induced Innovation: Technology, Institutions, and Development*, ed. H. Binswanger and V. Ruttan, 327–57. Baltimore, MD: Johns Hopkins University Press.

*Ruttan, V. (1984) Social science knowledge and institutional change, *American Journal of Agricultural Economics*, 66(5): 549–59.

Schmeidler, D. (1980) Walrasian analysis via strategic outcome functions, *Econometrica* 48(7): 1585–94.

Schotter, A. (1981) *The Economic Theory of Social Institutions*. Cambridge, MA: Cambridge University Press.

Shapley, L. and M. Shubik (1967) Ownership and the production function, *Quarterly Journal of Economics*, 81(1): 88–111.

Stiglitz, J. (1974) Incentives and risk sharing in sharecropping, *Review of Economics Studies*, 41(2): 219–55.

Walker, M. (1981) A simple incentive compatible scheme for attaining Lindahl allocations, *Econometrica*, 49(1): 65–71.

*Weitzman, M. (1974) Prices vs. quantities, *Review of Economics Studies*, 41(4): 477–91.

Williamson, O. (1975) *Markets and Hierarchies*. New York, NY: The Free Press.

Williamson , O. (1985) *Economic Institutions of Capitalism*. New York, NY: The Free Press.

*This work is relevant to the paper although not specifically cited.

13

Toward a Framework for Analyzing Institutions and Institutional Change

Introduction

In an era of major changes across the globe in economic as well as political institutions, there should be little argument about the need for an analytical framework to help us understand the observed phenomena. In the past, the development of such a framework was obstructed by imperfect communication between 'theorists' and 'institutionalists.' Our objective here is to facilitate communication by integrating institutional phenomena into models that have been developed for the study of economies, voting systems, and organizations. Primarily, we are interested in economic institutions, but certain aspects of the model are general enough to be applicable to political and other social institutions as well. Indeed, these non-economic aspects cannot be ignored, since introduction, implementation, and enforcement of the rules are essential features of the model.

Our point of departure will be the theory of economic mechanisms (formalized, for example, as adjustment processes or game-forms). Although this theory has had a normative orientation, we intend our framework to be usable for descriptive and explanatory analysis as well. We do not share the view that at the present stage, formalization is premature. It seems important to make institutional phenomena amenable to analysis with tools that have resulted in progress in many areas of economics and other social sciences.

Before proceeding with details, let us clarify the intended meaning of the term 'institution.' In common parlance, this term has two distinct meanings.

From *Markets and Democracy: Participation, Accountability and Efficiency*, ed. S. Bowles, H. Gintis, and B. Gustafsson, 51–67. ©1993 Cambridge University Press: Cambridge, MA. Reprinted by permission of Cambridge University Press. The author wishes to express his appreciation for insightful comments to his discussant Gil Skillman, as well as to Samuel Bowles and Herbert Gintis.

Toward a Framework for Analyzing Institutions and Institutional Change In: *The Collected Papers of Leonid Hurwicz Volume 1.* Edited by Samiran Banerjee, Oxford University Press.

To illustrate by example, we refer to such organizational entities as a university, a central bank, an ombudsman's office, or a state as institutions. On the other hand, we also call institutions certain arrangements, rules, or behavior patterns such as private property, marriage, representative democracy, antimonopoly laws, or markets. In this chapter, the term 'institution' is intended to refer to the latter meaning, i.e., an *institutional arrangement*, rather than the former (which can be called an *institutional entity*). Although some writers find the distinction unnecessary, it is useful in the present context.

Institutions (in the sense of institutional arrangements) do play an important role in models of economies or voting systems. The latter often presuppose a representative democracy, while the former, implicitly at least, postulate the existence of certain forms of ownership, markets, or central planning processes. But when it comes to formal treatment, the typical models contain only implications or consequences of the existence of an institution but do not formalize the institution itself. Thus neoclassical models presuppose the existence of markets, and the Arrow-Debreu model, with its profit shares going to consumers, presupposes private ownership of the means of production.[1] A study by Grossman and Hart (1986) explores the implications of ownership for vertical and lateral integration. But the institution of ownership itself is, in my view at least, not formalized in any of these models. However, there are contributions where specific institutions are modeled. An important example is Stiglitz's work (1974) providing a basis for distinguishing such institutions as sharecropping, renting, and wage labor.

We shall approach the concept of an institution by stages, through two intermediate concepts: an adjustment process and a mechanism.[2] This approach takes advantage of our familiarity with an example of an adjustment process, the Walrasian (perfectly competitive)[3] tâtonnement process.[4] Similarly, examples such as second-price auctions and procedures proposed for making decisions concerning public goods (e.g., Groves and Ledyard, pivotal, Groves mechanisms) can be helpful in gaining an insight into the notion of a mechanism.

More fundamentally, we shall be proposing a concept of institution based on that of a mechanism, namely as a particular type of a class of mechanisms. Hence it is essential that a foundation be laid by clarifying the notion of a 'mechanism' and of the closely related (but not identical) concept of an 'adjustment process.' This will be attempted in the next section.

---

1 Indeed, Debreu (1959) uses the label 'private ownership economy'.

2 A warning to the reader: even though the term 'process' is used, we shall largely confine ourselves to its static, i.e., equilibrium, properties.

3 From now on 'competitive' will be understood to mean perfectly competitive, i.e., where prices are treated parametrically.

4 Whose equilibrium is, of course, the perfectly competitive equilibrium configuration of prices and quantities.

Our indirect approach to theorizing about institutions may seem cumbersome, but it enables us to build on an analytical framework whose many properties are already known in considerable detail, and to integrate the theory of institutions with the existing body of theory.

Mechanisms and Adjustment Processes

First, a few words about the need for 'embedding' the notion of a competitive process in a more comprehensive concept. From the *descriptive* point of view, at least since Cournot's time, economics has modeled various *market* phenomena other than perfect competition—including monopoly (single and bilateral) oligopoly, oligopsony, monopolistic competition (with product differentiation and discriminatory pricing), etc. But both in the present-day world and in earlier epochs a variety of *non-market* systems, including government regulation, central planning, and feudalism, have been observed. Hence just for descriptive purposes we need a concept capable of covering these varied structures, and having enough flexibility and generality to accommodate various mixtures as well as new structures that might be observed in the future.

Normative aspects

The need for such a general concept is at least equally evident from a *normative* point of view. Clearly, for normative purposes we want to be able to cover known candidates (in particular, perfect competition) for some notion of optimality, as well as to cover alternative systems (such as central planning) that have been advocated as desirable. But more important, one wants to have a concept that can accommodate economic processes or structures that are potentially superior to those already tried or known. This need becomes especially obvious when we consider some of the well-known normative deficiencies of perfectly competitive equilibria, not to mention dynamic instability.

First, accepting for a moment Pareto optimality as the 'evaluation criterion,' competitive equilibria are guaranteed to exist and be optimal only in a class of *environments* that excludes externalities, indivisibilities, infinite horizons, and increasing returns to scale, i.e., only in *'classical'* environments.[5]

---

[5] A standard interpretation of 'environment' includes the structure of the commodity space, initial endowments, technology, and preferences. The general idea covers those aspects of the economy that cannot be affected by policy or institutional changes.

Yet one wishes to consider whether there might be economic processes that yield optimal outcomes even in 'non-classical' environments.[6]

Second, the Pareto criterion is neither sufficiently specific nor universally accepted as having priority over egalitarian and minimum standards criteria. Greater specificity can be achieved by a social welfare function compatible with Pareto optimality, but we are then faced with the dilemma implied by Arrow's impossibility result. It is at least partly for this reason that a more general vehicle for formulating social desiderata has been developed, here to be called a *goal correspondence*.[7] This set of normative considerations also argues in favor of broadening one's horizon beyond that of the Walrasian process.

Third, the behavior of economic agents implicit in the definition of Walrasian equilibrium is not 'natural' for any agent that is not infinitesimal as compared with the market as a whole, hence not plausible in economies with few agents. While profit and utility-maximization may create an impression that perfectly competitive equilibrium is consistent with selfish motivations, the requirement that prices be treated parametrically means that agents are supposed to ignore, and refrain from using, their 'market power.' Indeed, models of monopoly and oligopoly have been developed to deal more realistically with such situations. It follows that even if perfectly competitive outcomes are desired it is necessary to introduce additional incentive structures to attain such results. The latter point also applies to proposals for marginal cost pricing in economies with increasing returns (Hotelling, Lange, Lerner) where parametric treatment of prices is postulated.

The preceding observations should not be interpreted as detracting from the important, indeed central, role played in economic theory by the Walrasian and Arrow-Debreu models of a perfectly competitive economy. Our point is rather that a broader framework is necessary and that there is a need for a general concept of the economic process. Obviously, this concept must include the market structures (in particular, perfect competition) as well as forms of central planning. It is also clear that there is a great deal of arbitrariness in formulating such a concept.

---

[6] Indivisibilities and increasing returns seem particularly important for economies developing their infrastructures. That detrimental externalities are universally important needs hardly to be pointed out in an era of major concerns with global warming, integrity of the ozone layer, and various forms of pollution. Education and health are among important examples of positive externalities.

[7] We use this term in preference to the more usual 'social choice correspondence', in order to avoid terminological ambiguities associated with the term 'choice.' A *correspondence* is simply a multi-valued, i.e., set-valued, function. A single-valued function is viewed as a special case of a correspondence.

Formulating a Generalized Concept

In constructing a generalized concept, we start by distinguishing two aspects of the economic process: the *rules* governing the process and the *behavior* induced by (or at least compatible with) those rules.

There are two elements typically involved in the specification of the rules: the class of *admissible choices* and an outcome function specifying the outcome produced by the choices made. These choices may be actions or messages (e.g., proposals, bids, production plans, preference revelations), or—in the language of game theory—moves or strategies. The rules may also impose restrictions on the agent's choices given the agent's *characteristic*. Typically, the agent's characteristic is described by its admissible consumption set, its preferences, its initial endowment, and its production possibility set. The *environment*[8] is the configuration of all the agents' characteristics. To complete the description of the economic process we must specify the relation defining agents' choices given the agents' characteristics. (In static models, this relation is called the *equilibrium correspondence*.) This relation is affected by the behavioral properties of the agents and is here called 'behavior' for short. It includes, in particular, the game-theoretic solution concepts such as Nash, dominance, or maximin.

To illustrate: in a typical Walrasian market tâtonnement model, the admissible choices are messages consisting of price and/or quantity proposals; the outcome function accepts the equilibrium quantities proposed; behavior involves maximization (of profit or utility) with prices treated parametrically. (The consumer's preferences and endowments, as well as a firm's production function, i.e., their characteristics, enter into the maximization process.) But in a Hotelling-Lange-Lerner model profit-maximization (or, more generally, marginal cost pricing) is prescribed by the rules, hence is not to be viewed as 'behavior' in the sense of our definition, but rather as a restriction on permissible strategies.

---

[8] A word of explanation for what may seem somewhat artificial terminology used here. Informally, the term 'economy' is used in two meanings that [are] important to distinguish. On the one hand we speak of an economy as defined by properties such as preferences, technology, etc.; for example, we speak of a 'regular' or 'convex' economy. In this sense, the term 'economy' refers to those properties that are to be taken as given in the context of institutional or structural change. To avoid confusion, we use the term 'environment' (originally suggested by Jacob Marschak) as a synonym for this meaning of 'economy.' The other sense in which 'economy' is used is that of the economic system, e.g., a capitalist or a socialist economy, more generally those aspects that are subject to deliberate change. For this meaning of 'economy,' we shall use 'mechanism' as a substitute. Finally, the term 'adjustment process' is meant to encompass the mechanism together with behavior. The observed phenomena are viewed as determined by the three elements: environment, mechanism, and behavior. (Equivalently, by the environment and the adjustment process.) Conventional treatments, in listing their postulates, often fail to distinguish these categories, but for our purposes the distinctions are essential and this explains the terminological devices adopted here.

In a revelation model of public choice with preferences assumed transferable (so that the Pareto optimal level of the public good is uniquely defined by the valuation functions), an agent's admissible choices are statements (claims) about valuation functions; the outcome function picks the level of public good that is Pareto optimal for the claimed (not necessarily true) valuations, and monetary payments defined by the transfer rules (e.g., a Groves mechanism such as the pivotal mechanism). The agent's behavior consists in its choice of the statement (i.e., claimed preferences) given the truth. It is known that, for a Groves mechanism, the agent will in fact choose to tell the truth.

Formalization

At this point it seems desirable to introduce some notation and formalize to some extent the concepts just introduced, confining ourselves to economies with a finite number n of agents. The set of agents is denoted by N. Thus $N = (1, \ldots, n)$. With each agent we associate its characteristic; the characteristic of agent i is denoted by e^i. Typically, e^i is defined by the commodity space, the initial endowment, admissible consumption, set, preferences, and the production possibility correspondence.[9] The environment, denoted by e, is defined as the configuration of the individual characteristics, i.e., $e = (e^1, \ldots, e^n)$. The class of a priori admissible environments is denoted by E. We assume (as is customary, though unrealistic) that it is the Cartesian product of a priori admissible sets of individual characteristics denoted by E^i. That is, $E = E^i \times \cdots \times E^n$. This means that whether a particular individual characteristic is admissible for a given agent is independent of the characteristics of other agents.

We shall denote by C the space of possible choices and by Z the space of conceivable outcomes. In economic models, the space Z typically consists of conceivable (not necessarily feasible) resource allocations, including consumption, input-output vectors, and public goods levels. In political models, the space Z may consist of potential candidates for office or alternative answers in a referendum. The importance of the outcome space lies in the fact that, in normative models, social goals are formulated in terms of what happens in it. For instance, in Arrow's model, the social welfare function has as its domain the environment space[10] E and its value is a social

---

[9] In the absence of externalities on production side, we need only a production possibility set. But when productivity of a unit is affected by the activities of others, the more general concept of a correspondence (suggested by Antonio Camacho, 1970) is appropriate. A similar correspondence might also be required in the presence of certain types of externalities on consumption side, or between production and consumption.

[10] More precisely Arrow's SWF is defined on the space of possible preference profiles, which may be viewed as a sub-space of E.

ordering on the outcome space Z. A more general normative concept is that of a *(social) goal correspondence* (often called social choice correspondence[11]) denoted by F, which associates with a given environment e a subset $F(e)$ of the outcome space Z. The outcomes belonging to the subset $F(e)$ are thought of as F-optimal given the environment e. For example, if $F(\ )$ is the Pareto-correspondence, then $F(e)$ is the set of Pareto optimal outcomes given the feasibility conditions and preferences implicit in e.

An Arrow welfare function f generates a goal correspondence as follows. Let $R^S = f(e)$ be the social ordering for the environment (preference profile implicit in) e. Then the goal correspondence, say F_f, is defined by the relation $F_f(e) =$ the set of feasible outcomes in Z that maximize R^S. Thus a normative approach based on an Arrovian social welfare function can be subsumed under the social goal formulation. The converse, however, is not true because it may be impossible to rationalize the F correspondence in terms of any social choice function f. Hence the social goal correspondence formulation has greater generality. In particular, it can embody various egalitarian and minimum standards criteria, and it need not be compatible with the Pareto criterion.

There are various possible interpretations of what we have called the *choice space C*. In tâtonnement-type (not necessarily Walrasian) models, C may be interpreted as the *message space M*. In game-theoretic models, C may be interpreted as the *strategy space S* or (for games in extensive form) the space of histories of all agents' moves. In any case, the outcome function is defined as a function, denoted by h, from C into Z. That is, it associates a specified outcome with choices made by agents. In the terminology of game theory, the strategy space together with the outcome function, i.e., the pair (S, h), is called a *game-form*.[12] In other literature the game-form is usually identified with the notion of a *mechanism*.

To complete the picture, we must describe the transition from the environment to choices. We do so by introducing the concept of an *equilibrium correspondence* μ, which is a correspondence from the space of environments E into the choice space C. That is, $\mu(e)$ is the set of equilibrium choices that can prevail in the environment e. But what determines the nature of the correspondence μ? The answer depends on the model.

For example, in a game-theoretic model it depends on the solution concept, which we view as a behavioral postulate. Thus if we postulate

---

[11] To repeat an earlier comment, we prefer the term 'goal' to 'choice' as the name of this correspondence because of its clear normative connotation. The term 'choice' might be misinterpreted as referring to actions or decisions.

[12] In everyday language, this might be called a 'game.' But in game theory the term 'game' is reserved for the pair consisting of S and the n 'payoff functions' that are being maximized by the players. To obtain the i-th payoff function, it is necessary to apply the i-th utility function to the outcome function h.

Nash-behavior of the players, then the set $\mu(e)$ consists of Nash-equilibrium strategies given the players' preference profile implicit in e. But with alternative behavioral assumptions this set might represent various Nash-refinements or the dominant strategies, or maximin strategies.

It may, however, be the case that the equilibrium correspondence is constrained by restrictions on strategies. For example, in a Hotelling-Lange-Lerner economy, the enterprise is required to choose an input-output vector resulting in the equalization of output prices and marginal costs (with prices treated parametrically). In an extreme case, the equilibrium correspondence may be totally prescribed by the rules; furthermore, it may be singleton-valued (i.e., equivalent to a function). In the latter case, choice is completely determined by the rules.

We are now in a position to introduce formally the notion of an *adjustment process* as defined by the three entities: the choice space C, the outcome function h, and the equilibrium correspondence μ, i.e., the triple (μ, C, h). Of course, this presupposes the specification of the two underlying spaces, the environment space E and the outcome space Z.[13]

---

13 What we call an 'adjustment process' here is the stationary solution of the dynamic (tâtonnement) version of such a process. (It should be stressed that the term 'tâtonnement' as here used has a much broader scope than Walrasian tâtonnement: it refers to the fact that physical actions such as production or consumption do not take place until the 'dialogue' phase of the process has been terminated—either by a deadline or because equilibrium has been achieved.) Dynamically, the process consists of two phases: the dialogue and transition from dialogue to outcomes. The choices are messages. The i-th agent chooses a message m^i from its *language* M^i. The process constitutes a system of first-order temporally homogeneous difference equations. (This, of course, is a special case, chosen for the sake of simplifying exposition.) The message emitted by agent i at time t is denoted by m_t^i. Each agent has a *response function* f^i which determines the i-th agent's message emitted at time $t + 1$ given the n-tuple m_t of messages emitted by the n agents at time t and the environment e, i.e.,

$$m_{t+1}^i = f^i(m_t, e) \quad i = 1, \ldots, n \text{ and } t = 0, 1, \ldots$$

where $m_t = (m_t^1, \ldots, m_t^n)$.

The process is called *privacy-preserving* if the i-th response function, depends on e^i only; that is, if in the above equation the symbol e can be [replaced] by e^i. *Informational decentralization* can be defined as requiring the privacy-preserving property together with certain other features.

The n-tuple $m = (m^1, \ldots, m^n)$ constitutes a *stationary* (or *equilibrium*) value of the above difference equation system if

$$m^i = f^i(m; e) \quad i = 1, \ldots, n.$$

(When messages belong to an additive group, the preceding equation can also be written as

$$g^i(m; e) = 0^i,$$

where 0^i is the null element of the i-th language, M^i.)

Let $m(e)$ denote the set of stationary values compatible with environment e. Then the correspondence associating with each e in E the set $m(e)$ is the *equilibrium correspondence* (elsewhere denoted by μ). The choice space, elsewhere denoted by C, here is the joint *message space*, i.e., the Cartesian product $M = M^1 \times \cdots \times M^n$. The outcome function h then associates an element z of the outcome space with an equilibrium message m; i.e., $z = h(m)$ where m is a stationary n-tuple.

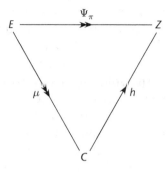

Fig. 1.

Performance, Realization, and Implementation

We now proceed to define the value of the *performance correspondence* Ψ_π of an adjustment process $\pi = (\mu, C, h)$ as the set of equilibrium outcomes associated with an environment e. In set notation, $\Psi_\pi(e) = \{z \in Z: z = h(c)$ for some c satisfying $c = \mu(e)\}$. The situation can be represented diagrammatically by the Mount-Reiter triangle shown in Figure 1.

Clearly, the performance correspondence specifies the possible equilibrium outcomes given the environment. But in addition to its descriptive value it is of central importance in the normative context. Given the environment e, it enables us to compare the outcomes generated by an adjustment process with the desired outcomes defined by a goal correspondence. We say that an adjustment process π *realizes* the goal correspondence F on the class of environments E if the following two conditions are satisfied: (i) an equilibrium exists for every environment in E; and (ii) the outcomes generated by π at e are among those defined as desirable by F. That is: (i) $\mu(e)$ is nonempty for all e in E; (ii) $\Psi_\pi(e)$ is a subset of $F(e)$ for all e in E.[14] Informally, this means that the equilibrium outcomes generated by the process satisfy the F-optimality criterion, and that the existence of equilibrium is guaranteed whenever the environment is within the specified class E, so that the guarantee is non-vacuous.

---

[14] Condition (i) is the requirement of existence of equilibrium, familiar from the theory of competitive equilibrium. The second condition can be illustrated by taking the goal correspondence to be Pareto. In that case condition (ii) requires that all equilibrium outcomes be Pareto optimal, i.e., that the conclusion of the first theorem of welfare economics hold for the given adjustment process. (Occasionally, a stronger requirement is proposed, that $\Psi_\pi(e) = F(e)$ for all e in E. This requirement is so strong that it is not satisfied by the Walrasian adjustment process when F is the Pareto-criterion. On the other hand, requirements (i) and (ii) are satisfied by the Walrasian adjustment process over the set of 'classical' environments, i.e., environments satisfying the familiar assumptions of absence of externalities, of convexity, continuity, etc., as formulated by one of the well-known existence theorems together with a version of the first welfare economics theorem.)

A case of special interest is that of the Nash-equilibrium correspondence $v(\cdot)$. This correspondence is completely determined by the mechanism, i.e., by the game-form (S, h).[15] Therefore, the adjustment process is completely determined by the mechanism and one could ask whether a particular mechanism (rather than the adjustment process it defines) Nash-realizes a given goal correspondence. Following the terminology introduced by Maskin (1977), it is now customary to speak of *Nash-implementation*, rather than Nash-realization. That is, we shall say that a mechanism (S, h) Nash-implements a goal function F over the class E of environments if, for every e in E: (i) there is a Nash-equilibrium strategy; and (ii) every Nash-equilibrium outcome in an environment e is an element of $F(e)$.[16] An analogous terminology is used for other game-solution concepts.[17]

Institutions

In the literature, there are various approaches to the theory of institutions. For our purposes, there are two important, and related, distinctions: (a) endogenously developed versus consciously created (designed), and (b) viewing institutions (in the sense of institutional arrangements rather than entities) as stable behavior patterns versus seeing them as sets of rules governing behavior. There is no doubt that there are many instances of endogenous development of institutions, and ideas such as those of Hayami and Ruttan (1985) concerning demand for institutional change throw light on an important aspect of such phenomena. My own interest is focused to a greater extent on the design of new or modified institutions, but there is no conflict between the two aspects of the process of institutional change. Indeed, when underlying conditions (e.g., technology, tastes, or attitudes) change, this may create a need, and demand, for institutional innovation, and the process of satisfying this demand may involve conscious design activities. Legislation is one example of such a process.

As for the distinction between the rules and behavior pattern interpretations, again, it need not be regarded as implying a contradiction, since behavior is affected, and in certain situations determined, by rules and so likely to remain stable as long as the rules are unchanged. As for semantics,

---

15 Note the equilibrium strategy s^* depends on the environment, i.e., $s^* = v(e)$, since strategies chosen are determined by the players' preferences as well as the game rules represented by S and h. But, of course the equilibrium correspondence $v(\cdot)$ itself does not depend on e.

16 Some writers refer to this concept as 'weak' implementation. The corresponding 'strong' concept requires that the set of equilibrium outcomes possible for a given environment e be equal to $F(e)$.

17 As we shall see, there might be an advantage in reserving the term 'implementation' for a somewhat different concept.

the term 'institution' may be applied either to the rules or to the resulting behavior, the (institution of the) market is an example. But from the point of view of policy choices and design, it seems clear that it is the rules that are susceptible to conscious change, with the behavior changes as a consequence. It is for this reason that we opt for a concept of an institution involving rules rather than behavior patterns.[10]

Within the framework discussed in the earlier sections of this chapter it is tempting to identify a set of rules defining an institution with a mechanism, specifying the set C of admissible choices and the outcome function h associating outcomes z with choices c.[19] In some cases this formulation might be adequate, but in general it is too narrow for the following reason. Suppose we adopt as our model of interactions that of a non-cooperative game with Nash-equilibrium as the solution concept. Suppose we identify an institutional arrangement with a game-form (S, h). Then, given the environment (i.e., specifying individual characteristics such as preferences, production functions, [and] initial endowments), the set of equilibrium strategies is uniquely determined. But in many examples of institutional arrangements, behavior patterns are not uniquely determined by these arrangements.

To illustrate the point: it seems reasonable to think of price controls as an example of an economic institution. But to determine the behavior of economic agents it is not enough to know that there are some price ceilings; one must know their numerical levels. Once such levels have been specified, we may consider that the i-th seller's choice domain C^i has been defined, say, as the numerical interval $[0, k]$ where k is the ceiling price the seller is permitted to charge. Assuming that the other agents' choice domains have also been specified and the outcome function h defined to represent the rules governing market transactions, the Nash-equilibrium set is uniquely determined. But a different Nash-equilibrium set would be obtained if the price ceiling k were chosen at a different level. Yet we would not say that changing the value of k changes the institutional setup: we have price controls regardless of the ceiling level. This leads to the idea that, in this example, the institutional arrangement (price controls) does not involve a particular choice domain but rather a *type of choice domain*, namely a choice domain for sellers which is an interval bounded from above.[20] Now we note

---

[18] To the extent that the two can be clearly distinguished. There may be cases where the dividing line is quite ambiguous.

[19] We recall that a mechanism (also called a game-form) is defined as the pair (C, h), where C is the space of choices and h a function from C into the outcome space Z, so that $z = h(c)$. In the game context, $C = S = S^i \times \cdots \times S^n$; here S is the ('joint') strategy space, assumed to be the Cartesian product of (independent) individual strategy spaces S^i.

[20] While in the absence of price ceilings that choice domain may be thought of as the infinite half-line $(0, \infty)$.

that when only the *type* of choice domain is specified, we wind up not with a single mechanism but a whole *family of mechanisms*.[21]

While the price control example identifies an economic institution with a family of choice domains, there are also examples of economic institutions that can be identified with a *type of outcome function*. As an illustration, we borrow a model from Stiglitz (1974); this paper considers the reward of a person working the land belonging to someone else. The reward (which we interpret as the outcome for the worker) is given by the formula

$$r = ay + b,$$

where r is the reward, y the worker's output (or, perhaps, value added), while a and b are real numbers. Three institutional arrangements are defined by selecting certain sets of values for the parameters a and b. Thus the worker is a sharecropper if $b = 0$ while a is a number between zero and one. The worker is on wages if $a = 0$ while b is some positive number; he/she is a renter if $a = 1$ while b is some negative number. Now to specify uniquely, it is necessary to specify the outcome function,[22] i.e., the numerical values of the two parameters. But we note that each of the three economic institutions (sharecropping, wage labor, renting) is identified with a range of values for one of the two parameters, i.e., with a set of points in the (a, b)-plane, not a single such point. This means that each institution is identified not with a single outcome function but with a family of outcome functions, hence—as in the price control example—with a *family of mechanisms*. It is important to note that other sets of points in the (a, b) plane might define either entirely new institutions or mixtures of the three ones previously described.

It is not difficult to think of other examples of institutions which are identified with a type of choice domain and a type of outcome function, where neither the choice domains nor the outcome function are uniquely defined. This, then, leads to the concept of an *institution as a family of mechanisms*, rather than a single mechanism.[23] But, of course, not every family of mechanisms is an institution.

We have seen in the preceding examples that a convenient way of identifying an institution with a family of mechanisms is to consider it as restricting the type of mechanism that is admissible. It is a rule about rules. This

---

[21] This would be true even if the institutional arrangement were characterized by a unique outcome function.

[22] As well as the choice domains.

[23] The term 'family' is used here as a synonym for 'set.' A one-element set (a singleton) is a legitimate special case. Hence, we are not saying that an institution can never be identified with a single mechanism, but rather that, in general, it is more natural to identify it with a set consisting of many (perhaps an infinity of) mechanisms.

means specifying which type of choice domain or of outcome function is admissible. But there are various possible sources of inadmissibility. The most obvious is physical impossibility. Obviously, restrictions due to the laws of physics would not be viewed as institutional. Only those restrictions that are due to human actions or behavior patterns are candidates for institutional interpretation, but not even all of these.[24]

It was mentioned earlier that the legislative process is a source of new or modified institutions. An example would be a law introducing price controls. Here the institution introduced is a system of price controls, and the human action generating it is the legislative process culminating in the price control law being passed. This pattern suggests a paradigm for modeling institutional change as a two-phase phenomenon. In the first phase, the institution is formed (in our example, by legislative act). But this does not uniquely specify the mechanism. For that to occur, the specific price ceilings (as well as a variety of regulatory details) must be decreed.[25,26] Typically, that will be done by an agency—either an existing one or one created for this special purpose, such as the US Second World War Office of Price Administration (OPA).[27]

Such process of institutional change can be modeled in various ways. Indeed, there are several possibilities even within the framework of game theory. The route adopted in a pioneering paper by Reiter and Hughes (1981) is that of a sequence of two games, the first corresponding to the legislative stage and the second to the regulatory stage.[28] But there is an alternative, so far not yet explored in detail, of regarding the phases as stages in a single game in extensive form. Here, again, the early stages of such a game would result in restrictions on the nature of the mechanism to be crystallized in the later stages.[29]

---

[24] There may be restrictions other than physical (or physiological) on the admissibility of mechanisms that would not qualify for institutional interpretation. Instinctive aversions or inclinations to certain actions as well as psychological factors may play a role analogous to physics in excluding or compelling certain choices.

[25] The term 'implementation' would seem appropriate for this phase of the process.

[26] The economic process (trading, production, etc.) might be a third game in this sequence, but neither it nor the second stage (the transition to a unique mechanism) would constitute a part of institution formation process.

[27] This example illustrates an important phenomenon, namely, that in order that an institutional arrangement (here price control) become effective, it may be necessary to create an institutional entity (here the OPA) whose mission is to implement (in the ordinary, not game-theoretic, sense of this word) the institutional rules. Thus there is an intimate relationship between institutions in the 'arrangements' and 'entity' senses.

[28] The two stages in the Reiter-Hughes model do not correspond precisely to the two phases of our example. It may also be noted that in their model, the first game is cooperative, the second non-cooperative.

[29] Some aspects of the extensive form approach are discussed in Hurwicz (1987). The extensive form approach provides a natural framework for introducing the informational aspects of the institution formation process. The extensive game model involves a sequence of moves some of which are actions producing outcomes (e.g., transaction costs) before the game is completed, while others are in the nature of messages (e.g., proposals). From the economist's viewpoint, this

A different view, in the nature of a generalization of the Reiter-Hughes approach, is to view the process of institutional change as a (finite) sequence of games, say $1, 2, \ldots, T$, where for $t = 1, \ldots, T - 1$ the outcome function specifies, in increasing detail, the rules for game $t + 1$. Then the T-game determines the 'substantive' outcome, e.g., resource allocation, or who gets elected (while the earlier games only determine the electoral rules). As an illustration, game 1 might result in formulating the country's constitution, games $2, \ldots, t - 2$ legislation, and $t - 1$ the rules specified by a regulatory agency. We may think of such a sequence as a *cascade* of games.

Suppose that we have designed a mechanism that Nash-implements (in the sense of the above technical definition) a given goal correspondence, and that the mechanism has been adopted. This implies that any Nash-equilibrium outcome is consistent with the stated goals and, furthermore, that equilibria do exist. Leaving aside the problem of dynamics, are we now entitled to expect the desired equilibria to prevail? Clearly, this depends on what is meant by the mechanism being 'adopted.' In the most favorable circumstances, one could imagine that all players are willing to stay within the prescribed choice (strategy) domains and that there is a procedure for making the outcome function effective. It is then correct to say (as is often said) that a Nash-equilibrium is 'self-enforcing.' The meaning of 'self-enforcing' in this context is interpreted as implying that there is no need for external policing because (by definition of a Nash-equilibrium) no player has an incentive to depart from his/her equilibrium strategy given the others' choices.[30]

But rules implicit in an institutional arrangement are not necessarily internalized by the player. Also, there are problems with putting an outcome function into effect, unless one can expect players to volunteer monetary transfers, paying fines, etc. Taking these problems into account, Schotter (1981, p. 11) proposes the following definition of a social institution:

> A social institution is a regularity in social behavior that is agreed to by all members of society, specifies behavior in recurrent situations, and is either self-policed or policed by some external authority.

---

is a mixture of tâtonnement and non-tâtonnement. (In another context, a suggestion for such a mixed model was put forward some years ago by Tom Marschak.)

Interim outcomes (i.e., outcomes produced before the completion of the game), especially transaction costs, play an important role in modern 'institutionalist' theory (see Williamson, 1985). They are also implicit in the informational theory of message exchange adjustment processes, where requirements such as the privacy-preserving property or limits on complexity may be attributed, in part at least, to communication or computation costs.

[30] This may sound like a tautology, but I prefer to interpret it as a behavioral assumption (that players do not unilaterally depart from their Nash-equilibrium strategies).

Although not all elements of this definition are in agreement with ours,[31] Schotter's concept is valuable for its stress on the enforcement (policing) aspect.

The problem of modeling the enforcement aspect of an institutional arrangement presents some conceptual difficulties. Elsewhere (Hurwicz, 1989) we have suggested a possible approach, involving an *'augmented game-form.'* To enforce a given (not self-policing) mechanism we introduce additional players, whose mission is to perform the policing functions. These additional players may be either physical persons or institutional entities (courts, police, ombudsmen, etc.). These additional players must be given appropriate incentives to perform their mission. Thus we have designed a game including both the original players (e.g., the traders or other economic agents) and the additional ones, and the situation thus created is viewed as the augmented game. This game must have a game-form (i.e., a governing mechanism) which, inter alia, prescribes the choice domains and outcomes for the additional players. The hope, of course, is that the equilibrium outcomes of the augmented game agree with the goal function which was being Nash-implemented by the mechanism designed for the original players (e.g., the traders).

But two problems arise. First, even if the new players abide by the rules of the augmented mechanism, the enforcement system calls for the use of social resources. This limits resources remaining for the satisfaction of the original goal function, e.g., production of food. Consequently, the resulting outcome cannot be Pareto optimal with regard to the total endowment.[32] Hence it becomes necessary to reformulate the goal criteria taking into account the costs of 'operating the system.' Some ideas along these lines were introduced in Hurwicz (1972a, 1972b).

But, again, why should one expect that the enforcers will be carrying out their missions rather than, say, trying to enrich themselves through corrupt activities? There is no more reason to expect the augmented mechanism to be self-enforcing than the original one. One way to view the problem is to think of the 'natural' game-form which includes not only the permitted choices but all those that are physically or psychologically possible for the participants, and where the 'natural' outcome function simply reflects the

---

[31] In particular, our concept is formulated in terms of rules governing behavior rather than the behavior itself. Also, to require the agreement on the part of *all* members of society seems too strong.

The requirement that an institutional arrangement apply to specific recurrent situations can perhaps be put in a more general form, namely that the institutional rules apply to a category of situations rather than to a particular one. (This excludes a 'bill of attainder' type of rule.) We shall call this property of rules 'categoricity,' and regard recurrence as a special case.

[32] The same issue arises with regard to costs of communication, other information processing, or other 'transaction costs.' This includes the costs of operating markets as well as those of a central planning bureaucracy.

necessary effects of actions taken. Thus one does not postulate an outcome function which automatically results in a fine being paid by a transgressor but rather describes the actions of all the participants (including the police, courts, etc.) that would have to be taken in order that the transgressor actually be made to pay the fine, or a lottery winner to collect his/her prize.

Needless to say, conceiving or announcing institutional modifications will not necessarily result in the desired behavior. The difficulties encountered in criminal law enforcement (e.g., drug interdiction) in various parts of the world is one obvious example. The obstacle to economic reform in various communist countries is another. How can analysis deal with this issue?

One possible approach is to consider in some detail the first phase of the institutional change process discussed above. If we view this phase as a game (whether cooperative or not), it seems appropriate that the outcomes of this game (i.e., what the players care about) be the institutional rules to be adopted. For a given institutional change to be adopted it is necessary that there be players who desire that particular institutional change, and secondly that they have the means to prevail. We may refer to these means as 'assets.' An example might be the role played by the international institutions (e.g., IMF or World Bank) desiring changes away from command centralized planning systems and subsidies, and which possess financial assets helping them prevail. But our interpretation of the term 'assets' in this context is broader: it may involve political power or even personal charisma. It is convenient to have a term referring to players with both a desire and assets for effecting institutional change; they may be called 'intervenors.' An intervenor may be an individual, an institutional entity, an organization, a social class, or even an unorganized human mass. Recent events provide examples of all these types. When the intervenors' assets are strong enough as compared with those of the opponents, institutional change is likely to occur. The existence of a 'demand' for institutional innovation will, of course, increase the probability of the intervenors' success.

The intervenors' role is not confined to the first phase, that of effecting institutional change. We have noted that in the augmented game there is a possibility that, due to the failure of the enforcement system, the equilibrium outcome will not be the intended one. By joining the augmented game and using their assets, the intervenors may be able to see to it that the enforcement system works as intended.[33]

---

[33] An interesting example of an intervenor is an experimenter testing, e.g., alternative hypotheses concerning the likely behavior of economic agents in game situations. The experimenter prescribes rules of the game. It is important for the experimenter that the human subjects abide by the rules of the game (otherwise the experimental results lose validity) and he/she presumably has the means ('assets') to make certain that they do—for instance, by being able to control their communications and actions, as well as motivating them by monetary rewards or other methods.

A few further remarks concerning the role of the intervenor in my model may be helpful here. First, although there may be some relationship between the role of an intervenor and of what some have called a 'political entrepreneur,' I do not identify the two. This is especially clear when we think of the intervenor as participating in the enforcement (as distinct from the institutional innovation) process.

Second, why introduce the intervenor into the model at all? One possible answer: that it seems to be a realistic element of many observed phenomena of institutional change and of enforcement. It may also help explain why certain reform efforts change—either through lack of adequate 'assets' on the part of would-be reformers, or due to lack of clarity or intensity in their preferences for the relevant institutions.

It seems less controversial that a presence of successful intervenors is helpful in effecting change and/or maintaining institutions. The question is whether it is necessary to have such intervenors. On [the side of preferences], the issue is whether in the cascade of games suggested above it is necessary to have players in game t whose preferences are defined on the space of rules for game $t + 1$ and/or subsequent games (rather than some discounted expected payoffs in the substantive game T). The presence of such preferences may be characterized as ideology, extended sympathy, or by treating rule outcomes as proxy variables for the final expected substantive outcomes. Whether, or under what circumstances, such phenomena are essential in models of institutional innovation and maintenance seems to me still an open question.

Finally, a comment concerning the possible application of existing results from the theory of adjustment processes and mechanisms to the institution formation problems discussed here.

First, the relevance of adjustment process results for mechanism theory. These results are mostly to be viewed as informational possibility and impossibility findings. In particular, there are interesting results showing that finite-dimensional spaces are inadequate in economies with non-convexities (e.g., increasing returns) and infinite horizons (Hurwicz, 1972a; Calsamiglia, 1977; Hurwicz and Weinberger, 1990). If no finite-dimensional adjustment process of the required type exists, it follows that no such mechanism exists. In general, negative results in adjustment process theory carry over to mechanism theory, and indirectly also apply to institutions. On the other hand, the fact that a certain type of adjustment process is possible does not imply the feasibility of a corresponding mechanism, since the adjustment process may be postulating behavior inconsistent with the agents' incentives. However, such positive results are not without value for mechanism design in that they suggest directions in which appropriate mechanisms can be sought.

A similar relationship exists between results in mechanism design and those in institutional theory. Negative results in mechanism theory carry over into institutional theory, positive results are suggestive but inconclusive. This may be so because a desirable mechanism may be either impossible to put into operation, or so costly in resources for enforcement and implementation that its net efficiency is lower than that of alternative mechanisms whose 'gross' efficiency is higher. Aside from these purely economic considerations, even efficient operation may be undesirable in terms of ethics, human rights, or other social and political consequences.

References

Calsamiglia, X. (1977) Decentralized resource allocation and increasing returns, *Journal of Economic Theory*, 14(2): 263–83.

Camacho, A. (1970) Externalities, optimality and informationally decentralized resource allocation processes, *International Economic Review*, 11(2): 318–27.

Debreu, G. (1959) *Theory of Value*. New Haven, CT: Yale University Press.

Grossman, S. and O. Hart (1986) The costs and benefits of ownership: A theory of vertical and lateral integration, *Journal of Political Economy*, 94(4): 691–719.

Hayami, Y. and V. Ruttan (1985) *Agricultural Development: An International Perspective*. Baltimore, MD: Johns Hopkins University Press.

Hurwicz, L. (1972a) On informationally decentralized systems, in *Decision and Organization*, ed. C. McGuire and R. Radner, Amsterdam: North-Holland. Second edition, 1986, 297–336. Minneapolis, MN: University of Minnesota Press.

Hurwicz, L. (1972b) Organizational structures for joint decision-making: A designer's point of view, in *Interorganizational Decision-Making*, ed. M. Tuite, R. Chisholm, and M. Radnor, 37–44. Chicago, IL: Aldine Publishing Co.

Hurwicz, L. (1987) Inventing new institutions: The design perspective, *American Journal of Agricultural Economics*, 69(2): 395–402.

Hurwicz, L. (1989) On modeling institutions, Universitat Autònoma de Barcelona, mimeo. Reprinted as Chapter 12, this volume.

Hurwicz, L. and H. Weinberger (1990) A necessary condition for decentralization and an application to intertemporal allocation, *Journal of Economic Theory*, 15(2): 313–45.

Maskin, E. (1977) Nash equilibrium and welfare optimality, mimeo. Published as Maskin, E. (1999) Nash equilibrium and welfare optimality, *Review of Economic Studies*, 66: 23–38.

Reiter, S. and J. Hughes (1981) A Preface on modeling the regulated US economy, *Hofstra Law Review*, 9(5): 1381–1421.

Schotter, A. (1981) *The Economic Theory of Social Institutions*. Cambridge, MA: Cambridge University Press.

Stiglitz, J. (1974) Incentives and risk sharing in sharecropping, *Review of Economics Studies*, 41(2): 219–55.

Williamson, O. (1985) *Economic Institutions of Capitalism*. New York, NY: The Free Press.

14

Economic Design, Adjustment Processes, Mechanisms, and Institutions

First of all, a word of deep appreciation for the title [of Honorary Editor] bestowed upon me by the editors and publishers of *Economic Design*, an honor I shall always treasure. I have accepted it not just on my own behalf, but also for the outstanding group of researchers whose accomplishments have amply justified Murat Sertel's initiative in creating this journal. Second, a warning and an apology for a highly subjective perspective of this essay. My aim is not to be encyclopedic nor to apportion merit, but merely to share my personal view and recollections of some of the developments. No doubt I give disproportionate weight to those whose contributions have influenced me most.

The name *Economic Design* is, I think we all agree, much narrower than the scope of research to be covered. To begin with, it is not just about design, if by design we mean a conscious creation of a model of a new mechanism. Although I may be responsible for having spoken of 'the designer's point of view', and of 'the design of resource allocation mechanisms', my thought was to stress that there was room and need for an approach where the mechanism was the *unknown of the problem* rather than a given. That is, of course, the case when we try to design a mechanism to some specifications, but not only there.

In fact, the stimulus that originally led to design issues was much more limited. It was Koopmans's emphasis[1] on the decentralization aspect of his resource allocation 'game'[2] with its custodians, managers, and a helmsman.

Reprinted from *Economic Design*, 1994, 1(1): 1–14.

[1] See Koopmans (1951), p. 93ff. Among other important influences for me was the collaboration with Kenneth Arrow on decentralization and computation in resource allocation, as well as the theory of teams developed by Jacob Marschak and Roy Radner (1972).

[2] I use quotation marks because, although Koopmans called it 'our allocation game', what he had (yes!) designed was not a game in the technical sense of the term. In fact, in view of its

Economic Design, Adjustment Processes, Mechanisms, and Institutions In: *The Collected Papers of Leonid Hurwicz Volume 1*. Edited by Samiran Banerjee, Oxford University Press.
© Oxford University Press 2022. DOI: 10.1093/oso/9780199313280.003.0014

Intuitively, it seemed clear that this 'game' deserved to be called decentralized, but a formal concept of decentralization was not introduced. His comments made clear that decentralization involved dispersion of information among the decision-makers, specifically where the knowledge of input-output coefficients for a particular activity is available only to the individual who determines the level of that activity. Thus decentralization was an informational feature, closely related to Hayek's characterization of the advantages of market processes[3] and, indeed, a lineal descendant of the debates in the 1930s with Mises, Hayek, Lange, and Lerner concerning market socialism. But to provide a rigorous definition of decentralization, it was necessary to define a class of objects, including—but not necessarily limited to—Koopmans's 'game', tâtonnement in competitive markets and central planning in command economies, that might or might not qualify as (informationally) decentralized. Only then could one determine whether, say, the allocation 'game' designed by Koopmans was in some sense the best possible decentralized one in such a class.

Adjustment Processes

An attempt in that direction was the definition of an *adjustment process*. Such a process was defined by a system of difference equations in which the participants exchanged informational messages or orders and which resulted in decisions about actions to be taken. Each participant had a *language* M^i, not necessarily quantitative, from which he/she could draw messages. If there were n participants, each period of time t produced an n-tuple $m(t) = \langle m^1(t), ..., m^n(t) \rangle$ of messages. In a simple first-order model, the response by the i-th participant in the next time period was determined by the difference equation

$$m^i(t+1) = f_t^i(m(t), e), \tag{1}$$

where e represents the (economic) *environment*[4] and f_t^i is called a *response function*. Once the process reached a terminal time message n-tuple $m(T)$ or (for temporally homogeneous processes) a stationary value m^*, an *outcome function* $h(\cdot)$, whose argument is the n-tuple $m(T)$ or m^* prescribes the

dynamic features and prescriptions for the behavior of the participants which left little if any room for strategic behavior, it would qualify as what had later been called an *adjustment process*.

3 See Hayek (1945).

4 The environment is defined by the endowments, production possibility sets, and preferences. The term 'environment' was used instead of the more common 'economy' because the latter term is often applied to a mechanism (e.g., a socialist economy). Our purpose was to avoid the ambiguity between the (given) data (endowments, etc.) and the unknown of the problem, viz., the mechanism.

outcome $z = h(m)$, e.g., the resulting resource allocation. Thus an *adjustment process* is defined by the ordered triple $\langle M, f, h \rangle$ where M is the set of individual languages, f the set of response functions, and h the outcome function. It is now possible to define a subclass of adjustment processes that qualify as decentralized. A somewhat broader class was that of *privacy-preserving*[5] processes where the i-th response function $f^i = (f^i_t)$, $t = 1, 2, \ldots$, depends only on the i-th component of $e = (e^1, \ldots, e^n)$, i.e., on the i-th person's own characteristic[6] only. Thus (1) becomes

$$m^i(t+1) = f^i_t(m(t), e^i). \tag{2}$$

Since much classical microeconomics was focused on statics, a static version of the above model came to be given particular attention. Assuming that the response functions do not vary over time, the subscript t attached to the response functions may be omitted. A *stationary message n-tuple* $m^* = (m^{*1}, \ldots, m^{*n})$ for the process is then defined by

$$m^{*i} = f^i(m^*, e^i), \qquad i = 1, \ldots, n, \tag{3}$$

which, with $f = (f^1, \ldots, f^n)$, can be written as

$$m^* = f(m^*, e).^7 \tag{4}$$

If we further assume that the n-tuples m are elements of an additive (Abelian) group,[8] we obtain the usual equilibrium condition

$$g^i(m^*, e^i) = 0 \qquad i = 1, \ldots, n, \tag{5}$$

or

$$g(m^*, e) = 0.^9 \tag{6}$$

It is important to keep in mind that these static relations do not represent a method of finding equilibria but rather what has been called a *verification*

---

[5] The definition of (informational) decentralization involved other restrictions, in addition to the privacy-preserving property.

[6] In resource allocation models the i-th characteristic is given by the i-th person's endowment, production possibility correspondence, consumption set and preference relation. (Externalities are not excluded.)

[7] In (4) it is understood that each component f^i of f depends only on the corresponding component e^i of e.

[8] So that they can be added and subtracted in the usual ways. They need not be elements of a vector space. In particular, they might only admit integer-valued sequences of entries (i.e., indivisibilities).

[9] The symbol 0 in the right hand side of (6) represents the identity element of addition for the group. Again, in (6) it is understood that each component g^i of g depends only on e^i.

scenario, i.e., a procedure where a candidate m^* for a stationary value is being tested and each participant is asked to indicate whether his/her component condition (the *i*-th relation in (3) or in (5)) is satisfied. Equilibrium is present if and only if each participant responds in the affirmative. The privacy-preserving (hence, informational decentralization) property consists in the fact that, to respond, it is sufficient for each participant to know his/her own characteristic e^i (as well as the equilibrium function g^i which is part of the adjustment process, i.e., in the nature of the 'rules of the game'). It is not necessary to know the others' characteristics.

Once the concepts of an adjustment process and informational decentralization were defined, it became possible to ask certain questions going beyond those concerning the Pareto optimality properties of Walrasian equilibria in classical environments. First, is it possible, while staying in classical[10] environments and retaining the optimality properties, to find decentralized mechanisms that are informationally superior[11] to Walrasian tâtonnement? Second, are there decentralized processes with the optimality properties valid over classes of environments broader than classical—e.g., with indivisibilities, non-convexities, etc.—and if so, what is the tradeoff in terms of information processing costs? Third, are there decentralized processes whose performance satisfies criteria of optimality other than Paretian—e.g., fairness—and, again, what of the informational cost tradeoff?

A great deal of subsequent research established the precise nature of the informational 'price' (in terms of the minimum size of dimension of the message space[12])to be paid for the optimality properties. In particular, it was shown[13] that among processes guaranteeing the Pareto optimality of outcomes in classical environments was a version of the Walrasian process using a message space of minimal dimension, thus providing an answer to the first question. But, unfortunately, it also turned out[14] that in non-classical (in particular, non-convex) environments an infinite-dimensional message space was needed to guarantee Pareto optimal outcomes.[15]

The second question posed was whether there were decentralized processes sharing with Walrasian tâtonnement the desirable (static) properties embodied in the classic theorems of welfare economics in classical environments—but (unlike the Walrasian) performing optimally in non-classical as well

---

[10] *Classical environments* are those having the properties usually assumed in the welfare and existence theorems for Walrasian equilibria, such as absence of externalities, perfect divisibility of commodities, convexity and continuity of preferences and production relations, etc.

[11] Or involving lower information processing (transaction) costs.

[12] When the response functions were assumed to have certain continuity or smoothness properties.

[13] Mount and Reiter (1974); Osana (1978).

[14] Calsamiglia (1977).

[15] Which throws some light on the known difficulties with marginal cost pricing.

as classical environments. A partial answer, initially quite surprising, was obtained by designing an adjustment process (called the 'greed process') which turned out to have the desired performance properties in a wide class of environments, free of externalities but possibly having indivisibilities, non-convexities, and discontinuities. This universality of coverage was, however, achieved at very high informational cost. It was clear that the problem of design involved tradeoff between performance (e.g., the Pareto optimality of equilibrium allocations) and informational cost, be it the cost of communication (as measured by the size or dimension of the message space) or the complexity of response rules.

A further line of research involving Reiter and Saari has broadened the field of investigation by seeking algorithms[16] that would yield processes (or more precisely, verification scenarios) *realizing* a given goal function f (or, more generally, a correspondence F) over a given class E of environments such that, for every e in E, the outcome associated with any equilibrium message equals the desired value, i.e., $h(m^*(e)) = f(e)$ for all e in E.[17] Mechanisms with stochastic components have been studied by Radner and Reiter, and problems of approximate realization in discrete message spaces by T. Marschak (1986). Jordan (1987) and Mount and Reiter (1987) have investigated the informational requirements for stable processes.

Mechanisms

One serious limitation of the adjustment process concept was that the participants' behavior was prescribed (by the response functions) rather than freely chosen by the participants on the basis of their preferences and strategic considerations. This feature was inherited from the customary analytical approach in microeconomics, where the agents' behavior is also prescribed—although we tend to be less aware of this fact because these behavioral assumptions are incorporated into the definitions of equilibria. Thus Walrasian equilibrium postulates the parametric treatment of prices, profit maximization by firms, and satisfaction maximization, subject to budgets, by households. These elements of the definition are in fact assumptions prescribing at least certain aspects[18] of behavior.

---

[16] E.g., by techniques using integrability, differential ideals (Saari 1984) or procedures inspired by geometry such as the 'method of rectangles'.

[17] This concept of 'realization' is analogous to that of 'implementation' discussed below, except that it applies to adjustment processes rather than to mechanisms (game-forms). It broadens the class of desirability criteria beyond those traditionally considered in economics, such as Pareto optimality.

[18] The assumptions deal only with the static aspects of the response rules and leave open their dynamic properties (e.g., velocities of adjustment).

An illustration of a different type is provided by the marginal cost pricing proposals. Here the normative aspect is quite evident, since the proposal requires the managers to operate at levels where the resulting marginal cost equals the price of the product. This example is of historical interest because it is one of the earliest processes specifically "designed" to assure efficiency of performance in non-classical[19] environments.

The issue of possible strategic behavior on the part of economic agents was brought out with particular force by Samuelson's (1954, 1955) critique of the Lindahl solution[20] for economies with public goods. In addition to stressing the likelihood of misrepresentation of preferences, Samuelson stated that similar difficulties (the 'free rider' problem) would befall any other 'decentralized' solution, although the precise meaning of the term 'decentralized' was not spelled out. It became obvious that the adjustment process concept would not be adequate to deal with this type of problem. On the other hand, a game model was a 'natural'. Since the game was non-cooperative, a Nash equilibrium seemed an appropriate solution concept, and since the problem was that of misrepresentation of preferences, the appropriate strategy domain for each player was a class of preference relations including not only the truth but also preference relations with lower marginal rates of substitution, representing less eagerness for the services of the public good. I.e., the Lindahl rules defined a game of 'direct revelation'. Samuelson's assertion amounted to the claim that, under the Lindahl rules of the game, truth telling would not be a Nash equilibrium.

As it turned out, the phenomenon was much broader than the 'free rider' economies with public goods. According to a theorem proved subsequently, if truth telling is a Nash equilibrium in a game of direct revelation, it follows that it is also a dominance equilibrium. I.e., if in a direct revelation game universal truth telling is a Nash equilibrium, then for any player truth telling is an optimal strategy regardless of whether others are telling the truth or not. But that is asking for a lot! In fact in turned out that, in general, there are no truth telling equilibria in direct revelation games in economies with public goods, but that similar failures occur in private goods exchange economies with a finite number of players—if the rules are so designed that truth telling would result in Pareto optimal individually rational outcomes. Subsequently it was shown that, generically, there is a conflict between truth telling (or, more generally, dominance) equilibria and Pareto optimality.[21]

---

[19] Specifically, for firms exhibiting increasing returns to scale (hence non-convexity) of the production possibility set) where Walrasian equilibrium is impossible.

[20] A 'designed' mechanism.

[21] It should be noted that there are those who would invoke the revelation principle to argue that this is not a serious problem because any outcome obtainable at a Nash equilibrium of an arbitrary mechanism can also be obtained as an equilibrium outcome of a revelation game.

A way out was offered by Groves and Ledyard (1977) who designed a game—more precisely a mechanism[22] or game-form—that was not of the direct revelation type but guaranteed the Pareto optimality of Nash equilibrium outcomes in economies with public goods. Although the equilibrium outcomes produced by this mechanism were not Lindahl, in fact not individually rational, they paved the way for the design of other mechanisms that did produce all Lindahl (and no other) outcomes in economies with public goods, as well as mechanisms producing all Walrasian (and no other) outcomes in private goods exchange economies,[23] hence in both cases Pareto optimal and individually rational.

The emphasis on the Pareto criterion (PO) in early mechanism design attempts is hardly surprising in view of the role the criterion has played in much of welfare economics since the 1930s. Indeed the two classical theorems of welfare economics refer to no other. But another postulate, satisfied both by the Walrasian and Lindahl allocations, that of individual rationality (IR), was perhaps often taken for granted. However, distributional considerations might argue in favor of allocations that, while satisfying the PO and IR criteria, differ from Walrasian (resp. Lindahl). In fact, the second theorem of welfare economics might create an expectation that such alternatives would be possible to attain, for instance by suitable fiscal measures. On the other hand, frequent (theoretical) resort to lump sum taxes and subsidies might induce a certain level of skepticism. It was natural, therefore to ask whether mechanisms can be designed that would produce Nash

However, the 'revelation' may involve not only one's own preferences but also those of others (as in Maskin's preference profile messages, see Postlewaite and Schmeidler 1987), and also some additional device (perhaps a persuasive argument or an integer component in the strategic message) for eliminating unwanted (non-truthful) equilibria that might also be present. (But see Jackson 1989 on the use of integers.) Whether this can be accomplished without destroying the dominance nature of equilibria may be an open question. On the issue of manipulation, see Thomson (1987).

[22] A *game* is defined by an assignment of a *strategy domain* S^i and of a payoff function $\pi^i : S \to \mathbb{R}$ each player. Here S is the joint strategy space of the individual players, i.e., the Cartesian product $S = S^1 \times \cdots \times S^n$ when there are n players. $\mathbb{R}$ denotes the space of real numbers. The value of $\pi^i(s^1, \ldots, s^n)$ is interpreted as the utility level experienced by player i when the players choose respectively the strategies $s^1, \ldots, s^n$. On the other hand, a *mechanism* (game-form), representing the *rules of the game*, is defined by the n strategy domains S^i together with the *outcome function* $h : S \to Z$ where Z is the outcome space, e.g., the space of resource allocations. (Thus the outcome function specifies the physical consequences of the chosen strategies, but not the feelings of the participants.) This is, of course, a close relationship between a game and the underlying mechanism. Let $u^i : Z \to \mathbb{R}$ denote the utility function of the i-th player. Then the i-th payoff function is the composition of the utility function with the outcome function. I.e., $\pi^i(s^1, \ldots, s^n) = u^i(h(s^1, \ldots, s^n))$. It is worth noting that in informal language the term 'game' is used in the sense of a mechanism (i.e., rules of the game) rather than of a game in the above technical sense.

[23] First constructed by Schmeidler (1976, 1982). But note that even though the outcomes were Walrasian (resp. Lindahl), the mechanisms that produced such equilibria were not of the Walrasian tâtonnement (resp. Lindahl revelation process) type.

equilibrium allocations other than Walrasian (resp. Lindahl) satisfying the PO and IR.[24] Rather surprisingly, the answer—subject to certain restrictions—turned out to be negative. More precisely, subject only to a continuity condition, if a mechanism guarantees that all Nash equilibrium outcomes will be PO and IR, then every Walrasian[25] (resp. Lindahl) allocation will be among the equilibrium allocations.[26] Thus, in particular, if there is a unique Nash equilibrium for an economy in which a unique Walrasian equilibrium exists, such a mechanism will produce the Walrasian allocation only, making any redistribution infeasible except by violating either Pareto optimality or individual rationality.

These facts open two more general questions: (i) which allocations are at all attainable as Nash equilibria, and (ii) does it make a difference if, instead of accepting all Nash equilibria, one limits oneself to some of their refinements? As for the second question, it has been shown[27] that few limitations remain if we confine ourselves to either subgame perfect or undominated Nash equilibria. However, the proofs are accomplished by the use of mechanisms with hugely expanded strategy spaces, i.e., at serious informational costs. It is not clear to me whether this tradeoff is unavoidable.

To formulate precisely the first question, we first note that (as illustrated by the PO and IR criteria) the desirability of an allocation depends on the environment.[28] This dependence is represented by a *desirability correspondence*,[29] denoted by F, specifying the set $F(e)$ of desirable outcomes when the environment e prevails. On the other hand, given a mechanism (S, h), the set of Nash equilibrium outcomes it produces also depends on the environment. Hence it can be written as $N_{S,h}(e)$. The problem of implementation, as defined by Maskin, involves the relationship of the two sets, the F-desirable set $F(e)$ and the Nash equilibrium outcome set $N_{S,h}(e)$ produced by the mechanism (S, h) in the environment e. Clearly, one is interested in mechanisms for which the outcome equilibrium set is non-empty (i.e., equilibrium existence is assured) and does not extend beyond the F-desirable set. Furthermore, the judgment concerning a mechanism must usually be made before it is known precisely which environment e will prevail. This is often expressed by saying

---

24 As noted above, if the same question were asked about dominance (in particular, truth telling) equilibrium outcomes, the answer would be, generically, in the negative. But the Nash equilibrium requirements are less demanding and one might be more optimistic about a positive answer.

25 Indeed, every constrained Walrasian.

26 A converse also holds, but with an additional condition of convexity on the outcome function.

27 Moore and Repullo (1988); Palfrey and Srivastava (1991).

28 I.e., on preferences, endowments, and production possibility sets.

29 Usually called a social choice rule.

that the designer does not know[30] the environment e but only knows a class E of environments in which e lies.[31] It is then said that the mechanism (S, h) *implements*[32] (in Nash) the desirability correspondence F *over* the class of environments E if, for all e in E: (i) the set of Nash equilibrium outcomes $N_{S,h}(e)$ is non-empty, and (ii) this set, $N_{S,h}(e)$, is a subset of $F(e)$

Given a particular mechanism, a specified class of environments, and a desirability correspondence, one can ask whether that mechanism implements the correspondence over that class. Indeed, if we overlook the fact that the Walrasian auctioneer scenario does not quite qualify as a game-form, the essence of the two standard theorems (existence and the first welfare theorem) is that the Walrasian 'mechanism' implements (although not in Nash!) the Pareto (desirability) correspondence. But when one does insist on a rigorous game-theoretic formulation, the question arises as to which correspondences are Nash implementable. As shown by Maskin, a necessary condition is a property of the desirability correspondences called 'monotonicity'. On the other hand, monotonicity together with the 'no veto-power', was shown to be sufficient when there are at least three participants.[33] The constructive proofs of sufficiency provided 'recipes' for designing a mechanism given an admissible desirability correspondence to be implemented. A recipe with such almost universal coverage might seem to make any further research on mechanism design unnecessary. But the strategy spaces used in these recipes are so huge[34] that a search for informationally less onerous mechanisms, at least for narrower classes of desirability correspondences,[35] is bound to continue. Nevertheless, the great importance of this approach lies in extending our horizon from the narrow

---

[30] This is distinct from the question of what it is that the players are assumed to know about the environment and, in particular, about other players' preferences. A widely accepted view is that, unless a Bayesian approach is used, one must assume complete information about others' preferences to be available to every player, since the location of Nash equilibria cannot be determined without the knowledge of all payoff functions, and the knowledge of all utility functions (more generally, all preferences) is necessary (in addition to the outcome function) to obtain the payoff functions. It should be noted, however, that a 'verification scenario' interpretation of Nash equilibria only requires that each player know the strategies used by other players as well as his/her own preferences.

[31] For instance, the designer might know that the environment is classical.

[32] Or, *weakly* implements. *Full* implementation requires that the two sets be equal.

[33] Maskin (1977); Saijo (1988).

[34] A Maskin-type strategy message of the i-th agent is of the form $(R_1^i, \ldots, R_n^i, a^i, m^i)$, where R_j^i is i's 'estimate' of j's preference relation, a^i is a proposed outcome, and m^i is an integer whose function is to weed out undesirable equilibria. Maskin's model assumes the feasible set to be known to the designer. In work involving Maskin and Postlewaite this assumption has been eliminated, at the cost, of course, of further complicating the mechanism. Jackson (1989) has discussed problems connected with the use of integer components in strategic messages.

[35] Mechanisms already designed for Walras and Lindahl correspondences in classical environments are of simpler type, with the required dimension of the message space determined by a function of the number of goods and participants, but independent of the number of parameters in the utility functions.

focus on Pareto optimality and a few other selected desirability criteria to the broader class of those desirability criteria that might be implementable.

A comment on the relationship of the results concerning mechanisms to those discussed in the previous section. If an adjustment process realizes a given desirability correspondence over a given class of environments, it does not follow that it defines a mechanism implementing that correspondence over that class of environments. However, the results specifying minimum informational requirements for realization do carry over to implementation. To see this in a simple setting, consider a mechanism (S, h), $S = S^1 \times \cdots \times S^n$, with each $S^i = \mathbb{R}$ (the reals), a k-dimensional Euclidean outcome space Z, and the outcome function $h : S \to Z$ concave and differentiable. Furthermore, let all utility functions $u^i : Z \to \mathbb{R}$ be strictly concave and differentiable. Then so is each payoff function $\pi^i(s) = u^i(h(s))$, s in S. Hence for a Nash equilibrium n-tuple of strategies $(s^{*1}, \ldots, s^{*n})$, the necessary and sufficient first-order conditions are

$$\partial/\partial s^i[\pi^i(s^i, s^{*-i})]\big|_{s^i=s^{*i}} \qquad i = 1, \ldots, n, \tag{7}$$

which is (using vectorial notation) equivalent to

$$u^{i'}(s^*) \cdot h_i(s^*) = 0, \qquad i = 1, \ldots, n, \tag{8}$$

where the first symbol denotes the k-vector of the partial derivatives of u^i with respect to the components of z in Z, the symbol h_i represents the k-vector of the components of $h(s)$ with respect to s^i, and the dot denotes the inner product, But (8) is of the form $g^i(m^*, e^i) = 0$, with s^* corresponding to m^*, the function $u^i(\cdot)$ corresponding to e^i, and the left hand side of (8) viewed as operating on s^* and $u^i(\cdot)$, corresponding to g^i operating on m^* and e^i. Thus in this case the Nash equilibrium conditions constitute a special case of the verification scenario conditions for stationary values of adjustment processes, and it follows that impossibility theorems established for the adjustment processes apply to Nash equilibria. In particular, they provide lower bounds for the dimensionality of strategy spaces, but these lower bounds are not in general achievable.[36,37]

One more comment. Although our illustrations have drawn on resource allocation problems, mechanism theory itself is applicable in a much broader arena. In particular there is a rich field of contributions to mechanism design

---

[36] Reichelstein and Reiter (1988) have studied dimensional requirements for Nash equilibria.

[37] A similar relationship exists between mechanism and institutional models when institutions are defined as classes of (certain types of) game-forms. That is, impossibility results for mechanisms carry over into the theory of institutions. This, it seems to me, is an advantage of the approach used below to the modeling of institutions.

theory in the context of voting theory problems, just as was true of Arrow's theorem on social welfare functions.

Institutions

Here I enter what I regard as the third phase of development of the design field, dealing with institutions. It is most subjective and programmatic. On the one hand, those dealing with mechanisms, or even adjustment processes, have often aimed at bridging the gap between traditional microeconomics and institutional approaches. Koopmans, in the above cited passage referred to his 'helmsman-custodians-managers' allocation game as an institutional arrangement alternative to central planning. Many other models, including particular variants of the principal-agent problem, were designed to represent alternative institutional arrangements. But, for a variety of reasons, it seems that the theory of mechanisms has not as yet succeeded in bridging the gap. The purpose of the remarks that follow is to present a view of the relationship between mechanism theory and ideas that seem to be implicit in much of the institutional analysis.

First, a distinction. The term 'institution' has two meanings: (i) that of an entity, e.g. a university, the office of ombudsman, etc.; (ii) institutional arrangements governing a variety of social interactions. Initially, I shall be using the term only in its second meaning, that of institutional arrangements. There are two interpretations in the literature, that—on the surface— are in conflict: institution arrangements as (A) rules of the game (e.g., North 1990, 1992; Ostrom 1986) and (B) institutional arrangements as solutions (equilibrium strategy behavior) in (super-)games (Schotter 1981).

Consider the first interpretation (A). If institutions are rules of the game, are they not to be identified with game-forms, i.e., mechanisms—since these are indeed formalizations of rules governing a game? There are several reasons why a simple identification of institutions with game-forms is not appropriate. The literature of institutions stresses two special features, relevant for both interpretations A and B. One is that there must be a system of enforcement or policing in order that the rules be obeyed, unless they are internalized. Second, institutional arrangements are what one may call 'categorical', in the sense that they apply to a category of situations and/or agents, rather than to specific cases and places. This amounts to regarding institutional arrangements as particular kinds of game-forms, rather than arbitrary ones.

But there is another point. Consider an institution (an institutional arrangement) such as price control. Its essence is that the seller's strategy domain (the choice of price) has an administratively imposed upper bound.

It would be price control regardless of the numerical value of that bound. But to define a game-form, one must completely specify the seller's strategy domain, hence the numerical value of that bound. My conclusion is that a natural correspondence is not between an institution and a single game-form but rather between an institution and *a class of game-forms* sharing certain characteristics, in this example the upper bound imposed by an administrative body. If a game is defined in extensive form, an institution may well be defined as the class of (extensive)[38] game-forms having some subgame in common.

As for the property of categoricity, it is characteristic of legal or customary rules that they are formulated for persons in certain roles, say buyer, seller, parent, spouse, etc. Hence a game-form representing the functioning of such rules must provide procedures for determining that specific individuals qualify for the claimed roles.

Next, the problem of modeling enforcement. The issue is much broader than this term implies. Consider the introduction of the institution of social security. It requires not just enforcement to make people obey the rule, but a complex apparatus, providing the required information and facilities for the collection of taxes and the disbursement of payments. I have sometimes used the term '*genuine*[39] *implementation*' to refer to the procedures to make such an institutional arrangement effective. One aspect of genuine implementation of institutional arrangements (i.e., institutions in the sense (ii)) is the frequent utilization of institutional entities (institutions in sense (i)) to accomplish this. Examples, such as the agencies administering the social security system, abound. But one can think of institutional arrangements created by long-standing custom and enforced by spontaneous actions of a group where there is no institutional entity in charge of its administration or enforcement.

The problem of modeling enforcement poses some difficult problems. To begin with, there is a view that Nash equilibria are self-enforcing, by definition. What, I believe, is meant, is that if the genuine implementation apparatus is in place so that the rules of the game are obeyed and the outcome function is effective, then no player has an incentive unilaterally to defect. But, in general, there is nothing in a specific game-form, prescribing particular strategy domains and outcome functions that would prevent players from

---

[38] An extensive game-form is the analog of an extensive game, except that instead of payoffs, certain nodes specify physical outcomes rather than numerical (utility) payoffs. Also, it seems desirable that the outcomes be (in general) associated with intermediate, as well as terminal, nodes. (An example would be the required payment of a fee to proceed to the next stage.) This feature may be helpful in accommodating the role of transaction costs that are so important in the 'new institutionalist' approach.

[39] To distinguish it from the term 'implementation' as used in the theory of mechanisms (see above).

resorting to 'illegal' strategies, nor is there automatic assurance that outcomes specified by the outcome function will occur unless the required apparatus is in place.

Nor is it enough to expand the game-form so as to prescribe the procedures governing the enforcement process, since similar objections can be raised with respect to this expanded game-form. This is the so called 'infinite regress' problem.

My feeling is that a way out is to embed the 'desired'[40] game-form in what I call the 'natural' game-form, including all feasible behaviors (and not merely those that are 'legal' according to the desired game-form) and their natural consequences as the 'natural' outcome function. Because the natural game-form is, in a sense, maximal, there is—it seems to me—no problem of infinite regress.

An important issue in the analysis of institutional arrangements is the genesis of the rules in the game. Some (as Schotter) have stressed the endogeneity of institution formation, interpreting the institutional arrangements, including enforcement, as Nash equilibrium behavior in a supergame consisting of the infinite repetition of a particular stage ('constituent') game. But there are certainly institutions that result from conscious decisions— often made by legislative bodies—as to what the rules of the game should be. This type of development in the context of regulatory processes was modeled by Reiter and Hughes (1981) as a sequence of two games, in which the rules of the second (economic) game are determined as the outcome of the first game. Those playing the first game (say, the legislators) have an interest in the outcome of the second game (played by firms and regulators). The process could presumably also be represented by a single multi-move (extensive form) game, with a totally new set of players in the second stage. Coming back, however, to the two-game model, it would seem appropriate to enrich the model by specifying that the outcome of the first game includes not only the formulation of the rules for the second game but also an effective change in the environment that would change the natural game for the second stage to result in genuine implementation. Otherwise, the adopted rules might remain on paper only—which of course often happens.

The two-game model may also provide for a reconciliation of the two interpretations (A and B above) of institutional arrangements. The stage A can, but need not always, involve legislative decision-making. Instead, it may be the kind of repetitive process envisioned by Schotter. But the rules of behavior evolved in this process may in effect constitute the game-form for the second stage, even though it is played by a different set of participants.

---

[40] I.e., the game-form that is supposed to govern the behavior of the players.

A comment now about aspects of institutional arrangements that are particularly important for new institutionalist analysis (Coase 1937, 1960; North 1990, 1992; Williamson 1975, 1985). Two elements stand out: (a) the assignment of rights and obligations, and (b) transaction costs. As for (a), it has been suggested that in certain problems it can be modeled as the location, in an appropriate 'commodity' space, of the initial endowment.[41] However, there are examples, such as alternative land tenure forms (Stiglitz 1974) where an appropriate representation is in terms of different parameter values in outcome functions. As for (b), it may be noted that the study of informational requirements in adjustment processes deals precisely with an important class of transaction costs and their implications for realizability or implementability of various desiderata. I do not know to what extent the costs of genuine implementation in their non-informational aspects have been subject to systematic study.

I hope that this new journal, *Economic Design,* will play a constructive role in facilitating better mutual understanding and a rapprochement between those pursuing formalized design theory and those studying institutions from a historical or descriptive point of view, thus sharing the best insights of both.

References

Calsamiglia, X. (1977) Decentralized resource allocation and increasing returns, *Journal of Economic Theory*, 14(2): 263–83.

Coase, R. (1937) The nature of the firm, *Economica* 4(16): 386–405.

Coase, R. (1960) The problem of social cost, *The Journal of Law and Economics*, 3(1): 1–44.

Groves, T. and J. Ledyard (1977) Optimal allocation of public goods: A solution to the 'free rider' problem, *Econometrica*, 45(4): 783–809.

Groves, T., R. Radner, and S. Reiter, ed. (1987) *Information, Incentives, and Economic Mechanisms*. Minneapolis, MN: University of Minnesota Press.

Hayek, F. (1945) The use of knowledge in society, *American Economic Review*, 35(4): 519–30.

Jackson, M. (1989) Implementation in undominated strategies: A look at bounded mechanisms, mimeo, Northwestern University. Published as Jackson, M. (1992) Implementation in undominated strategies: A look at bounded mechanisms, *Review of Economic Studies*, 59(4): 757–75.

Jordan, J. (1987) The informational requirements of local stability in decentralized allocation mechanisms, in *Information, Incentives, and Economic Mechanisms*, ed. T. Groves, R. Radner, and S. Reiter, 183–212. Minneapolis, MN: University of Minnesota Press.

---

[41] See, e.g., Eggertsson (1990).

Koopmans, T. (1951) Analysis of production as an efficient combination of activities, in *Activity Analysis of Production and Allocation*, ed. T. Koopmans, 33–97. Santa Monica, CA: Rand Corporation.

Marschak, J. and R. Radner (1972) *Economic Theory of Teams*. New Haven, CT: Yale University Press.

Marschak, T. (1986) Organization design, in *Handbook of Mathematical Economics, volume III*, ed. K. Arrow and M. Intriligator, 1359–1440. Amsterdam: North-Holland.

Maskin, E. (1977) Nash equilibrium and welfare optimality, mimeo. Published as Maskin, E. (1999) Nash equilibrium and welfare optimality, *Review of Economic Studies*, 66: 23–38.

Moore, J. and R. Repullo (1988) Subgame perfect implementation, *Econometrica*, 56(5): 1191–1220.

Mount, K. and S. Reiter (1974) The informational size of message spaces, *Journal of Economic Theory*, 8(2): 161–92.

Mount, K. and S. Reiter (1987) On the existence of a locally stable dynamic process with a statically minimal message space, in *Information, Incentives, and Economic Mechanisms*, ed. T. Groves, R. Radner, and S. Reiter, 213–40. Minneapolis, MN: University of Minnesota Press.

North, D. (1990) *Institutions, Institutional Change and Economic Performance*. Cambridge, MA: Cambridge University Press.

North, D. (1992) *Transaction Costs, Institutions, and Economic Performance*. San Francisco, CA: ICS Press.

Osana, H. (1978) On the informational size of message spaces for resource allocation processes, *Journal of Economic Theory*, 17(1): 66–78.

Ostrom, E. (1986) An agenda for the study of institutions, *Public Choice*, 48(1): 3–25.

Palfrey, T. and S. Srivastava (1991) Nash implementation using undominated strategies, *Econometrica*, 59(2): 479–501.

Postlewaite, A. and D. Schmeidler (1987) Differential information and strategic behavior in economic environments: A general equilibrium approach, *Information, Incentives, and Economic Mechanisms*, in ed. T. Groves, R. Radner, and S. Reiter, 330–48. Minneapolis, MN: University of Minnesota Press.

Reichelstein, S. and S. Reiter (1988) Game-forms with minimal message spaces, *Econometrica*, 56(3): 661–92.

Reiter, S. and J. Hughes (1981) A preface on modeling the regulated U.S. economy, *Hofstra Law Review*, 9(5): 1381–1421.

Saari, D. (1984) A method for constructing message systems for smooth performance functions, *Journal of Economic Theory*, 33(2): 249–74.

Saijo, T. (1988) Strategy space reduction in Maskin's theorem: Sufficient conditions for implementation, *Econometrica*, 56(3): 693–700.

Samuelson, P. (1954) The pure theory of public expenditure, *Review of Economics and Statistics*, 36(4): 387–89.

Samuelson, P. (1955) Diagrammatic exposition of a theory of public expenditure, *Review of Economics and Statistics*, 37(4): 360–66.

Schmeidler, D. (1976) A remark on microeconomic models of an economy and on a game theoretic interpretation of Walras equilibria, University of Minnesota Discussion Paper No. 76–68.

Schmeidler, D. (1982) Walrasian analysis via strategic outcome functions, *Econometrica*, 48(7): 1585–94.

Schotter, A. (1981) *The Economic Theory of Social Institutions*. Cambridge, MA: Cambridge University Press.

Stiglitz, J. (1974) Incentives and risk sharing in sharecropping, *Review of Economics Studies*, 41(2): 219–55.

Thomson, W. (1987) The vulnerability to manipulative behavior of resource allocation mechanisms designed to select equitable and efficient outcomes, in *Information, Incentives, and Economic Mechanisms*, ed. T. Groves, R. Radner, and S. Reiter, 375–96. Minneapolis, MN: University of Minnesota Press.

Williamson, O. (1975) *Markets and Hierarchies*. New York, NY: The Free Press.

Williamson, O. (1985) *Economic Institutions of Capitalism*. New York, NY: The Free Press.

15

Institutional Change and the Theory of Mechanism Design

Abstract. The aim of the paper is to construct a model useful for rigorous analytical treatment of economic and political institutions. An institution is defined as a class of game-forms ('rules of the game') having the following special attributes: they are the result of human actions; there are arrangements for making the rules effective (including enforcement); they apply to categories of situations or persons. An appendix illustrates the concepts by an example involving inventions and patents.

Introduction

My current interest in this topic stems from two sources: (a) the important institutional changes that have been taking place in Asia and Europe during the recent decades, and (b) the inadequacy of traditional (neoclassical) welfare economics in dealing with such phenomena.

The important trend observed in most formerly communist countries has been a movement away from command and toward a market-oriented system, while in many free enterprise or capitalist countries there has been a tendency toward deregulation and a lessening of the state's role in influencing the economy.

It is therefore natural to seek a theoretical framework in which the institutions (the system) are viewed as a 'variable', and even an 'unknown' of

Reprinted from *Academia Economic Papers*, 1994, 22(2): 1–27. I am grateful to Dr. Tzong-shian Yu, President, Chung-Hua Institution for Economic Research, and Dr. Jia-dong Shea, Director, Institute of Economics, Academia Sinica for the opportunity of developing and presenting the ideas of this paper and for their comments, as well as for the comments of other members' of the two institutions. An earlier version of this paper was presented in the Chung-Hua series of lectures on May 8, 1992, at the Institute of Economics, Academia Sinica.

the problem, rather than something given and fixed. Yet much traditional welfare economics usually postulates a particular mechanism or set of institutions (e.g., perfect competition, monopoly, oligopoly) and then proceeds to analyze the implications of these assumptions. Institutional aspects of an economy have often been viewed as not amenable to analytical treatment. It is our objective to show how a sequence of concepts, including adjustment processes, economic mechanisms, and institutions (defined as certain classes of mechanisms) makes it possible to broaden the traditional approach while providing a framework within which economic analysis can be carried out.

An adjustment process is a generalization of the notion of tâtonnement. It completely specifies the hypothetical behavior of the economic agents, thus making it possible to study its equilibrium and dynamic properties, as well as its informational requirements. However, by specifying the behavior it leaves open the question of incentives and motivations that would induce the postulated behavior. The study of incentives is undertaken with the aid of tools borrowed from the theory of games of strategy. In particular, a mechanism is defined as a 'game-form,' i.e., a specification of the rules of the economic game—more precisely, the permissible strategies and the consequences of those strategies (in technical language, strategy domains and outcome functions). A good deal of recent research work has been devoted to the problem of 'implementation', i.e., the question whether a given mechanism produces results compatible with certain given desiderata—e.g., efficiency or fairness. In turn, an institution (in the sense of an institutional arrangement—not in the sense of an organization that is sometimes also called an institution) is defined as a particular type of a class of mechanisms. To qualify as an institution, a class of mechanisms must have been generated by human behavior (rather than, say, laws of physics), its rules must be either internalized or subject to effective enforcement procedures, and they must apply to a category of situations (e.g., across persons or time).

Institutional change can be modeled by an evolutionary process. In particular, it can be viewed a sequence of games, some cooperative, some not. Some change may be viewed as endogenous or 'organic', and some as subject to (or the result of) design. The great transformations the world has been observing have posed unique and often totally unanticipated problems. This is the area of greatest need for new research.

Institutions: The Concept

In many countries the recent period has been characterized by significant changes in their institutional structure or by search for and conflict over institutional reforms. Current economic literature abounds in statements about the importance of institutions. But the term 'institution' has many meanings. Thus the term 'institution' is applied to a university but also to property rights. These two are in conceptual spheres so different that it seems natural to place them in separate categories. Indeed most writers do draw a distinction. Ruttan (1978, pp. 328–29), however, calls it "a distinction without a difference",[1] and uses the term 'institution' to include organizations. On the other hand, North (1992, p. 9) characterizes the distinction between 'institutions' (such as the US Constitution or the common law) and 'organizations' (such as a university or the Senate) as "crucial" (North, 1990, p. 4), and deems it "...essential to any understanding of institutions and institutional change...".

Given the objectives of the present paper, I share North's view on the importance of the distinction, even though the correspondence between his pair of concepts (institutions, organizations) and mine (institutional arrangements, institutional entities) is less than complete. Different terminologies are used to express this distinction. When it is necessary to avoid ambiguity, my choice is to distinguish between institutional entitles[2] (such as a university) and institutional arrangements (such as property rights).

I am in essential agreement with North (1992, p. 10) when he says that "If institutions are the rules of the game, organizations are the players", typically with a common purpose or "mission". But what I call institutional entities is a class of players somewhat broader than North's. It includes artificial or juridical (legal) persons of various types, conceivably not even identified with a particular set of persons (e.g., the estate of a decedent) as well as one-person entities such as an ombudsman or a country's president.

North (1990, p. 5), on the other hand, views organizations as "...groups of individuals bound by some common purpose to achieve objectives". For me the ombudsman is an 'institution' in the sense of an institutional entity even though not an organization. Even if we admitted [a] one-person 'group', this would still not capture the distinction between, say, the personal (private) actions of the ombudsman and actions carried out in his/her institutional capacity.

Furthermore, even when more than one individual is involved, there may be a problem in identifying an organization with the membership group. Thus two different entities (or even organizations) may have the same membership. To retain the spirit of North's framework, one might require the definition of an organization to refer not only to its constituent group

---

[1] See also Ruttan (1978, pp. 328–29, footnotes 2 and 4) for references to related distinctions due to Frank H. Knight, Samuel P. Huntington, Lance E. Davis, and Douglass C. North.

[2] The term entity corresponds to what in economics is often called a unit or an agent, e.g., a person, firm, government office. Entities can make decisions and have rights and duties. But not every agent is an institutional entity.

211

but also to its purpose. It is for such reasons that I prefer not to identify institutional entities with organizations, or organizations with groups of individuals. But in our formal models, the institutional entities will indeed have the role of players, even though there will also be non-institutional players such as ordinary live persons.

As for institutional arrangements there are many examples of fundamental importance for economics. Private property rights were already mentioned. The distinction between a market economy and a centrally planned economy involves two alternative institutional arrangements. Among alternative institutional arrangements when persons other than the owner work the land are renting, wage labor, and sharecropping.

From now on, unless the contrary is specified, we shall use the term 'institution' to mean 'institutional arrangement'.

There is a further important dichotomy in the way institutions[3] are viewed in the existing literature, with institutions being viewed by some (e.g., North[4]) as rules governing behavior or conduct, and by others (e.g., Schotter) as regularities (or norms or standards) of behavior. In the language of game theory, this dichotomy has been interpreted by Schotter as corresponding to the distinction between the game-form[5] and the solution (in particular, equilibrium) of a game.

This distinction was made by Schotter (1981, p. 155):

> For us, however, what we call social institutions are not the rules of the game but rather the alternative equilibrium standards of behavior or conventions of behavior that evolve from a given game described by its rules. In other words, for us, institutions are properties of the equilibrium of games and not properties of the game's description.

In (1989, pp. 50–51), Schotter proposed a terminology to reflect this distinction, calling institutions interpreted as rules "institutions of type I", while those defined as regularities of behavior are called "institutions of type II".[6]

---

[3] This term being here used already in the narrower sense of institutional arrangements rather than entities.

[4] Also Riker (1982, p. 4), Plott (1979, p. 156), and E. Ostrom (1986, p. 5).

[5] The game-form specifies the players' individual strategy domains and the outcome function. In the economic literature it is often referred to as the mechanism.

[6] A related but distinct dichotomy, based on the genesis of institutions, is formulated in Schotter (1986, pp. 117–18). Here, what he calls the "rules view" (presumably intended to correspond to institutions of type I) is associated with the "design and implementation school of social institutions", in whose literature "...institutions are planned and designed mechanisms given exogenously to or imposed upon a society of agents. Institutional change is a process of social engineering that takes place through the manipulation of rules". This is contrasted with the "behavioral view" (presumably intended to correspond to institutions of type II) whose representatives "...look at social institutions not as sets of predesigned rules, but rather as unplanned and unintended regularities of social behavior (social conventions) that emerge

It is important to see why it is the 'game-form' (here hyphenated to avoid interpretations inconsistent with its technical meaning) and not the 'game' (as defined in the theoretical literature) that is considered to correspond to 'rules of the game'. The common features of the two terms are that they both specify the set of players and the class of strategies[7] the players are permitted to use. But beyond this, the two concepts differ. A game-form is further characterized by an *outcome function* which—given the players' strategy choices—defines the (physical) consequences of these choices. For instance, the outcome function may specify who gets elected given the votes cast, or the resource allocation (both private and public goods) resulting from the participants' trade and payment choices.[8] By contrast, a game is characterized by as many *payoff functions* as there are players. A player's payoff function specifies his/her utility (a single number) given the strategies chosen by the players. I.e., the payoff functions describe how the players feel about the consequences of the group's strategic choices, while the outcome function only describes these consequences.

In the language of set theory, the two kinds of functions have the same domain, viz., the joint strategy domain[9] of the players, but different ranges: the outcome function takes its values in the space of (physical) consequences or outcomes of the strategy choices made by all the players, while the value of each player's payoff function is a real number indicating that player's utility associated with all players' strategy choices. But, of course, a player's payoff function is not the same as his/her *utility function*—because a utility function represents preferences as a function of outcomes, while payoff functions have strategy choices as their (common) domain. In fact a player's payoff function can be constructed given the knowledge of the outcome function and of that player's utility function: given the players' strategy choices, the numerical value of the player's payoff equals the numerical utility (specified by the utility function) of the outcome (specified by the outcome function) of these strategy choices.[10]

'organically' (to use Menger's term). Institutions are outcomes of human action that no single individual intended to occur".

[7] Actually, rules and laws are usually formulated in terms of prohibited or permitted actions and behaviors, i.e.,—in the language of game theory—in terms of (sequences of) moves rather than strategies. Hence it would be more appropriate to model institutions as 'extensive form' games, making explicit reference to moves and actions. But rules concerning moves and actions can be translated into rules about strategies in a 'normal form' representation of the game. To simplify exposition, the discussion in the text is carried out in terms of the normal form, hence references to strategies rather than to moves or actions.

[8] See another illustration of the concept of an outcome function in the Appendix.

[9] I.e., the Cartesian product of the individual players' strategy domains.

[10] I.e., the player's payoff function is the composition of his/her utility function with the outcome function (see a more formal statement below).

The common sense interpretation of the term 'rules of the game' involves the specification of permissible and prohibited behaviors, but in no way refers to the players' feelings. Hence it is the 'game-form' rather than the 'game' that is the natural technical counterpart of the everyday meaning of 'rules of the game'.[11]

Before proceeding to formalize the concept of an institution (in the sense of an institutional arrangement) let us examine some verbal definitions found in the literature. As a representative of the 'rules' view of institutions[12] consider the definition in North (1990, p. 3):

> Institutions are the rules of the game in a society or, more formally, are the humanly devised constraints that, shape human interaction.[13]

The 'regularities' view of institutions is most explicitly formulated by Schotter (1981, p. 11)[14] who modifies the definition of a 'social convention' due to Lewis (1969, p. 58) and arrives at the following definition of a 'social institution':

> A social institution is a regularity in social behavior that is agreed to by all members of society, specifies behavior in specific recurrent situations, and is either self-policed or policed by some external authority.[15]

Let us note that the two views have important aspects in common. First, although North's definition contains no explicit reference to policing, he does stress elsewhere (e.g., 1990, p. 4) the role of enforcement:[16]

> ...an essential part of the functioning of institutions is the costliness of ascertaining violations and the severity of punishment.

---

[11] One does occasionally encounter contrary usage, as in Shubik (1982, p. 8).

[12] In the sense of institutional arrangements.

[13] In a somewhat similar spirit, Eggertsson (1990, p. 70) speaks of institutions "as sets of rules governing interpersonal relations, noting that we are talking about formal political and organizational practices". However, the requirement of formality is absent from North's definition. Indeed, North (1990, p. 4) stresses that his concept of an institution includes not only formal written rules but also unwritten codes of conduct.

[14] Two more detailed verbal definitions are given by Berman and Schotter on pages 52 and 78 of Schotter (1981), ch. 3. This chapter also contains a mathematical formalization of the concept of an institution as Nash equilibrium of a supergame.

[15] The main difference between Lewis's 'social convention' and Schotter's 'social institution' is that a social convention is self-policed while a social institution may require policing by an external authority. However, while using the institution of property rights to illustrate the need for enforcement by an external authority, Schotter remarks (p. 165, note 8) that "...if the situation were modeled as a supergame, it could be shown, using certain discount rates, that property rights are a noncooperative equilibrium institution in the supergame and need no external enforcement". (Presumably, the term "noncooperative equilibrium" refers to a Nash equilibrium.)

[16] Indeed the whole ch. 7 of North (1990) is devoted to enforcement.

In addition, North also stresses (e.g., 1990, pp. 40–42, 60) the role played by "internally enforced codes of conduct" and "self-enforcing standards of conduct".

Schotter's definition, as just seen, requires policing or self-policing. He refers to certain strategies in an infinitely repeated game (i.e., a supergame) as "policing" strategies because they are designed to discourage non-cooperative behavior.[17]

Second, institutions deal with *categories or classes of situations* rather than single cases. I refer to this attribute of institutions as categoricity. Schotter (1981, p. 11) says that "A social institution...specifies behavior in specific recurrent situations...". Ostrom (1986, p. 5) refers to institution-defining rules as prescriptions designed to order "repetitive interdependent relation-ships".[18]

One important consequence of the categoricity of institutions is that rules, whether formalized as game-forms or in other ways, refer not to specific (named) individuals but to their personal *status* (e.g., age, race, caste, religion) and/or *role* played by agents in specific situations (e.g., as spouses, parents, buyers, sellers, or holders of specific offices; in chess, whether a player has black or white). The actions individuals are permitted to take, as well as the consequences of these actions, may depend on their status and roles. Hence a prerequisite to the application of the rules in a specific situation is the determination of the participants' status and the roles they play in that situation.[19]

Third, both view institutions as human creations or consequences of human actions and behavior, although there is varying emphasis on the process of genesis: conscious design versus 'organic' emergence, Schotter's definition is explicitly formulated in terms of the regularities of social behavior. In (1989, p. 118), he characterizes what he calls the "behavioral view" as follows: "Institutions are outcomes of human action that no single individual intended to occur".

North uses the *"humanly* devised constraints" (italics added), and uses illustrations such as the US Constitution and common law. The human

---

[17] Difficult problems arise in connection with modeling enforcement, including that of 'infinite regress'. I have proposed an approach that views the 'desired' game-form (the way the mechanism is supposed to work, including the specification of what we might term 'legal' moves or strategies) as embedded in the 'natural' game-form that includes all moves and strategies that are feasible (although possibly 'illegal'). See Hurwicz (1993a).

[18] I am less clear as to North's view on this point because of his references (e.g., 1990, pp. 47, 52) to contracts containing "provisions specific to a particular agreement in exchange" as included in the hierarchy of rules.

[19] This is implicit in many applications of game theoretic models. In extensive form games, the determination of role or status could be modeled as moves.

action genesis of the institution in its 'rules' version is made explicit in Ostrom (1986, pp. 5–6):

> Rules, as I wish to use the term, are distinct from physical and behavioral laws. I use the term differently than a game theorist who considers linguistic prescriptions as well as physical and behavioral laws to be "the rules of the game". If a theorist wants only to analyze a given game or a situation, no advantage is gained by distinguishing between rules, on the one hand, and physical or behavioral laws, on the other hand. To change the outcomes of a situation, however, it is essential to distinguish rules from behavioral or physical laws.... Theoretically, rules can be changed while physical and behavioral laws cannot.... That rules can be changed by humans is one of their key characteristics.[20]

Ostrom's distinction between physical and behavioral laws versus rules has an important implication for modeling institutions as rules. In my interpretation, the game theorist's "rules of the game" in Ostrom's comment correspond to the 'game-form'. Her point can therefore be interpreted as stressing that the *game-form consists of two 'components':* (a) those that are subject to change by human intervention, and (b) those, like physical and behavioral laws that are not, and consequently that institution-defining rules are only those belonging to the (a)-*component.*

An example of formalization of the genesis of institutions is found in the Reiter and Hughes (1981) model of regulation. Their model consists of a sequence of two games: (1) the political (e.g., legislative) process game (e.g., played by legislators), which results in the legal and budgetary framework that governs (2) the (economic/administrative) process game, the latter to be played by business firms and regulatory agencies. Here the regulatory legislation creates the institutional *arrangements* such as antitrust laws which are then to be implemented by institutional *entities* in the form of regulatory agencies. Technically, the outcome of the first game is to modify the (a)-component of the game-form of the second (economic/administrative) game.[21]

The two-stage process of the Reiter-Hughes model is a special case of a more general phenomenon, that of a sequence[22] (sometimes to be called a cascade) of games where, except for the final stage, the outcome of each stage is the creation or modification of the game-form of the next stage. This typically results in a hierarchy of rules, illustrated in North (1990, p. 47) by

---

[20] Analogous distinctions are emphasized in Gardner and Ostrom (1991), pp. 121–22.

[21] For such modification to be effective, more is required than to have the first game define a new 'desired' game-form for the second (economic/administrative) game. In my view, the outcome of the first game must, in general, change the 'natural' game-form of the second game, e.g., by making certain changes in the environment that affect the feasibility of moves in the second game.

[22] Of arbitrary length.

216

the sequence consisting of constitutions, statutes and common laws, specific bylaws, and finally individual contracts.[23]

When the cascade view of institution formation is adopted, the contrast between Schotter's institutions of type I and II appears in a different light. Consider the Reiter and Hughes model. Are the antitrust regulations, which constitute an institutional arrangement, of type I or II? From the point of view of the second (economic/administrative) game, they are rules of the game (a game-form), hence of type I. But this game-form is the outcome of the first (political process) game, hence essentially[24] of type II. Thus the same institution qualifies as type I relative to the second game and of type II relative to the first game. The classification is not absolute but relative to the game in the sequence.

In the search for an appropriate definition of an institutional arrangement more is at issue than semantics. When our attention is focused on actual behavior (Schotter's "institutions of type 2",[25] technically strategies that constitute game solutions or equilibria), our conclusions as to likely behavior by the participants depend not only on the game played (i.e., the set of players, strategy domains, and payoff functions) but also on the concept of solution used. For instance, different researchers may obtain different solutions or equilibria for the same game depending on whether the equilibrium concept they have used is maximin, or (simple) Nash, or "perfect Nash", or one of the many other refinements of the equilibrium concept recently proposed. Therefore I feel that even if [the] main interest is in explaining observed behavior, our analysis should distinguish between postulates concerning the game itself and those concerning the nature of solutions.

But, as we have seen, the payoff functions which define the game are themselves determined by two factors: the "rules of the game" (formalized as the game-form, i.e., strategy domains and the outcome function) and individual preferences (represented by utilities). To understand the causation of behavior in a given game it is natural to want to separate the influence of these two factors. For instance, in studying behavior changes over time or behavior differences across countries we want to know the respective roles

[23] In a private 1992 communication, Andrew Schotter has pointed out that the earlier stages of a cascade may well produce, in addition to rules for subsequent games, also substantive outcomes with immediate utility payoffs.

[24] I say "essentially", because Schotter defines an institution of type II in an n-player game as the an n-tuple $s = (s^1, \ldots, s^n)$ of equilibrium strategies, whereas, in the Reiter and Hughes model, the institution is the outcome, say $z = h(s)$, where z is an element of the outcome space of the first game (here actually a game-form or a class of game-forms for the second-game) and h is the outcome function for the first game. (z would be a *class* of game-forms if the legislative process left certain parameters of the antitrust rules up to the determination in the second game.)

[25] Let us keep in mind that both type I and type II institutions in Schotter's terminology are what we have called institutional arrangements (rather than "institutional entities").

played by preferences and rules of the game. A closely related[26] point is made by North (1990, p. 5):

> Separating the analysis of the underlying rules from the strategy of the players is a necessary prerequisite to building a theory of institutions.

Schotter (1981, p. 155) suggests that the two concepts, labeled by him institutions of type I ("rules") and II ("behavior regularities"), are complementary, with type II concept being appropriate for positive (descriptive) analysis while type I is relevant for normative (prescriptive) purposes.

To the extent that rules of the game constitute an instrument envisaged in normative analysis, it is certainly necessary that normative analysis must deal with type I institutions. But, as argued above, type I institutions are also of interest for historical and cross-country comparative analysis aimed at causal explanation rather than prescription, hence are also relevant for positive analysis.

On the other hand, normative analysis (in Maskin's terminology, the theory of implementation) is the search for rules of the game (game-forms) that would result in behavior (equilibrium strategies) that would be deemed desirable in terms of specified performance standards or optimality criteria.[27] Thus the theory of implementation involves a study, in the light of various optimality criteria, of the relationship between institutions of type I and type II. These considerations make Schotter's case for complementarity of the two concepts or approaches even stronger.

Returning to the notion of institutions as rules, how is the term "rules" to be understood? North speaks of institution-defining rules as "*constraints* that shape human interaction". (Italics added.) Ostrom (1986, p. 5) defines rules as "... potentially linguistic entities ... that refer to prescriptions ... [that] ... refer to which actions (or states of the world) are *required, prohibited, or permitted*". (Italics in the original.)[28] As I interpret them, these definitions amount to identifying rules with restrictions on the players' strategy domains.[29] But then 'rules of the game' becomes a narrower

---

[26] But not identical—because North is contrasting rules of the game with strategy choices, while our distinction at this point was between rules of the game and preferences. However, since strategy choices are determined by rules of the game and preferences, the two distinctions are closely related. What makes the issues somewhat complicated is that we are dealing with four separate "variables": rules of the game (game-forms), preferences, solution concepts, and resulting behavioral implications (equilibrium strategies).

[27] Such optimality criteria are sometimes referred to as social choice rules. They should not, of course, be confused with rules of the game.

[28] Similarly, Gardner and Ostrom (1991, p. 121) speak of "*Deontological statements* [that] tell what players are expected to find obligatory, permitted, or forbidden to do". (Italics in the original.)

[29] By contrast, Gardner and Ostrom (1991, pp. 125–26) in their listing of rules include those that directly affect the benefits and costs assigned to actions. These rules do not involve preferences and hence, in our terminology, qualify as aspects of outcome functions (although

concept than that of a game-form, since a game-form involves not only strategy domains but also an outcome function specifying the consequences of strategy choices.

My feeling is that a definition identifying rules of the game with constraints, i.e., strategy choices) is somewhat too narrow for purposes of economic (or political) analysis because, in general, rules specify not only what is or is not permitted but also the consequences of agents' choices.

Admittedly, consequences of actions taken by a given set of players may be due (aside from the workings of the laws of physics and other '[natural]' factors) to constraints on the actions of other players. For example, if the consequence of committing an act of theft is the serving of a jail sentence, this is—in part—at least-due to the actions of those in the enforcement personnel. These actions, in turn, can be interpreted as dictated by the enforcement agents' professional obligations, i.e., by constraints on their behavior imposed by the rules of the system. That is, we may enlarge the original game (that did not include enforcement agents as players) to a game including the enforcement agents as players. It may then be possible to interpret the outcome function of the original game as constraints on the actions (restrictions on strategy domains) of players in the enlarged game. However, such enlargement, even when legitimate, may complicate analysis and make the model less tractable.

Furthermore, it is not clear that the enlargement device would always permit the interpretation of consequences in the original game as constraints on actions in the bigger game. For instance, in chess certain moves result in the loss of a piece and others in the loss of a game. The abdication by the reigning monarch may have as consequence the succession to the throne by the oldest child. It does not seem natural to view these consequences as restrictions on strategies, i.e., as constraints on behavior. The introduction of social insurance may result in new opportunities for some people. Thus, in general, rules may produce an expansion rather than restriction in strategy domains. For these reasons, when thinking of type I institutions, along with Schotter, I find it more congenial to think of institution-defining rules as game-forms rather than constraints, thus including not only restrictions on strategy domains but also outcome functions.

To summarize, we have argued that the appropriate technical counterpart of institutional arrangements as rules of the game are neither more nor less than the game-forms. Not more—in the sense that the concept of a game embodies (through the payoff functions) not only strategies and outcomes but also preferences, which do not qualify as rules. And not less—in the sense

the authors call them 'payoff rules'). Thus in this paper the concept of rules goes beyond constraints and is close to that of a game-form.

that to interpret rules merely as constraints on permissible actions ignores the role of the outcome function and is thus too restrictive.

But while game-forms serve as the basic game theory concept to be used in modeling institutions, I shall not be establishing a one-to-one correspondence between institutions and game-forms. Rather, an institution (in the sense of Schotter's type I) will be identified not with a single game-form but rather with a class[30] of game-forms. Two examples may illustrate the reason.

As first example of an institution, consider price control. Formally, we may think of it as restricting the seller's strategy domain by imposing a finite upper bound on the price that can be charged. Thus in the corresponding game-form the seller's strategy domains S^1 may be described as a closed interval of the form $[0, k]$, where $k > 0$ is the price ceiling chosen by a regulatory authority. To specify the game-form, we must specify the numerical value of k. Two different values of k define two different game-forms. But we would naturally say that a regime or institution of price control prevails regardless of the numerical value chosen for the ceiling. Thus, in this simplified example, the institution of price control can be defined as a *class* of game-forms in which the seller's strategy domain is a bounded interval of the form $[0, k]$, with k ranging over positive numbers.

A second example involves land tenure arrangements. It is based on a Stiglitz (1974) model. Consider a two-person situation in which agent 1 (the landlord) owns land to be worked by agent 2. The strategy domain S^2 of agent 2 is the level of effort, as measured by the level of output y.[31] Agent 2's reward, denoted by r^2, is a function of the output, $r^2 = f(y)$, with the reward function f chosen by the landlord. The landlord's strategy space S^1 is the class of reward functions he/she can choose from. The landlord's reward is the remainder, i.e., $r^1 = g(y) = y - f(y)$. The two functions f and g together constitute the outcome function for the game-form of this example. Thus the game-form is specified by S^1, S^2, f, and g. More specifically, we shall assume with Stiglitz that the function $f(y)$ is linear so that

$$r^2 = ay + b, \qquad (*)$$

where a and b are fixed parameters. In turn, $r^1 = y - (ay + b)$.

The three alternative institutional structures under consideration are renting, wage labor, and sharecropping. *Renting* may be viewed as a special case of formula $(*)$: the agent 2 pays a fixed rental fee, so $b < 0$, and he/she gets the whole crop, so $a = 1$; hence under renting, $r^2 = y + b$, $r^1 = -b$, with $b < 0$. The situation is reversed under the *wage system*: the landlord gets the

---

30 In special cases it may be a one-element class.
31 Formally, we may take S^2 to be a (feasible) subset of the set of positive numbers.

whole crop minus the fixed amount of the wage, so that $a = 0$, $r^2 = b > 0$, [where] b [is] the wage, while $r^1 = y - b$. Finally, under *sharecropping*, agent 2 gets a fixed fraction $1 > a > 0$ of the output. Hence here $b = 0$, $1 > a > 0$, $r^2 = ay$, and $r^1 = (1 - a)y$. Under the assumption of linearity, a game-form for this example is defined if and only if the parameters a and b have been specified. But the *institution of renting* is present whenever $a = 1$ and b is negative. Each selection of the numerical value of b defines a different game-form. Hence the institution of renting is defined by the *class of game*-forms for which $a = 1$ and $b < 0$ with b ranging over negative reals. Similarly, the institution of wage labor corresponds to the class of game-forms for which $a = 0$ and $b > 0$. Finally the institution of sharecropping corresponds to the class of game-forms with $b = 0$ and a *between* 0 *and* 1.

In each case a particular institutional arrangement corresponds to a class of game-forms, not to a single game-form. This should not be surprising because the intuitive notion of an institution is of a qualitative non-numerical character.[32] But, for the same reason, it does not follow that any collection of game-forms is the natural counterpart of what we think of as a specific institutional arrangement. Intuitively, there should be some qualitative similarity between game-forms corresponding to the same institutional arrangements. We shall refer to such similarity as institutional equivalence. Thus in our first example, game-forms that only differ by the level of the price ceiling k are considered institutionally equivalent. In the second example, the various rental system game-forms (with $a = 1$ and $b < 0$) are institutionally equivalent, and so are the various wage system game-forms (with $a = 0$ and $b > 0$). But since renting system is viewed as a different institution from the wage system, a game-from with $a = 1$ and $b < 0$ is not institutionally equivalent to a game-from with $a = 0$ and $b > 0$.

How to Model Game-Forms[33]

As we have seen, the game-form or mechanism[34] is the basic concept use in modeling institutions. We must therefore be precise about the notion of the game-form.

It makes a difference whether we do this in normal form or in extensive form. Although the extensive form is more informative it will be simpler to start with the normal form of a mechanism. In normal form the mechanism is defined by the set N of n players, the individual strategy domains $S^1, \ldots, S^n$, the outcome space Z, and the outcome function $h: S \to Z$, where S (called the joint strategy space) denotes the Cartesian product of the individual strategy

---

[32] See Katzner (1989).
[33] See also Hurwicz (1993b).
[34] From now on we shall treat 'game-form' and 'mechanism' as synonyms.

domains, i.e., $S = S^1 \times \ldots \times S^n$. Elements of S^i and S are respectively denoted by s^i and s.

For the moment, the outcome space Z and the strategy domains S^i, $1 = 1, \ldots, n$, are arbitrary sets. The outcome space Z is interpreted as the space of physical events or states resulting from the players' strategy choices. In microeconomic models the outcome space Z might be the space of resource allocations, hence a vector space of possibly high dimension. In voting models the outcome space Z might represent the set of candidates or issues, hence a finite set.[35]

The relation $z = h(s) = h(s^1, \ldots, s^n)$ states that if players $1, \ldots, n$, respectively choose strategies $s^1, \ldots, s^n$, then the physical result will be the outcome z in Z.

A mechanism in normal form can be written as $\langle N, S, Z, h \rangle$, sometimes more briefly as $\langle N, S, h \rangle$.

A mechanism is to be distinguished from the corresponding game in normal form. Denoting by R the set of real numbers, such a game is defined by N, S, and n payoff functions $\pi^i \colon S \to R$, $i = 1, \ldots, n$. The relation $r^i = \pi^i(s) = \pi^i(s^1, \ldots, s^n)$ states that if players $1, \ldots, n$, respectively choose strategies $s^1, \ldots, s^n$, then as a consequence player i will experience the utility level r^i (a real number).[36]

Define the joint payoff function π as the n-tuple of the individual payoff functions, i.e., by the relation $\pi(s) = \langle \pi^1(s), \ldots, \pi^n(n) \rangle$ for all s in S, written also as $\pi = \langle \pi^1, \ldots, \pi^n \rangle$, where $\pi \colon S \to R^n$. Then this game can be written as $\langle N, S, \pi \rangle$.

The mechanism $\langle N, S, h \rangle$ and the game $\langle N, S, \pi \rangle$ have the first two components (N and S) in common. Furthermore, the two functions h and π have the same domain S. But their ranges are different: the range of π is the n-dimensional vector space R^n, while the range of h is the outcome space Z which can be very different from R^n. However, there is a special case where the two become indistinguishable, namely when Z itself is R^n, with $z = (z^1, \ldots, z^n)$, where z^i is a real number, and the i-th player's utility function is of the form $\phi^i(z) = z^i$ for all z in Z.[37] (For example, the outcome

---

[35] Sometimes, as when it represents the resource allocation in a private goods economy, an outcome z (an element of Z) may be decomposed as $z = (z^1, \ldots, z^n)$ where z^i is the commodity bundle of agent i. But such decomposition may not by possible or appropriate in other cases such as economies with public goods or in voting models.

[36] It is easy to formulate the definition of a game in purely ordinal terms rather than in terms of utilities. Thus if R^i is the (weak) preference ordering relation of agent i, we define the corresponding 'payoff ordering' of that agent as the weak ordering relation R^{*i} on S by $s'R^{*i}s''$ if and only if $h(s')R^ih(s'')$. However, in the present context, this slight extra generality would not justify the additional complexity of notation.

[37] See the next paragraph showing the derivation of the payoff functions from outcome and utility functions.

consists of monetary payments to players who are risk-neutral.) This special case is often assumed (explicitly or implicitly), thus making it difficult to separate the game from the mechanism. But for our analysis the distinction is important and we shall not be making such special assumptions.

To relate this game to the mechanism $\langle N, S, Z, h \rangle$ we introduce the n individual utility functions ϕ^i where $\phi^i \colon Z \to R$. The relation $r^i = \phi^i(z)$ states that, when outcome z occurs, player i will experience the utility level r^i (a real number).

Using this framework we can express, for each $i = 1, \ldots, n$, the i-th payoff function π^i in terms of the outcome function h and the i-th utility function ϕ^i by the relation

$$\phi^i(s) = \phi^i(h(s)) \quad \text{for all } s \text{ in } S.$$

That is, the payoff function is the composite of outcome function and the utility function; hence the preceding relation can be written as

$$\pi^i = \phi^i \circ h, i = 1, \ldots, n,$$

where $\circ$ is the composition symbol.

Write $s_{-i} = (s^1, \ldots, s^{i-1}, s^{i+1}, \ldots, s^n)$.[38] Then a Nash equilibrium of the game $(N, S, \pi^1, \ldots, \pi^n)$ is defined as an element $s = (s^1, \ldots, s^n)$ of the joint strategy space such that, for every $1 = 1, \ldots, n$, the inequality

$$\pi^i(s) \geq \pi^i(s'^i, s_{-i}) \quad \text{holds for all } s'^i \text{ in } S^i.$$

When s is a Nash equilibrium of a game, the outcome $z = h(s)$ is called the (corresponding) equilibrium outcome.

To find the equilibrium of the game it is sufficient to have the payoff functions without knowing how they can be decomposed into utility and outcome functions. But the situation is different for normative, comparative, historical, or causal analysis. In the normative context of economics we typically assume that the outcome function (say, representing the tax and subsidy system) is subject to change by human intervention (e.g., legislation), while preferences represented by the utility functions are not. In comparisons across states we may want to assume that preferences are the same while the outcome function differ. In other cases it might be that outcome functions are the same but preferences differ. In all such situations, it is necessary to decompose the payoff functions into their utility and outcome components to carry out the analysis.

---

[38] I.e., s_{-i} is the $(n-1)$-tuple obtained from s by omitting s^i.

To display in detail the time and information structure of a game, it is found helpful to use the so-called extensive form whose graphical representation is the familiar tree diagram. In the usual terminology the intermediate decision points are represented by decision nodes and the end of the game is represented by terminal nodes.

As a very simple example, consider a 2-person 2-move game in which player 1 has the first move and chooses between moves A or B. Player 2 has the second move and chooses between moves C or D. The tree diagram starts with node ('root') labeled '1' representing the point at which player 1 chooses between A and B. From this node issue two 'branches' (labeled respectively $1A$ and $1B$) corresponding to 1's choice of A or B. At the ends of the two branches there are nodes which we may label respectively '$2A$' and '$2B$' corresponding to 2's choice point between C and D. Thus from each of the nodes $2A$ and $2B$ issue two branches corresponding to 2's choices. The branches issuing from node $2A$ are labeled $2AC$ and $2AD$; those from $2B$ are $2BC$ and $2BD$. At the end of each of these four branches there is a terminal node, labeled by the sequence of choices that lead to it. Thus if 1 chose A and 2 chose C, the terminal node is labeled AC, etc.

Now in the usual extensive form representation of an n-person game, the information associated with each terminal node consists of real numbers representing the utilities experienced by the players when the history of the game led to that node. In our example, the node AC would have associated with it the pair of numbers (r^1, r^2) representing the respective utilities of the players attained when the history of the game was A followed by C. That is, the information represents the players' respective payoffs but as functions of game history (the sequence of moves) rather than as a function of strategies (as was the case for the normal form).

But, as we have seen, payoffs are a composite of outcome functions and utilities, and for our purposes the two should be separated. This is very simple to achieve. By analogy with the extensive form *game* we introduce the notion of extensive form *mechanism* (i.e., extensive form *game-form*). As far as moves are concerned, the extensive form mechanism has the same data as the extensive form game. But the difference is that instead of providing data about utilities (i.e., payoffs) it will specify the (physical) outcomes associated with the different nodes of the game-tree. Thus, in the above example, the information associated with node AC would be not the two utility numbers, but the (physical) outcome associated with that node. This could be the description of the resulting resource allocation in an exchange model, or the name of the candidate elected in a voting model.[39]

---

[39] Of course, given the knowledge of utility functions (defined on these outcomes), one could then calculate the respective utility numbers.

One reason for defining the extensive form mechanism is, as indicated above, to separate the roles played by aspects that can be changed through human intervention (institutional change) from those that cannot be so changed, namely preferences.[40]

But there is another reason of particular importance in any attempt to model institutions. Following Coase (1937 and 1960), the literature dealing with institutions puts considerable emphasis on the role of transaction costs.[41] It has been argued by North (e.g., 1990, p. 3)—as well as others—that "... there as yet has been no analytical framework to integrate institutional analysis into economics and history". In particular, in the context of the theory of exchange (1990, p. 27), North attributes this failure to the theorists' disregard for the costliness of the transaction costs. To the extent that this charge is valid, it is necessary to develop a framework for analyzing institutions that would have room for recognizing the role of transaction costs.[42] Now, as indicated above, many aspects of institutional analysis can be captured by formalizing them as properties of normal form mechanisms (i.e., game-forms). But, it seems to me that in order to model the effects of transaction costs, it is necessary to go over to the extensive form of mechanisms introduced above. This is particularly evident in the analysis of informational costs in message exchange mechanisms (adjustment processes) which are formulated as systems of difference equations and are in close correspondence with extensive forms.

We have defined the extensive mechanism form as differing from the extensive form game in that the utility data are replaced by outcome data. But now let us consider a further change. Instead of associating the outcome data exclusively with the terminal nodes, let some of the outcome data be associated with certain branches or intermediate nodes of the tree. Thus in the above 2-person example, suppose that the choice of A by player 1 requires the payment of a license fee of 10 and a personal appearance at a specified government office to apply for that license. Then branch A, connecting node 1 with node $2A$, would have associated with it the outcome vector written, say, as $c = (-\$10,$ appearance at government office). Formally, vector c is an element of the appropriately defined outcome space, but it can be

---

[40] In assuming that preferences are not changed by human intervention, we are ruling out such forms of intervention as education, advertising, and propaganda.

[41] Transaction costs are a major factor in explaining the development of institutional arrangements, but it does not follow that institutions are without importance when transaction costs (or their differentials) are absent or insignificant, unless one ignores income effects and distributional phenomena (see Hurwicz, 1993c).

[42] However, in the theory of mechanism design a great deal of attention has been paid to the size the message space and the complexity of a mechanism, two factors affecting the informational transaction costs. There has been less attention given to other factors—such as those affecting the costs of enforcement.

interpreted as the cost of the 'transaction' consisting in choosing A. Similarly, it might be the case that choosing B requires various types of effort, perhaps to acquire needed information. These requirements would constitute the outcome associated with branch B, connecting the nodes '1' and 2B, Again this outcome can be interpreted as transaction 'cost'.[43]

The formulation being proposed amounts to defining the extensive form *mechanism* as represented by a tree which differs from the customary extensive form *game* tree in that it (1) associates outcome information with (some) branches as well as (some) terminal nodes, and (2) does not provide utility data.[44]

It is true that for a game with a finite number of moves, it is possible to use an alternative tree representation where the costs (or other outcomes) would be accumulated along each sequence of moves and associated with the terminal node corresponding to that sequence. Thus modification (1) would be avoided. But such alternative representation is further removed from a 'natural' description of the mechanism; it also seems less satisfactory because it conceals the time structure of costs that may be an essential element of the picture.

Finally, a comment concerning the contents of the rules involved in institutional arrangements. The emphasis, especially on the economic literature, is on the assignment of rights and obligations. A classic example is that of the assignment of pollution rights and liability for damage caused by pollution. It turns out that there often is a very simple and natural way of representing the assignment of rights by the standard techniques of microeconomics, namely as defined by the location of the initial endowment point, with the understanding that an agent is always entitled to remain at that point.[45]

---

[43] The example of effort shows that the transaction 'cost' is not necessarily expressible in purely monetary terms; nor is it equivalent to utilities.

[44] It is to be noted that a need for associating data with branches and not merely terminal nodes arises already for games with infinite time horizon which do not have terminal nodes. What is usually done in modeling these games is to express the utility as the infinite summation of discounted instantaneous utilities ('felicities'). But these felicities are in effect payoffs associated with branches of an infinite tree that would represent such a game. Hence there is precedent for modification (1) above even in the context of extensive form games.

[45] This is described on p. 104ff. of Eggertsson (1990) and attributed to Haddock and Spiegel (1994). I have not seen the latter paper, but I have found the technique very helpful in analyzing the Coase Theorem in Hurwicz (1993c). A very special case of this technique can be seen in the 'no-trade option' property introduced in Hurwicz (1972), p. 327. It may be noted that this option implies 'individual rationality' of a social choice rule (the guarantee that no player will be pushed below the initial utility level)—but the converse is not true. In the context of institutional analysis, the no-trade option seems the more appropriate assumption—because it is a right. In contexts other than trade models, the no-trade option would naturally be replaced by status quo or a threat point.

Appendix

The following is an example of a normal form game-form which is 'natural' because it includes the possibility of illegal behavior and corresponding enforcement measures.

The players are the inventor (player 0) and users of the invention: A (player 1), B (player 2), etc. However, the model below represents only the outcome when there is only one user, A.

The inventor has the following strategies: 0.1 do nothing; 0.L make a low effort; 0.H make a high effort. Without effort there is no invention, hence no patent and no use. With effort there is an invention whose value corresponds to the level of effort, and a patent is obtained. Once the patent is obtained, the inventor either grants the license when asked to (strategies 0.L.1 and 0.H.1 respectively) or not (strategies 0.L.2 and 0.H.2, respectively).

User A has the following strategies: 1.1 do not use the invention; 1.2 use the invention (if there is one) legally (and pay the required license fee); 1.3 use the invention (if there is one) illegally (without paying the fee).

We shall denote the outcome (over and above the status quo) by $z = \langle z^0; z^1 \rangle$ where z^i is the outcome for player i, with $i = 0, 1$. Hence, the outcome function can be written as $z = h(s) = h(s^0; s^1) = \langle z^0; z^1 \rangle = \langle h^0(s^0; s^1), h^1(s^0; s^1) \rangle$ where h^i is the outcome function for player i.

The following are examples of the entries in the outcome function table (in $\langle a, b \rangle$ below, a represents the outcome for player 0 and b the outcome for player 1; the symbol ϕ means status quo (no change)):

- $h(0.1; s^1) = \langle \phi; \phi \rangle$ for all s^1; i.e., if the inventor makes no effort, there is no invention and status quo prevails.

- $h(0.j.1; 1.1) = \langle k^j; \phi \rangle$ where k^j represents (say) the inventor's fatigue at level $j = L, H$ corresponding to the level of effort (low or high); this is the outcome when the user's strategy is 'do not use even if there is an invention available'.

- $h(0.j.1; 1.2) = \langle k^j; b^j, -f \rangle$ where b^j is the result for the user (not necessarily monetary) of using the j-level invention, and f the license fee received by the inventor and $-f$ the fee paid by the user.

- $h(0.j.1; 1.3) = \langle k^j; p; -p \rangle$ where p is the damage paid by the user to the inventor for an (assumed unsuccessful) attempt to use the invention illegally.

[The last item], of course, presupposes an effective enforcement system. In the absence of such a system, the outcome would be $\langle k^j; b^j \rangle$. I.e., the inventor only has fatigue to show for his/her effort, while the user gets the benefit without either having to pay fee or damages. Note that the outcomes may but need not be monetary in nature and they do not represent utilities, only physical outcomes. By replacing these physical outcomes with their utility numbers we would obtain the two players' payoff functions.

References

Berman, S. and A. Schotter (1981) A mathematical theory of institution creation, in *The Economic Theory of Social Institutions*, A. Schotter, 52–108. Cambridge, MA: Cambridge University Press.

Coase, R. (1937) The nature of the firm, *Economica*, 4(16): 386–405.

Coase, R. (1960) The problem of social cost, *The Journal of Law and Economics*, 3(1): 1–44.

Eggertsson, T. (1990) *Economic Behavior and Institutions*. Cambridge, MA: Cambridge University Press.

Gardner, R. and E. Ostrom (1991) Rules and games, *Public Choice*, 70(2): 121–49.

Haddock, D. and M. Spiegel. (1984) Property rules, liability rules, and inalienability: One view of the Edgeworth Box, in *Papers Presented at the First Meeting of the European Association for Law and Economics*, ed. G. Skogh, 97: 47–75. Lund, Sweden: Nationalekonomiska Institutionen.

Hurwicz, L. (1972) On informationally decentralized systems, in *Decision and Organization*, ed. C. McGuire and R. Radner, Amsterdam: North-Holland. Second edition, 1986, 297–336. Minneapolis, MN: University of Minnesota Press.

Hurwicz, L. (1993a) Toward a framework for analyzing institutions and institutional change, in *Markets and Democracy: Participation, Accountability and Efficiency*, ed. S. Bowles, H. Gintis, and B. Gustafsson, 51–67. Cambridge, MA: Cambridge University Press.

Hurwicz, L. (1993b) Implementation and enforcement in institutional modeling, in *Political Economy: Institutions, Competition, and Representation*, ed. W. Barnett, M. Hinich, and N. Schofield, 51–59. Cambridge, MA: Cambridge University Press.

Hurwicz, L. (1993c) What is the Coase Theorem?, mimeo. Published as Hurwicz, L. (1995) What is the Coase Theorem?, *Japan and the World Economy*, 7(1): 49–74.

Katzner, D. (1989), Institutionally determined parameters, mimeo. Published as Katzner, D. (1990) Institutionally determined parameters in economic equations, *Économie Appliquée*, 43(3): 35–52.

Lewis, D. (1969) *Convention: A Philosophical Study*. Cambridge, MA: Harvard University Press.

North, D. (1990) *Institutions, Institutional Change and Economic Performance*. Cambridge, MA: Cambridge University Press.

North, D. (1992) *Transaction Costs, Institutions, and Economic Performance*. San Francisco, CA: ICS Press.

Ostrom, E. (1986) An agenda for the study of institutions, *Public Choice*, 48(1): 3–25.

Plott, C. (1979) The application of laboratory experimental methods to public choice, in *Collective Decision-Making: Applications from Public Choice Theory*, ed. C. Russell, 137–60. Baltimore, MD: Johns Hopkins University Press.

Reiter, S. and J. Hughes (1981) A preface on modeling the regulated U.S. economy, Hofstra Law Review, 9(5): 1381–1421.

Riker, W. (1980) Implications from the disequilibrium of majority rule for the study of institutions, *American Political Science Review*, 74(2): 432–46.

Ruttan, V. (1978) Induced institutional change, in *Induced Innovation: Technology, Institutions, and Development*, ed. H. Binswanger and V. Ruttan, 327–57. Baltimore, MD: Johns Hopkins University Press.

Schotter, A. (1981) *The Economic Theory of Social Institutions*. Cambridge, MA: Cambridge University Press.

Schotter, A. (1986) The evolution of rules, in *Economics as a Process*, ed. R. Langlois, 117–33. Cambridge, MA: Cambridge University Press.

Schotter, A. (1989) Comment (on *Market and Institutions* by Siro Lombardini), in *Economic Institutions in a Dynamic Society*, ed. T. Shiraishi and S. Tsuru, 50–55. New York, NY: Macmillan.

Shubik, M. (1982) *Game Theory in the Social Sciences: Concepts and Solutions*, Cambridge, MA: M.I.T. Press.

Stiglitz, J. (1974) Incentives and risk sharing in sharecropping, *Review of Economics Studies*, 41(2): 219–55.

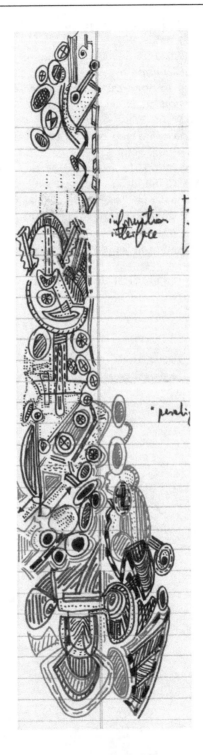

16

Institutions as Families of Game-Forms

1 Introduction

Recent decades have witnessed a revival of interest in the role of institutions in economic processes. The importance attached to the work of Coase, North, Williamson and others attests to this. The works of these authors contain illustrative examples of institutions: property rights (common or private property), the state as guarantor of rights, law, markets (competitive oligopolistic, monopolistic), money (commodity or fiat money), liability for damage by smoke, state regulation of economic activities (e.g., price controls, anti-trust laws), various forms of land tenure (sharecropping, renting, utilization of wage labor), various forms of business organization (corporations, partnerships, non-profits), company towns, franchise systems, and many others—including even the week, viewed as an institution.

Specific institutions have been studied with the help of familiar analytical tools: demand and cost functions, principal-agent, and game-theoretical models. The comparison of sharecropping (métayage or on 'shares') system with renting (the 'English' system) is already found in Marshall's 1890 edition of his *Principles of Economics* (Book VI, Ch. X, §§4, 5, 6, pp. 642–49). But serious analytic study of institutions as a general phenomenon calls for a rigorous definition of the concept of an institution within the framework of a formal model. Ideally, the definition should fit most if not all of the examples such as those above.

Not all those stressing the importance of institutions have attempted to provide such a definition. Those who did, as pointed out by Ostrom (1986),

Reprinted from *The Japanese Economic Review*, 1996, 47(2): 113–32. The present paper is an expanded version of my comments at the First Decentralization Conference in Japan, held at Keio University in November 1994. Due to its expository nature, it overlaps parts of some of my earlier papers cited in the references. Thanks are due to Professors Tatsuyoshi Saijo and Takehiko Yamato for numerous helpful suggestions. Responsibility, as always, remains the author's.

Institutions as Families of Game-Forms In: *The Collected Papers of Leonid Hurwicz Volume 1.*
Edited by Samiran Banerjee, Oxford University Press. © Oxford University Press 2022.
DOI: 10.1093/oso/9780199313280.003.0016

had to face the multiplicity of meanings of the term and to make choices among them.

2 Institutions and Game-Forms

2.1 Meanings A and B of the term 'institution'

For North (1990, pp. 3, 4) who views institutions as rules of the game in a society, a basic dichotomy is between the meaning of institutions as such rules and the players whom he calls 'organizations'. But these players are often also called institutions. They are entities or bodies, usually mission oriented and treated as juridical persons. Examples abound: a university, a church, a country's legislative body. Although most 'player'-institutions involve many (physical) persons and can be classified as organizations, there are also one-person 'player'-institutions, as for instance a country's presidency or an agency's ombudsman.[1] We shall refer to 'player'-institutions as the *A-institutions*.

The other meaning of 'institution', to be referred as the B meaning, and often called an *institutional arrangement*, is a matter of some controversy. As noted above, for North and many others[2] it consists of rules (in the language of game theory, *game-forms*). For others, in particular Schotter (1981, p. 155), social[3] institutions are regularities or standards of behavior.[4] In the language of game theory, they are for him the *solutions* rather than rules of the game.[5]

In what follows I shall be dealing primarily with the B meaning of the term 'institutions', i.e., 'institution' is to be interpreted as synonymous with institutional arrangement (a *B-institution*), unless the contrary is specified. As for a formal definition of a B-institution, mine will be close to the 'rules (game-forms)' interpretation, but when an institution's genesis is taken into account it will incorporate some of the regularities approach as well. To make this clear, some formal apparatus is needed.

---

[1] In one-person player-institutions one must distinguish between the player-institution and its incumbent.

[2] In particular Riker (1982, p. 4) and Ostrom (1986). For an approach synthesizing the different concepts see Crawford and Ostrom (1995).

[3] Although North, unlike Schotter, does not use the term 'social', he speaks of the rules of the game *in society*, so the intent seems the same.

[4] It is interesting to note that von Neumann and Morgenstern (1944, pp. 41, 512) use the term 'standards of behavior' as representing the solution of a game. On the other hand, when using the term 'institutions' (as on p. 225, footnote 3), identified with forms of social organization (the example being laissez-faire), they seem to be referring to rules of the game rather than to solutions.

[5] In (1989, pp. 50–51), Schotter speaks of institutions of type I (rules) and of type II (regularities of behavior).

2.2 Notation for games in normal form

In order to be clear about the formalization of the notion of rules of the game, we must be careful about distinguishing between a *game* and a *game-form*.[6] Games, as is well known, have different forms of representation, in particular the so-called *extensive form* specifying the individual moves and their consequences, and the *normal form* formulated in terms of admissible *strategies* and the outcomes they produce.

We shall mostly be dealing with the normal form, assuming a finite number n of players. The term 'game' in its technical sense is applied to the ordered pair consisting of two n-tuples: that of *individual admissible strategy domains*, $S^1, \ldots, S^n$, and that of (real-valued) payoff functions, $\pi^1, \ldots, \pi^n$. Denote by $S = S^1 \times \cdots \times S^n$, the *(joint) strategy space*, i.e., the Cartesian product of the individual domains, and by $N = \{1, \ldots, n\}$ the set of players. For all i in N, the i-th payoff function has the (joint) strategy space S as its domain and takes its values in the reals. Let $s = (s^1, \ldots, s^n)$, s in S, s^i in S^i for all i in N, be the n-tuple of strategies adopted by the players. The result is that the i-th player obtains the payoff $\pi^i(s)$, usually interpreted as the utility derived by the i-th player when s prevails. It is its payoff that each player is trying to maximize.

Formally, a game Γ then is defined as the double n-tuple, $\Gamma = (S^1, \ldots, S^n; \pi^1, \ldots, \pi^n)$ where, for each i in N, $\pi^i : S \to \mathbb{R}$. (Here $\mathbb{R}$ represents the reals.)

2.3 Game-forms vs. games

Since the payoff values represent the players' utilities, they depend both on rules of the game and on the players' preferences. To represent this situation, we first introduce the notion of an *outcome space*, denoted by Z, whose elements are the (physical) outcomes of the strategic decisions. In economic environments, the generic element of Z might be a resource allocation; for example, in a pure-exchange economy with m goods, a point z of the outcome space is a vector with $m \cdot n$ real components z_j^i, where z_j^i is the total amount of good j held after trading by trader i, so that Z is a vector space of dimension $m \cdot n$. In a voting model, the outcome space might consist of the set of candidates. In a social game, Z might be the set of prizes that might be given to players. Just who gets which prize depends, of course, on the strategies chosen by the players. The relationship between the strategies chosen and the resulting outcomes is defined by the outcome function, denoted by h. The *game-form*[7] G is formally defined as $G = (S^1, \ldots, S^n, h)$, or more briefly as (S, h) where S is the Cartesian product of the S^i's and $h : S \to Z$.

---

[6] Although this is not customary, we sometimes hyphenate the term 'game-form' in order to avoid misunderstandings that might arise, e.g., when we speak of game-forms in extensive form.

[7] In the economic literature often called the *mechanism*.

To express the relationship between game-forms and games, we introduce utility functions to represent preferences.[8] The i-th player's *utility function* ϕ^i associates a real number, say u^i, with the outcome (e.g., resource allocation[9] or candidate elected) resulting from the strategies s chosen by the players. I.e., $u^i = \phi^i(z)$ where $z = h(s)$, and so $u^i = \phi^i(h(s))$. Hence the real number u^i represents the i-th player's utility resulting when the strategy n-tuple s prevails, so that u^i is the value of the i-th payoff function associated with s. It follows that the payoff function is the composite of the utility function and the outcome function. This can be written as

$$\pi^i(s) = \phi^i(h(s)) \quad \text{for all } i \text{ in } N \text{ and all } s \text{ in } S,$$

or, more compactly, as $\pi^i = \phi^i \circ h$.

2.4 'Rules of the game' are represented by game-forms, not by games

We have been somewhat pedantic in formalizing the concepts of a game and of a game-form, because the distinction between the two is crucial for understanding the meaning of the 'rules of the game'. Since the players' preferences are not part of the rules, it is the game-form, rather than the game, that corresponds to the intuitive notion of the 'rules of the game'.[10] Hence 'game-form' is the important concept in defining institutions in terms of rules.[11]

In the literature, the models under consideration frequently involve numerical outcomes—e.g., monetary payments to individual consumers. Thus an element of the outcome space is $z = (z^1, \ldots, z^n)$ where z^i is the payment to person i (a real number). Further, suppose that every individual is selfish, so that i's utility depends only on the i-th component of z, say $u^i = \phi^i(z) = \psi^i(z^i)$ where ψ^i is a strictly increasing function. Finally, suppose that every one is 'risk-neutral', i.e., that the ψ^i is a linear (or affine) function of the payment z^i. Then, without loss of generality, one may take the function ψ^i to be identity, so that $u^i = \phi^i(z) = \psi^i(z^i) = z^i$ for each person i. Let h denote the outcome function, so that $h(s) = (z^1, \ldots, z^n)$, and define $h^i(s) = z^i$. Then the payoff function in this model is given by $\pi^i(s) = z^i = h^i(s)$, and the n-tuple $\pi(s) = (\pi^1, \ldots, \pi^n)$ is identical with the outcome function $h(s) = (h^1(s), \ldots, h^n(s))$. It is easy to see that in this case the distinction between the outcome function (the n-tuple of the h^i's) and the i-th payoff

---

[8] At the cost of complicating exposition, it is possible to avoid the assumption (implicitly made here) that the preferences can be represented by utility functions.

[9] This formulation allows for the possibility of non-selfish preferences. When preferences are selfish, the i-th player's utility in fact depends only on the subvector or 'bundle' $z^i = (z^i_1, \ldots, z^i_m)$ of the resource allocation z.

[10] On the other hand, since institutions will be defined as the results of human activities, not all aspects of the game-form are to be viewed as institutional.

[11] I.e., corresponding to Schotter's 'type'!

function (identical with the i-th component of the outcome function) does not seem very important. But, of course, this is a very special case.

2.5 Representation of institutions by game-forms involves more than restrictions on strategy domains

When an institution is defined by restrictions on the individual strategy domains (the sets S^i) imposed by an authority, it is natural to call such an institution a *regulation*.[12] North's (1990, p. 3) initial definition of institutions appears to include little[13] beyond regulations so defined: "Institutions are the rules of the game in a society or, more formally, are the humanly devised constraints that shape human interaction."

But the notion of (B-) institutions as constraints is, in my view, too narrow—for two reasons. First, of the two components of a game-form (S, h), they only deal with the first (the strategy domains) and, even among the properties of strategy domains, they seem to cover only restrictions of the individual strategy domains while ignoring the possibility of expansions[14] of these domains by institutional arrangements. Second, it is difficult to see how certain important institutions (e.g., markets, social insurance) could be described just in terms of strategy domains but without reference to the outcome functions. It is natural to represent arrangements such as taxes, penalties, or subsidies as properties of outcome functions.[15]

2.6 An institution is a class of game-forms, not just a single game-form

An examination of examples of any phenomenon typically called an institution (in the sense of rules) shows, however, that it would not be natural to identify it with a particular game-form. For instance, the institution of sharecropping specifies that the crops will be divided so that the landlord

---

[12] The concept of a regulated economy in Reiter and Hughes (1981) is broader: it includes not only 'direct constraints on behavior' (corresponding to our concept of regulation) but also parameters θ^{ij} determining the agents' incentives (e.g., taxes or subsidies).

[13] It is somewhat broader because it refers to constraints that are 'humanly devised'—but not necessarily by an authority. This might, for instance, cover commodity money regarded as a (spontaneously developed) institution but not qualifying as regulation.

[14] Crawford and Ostrom (1995, p. 583), by contrast, do refer to opportunities as well as constraints.

[15] Admittedly, some of the arrangements mentioned above—such as taxes (or subsidies)—can alternatively be viewed as restrictions on (or expansions of) strategy domains, although this representation might make analysis more complicated. But in many cases, including these examples, there is additional machinery involved, needed for the processing and transmission of information as well as for enforcement. Representation through outcome functions (as well as addition of artificial players such as, e.g., the Internal Revenue Service agency, an A-institution) seems the appropriate way to represent such institutional arrangements.

gets a fraction, say k (with $0 < k < 1$) and the laborer $1 - k$.[16] Now when sharecropping is formulated as a game-form, the value of the share parameter k (entering the outcome function) must be specified, say $k = 1/2$. But to qualify as the institution of sharecropping any fractional value of k is acceptable. Hence the institution of sharecropping corresponds not to a particular game-form, say $G_{1/2}$ (with k specified to equal 1/2) but to a class of game-forms, say $\mathbb{G} = \{G_k : 0 < k < 1\}$.[17]

Another illustration of the same point is provided by price controls, more specifically price ceilings. In game-form representation, these define the seller's strategy (price) domain as having a finite upper bound, say p^{i*}, determined by the price control agency, say $S^i = \{p^i : p^i \leq p^{i*}\}$, where the seller is the i-th agent and p^i his/her strategy variable. To specify a game-form requires a particular numerical value of p^{i*}. Denote such a game-form by $G_{p^{i*}}$, characterized by a specific value of p^{i*} in the above formula for S^i. One would naturally say that price controls as an institution prevail regardless of the numerical value of the ceiling p^{i*}. Hence, again, the institution of (ceiling) price controls corresponds to a *class of game-forms*, say $\mathbb{G} = \{G_{p^{i*}} : p^{i*}$ ranging over (finite!) real numbers$\}$.[18]

Membership in a class of objects may be considered as equivalent to having a certain attribute (or collection of attributes) distinguishing members from non-members. Hence defining an institution as a class of game-forms may be viewed as equivalent with defining an institution as an attribute (or collection of attributes) of game-forms.

We may refer to the game-forms belonging to the class representing the same institution (i.e., sharing certain attributes) as 'institutionally equivalent'. Typically, this equivalence is based on similarity of the incentive structure it engenders for the participants, but there is a great deal of arbitrariness, sometimes depending on the issues under consideration. As an illustration, much of the analysis of incentive structures of the alternative

---

16 The 1969 *Nouveau Petit Larousse en couleurs* specifies (under *métayage*) that k should not exceed a third. Actually, the term *métayer* comes from a Latin word meaning 'a half'. Thus there might have been a time when $k = 1/2$ was the only permissible value under *métayage*. But in the present context, all values strictly between zero and one qualify as 'sharecropping'. (See Hurwicz 1979a, pp. 123–47, and esp. pp. 140–44, the section entitled 'Incentive structures for unilateral maximization', for a simple model in which one-half turns out to be the best value of k from the landlord's point of view when the laborer's effort cannot be measured or observed.)

17 Following Stiglitz (1974), let the laborer's reward, a component of the outcome function, be written as $r = ky + b$ where y is the size of the crop (regarded here as the worker's strategy variable) and k and b are real-valued parameters. Different forms of land tenure are defined by different regions in the (k, b)-parameter space. Thus (pure) sharecropping is defined by the conditions $b = 0$ and $0 < k < 1$; renting by $k = 1$, $b < 0$; wage-labor by $k = 0$, $b > 0$. Thus, under renting, $-b$ is the rental fee, while under wage-labor b is the wage.

18 Although the frameworks are different (dealing with imputations or strategy spaces), it is of interest to note the multiplicity of imputations in a single von Neumann-Morgenstern solution and the multiplicity of Nash solutions (e.g., in a coordination game) corresponding to the same institution in Schotter's treatment.

land tenure form reaches conclusions that are valid for all pure sharecropping game-forms, regardless of the value of the share parameter k, provided it is strictly between 0 and 1; similarly for all rental arrangements, regardless of the value of the parameter $b < 0$, and all wage-labor arrangements regardless of the value of $b > 0$. (See footnote 17 for notation.) Hence we speak of all pure sharecropping game-forms, regardless of the value of k as institutionally equivalent, etc.

2.7 Conditional game-forms ('humanly devised' aspects of game-forms)

2.7.1 Institutions as correspondences from environments to game-forms

Quite often a game-form has two aspects: (1) those that are behavioral in nature and are (potentially at least) subject to alternative design and embody the essence of the institutional arrangements, and (2) those that are considered as given, either because they are determined by the laws of physics or, more generally, by what we call the (economic) environment (in particular by the existing resource endowments, and the current state of technology). In such cases, it would be incorrect to identify the institutional arrangements with all of the game-form (S, h), and therefore a more refined definition of an institution must be formulated.

One example of such a game-form is seen in a mechanism proposed in Hurwicz, Maskin, and Postlewaite (1995) for situations in which no player knows the other players' endowments. The rules of the game call for each player to announce his/her own endowment (as well as estimates of the other players' endowments). This announcement is permitted to be an understatement but not an overstatement. The prohibition against overstatement is enforced by the requirement that the player 'put on the table' the resources claimed in the endowment. Assuming that borrowing is somehow ruled out, it is then physically impossible to exaggerate. But this means that a given player's strategy domain depends on his/her true endowment. (In the usual economic models, the endowments, preferences, and technologies determine the environment.) Thus the i-th strategy domain S^i is a function of the true value, denoted by $\mathring{\omega}^i$, of the i-th agent's endowment. Therefore, the i-th strategy domain is denoted more accurately by $S^i(\mathring{\omega}^i)$. Since $\mathring{\omega}^i$ is a component of the i-th characteristic e^i, and, in turn, e^i is a component of the environment $e = (e^1, \ldots, e^n)$, we see that the rules of the game specify the i-th strategy domain by a functional relation from the space E of environments into the space of strategy domains, hence into the space of game-forms. The institutional aspect, here the result of design ('humanly devised'), is this functional relation, rather than the strategy domain itself.

An instance where the outcome function of a mechanism depends on the existing technology, hence on the environment e, is given below in Section 6. Here the rules of the game specify (via the 'reward functions') how players are rewarded given the output. With y denoting output, consider (as in footnote 17—the Stiglitz model) the class of (the worker's) linear reward functions written $r^i = ky + b$. (However, unlike in footnote 17 and in Section 6, effort—not output—is considered the worker's strategy variable.) As in footnote 17, special cases of the reward functions (i.e., of the parameters k and b) produce alternative institutional arrangements (e.g., sharecropping, wage labor, renting) and are 'humanly devised'. The player's strategy may be his/her intensity of effort; this will determine the output via the production function. The outcome function, relating reward (outcome) to effort (strategy), has a 'humanly devised' aspect (the reward functions) and an aspect determined by the environment (the production function). Thus the institutional aspect is in this example represented by a functional relation from the space E of environments to the space of outcome functions, rather than the outcome function itself.

The preceding two examples illustrate the fact that institutional phenomena should, in general, be represented not as game-forms but as relationships between game-forms and the economic environment. But since we think of institutions as associated with *classes* of mechanisms, this relationship must be viewed as a correspondence rather than a function. Thus in the preceding example, the institution of sharecropping involves the worker's reward function ('humanly devised') of the form $r^i = ky$ where y is the output and k a number between zero and one. But suppose the strategy variable s^i is the worker's effort x^i, so that $s^i = x^i$, and the output is determined by the production function $y = cx^i$, where c is the technologically determined productivity of effort parameter, considered as part of the environment and not institutional in nature. Then the worker's outcome function is $h^i(s) = dx^i = kcx^i$, involving both the institutional aspect (k) and the environment aspect (c). Thus it is not the outcome function h^i that represents the institution of sharecropping, but rather the correspondence that associates with each environment (productivity parameter c) an outcome function $h^i(\cdot)$, where $h^i(s) = dx^i$ and d/c is a number between zero and one.

In formal notation, we have the following situation. Let $\mathbb{G}$ denote the class of conceivable game-forms. We may then consider an institution to be correspondence, say Λ, from the space of environments E into $\mathbb{G}$, i.e., $\Lambda:E \to \mathbb{G}$. Given an environment e, the resulting class of game-forms, $\mathbb{G} = \Lambda(e)$, embodies not only institutions but also the characteristics of the environment; it is the correspondence Λ itself that represents the purely institutional aspect of the game-forms. (See footnote 41 in Section 6 for an example of such a correspondence.)

We may note that a constant correspondence Λ may be identified with a class of game-forms. In fact, throughout the present paper, when we speak of institutions as represented by classes $\mathbb{G}$ of game-forms, they should be interpreted as correspondences Λ. (Alternatively, one can interpret such references as dealing with the special case of constant Λ.)

For the sake of brevity, we sometimes refer to *conditional game-forms* or *classes* $\mathbb{G}$ when the institutional aspects are represented by functions or correspondences such as Λ above. (The case of constant Λ may then be termed an *unconditional* game-form.)

2.7.2 *An alternative formalization of dependence on the environment*

As an alternative way of looking at the problem, consider again the class $\mathbb{G}$ of conceivable game-forms. Further, let $\mathbb{G}(e)$, a subset of $\mathbb{G}$, be the class of game-forms consistent with the laws of physics and other restrictions that cannot be modified by human action under the prevailing environment e. Thus human action can only result in choice among the game-forms in $\mathbb{G}(e)$. Thus an institution, say T, is represented by a subset, say G_T, of $\mathbb{G}(e)$.

In our interpretation of institutions as classes of game-forms, the set-theoretic difference $\mathbb{G}(e)\backslash G_T$ represents the game-forms that have been eliminated by human action. Full information about the effect of human action in this case is represented by the ordered pair $\langle \mathbb{G}(e), G_T \rangle$, showing both the field of choice and the choice made through human action.

Now the set $\mathbb{G}(e)$ is determined by the environment e. If the correspondence $\mathbb{G}(\cdot)$ is regarded as known, we are back to the ordered pairs (e, G) representing institutions, i.e., to conditional game-forms.

3 The Defining Attributes of Institutions

Not all classes of game-forms qualify as institutions. In this section we shall be considering some of the attributes of game-forms that, by almost unanimous consensus, characterize institutions. These are:

  (a) the genesis of institutions: human actions (behavior),
  (b) ensuring the effectiveness of institutions, and
  (c) the domain of applicability of institutional rules ('categoricity').

3.1 *The genesis of institutions: human actions (behavior)*

Clearly, the constraints (or outcomes) due to laws of physics would not be considered institutions. In one fashion or another, this is recognized by all writers and incorporated into the definition of institutions. Thus, as seen from the above quotation, North defines institutions as *humanly devised* constraints.

Ostrom (1986, pp. 5–6) says: "Rules, as I wish to use the term, are distinct from physical and behavioral laws.... That rules can be changed by humans is one of their key characteristics."

Schotter's definition (1981, p. 11) reads as follows:

> A social institution is a regularity in social behavior that is agreed to by all members of society, specifies behavior in specific recurrent situations, and is either self-policed or policed by some external authority.

Clearly, it is the human behavior or actions that generate the institutions. In Section 3.1.2 we consider a formalization (the concept of conditional game-forms) designed to separate the 'human design' from the 'environmental' aspects of game-forms.

The Reiter-Hughes (1981) model contains a sequence of two games, the first of which generates the (institutional) rules for the second. Again, human choices are involved. This formalization will be elaborated in Section 4 below.

3.1.1 *Conscious design vs. 'organic' (endogenous) origin*

It is to be noted that human actions are not synonymous with conscious design. While North speaks of 'humanly devised' constraints, Schotter (1981, p. 21) stresses the absence of conscious design (the 'organic' or 'behavioral' view, with roots in Carl Menger's 1883 discussion almost a century earlier):

> ... the institutional form will be an endogenous variable in the model. It emerges without any agent or group or agents consciously designing it—through human action but not human design.

In this context Schotter cites Hayek's (1955, p. 39) statement in a similar spirit:

> The problems which they [the social sciences] try to answer arise only in so far as regularities are observed which are not the result of anybody's design.

The point that not all institutions emerge without conscious design is made in Schotter, although he gives reasons (1981, pp. 28–29) (some quoted from Hayek, 1955) why he will not (subsequently) be discussing consciously created institutions. He says:

> ... many social institutions are created in one stroke by a social planner or by the agents of society meeting in a face-to-face manner and bargaining about the type of institution they would like to see created. Here the exact form of the institution

that emerges is the result of explicit human design (in the case of a planner) or multilateral bargaining (in the case of a legislature).[19]

The 'constitution creation game' is mentioned as an example of institutional rules created by such a process.

In his 1986 paper (pp. 117–18), Schotter correlates what he calls the 'rules view' ('type I' in his 1989 terminology) of institutions with the notion of *consciously designed* game-forms or mechanisms:

> The focus of attention here is on the possibility of designing sets of rules or game-forms (to use Gibbard's terminology) that when imposed on a set of social agents, leads to prespecified equilibrium outcomes. ... Throughout this literature, social institutions are planned and designed mechanisms given exogenously to or imposed upon a society of agents. Institutional change is a process of social engineering that takes place through the manipulation of rules.

But there is no logical basis for identifying the 'rules view' of institutions with the assumption of conscious design as genesis of the rules. Many questions studied in what is often called 'mechanisms design' or 'implementation'[20] literature deal with the *logical* compatibility of various attributes of game-forms or rules. The answers are as relevant to rules arrived at by consensus or majority vote of a group to whom the rules are to apply (and who respect the majority decision) as they are to rules "given exogenously or imposed upon a society of agents".

This is, in particular, true of the informational (im)possibility theorems, such as the theorem stating that Pareto optimality cannot be guaranteed by any informationally decentralized mechanism with a message space of dimension substantially lower than that need to verify that perfectly competitive equilibrium prevails (see Mount and Reiter 1974; Hurwicz 1977; and Osana 1978). It is also true of the theorem stating that the set of Nash equilibrium allocations of any mechanism guaranteeing Pareto optimality in an economy where participants are not forced to trade must include the perfectly competitive allocations.[21]

I see no reason why a set of rules under which a society or economy operates cannot be the outcome of some 'organic' process, free of conscious design. In fact, I believe that Schotter's (1981) supergame Nash equilibria may be viewed as an illustration of this possibility, showing that a rigorous

---

[19] In fact, the first of two games in the Reiter-Hughes model, the (cooperative) political game Π [whose outcome (p. 1399) is the framework for the second game (played by firms and regulators)], is envisioned as a bargaining game involving coalition formation.

[20] I probably am to blame for having popularized the 'design' term, while 'implementation' is probably due to Eric Maskin.

[21] Subject to a condition of continuity and a sufficiently broad class of economies for which the guarantee is to hold. See Hurwicz (1979b).

game-theoretic formulation can constitute a model of 'organic' or endogenous formation of rules governing behavior. It is for this reason that I see no conflict between the rules interpretation of institutional arrangements and the possibility of 'organic' genesis of such institutions.

However, the distinction between imposed and non-imposed rules does suggest a related and important dichotomy of institutions: (1. 'external') those, like rules contained in laws, that are binding on persons other than their creators (e.g., legislators), and (2. 'internal') those, like rules contained in contracts, that only bind those that participate in their creation (including heirs, assigns, etc.).[22] My intent is to formulate the concept of institution so that it covers both categories. Moreover, if I think of the process of creating an institution as a game (à la Reiter-Hughes, and perhaps even Schotter), this is not meant to exclude the possibility of less formalized genesis such as custom formation.

3.2 Ensuring the effectiveness of institutions

Although Schotter's concept of an institution differs from that proposed in the present paper,[23] it is valuable because of its explicit reference (1981, p. 11) to behavior being "either self-policed or policed by some external authority". North's definition does not mention enforcement but its importance is clear from subsequent discussion (e.g., 1990, pp. 28–33). Crawford and Ostrom (1995, p. 586) distinguish rules from norms by the role of sanctions for not following rules (their 'or else' element).

Schotter's notion of 'self-policed' may cover two phenomena: (1) behavior being policed by members of the group rather than an external authority,[24]

---

[22] It is interesting to note the part of Schotter's definition of a social institution as "... a regularity of social behavior that is agreed to by all members of society...". Taken literally, this would imply that all social institutions belong to class (2) above. The models of institution generation constructed by Schotter, including property rights, do satisfy this requirement. But one might not want to say that the institution of property rights does not exist if some members of the society are opposed to it.

[23] Schotter (1981, p. 11) defines an institution as regularity of behavior and calls it in Schotter (1989, pp. 50–51) an institution of type II, while labeling institutions defined in terms of rules as institutions of type I. Both type I and II are institutions in the B sense. (The terminology used in Crawford and Ostrom 1995 is 'institutions-as-equilibria' and 'institutions-as-rules' corresponding, at least roughly, to Schotter's type II and type I respectively.)

In the terminology of game theory, an institution of type II is an equilibrium strategy (e.g., a Nash equilibrium) of a game, hence an element of the space S, while an institution of type I is formulated in terms of the game-form which, together with the players' utility functions, defines a game.

As will be seen below, we take into account the equilibrium aspect of institutional phenomena by following Reiter and Hughes (1981) using a model consisting of a sequence of two games where the rules governing the second game are obtained as the equilibrium outcome of the first game. Thus an institutional arrangement is both a class of game-forms (of the second game) and an equilibrium outcome (of the first game). Note, however, that—except in special cases—the equilibrium outcome of the first game need not be an element of its strategy space.

[24] A situation studied by Elinor Ostrom and co-authors in a number of papers.

and (2) internalization of appropriate behavior, so that each person is, in effect policing himself/herself. In a variety of situations, any of these modes of enforcement (or their combinations) may be present. But it seems to me that enforcement is too narrow a category of phenomena serving to ensure the effectiveness of an institution (viewed as a class of game-forms) [25]

Enforcement is aimed at making sure that the strategy domains prescribed by the game-forms are being abided by. But to make a game-form (mechanism) effective, the results specified by the outcome functions must also be 'delivered'. Mechanisms such as markets or social insurance, illustrate the need for special machinery required to carry out, in addition to enforcement, the informational functions (in particular, communication) as well as the physical flow of goods and financial instruments. The totality of these required activities corresponds, I believe, fairly closely to everyday usage of the term 'implementation'. But since in recent literature this term has been given a different meaning,[26] I sometimes qualify it by an adjective and speak of *genuine implementation*, with the intention of covering the complex of all activities designed to make the outcome function effective, thus including much in addition to enforcement.[27]

3.3 The domain of applicability of institutional rules ('categoricity')

Here again, Schotter's definition has the merit of explicitly referring to social institutions being concerned with "behavior in specific recurrent situations". To put it in a somewhat more general form, a (B-) institution deals with a *category* of situations (whether recurrent or contemporaneous) and typically applies to a class (*category*) of actors rather than to specifically named persons.[28] Thus there are rules for buyers or sellers, for parents and children, for legislators, bureaucrats, etc. This is the property referred to as 'categoricity'.

---

[25] One occasionally hears the opinion that a Nash equilibrium is self-enforcing. But that is only true (presumably, by definition) if one assumes that players abide by the rules of the game. To make sure that they do, enforcement machinery may be necessary.

Another view exists, to the effect that enforcement is impossible because of the possibility of corruption on the part of those in charge of enforcement, as well as their superiors. ('Who will guard the guardians?') An infinite regress seems to be a possibility. A framework for avoiding this paradox, involving the notion of the "natural game-form" is discussed in Hurwicz (1993a).

[26] Following Eric Maskin, current literature uses the expression "to implement a social choice rule" in the sense of finding a game-form which, within a specified class of players' preferences, would produce equilibrium outcomes consonant with the desiderata embodied in the social choice rule. (The use of the term 'rule' in 'social choice rule' to represent the desiderata, although widespread, is somewhat confusing in the present context; hence we sometimes use 'goal correspondence' instead.)

[27] One frequent aspect of genuine implementation is the creation of an agency (e.g., the Social Security Administration, an A-institution) whose function is precisely to make the outcome function operational, and in some cases also to enforce the constraints on the strategy domains.

[28] As indicated above, some institutions (called above 'internal') govern only their creators; others ('external') are binding on others as well.

To determine that an institution applies in a given case, it must be verified that the situation and the actors belong to appropriate categories.

4 A Game Sequence Model

4.1 Three-game sequence model

To avoid ambiguity, we shall formalize some of the ideas discussed above. The formalization admittedly is narrower than the general situations discussed above; in particular, it may not cover the 'organically' generated institutions that constitute Schotter's primary interest. Specifically, we follow to a considerable extend the schema used by Reiter and Hughes, although we shall use a sequence of three games where Reiter and Hughes use two. It is the first of these three games, Γ_1, called *preliminary*, that results in creating the institution, i.e., a class of game-forms (denoted by $\mathbb{G}_{23} = \mathbb{G}_2 \times \mathbb{G}_3$) intended to govern the subsequent games.[29],[30] The second game, Γ_2 called *administrative* (although it may be involve judicial as well as administrative bodies as players), formulates detailed regulations and so narrows down the *class* $\mathbb{G}_3$ to a *single* game-form G_3, required to be an element of $\mathbb{G}_3$. This game-form G_3 will then govern the third game, Γ_3, called *substantive*.

For example, the preliminary game Γ_1 may be the legislative process resulting in the prohibition of cartels, the institution being created; this legislation would define a class of game-forms $\mathbb{G}_{23} = \mathbb{G}_2 \times \mathbb{G}_3$, assuming a law-abiding society, one can expect that the natural game-forms of the two subsequent games change appropriately, thus assuring compliance. Based on this legislation, in the course of the administrative game Γ_2, the administrative (and/or judicial) bodies then formulate detailed regulations, e.g., defining the term 'cartel' and specifying implementation and enforcement procedures consistent with the enabling legislation, thus producing a game from G_3 (an element of the class $\mathbb{G}_3$). Again, we shall assume a law-abiding society, so that game-form G_3 will in fact be effective in governing the substantive game Γ_3. This game consists of interactions between the regulators and the firms being regulated, as well as among the firms themselves. (If compliance with law could not be taken for granted, additional actions would have to be taken in the course of the first two games

---

[29] Unlike Reiter and Hughes, however, we do not require at this stage that the preliminary game be a cooperative game.

[30] Here $\mathbb{G}_2$ is assumed to be a one-element class (a singleton, its element denoted by G_2) representing the rules governing the administrative game Γ_2. (Otherwise, a longer cascade might be needed.) On the other hand, $\mathbb{G}_3$ will in general have many elements, thus creating the need for the administrative stage, whose function is to narrow down the class $\mathbb{G}_3$ to a single element G_3 of this class that will govern the substantive game Γ_3.

to assure the effectiveness of the prohibition of cartels.) Thus, whatever the details, for the (desired) game-form $G_3 = (S_3, h_3)$, the strategy domain S_3 excludes any 'legal' strategies that would result in the formation of a cartel among the participating firms, and h_3 imposes penalties for violations.

The question may be raised why a sequence of three separate games is considered preferable to a single game with three stages. One reason is that the preliminary, administrative, and substantive phases are very likely to involve different sets of players. On the other hand, for 'internal' institutions, a single multi-stage game model may be more appropriate.[31] Much of our formulation could be adapted to such a model.

The fact that we restrict ourselves to a sequence of just three-game models is mainly an expository simplification. In general, we might consider a 'cascade' of T games, $\Gamma_1, \ldots, \Gamma_T$, $T \geq 2$, where each predecessor restricts the game-forms governing its successors, and it is only the last game, Γ_T, [that] is substantive. As an illustration, the sequence could consist of the country's constitution, statutes of successively greater specificity, judicial interpretations of the law, as well as regulatory actions of administrative bodies.

Let us return to the three-game ($T = 3$) sequence model. For $t = 1, 2, 3$, let the set of players of Γ_t be $N_t = \{(t, 1), \ldots, (t, n_t)\}$, the (joint) strategy space S_t, the outcome space Z_t, and the game-form $G_t = (S_t, h_t)$, where the symbol (t, i) denotes the i-th player in game Γ_t. In game Γ_t, let the payoff function of player (t, i) be denoted by π_t^i obtained as the composition $\pi_t^i = \phi_t^i \circ h_t$, where ϕ_t^i is the utility function of player (t, i) and h_t the outcome function of Γ_t. Then we may write $\Gamma_t = \langle N_t, S_t, (\pi_t^1, \ldots, \pi_t^n) \rangle$, or, for short, $\Gamma_t = \langle N_t, S_t, \pi_t \rangle$, where π_t is the n_t-tuple of payoff functions of the game Γ_t.

The generic element z_1 of Z_1 (the outcome space of the preliminary game) is assumed to consist of two elements, say $z_1 = (\mathbb{G}_{23}, b_{23})$, $\mathbb{G}_{23} = \mathbb{G}_2 \times \mathbb{G}_3$, with $\mathbb{G}_2$ consisting of the one-element G_2. Here $\mathbb{G}_3$ is a class of 'desired game-forms' for the substantive game Γ_3. A rough interpretation of this concept is that players of the preliminary game want the substantive game Γ_3 to be governed by one of the game-forms in $\mathbb{G}_3$.[32] The b_{23} component of z_1 represents actions or behavior of preliminary game players intended to have this effect on the environment prevailing during the subsequent games, and hence the 'natural' game-forms $\hat{G}_2$ and $\hat{G}_3$,[33] of the administrative and

---

[31] But even for 'internal' institutions the sets of players in different phases may vary, as when, e.g., heirs of the contracting parties are involved.

[32] More precisely, it is the result of strategy choices (bargaining, etc.) by members of N_1 each of whom is 'pushing' toward his/her favorite game-form for Γ_2. Of course the equilibrium outcome $\mathbb{G}_2$ need not be to everyone's liking.

[33] Write the 'natural' game-form as $\hat{G} = (\hat{S}, \hat{h})$. The ('natural') strategy domain $\hat{S}$ of $\hat{G}$ contains not only the strategies permitted by a desired game-form but also all others that are physically

substantive games, [so] as to make some game-form from $\mathbb{G}_2$ effective for Γ_2, and some game-form from $\mathbb{G}_3$ effective for Γ_3. The introduction of the element b_{23} is motivated by the idea that the desired game-forms in $\mathbb{G}_2$ might remain 'on paper' and not become effective unless the natural game-form of the substantive game was suitably changed by some action or behavior. Examples of b_{23} components are: physical barriers (preventing or deterring the use of 'illegal' strategies), education and propaganda, and, of course, the existence or creation of reliable and effective implementation (in particular, enforcement) organs.[34] These activities would involve diversion of resources (a component of transaction costs). A more sophisticated (probabilistic) model would explicitly take into account the fact that enforcement typically is less than 100% successful. It is interesting to note that in experimental settings great effort is made to make the rules of the game completely effective (there is genuine implementation), often by the nature of physical arrangements.

The outcome z_2 of G_2 is of the form (G_3^*, b_3), where G_3^* is the game-form (no longer a class!) designed to govern the substantive game Γ_3, and b_3^* is again an action aimed at modifying the environment E_3, and hence the natural game-form $\hat{G}_3$ prevailing during the substantive game so as to assure effectiveness.

In certain situations or societies, the mere fact that the preliminary game had produced the class $\mathbb{G}_{23}$ might have sufficient authority to make one of its constituent game-forms effective. (We speak of law-abiding societies and say that the rule of law prevails.) In such cases, b_{23} might be interpreted

and psychologically feasible. If we think of the desired strategies as the legal ones, $\hat{S}$ contains not only the legal strategies but also all feasible illegal strategies. By definition, the ('natural') outcome function $\hat{h}$ of $\hat{G}$ represents those strategy choices from $\hat{S}$ that are in fact likely to occur. In general, even when desired strategies are used, the natural outcomes may differ from those desired. (See Hurwicz 1993a for a fuller discussion of these concepts.)

Consider games with two players and finite strategy spaces, so that the outcome functions are represented by matrices. We may want to suppose that the desired outcome matrix is a submatrix of the natural outcome matrix, i.e., that at least the legal strategies have the desired outcomes. However, this need not always be so. It may easily happen that the desired outcome function is not effective, so that the actual (natural) outcome associated with a 'legal' joint strategy s is different from the prescribed outcome; i.e., in symbols, for some $s \in S$, $\hat{h}(s) \neq h(s)$ where $\hat{h}$ denotes the natural outcome matrix and h the desired outcome matrix; thus in this case, the desired outcome matrix h is not a submatrix of $\hat{h}$.

A desired game-form $G^* = (S^*, h^*)$ is said to be a *effective* with respect to the natural game-form $\hat{G}$ over a class Φ of n-tuples of utility functions for players in N if, for every n-tuple of utility functions ϕ in Φ, the sets of equilibrium outcomes of the two games $\hat{G}$ and G^* are the same. (Here $\hat{G}$ is the composition of ϕ with the outcome function $\hat{h}$, while G^* is the composition of the same ϕ with the outcome function h^*; the set of players is N in both cases.)

The intent of this definition of the term 'effective' is to formalize the idea that even though the actual game being played is always the natural game, the outcomes will be the same as those that would have resulted from the desired game. In particular, even though participants could have used illegal strategies, they will not do so at an equilibrium. Thus enforcement works and we have 'genuine implementation'.

34 See Hurwicz (1993b) on the role of 'intervenors', and 'closed circles'.

simply as the announcement of the class G_{23} as the equilibrium outcome of the preliminary game. (Formally, in this case, $z_1 = (G_{23}, b_{23})$, with $b_{23} = $ the announcement of G_{23}, and similarly $b_3^* = $ the announcement of G_3^*.)

There is an important relationship between preferences of the players N_1 and N_3, respectively in the preliminary and substantive games of the sequence. Typically, a player of the preliminary game is interested in the expected or likely outcome z_3 of the substantive game, perhaps because he/she identifies with the interests and/or preferences of some players of the substantive game. Hence while the utility function ϕ_1^i has Z_1 as its domain, the value of $\phi_1^i(z_1)$ depends on the expected outcome z_3 generated (indirectly) by z_1.

4.2 Main features of the model

To summarize, among the important features of the preceding model are these: (a) the sequential structure of the process; (b) the preliminary game, if effective (i.e., genuinely implemented), determines a class of game-forms, here interpreted as the institutional arrangements, that will ultimately govern the 'proper' phase of the substantive game; (c) in order to achieve genuine implementation, it is, in general, necessary for the preliminary game to produce actions or behavior that will so modify the natural game-form of the substantive game as to make the rules produced by the preliminary game effective.[35]

It should perhaps be emphasized that the model is intended for a broad class of institutions, even though in many cases it would not be natural to represent the formative phase by game formalism. However, other aspects of the model might still be appropriate. Thus, for instance, the common features of the institution of marriage, with its many forms in many societies and historical periods, may be represented by a class G_3 of game-forms, while the formative phase would be represented by an 'organic' evolutionary process. However, the specific game from G_3^* prevailing in a country or state during a particular period (e.g., the prohibition of polygamy) often is the product of legislative, administrative, or judicial actions.

As for the internal structure of the substantive game, whether or not it includes the administrative phase, it may be most natural to represent it in extensive form. One reason is that in practice, rules are usually[36] formulated in terms of moves rather than strategies. Moreover, extensive form would make it simpler to accommodate an important aspect of New Institutional

---

[35] A formalization of 'effective' is given above in footnote 33.
[36] But not always: for instance, rules dealing with predatory competition concern strategies rather than separate moves.

Economics, viz. transaction costs. Therefore, for purposes of institutional analysis, it would be desirable to introduce the notion of *game-form in extensive form*. This could be represented by the usual tree diagram, but with outcomes (elements of the outcome space Z) instead of numerical (utility) payoffs. Furthermore, it would also seem desirable to depart from the usual procedure of associating the outcomes with terminal nodes only. In addition to the usual terminal outcomes, one could introduce *interim outcomes*, associated with progression from any node to the next. The various transaction costs would be among the components of such interim outcomes. An example might be the requirement of up-front payments for the filing of a law-suit.[37]

4.3 Definition of an institution

We have so far discussed different characteristics and models of (B-) institutions, but no formal definition of an institution has been given. A highly simplified definition might be that implied by the title of this paper: an institution is a class of game-forms. In the preceding example of the institution prohibiting cartels, it would be a class $\mathbb{G}_3$ of various game-forms all of which exclude strategy domains involving cartel formation and, perhaps, some limits on penalties for violations. But such a definition fails to embody the various attributes that qualify a game-form class as an institution. To begin with, in line our discussion in Section 2.7 above, in order to make sure that we are excluding the effects of the laws of physics, etc., we must use conditional game-forms (in effect, specifying classes of game-forms permitted by human actions given the prevailing environment). Second, there must be explicit reference to human actions creating the institution, the multi-stage or sequential aspect of the process. Third, since effectiveness (or genuine implementation) is considered to be essential, the element making for effectiveness must also be explicit in the formalization. Finally, there must be a formal expression of the categoricity aspect.

Clearly, this makes for a complex concept. In the interest of minimizing this complexity, we shall confine ourselves to the sequential structure described in Section 4.1. Formally then, a (B-) institution is defined as the following ordered sequence of elements:

$$\langle E_1, \Gamma_1, z_1; E_2, \Gamma_2, z_2; E_3 \rangle,$$

---

[37] Introducing interim outcomes is not a complete innovation. In games with infinite time horizon there are, of course, no terminal nodes; the so-called felicities are interim utilities associated with interim outcomes such as consumption in a given time period.

with

$$z_1 = (\mathbb{G}_{23}, b_{23}), \ \mathbb{G}_{23} = \mathbb{G}_2 \times \mathbb{G}_3, \ z_2 = (\mathbb{G}_3^*, b_3^*),$$

$$E_2 = \eta_2(E_1, b_{23}); \ E_3 = \eta_3(E_2; b_{23}, b_3^*),$$

all game-forms being 'conditional' (in the sense of Section 2.7)[38] and 'categorical' (in the sense of Section 3.3, i.e., applicable to categories of actors and situations rather than named individuals and situations), the unique element G_2 of $\mathbb{G}_2$ being effective in Γ_2, and the game form G_3^* being effective for the class $\mathbb{G}_3$ over E_3.[39]

The components b_{23} and b_3^* represent actions or behaviors so modifying the environment as to assure effectiveness in subsequent games. E_t represents the environment prevailing during game Γ_t and hence determines the natural game-form $\hat{G}_t$ prevailing during Γ_t. The symbols η_2 and η_3 denote functional relations representing the effects of the respective actions b_{23} and b_3^* on subsequent environments.

As it stands, the preceding formulation does not accommodate institutions whose 'organic' genesis does not lend itself to game-theoretic representation of the preliminary phase $(t = 1)$. To model this type of genesis, the preliminary game Γ_1 would have to be replaced by some non-game type of process. However, other elements of the above formal definition might still retain their relevance.

On the other hand there is a relationship, albeit imperfect, between Schotter's supergame model of institutions and our above framework, with the supergame corresponding to our preliminary game Γ_t, and the solution of the supergame corresponding to our game-form G_3^*.

5 Contents of Institutions

So far we have been discussing the more formal aspects of modelling institutions. But what of their substance? In particular, in economic settings, what aspects of the economic process do the rules deal with? The answer, of course, is: a tremendous diversity. Without attempting a complete treatment, it seems worthwhile to indicate two types of phenomena frequently treated in institutional literature: endowments and residuals.

---

[38] Hence, strictly speaking, we should be using the symbols Λ representing corresponding from the respective environment spaces into the space of conceivable game-forms rather than the symbols $\mathbb{G}$ representing classes of game-forms. However, as indicated in Section 2.7, we have opted for the somewhat ambiguous notation because the $\mathbb{G}$ symbols seem more suggestive, and, of course, correct in the case when the Λ's are constant.

[39] It may be noted that the class of environments, E_3, over which the institution represented by $\mathbb{G}_3$ is effective may be different from what had been aimed at by players in the preliminary game.

5.1 Institutions assigning initial endowments

A broad class of institutions dealt with by economists can be formalized in terms of the assignment of initial *endowments*, especially endowments of rights (see Eggertsson 1990, especially ch. 4). Among many examples are the following.

The alternative liability rules for damage caused by pollution can be represented by alternative assignments of initial endowments of the right to pollute or the right to enjoy clean air and water (see Hurwicz 1995).

The distinction between common and (individual) private property (central to the 'tragedy of the commons' problem) can be represented by distinguishing between endowments associated with a group of agents as against endowments obtained by individual agents. A property right may be viewed as a ternary relation involving a person, natural or artificial, the specific object owned, and a particular right, e.g., that of use, or alienation. Specifically, consider a particular aspect of property rights, the right of use, say the right of fishing in a commonly owned body of water. In general, more than one person may have the right of fishing there. But under exclusive individual property rights, only one person has such right. Denote by (i, x) the right of agent i to use the object x. In game-form formulation, this means that (i, x) is an element of i's strategy domain S^i. The absence of common ownership means that, for any $j \neq i$, the element (j, x) does not belong to S^j. So absence of common ownership is a relationship between the different players' strategic domains, hence an attribute of the (joint) strategy space S, and therefore of the game-form (S, h).

Primogeniture, considered by many an important institutional factor in England's economic history, is naturally represented as a rule concerning the endowment of heirs with the parents' estate. (Note that the rule is of 'categorical' nature: it applies to the actor defined as the oldest son, not to a specific person.) In some cases the rights endowments are of procedural nature (e.g., the burden of proof in torts),[40] materially affecting transaction costs.

5.2 Institutions assigning certain residuals

Another class of institutional phenomena deals with certain *residuals*. Thus Grossman and Hart (1986) explain the effects of vertical or lateral integration of firms by the residual rights of ownership with respect to vague residuals

---

[40] In the Napoleonic code, as well as in ancient Roman Law, when damage was due to actions of children, cattle, or was 'caused' by buildings, the burden of proof was on parent or owner, as an exception to the general rule. In French civil law before World War II, this reversal also applied to most cases of damage caused by automobile accidents.

due to the incompleteness of contracts caused by unavoidable complexity of contingencies. The different incentive effects of the various land tenure forms are due, at least in part, to the location of residual risks or opportunities. Similar considerations apply to alternative institutional structures of firms, both with respect to rewards (profits, etc.) and liabilities. The location of these residuals is often determined by the assignment of endowments, including those of liabilities. Hence, there is a relationship between the two aspects of institutional phenomena, and much of the principal-agent literature deals with them. Very tentative and incomplete ideas for certain aspects of these phenomena are discussed in the next section.

5.3 Institutions governing particular aspects of behavior

Institutions are not only due to human actions, they also deal with human actions, whether through the description of the strategy domains S^i or through the specified outcome functions h. One problem of formalization we have not yet faced is the fact that what is usually called an institution deals only with particular aspects of human activities, e.g., commerce, family status, punishment for crimes, etc., rather than with the totality of human behavior. To formalize this, consider again an institution T (say, rules governing commerce) represented by the class G_T of game-forms. Let the outcome space Z be the common range of all outcome functions in G_T, and let us think (in the present context only) of Z as a subset of a vector space, with sets of components of its elements corresponding to different aspects of human behavior. For such an element z, write $z = (z_T, z_{T'})$, an element of the Cartesian product $Z = Z_T \times Z_{T'}$. Here z_T represents the components dealing with behavior in commerce, while $z_{T'}$ represents all other aspects of behavior. If $(S^\#, h^\#)$ is an element of G_T, and if, for some s in $S^\#$, $h^\#(s) = (a^*, b^*)$ in $Z_T \times Z_{T'}$, then G_T must also contain all game-forms $(S^\#, h)$ where $h(s) = (a^*, b)$ and b ranges over all of $Z_{T'}$.

Similar factoring of the elements s of the strategy domains S is also to be carried out. Thus if s is in S, write $s = (s_T, s_{T'})$, an element of the Cartesian product $S = S_T \times S_{T'}$. Then if $(S^\#, h^\#)$ is an element of G_T, and $s^* = (c^*, d^*)$ is in $S^\#$, the G_T must also contain all game-forms $(S, h^\#)$ where S contains all elements of the form $s = (c^*, d)$, with d ranging over all of $S_{T'}$.

Let the different aspects of behavior be indexed by the set Θ, and let the family G_θ of game-forms represent the institution dealing with aspect θ of behavior. Then, clearly, the aggregate impact of the totality of institutions G_θ, with θ ranging over Θ, is represented by their intersection $\bigcap_{\theta \in \Theta} G_\theta$. If the requirements of the various institutions are not mutually inconsistent, the intersection is non-empty.

6 The Characteristic Function, the Support Set, and the Support Function

As an illustration of some of the preceding concepts consider the following situation, closely related to the principal-agent model, with the Stiglitz land tenure example of Section 2.6 and footnote 17 as an illustration.

There are two persons 1, 2, with strategy domains S^1 and S^2. The set S^0 is the strategy domain of the exogenous factors (e.g., weather). S^i includes effort expended by person i, $i = 1, 2$. The joint strategy space is $S = S^1 \times S^2 \times S^0$. Write $s = (s^1, s^2, s^0)$ for the generic element of S.

The generic outcome is written

$$z = (y, r^1, r^2),$$

where y is the output (or, e.g., value added) and r^i the reward (wealth increment) for person i.

The production function is

$$y = \eta(s);$$

in particular, the function η represents the extent to which the output depends on the level of effort of the two persons and on the exogenous factors. (The symbol η used here is not related to the same symbol used in Section 4.)

The reward functions f^i (defined by the prevailing institutions) are given by

$$r^i = f^i(y; s), \quad i = 1, 2.$$

(When the strategy, e.g., the level of effort, of person i is not observable to the other, it may be impractical to make the reward function f^i directly dependent on i's effort or, more generally, on s^i. A similar limitation applies to direct dependence of reward functions on exogenous factors, i.e., on s^0.)

Hence the outcome function $h(\cdot)$ can be written as

$$h(s) = \langle \eta(s), (f^i(\eta(s); s))_{i=1,2} \rangle.^{41} \tag{*}$$

---

41 Our interpretation here is that only the reward functions represent the institutional aspect of the model while the production function is an aspect of the environment. Consider, for example, the class L of reward functions affine in y, i.e., $f = (f^1, f^2)$, $f^2(y, s) = ky + b$, $f^1(y, s) = y - f^2(y, s)$, where the landlord is agent 1. Let the subset L^* of L be the class of reward functions corresponding to sharecropping, i.e., where $f^2(y, s) = ky$, with k ranging over the open interval $(0, 1)$. Then the institution of sharecropping is formally represented by the correspondence $\Lambda : E \to \mathbb{G}$ where an element e of the space E of environments can be identified with a particular production function η, $\mathbb{G}$ is a class of game-forms, and $\Lambda(e) = \lambda(\eta) = h(s)$, where h is given by the formula (*) in the text. (See Section 2.7 for a discussion of conditional game-forms.)

The utility functions are $u^i(r^i, s)$, $i = 1, 2$. It is natural to assume that u^i rises with r^i. The dependence of u^i on s represents phenomena such as the disutility of effort, the discomforts of bad weather, etc.

The production function η tells us who and to what extent strategies, in particular effort, can affect the output. On the other hand, the reward function f^i tells us to what extend i's reward is affected by variations in output, as well as directly by s. The relationship between the reward functions and the production function is a major factor in determining whether the given institutional setup does or does not promote 'efficiency' (as measured by output).

The situation can be analyzed with the help of certain concepts that seem of potential value in arriving at general propositions about the incentive structures engendered by alternative institutional arrangements.

The first of these is what we call the *characteristic function of an institution*, denoted by F. For instance, consider the Stiglitz land tenure example of Section 2.6 and footnote 17. Let the three forms of land tenure be abbreviated as a = wages, b = renting, c = sharecropping, and let the two persons be the landlord ($i = 1$) and the worker ($i = 2$). Then we define $F(x/i) = 1$ (or -1, or 0) if i's reward depends positively (or negatively, or does not depend) on i's s^i (e.g., effort) via the production function.

Thus, assuming that the worker's effort can increase output, $F(2/a) = 0$ while $F(2/b) = 1$. On the other hand, if the landlord's actions can increase the worker's productivity, one might expect that $F(1/a) = 1$ while $F(1/b) = 0$. Finally, if both sharecroppers can raise output by their effort, $F(1/c) = F(2/c) = 1$.

The *support set of an institution x* is defined as the set of agents i, denoted by $\psi(x)$, such that $F(i/x) \neq 0$. The *support function for a class X of institutions* (with the same set of agents N) is the set-valued function $\psi(\cdot)$ where $\psi(x)$ is the support set of x, and the argument of $\psi(\cdot)$ ranges over the class X. I.e., $\psi : X \rightarrow N$, where for a given institution x in X, $\psi(x) = \{N'$ a subset of $N : F(i/x) \neq 0$ for i in $N'\}$.

References

Crawford, S. and E. Ostrom (1995) A grammar of institutions, *The American Political Science Review*, 89(3): 582–600.

Eggertsson, T. (1990) *Economic Behavior and Institutions*. Cambridge, MA: Cambridge University Press.

Gardner, R. and E. Ostrom (1991) Rules and games, *Public Choice*, 70(2): 121–49.

Grossman, S. and O. Hart (1986) The costs and benefits of ownership: A theory of vertical and lateral integration, *Journal of Political Economy*, 94(4): 691–719.

Hayek, F. (1955) *The Counterrevolution of Science*. New York, NY: The Free Press.

Hurwicz, L. (1977) On the dimensional requirements of informationally decentralized Paretosatisfactory processes, in *Studies in Resource Allocation Processes*, ed. K. Arrow and L. Hurwicz, 413–24. Cambridge, MA: Cambridge University Press.

Hurwicz, L. (1979a) On the interaction between information and incentives in organizations, in *Communication and Control in Society*, ed. K. Krippendorff, 123–47. New York, NY: Gordon and Breach Science Publishers.

Hurwicz, L. (1979b) On allocations attainable through Nash equilibria, *Journal of Economic Theory*, 21(1): 140–65.

Hurwicz, L. (1993a) Toward a framework for analyzing institutions and institutional change, in *Markets and Democracy: Participation, Accountability and Efficiency*, ed. S. Bowles, H. Gintis, and B. Gustafsson, 51–67. Cambridge, MA: Cambridge University Press.

Hurwicz, L. (1993b) Implementation and enforcement in institutional modeling, in *Political Economy: Institutions, Competition, and Representation*, ed. W. Barnett, M. Hinich, and N. Schofield, 51–59. Cambridge, MA: Cambridge University Press.

Hurwicz, L. (1995) What is the Coase Theorem?, *Japan and the World Economy*, 7(1): 49–74.

Hurwicz, L., E. Maskin, and A. Postlewaite (1995) Feasible Nash implementation of social choice rules when the designer does not know endowments or production sets, in *The Economics of International Decentralization: Complexity, Efficiency and Stability*, ed. J. Ledyard, 367–433. Boston, MA: Kluwer Academic Publishers.

Marshall, A. (1890) *Principles of Economics*, Vol. 1. London: Macmillan.

Menger, C. (1883) *Untersuchungen über die Methode der Sozialwissenschaften und der Politischen Oekonomie insbesondere* (Investigation of the methods of the social sciences especially political economy). Leipzig: Duncker and Humblot. (Reprinted by the London School of Economics, 1933).

Mount, K. and S. Reiter (1974) On the informational size of message spaces, *Journal of Economic Theory*, 8(2): 161–92.

North, D. (1990) *Institutions, Institutional Change and Economic Performance*. Cambridge, MA: Cambridge University Press.

North, D. (1992) *Transaction Costs, Institutions, and Economic Performance*. San Francisco, CA: ICS Press.

Osana, H. (1978) On the informational size of message spaces for resource allocation processes, *Journal of Economic Theory*, 17(1): 66–78.

Ostrom, E. (1986) An agenda for the study of institutions, *Public Choice*, 48(1): 3–25.

Ostrom, E., J. Walker, and R. Gardner (1992) Covenants with and without a sword: Self-governance is possible, *American Political Science Review*, 86(2): 404–17.

Reiter, S. and J. Hughes (1981) A preface on modeling the regulated US economy, *Hofstra Law Review*, 9(5): 1381–1421.

Riker, W. (1982) Implications from the disequilibrium of majority rule for the study of institutions in *Political Equilibrium*, ed. P. Ordeshook and K. Shepsle, 3–24. Boston, MA: Kluwer-Nijhoff. Originally published as Riker, W. (1980) Implications from the disequilibrium of majority rule for the study of institutions, *American Political Science Review*, 74(2): 432–46.

Schotter, A. (1981) *The Economic Theory of Social Institutions*. Cambridge, MA: Cambridge University Press.

Schotter, A. (1986), The evolution of rules, in *Economics as a Process*, ed. R. Langlois, 117–33. Cambridge, MA: Cambridge University Press.

Schotter, A. (1989), Comment (on Market and Institutions by Siro Lombardini), in *Economic Institutions in a Dynamic Society*, ed. T. Shiraishi and S. Tsuru, 50–55. New York, NY: Macmillan.

Stiglitz, J. (1974) Incentives and risk sharing in sharecropping, *Review of Economics Studies*, 41(2): 219–55.

von Neumann, J. and O. Morgenstern (1944) *Theory of Games and Economic Behavior*. Princeton, NJ: Princeton University Press.

17

Issues in the Design of Mechanisms and Institutions

Introduction

Environmental and resource management issues pose very special problems for economic analysis. Externalities, common pool resources, infinite horizons, and exhaustibility (or sustainability) are among the labels that have been applied to some of these special issues. Common phenomena in such situations are inefficiency of competitive equilibria and thinness or absence of markets. For these reasons, such situations are often called 'market failures'.

However, there is no consensus among economists on either causes or remedies, or even on whether there really is a problem. While it may be accepted that any failures that do exist reflect the absence of appropriate institutions, there is no agreement on which institutions would be appropriate, nor on whether conscious social intervention is required to bring preferred institutions into being.

Some abhor 'social engineering' and favor a laissez-faire approach, perhaps counting on the spontaneous ('endogenous') development of needed institutions. Others see the need for intervention, but only for the purpose of clarifying individual property rights—assuming that market mechanisms would take care of the rest. (This view has been particularly widespread among many of those seeking to understand and remedy the overutilization of common property or common pool resources.)

Even in the presence of externalities, some argue that efficiency is guaranteed, if not by competitive trading then by negotiations, bargaining,

From *Designing Institutions for Environmental and Resource Management*, ed. E. Loehman and D. Marc Kilgour, 29–56. ©1998 Edward Elgar: Northampton, MA. Reprinted by permission of Edward Elgar Publishing.

and compensatory payments among parties—unless 'transaction costs' make such procedures impractical. In the forefront has been Coase, who not only postulated that negotiations and payments would result in efficient resource allocation under externalities (when transaction costs are absent) but also claimed that—except financially—institutions such as liability laws would have no effect on resource allocations. For example, the pollution level would be the same whether or not the polluter is liable for damage to neighbors.

I shall discuss the range of validity of such claims below, as well as the distributional issues that remain. Even if the level of pollution is unaffected by liability rules, the financial burden falls differently—on neighbors when the law imposes no liability for pollution damage, and on the (potential) polluter when it does. Thus institutional issues, and the potential need for design, arise not just from efficiency problems but also from considerations of distribution.

The importance of institutional arrangements is generally accepted when 'transaction costs' are significant, although disputes remain over whether such institutions are likely to develop spontaneously or require conscious design activity. The fact that transaction costs are always present calls for a re-examination of the standard concepts of efficiency. No matter how competitive and 'perfect', market operations incur social and private costs. For example, as is well known, markets require the regulation of weights and measures, and a system for enforcing contracts, but the costs of these features are not part of the classical analytical framework. These costs of regulation and enforcement machinery are too often ignored in comparing alternative economic institutions. Institutional arrangements that seem efficient when these costs are ignored may fail the test of efficiency when they are taken into account (see Hurwicz, 1972a, 1972b).

Not only are institutional costs ignored in classical models, but the institutions themselves, while brought in for motivation, are typically not part of the formal analytical framework. Therefore, my own recent focus has been on developing a framework in which institutional arrangements can be an explicit part of a resource allocation model.

This chapter discusses issues in the design of institutions relevant for problems of externalities, common pool resources, and temporal horizons. The design process for economic institutions should, of course, reflect the lessons of past experience and our accumulated knowledge of the behavior of economic agents. But—like the problem of designing a lunar landing craft—institutional design for situations in which there is no historic precedent must draw on a significant theoretical foundation. New theoretical constructs may be required, but fortunately the economist's toolbox already contains many appropriate models and techniques.

Approaches useful for institutional analysis are discussed below, including:[1]

(1) traditional microeconomic and welfare economic models, such as the Edgeworth Box;

(2) game theory, including principal-agent models;

(3) informational processes, such as information exchange.

Some of these may be viewed as subcategories of others; we make no attempt to provide a complete taxonomy at a high level of generality and abstraction. Nor do we study all approaches equally. A central issue is how to represent institutions in economic models for the purpose of analyzing the relative efficiency of alternative institutions.

Micro- and Welfare Economic Foundations

Externalities and public (or 'non-rivalrous')[2] goods were phenomena ruled out by the assumptions underlying classical or neoclassical general equilibrium models. An externality was viewed as separate from market processes. Hence there was no logical contradiction between the conclusions of the First Fundamental Theorem of Welfare Economics, guaranteeing the Pareto optimality of (perfectly) competitive resource allocations, and the evident inefficiencies of market allocations in the presence of, say, smoke pollution.

But why not think of smoke as a commodity? Then, the polluter can be a 'seller' and the victim a 'buyer', consistent with the new use of permit markets for pollution. Arrow's (1969) formalization implemented this view. Similarly, in an economy with a public good. Foley's model[3] of a Lindahl equilibrium has personalized commodities, each purchased separately by individuals but constituting a joint product from the supplier's point of view.

It is possible to interpret alternative institutional arrangements in an enlarged commodity space and to analyze them using some customary tools of microeconomics. But this approach is inadequate for many problems. For example, if there are non-convexities, inserting externalities or public

---

[1] Unless there is an explicit statement to the contrary, in what follows I shall use the term 'institution' in the sense of institutional arrangements rather than of institutional entities or organizations (such as universities, states, etc.) that participate as actors in social, political, or economic processes.

[2] In the literature, a public good is often defined as non-rivalrous and non-excludable. Here, excludability is not assumed; it may be present or absent.

[3] See Foley (1970, especially section 4), Blad and Keiding (1990, p. 265), Mas-Colell et al. (1995, p. 569), and Milleron (1972).

goods into a model as artificial commodities may not be consistent with the fundamental theorems of welfare economics. Existence of equilibrium, and in particular, the Second Theorem of Welfare Economics, may not hold without convexity conditions on both production and consumption. As Starrett[4] showed, because detrimental externalities may be associated with non-convexities, competitive equilibrium may not exist.

To provide a conceptual framework for thinking about policy design when pollution is viewed as a personalized commodity, two traditional types of microeconomic/welfare economics models are utilized below—contract curves and production possibility sets—to examine arguments about the Coase Theorem and non-convexities. These two issues are crucial to understanding externalities and other problems related to resources.

A Coase economy: Institutions without transaction costs

Representing institutional phenomena in a standard microeconomic framework makes them, and their economic consequences, susceptible to rigorous analysis. In particular, an Edgeworth Box analysis allows determination of the conditions for validity of the Coasian assertion. In my paraphrase, under the assumptions that (1) the economy is governed by some mechanism assuring Pareto optimality, and (2) there are no transaction costs, the assertion is that *the equilibrium level of pollution does not depend on the definition of liability.*[5]

As Hurwicz (1995) shows, the 'Coase Theorem' holds *if, but only if, both agents' preferences are free of income effects,*[6] i.e. their indifference curves are parallel, and their preferences are represented by quasi-linear utility functions.

The argument is as follows. Consider the interaction of two agents, a (potential) polluter, A, and a (potential) victim, B. For instance, A and B are neighbors, separated by a wall that is not soundproof. A enjoys singing loudly and B dislikes being forced to listen to A's singing. There are two goods: X ('money') and Y (pollution: A's singing). We avoid the complications resulting from concomitant production profits and abatement costs by assuming that A can costlessly produce Y, but only up to some level $y^{\#}$. Moreover, A enjoys both singing and money, so A's preferences are increasing in x^A and y^A, the amounts A 'consumes' of X and Y, respectively. The amounts 'consumed' by B are, respectively, x^B and y^B, where $y^B = y^A$ because Y is an externality—

---

[4] See Starrett (1972), as well as comments in Otani and Sicilian (1977).

[5] Both assumptions (1) and (2) are either explicitly used by Coase, or are implicit in his argument.

[6] It was shown by Chipman and Tian (2012) that it is not necessary for preferences to be free of income effects for the 'Coase Theorem' to hold, i.e., there is a narrow configuration of preferences whose indifference curves are not parallel under which the 'Coase Theorem' could still hold.—SB

when A sings, both A and B hear it. The initial money endowments are respectively ω_x^A and ω_x^B. Agent B also likes money, hence prefers more X to less, but finds singing a nuisance, so prefers less rather than more of Y. Such preferences can be represented in a diagram analogous to the Edgeworth Box with both agents having the same vertical coordinate.[7] Under the customary assumptions of convexity and smoothness, interior Pareto optima occur at the tangency points of indifference curves.

The *institutional aspect* of the problem considered by Coase (1960) and others is the presence or absence of A's liability for damage (or nuisance) to B caused by the pollution Y. To represent liability rules in diagrams, we reinterpret the Y axis to represent pollution rights as well as pollution level (see Hurwicz, 1996). Let A's initial entitlement level be denoted ω_y^A, and let B's initial entitlement level to *freedom from* pollution be denoted ω_y^B, with the understanding that $\omega_y^A + \omega_y^B = y^\#$. Thus the initial endowment point is $\omega = (\omega^A, \omega^B)$, where $\omega^A = (\omega_x^A, \omega_y^A)$, and $\omega^B = (\omega_x^B, \omega_y^B)$, with $\omega_y^B = y^\# - \omega_y^A$. In particular, if A's right to pollute (without liability for damages) is unlimited, then $\omega_y^A = y^\#$ and $\omega_y^B = 0$. On the other hand, if A is liable for damages, we set $\omega_y^A = 0$ and $\omega_y^B = y^\#$.

In this formulation, ω_y^A can be thought of as A's total endowment of pollution rights, which may range from $\omega_y^A = y^\#$ (A has no liability for pollution) to $\omega_y^A = 0$ (B has the right to freedom from pollution). When $0 < \omega_y^A < y^\#$, A has the right to pollute up to level ω_y^A, while B has 'freedom from pollution' rights in the amount $y^\# - \omega_y^A > 0$. Hence pollution rights behave just like an ordinary commodity in a pure exchange Edgeworth Box model; the total remains constant, while the distribution between the two agents varies. (For B, holding freedom from pollution rights is equivalent to holding A's pollution rights.) The economy may therefore be viewed as a two-good economy, with the goods being money and A's pollution rights.

As in Eggertsson's original Edgeworth Box exposition (1990), this mode of presentation has both advantages and limitations. The main advantage is its ability to capture one institutional factor simply as a component (i.e., ω_y^i, $i = A, B$) of the endowment point. It is then straightforward to analyze the implications of alternative liability rules, and to assess permit trading markets and their equilibria in terms of such characteristics as convexity, satiation, continuity of preferences, and relation to the initial endowments.

---

[7] See Hurwicz (1995) and Eggertsson (1990, fig. 4.3, p. 106). As indicated by Eggertsson (footnote 46), this presentation has been used by Haddock and Spiegel (1984), who assume a satiation level for A with respect to Y, rather than a maximum feasible level of pollution, $y^\#$, as assumed here. Our postulates simplify the subsequent exposition.

Note that the Coase Theorem implicitly assumes that the optimality of allocations is obtained by some process of negotiation or bargaining, but the nature of the mechanism that would achieve optimality is not made clear.

Market mechanisms for achieving optimality

For a contemporary economist it is natural to start by asking whether the competitive market mechanism could accomplish the task of resource allocation for externalities, in technical language whether—in the presence of externalities—a competitive equilibrium allocation is necessarily Pareto optimal. That the answer is negative was known before Pigou, but as early as 1912 he was instrumental in bringing the problem to the attention of economists, and he proposed—though not in detail—a system of remedies involving taxes and subsidies ('bounties').

What are now called Pigouvian taxes or subsidies are designed to serve as substitutes for damage payments or rewards for uncompensated disservices or services rendered to third parties. More specifically, and in their modern garb, they are supposed to motivate those responsible for generating externalities to behave so as to produce Pareto optimal resource allocations.

An alternative approach, formulated by Arrow (1969), involves creating artificial markets for externalities, which can be accomplished by introducing new, in general personalized, commodities. Each of these new commodities represents the effect of an externality (e.g., smoke) on a particular agent, and thus *augments* (increases the dimensions of) the *commodity space*.

In what follows, we shall illustrate the issues that arise in the context of a simplified class of examples, a special case of those discussed in detail by Malinvaud (1972, pp. 203–10), Baumol and Bradford (1972), Starrett (1972), and Baumol and Oates (1988).

Consider an economy with one consumer whose preferences are represented by a twice differentiable utility function, and two producers (firms), 1 and 2. A unilateral detrimental externality is generated by firm 1 and adversely affects firm 2. (For the sake of concreteness we can think of the externality as smoke pollution, and refer to firm 1 as the polluter and firm 2 as the victim.) The two firms use labor as input and produce two distinct goods, both of which enter the consumer's utility function. Denoting the labor input used by firm i by x_i, and its output by y_i, we write their respective production functions as $y_1 = F^1(x_1)$ and $y_2 = F^2(x_2, y_1)$, with $\partial F^i / \partial x_i > 0$, $i = 1, 2$. More precisely, the formulae should be understood as defining the respective production possibility *correspondences,* or 'conditional' production possibility sets (conditioned on the other firm's input/output as domain) by

$$\phi^1(y_2) = \{(x_1, y_1) \in \mathbb{R}_+^2 : y_1 \le F^1(x_1)\},$$

$$\phi^2(y_1)\{(x_2, y_2) \in \mathbb{R}_+^2 : y_2 \le \max\{F^2(x_2, y_1), 0\}\}.$$

The first correspondence is of course a constant, as there is no externality acting on firm 1. The externality acting on 2 would be absent if $\partial F^2/\partial y_1 = 0$, but, as we assume, is detrimental when $\partial F^2/\partial y_1 < 0$.

As for the role of labor in [the] consumer's preferences, we distinguish two types of economies: in type (A), the consumer's utility function is $u(y_1, y_2, z)$, where z denotes leisure remaining after the performance of work x, and the three marginal utilities are positive; total labor supplied is given by $x = x_1 + x_2 = \omega_z - z$; in type (B), the consumer is indifferent to leisure, so $\partial u/\partial z = 0$, and the supply of labor is fixed, say at the exogenously given level ξ.

First-order conditions for Pareto optimality

The optimality conditions differ according to the type of the economy. (Below, subscripts represent partial derivatives.) For type (A), they are (for interior solutions)

$$u_{y_1}/u_x = 1/F_{x_1}^1 - F_{y_1}^2/F_{x_2}^2, \tag{2.1}$$

$$u_{y_2}/u_x = 1/F_{x_2}^2. \tag{2.2}$$

On the other hand, at the 'natural' competitive equilibrium,

$$u_{y_1}/u_x = 1/F_{x_2}^1 \tag{2.3}$$

so that (2.1) must be violated, since, by hypothesis, $F_{y_1}^2/F_{x_2}^2 \ne 0$. I call a classical competitive equilibrium 'natural' to distinguish it from competitive equilibria with Arrovian artificial commodities or Pigouvian taxes or subsidies. However, if there are externalities, the definition of 'natural' competitive equilibrium goes beyond the usual textbook versions in that it assumes that the affected agent maximizes with respect to variables under his/her control, while treating others' choices, and prices, as 'parametric', i.e., exogenously given.

In type (B) economies, it is convenient to invert the production functions, solving them for (minimal) labor requirements, written as

$$x_1 = G^1(y_1) \quad \text{and} \quad x_2 = G^2(y_2, y_1), \quad \text{so that} \quad G^1(y_1) + G^2(y_2, y_1) = \xi,$$

with $\partial G^i/\partial y_i > 0$, $i = 1, 2$, and the detrimental externality expressed as $\partial G^2/\partial y_1 > 0.$[8]

Then the first-order conditions for Pareto optimality are

$$G^2_{y_2}/(G^1_{y_1} + G^2_{y_1}) = u_2/u_1 \qquad (2.4)$$

where $G^2_{y_1} > 0$ in the presence of a detrimental externality. (Here $G^2_{y_1}$ is the partial derivative of G^2 with respect to y_1, etc. $G^2_{y_1} = 0$ would mean the absence of externality.) At a 'natural' competitive equilibrium,

$$u_2/u_1 = G^2_{y_2}/G^1_{y_1}, \qquad (2.5)$$

so that again a competitive allocation is not Pareto optimal in the presence of an externality.

Artificial markets for externalities

Augmented Commodity Space. Suppose we follow Arrow (1969) and define an artificial personalized commodity, say Q_{isr} to represent the externality 'received' by firm r when firm s produces commodity i, with the commodities having different markets if the two agents (r and s) are not identical, even if the good i produced by firm s (e.g., smoke) is physically the same. The net output of commodity i entering the production function of firm r, usually written y_{is}, is now denoted y_{isr}; of course, $y_{isr} = y_{ist}$ for any two recipients r and t, since they both, by construction, receive what in the usual notation would be denoted by y_{is}.[9] It is assumed that there is a separate market for each commodity Q_{isr}, so the total number of commodities is now km^2. We refer to this enlarged commodity space as *augmented*, and the new commodity markets as *artificial*. The corresponding 'personalized' prices are denoted by p_{isr}. The crucial advantage of this construction is that, perhaps paradoxically, in the augmented commodity space there are no externalities.[10]

---

[8] A useful example given by Baumol and Bradford (1972), reproduced and further analyzed in Baumol and Oates (1988, p. 116), postulates the requirement functions $x_1 = y_1^2/2$ and $x_2 = y_2^2/2 + ky_1y_2$. Both own (conditional) sets are convex.

[9] Thus in the augmented commodity space the commodities Q_{ijr} and Q_{ijt} are joint products of firm j.

[10] As is often pointed out, the markets for the artificial commodities are 'thin', and in reality agents would not be likely to treat them parametrically. However, our analysis is devoted not to such motivations, but rather to the question of how the augmented space competitive equilibria work, on the assumption that agents do treat prices parametrically. In spirit, this is no different from the usual analysis of the existence and optimality properties of competitive equilibria, where prices are treated parametrically by the definition of competitive equilibrium. The number of agents does not affect the validity of the classical theorems, although it may, of course, affect their applicability in specific situations.

It follows that standard classical theorems concerning the optimality properties and existence of competitive equilibria are applicable, provided their hypotheses remain valid. The three classical theorems postulate absence of externalities, and as just noted, in the artificial markets there are no externalities. But what about other hypotheses of the classical theorems?

The answer is simplest with respect to the First Theorem of Welfare Economics, asserting the Pareto optimality of competitive allocations. It has only one assumption in addition to the absence of externalities, namely the local non-satiation of consumer preferences. If this condition holds, any equilibrium allocation in the augmented economy must be Pareto optimal.

Starrett's argument: Nonconvexity. Unfortunately, the situation is less simple for the Second Welfare and Existence Theorems, primarily because of their additional hypotheses, in particular of convexity of the production sets. In the example above, suppose that the production functions $F(\cdot, y_j)$ are concave in their respective own decision variables, y_i, so that their own (conditional) production sets are convex. Thus suppose that $F^1(\cdot)$ is concave in y_1 and, in the augmented space, that $F^2(\cdot, q_{212})$ is concave as a function of x_2 for any admissible value of q_{212}. Would the 'grand' production possibility set defined by $F^2(x_2, y_2)$,

$$P_2 = \{(y_2, x_2, q_{212}) \in \mathbb{R}^3_+ : y_2 \leq \max (F^2(x_2, q_{212}), 0)\},$$

be convex in the space of feasible triples (y_2, x_2, y_1), while q_{212} ranges over all nonnegative values?

In his 1972 paper, Starrett argues that P_2 cannot be convex if the externality is detrimental. Consider the cross-section of the production function F^2 with the labor input x_2 fixed at an arbitrary positive value, say x_2^*. Examine the function $F^{*2}(q_{212}) = F^2(x_2^*, q_{212})$, where the domain of q_{212} is the set of all non-negative reals; i.e., the output as a function of the quantity of smoke received, q_{212}, with labor input fixed at x_i^*, so $F^{*2}(0) > 0$. Since smoke is detrimental by hypothesis, it is necessarily the case that

$$0 < F^{*2}(q_{212}) < F^{*2}(0) \text{ for all } q_{212} > 0.$$

It is now not difficult to show that $F^{*2}(\cdot)$ cannot be concave, and hence the 'grand' production set P_2 cannot be convex.

Non-Existence of equilibria in artificial markets. While convexity of production sets cannot be dispensed with for the existence theorem and for the Second Theorem of Welfare Economics, it is not a necessary condition. That is, there are cases where the production sets fail to be convex and yet competitive equilibria exist. But, as Starrett shows, the artificial markets economy has no such luck.

The argument is quite straightforward. Let the input X be fixed, and consider the problem of equating supply with demand for the artificial commodity Q_{212} (smoke, or the right to emit smoke). If the price of smoke, P_{212}, were zero (or positive), the polluter would want to supply a positive amount, but the victim would not want to 'buy' any smoke. On the other hand, if the price of smoke is negative, $p_{212} < 0$, the polluter pays to the victim the total of $-p_{212} \cdot q_{212} > 0$ when the quantity q_{212} of smoke is 'bought' by the victim from the polluter. (The purchase of smoke may be interpreted as the sale of pollution rights by the victim to the polluter.)

Then the victim can raise its profit to any arbitrarily high level by demanding a sufficiently large amount of smoke while keeping the labor input fixed (possibly at zero). Thus there is no price of the artificial commodity (smoke) at which supply equals demand, so there can be no equilibrium in the augmented economy with artificial markets. Because this non-existence phenomenon is unavoidable in the presence of detrimental externalities, and not just a feature of a special example, Starrett refers to the non-convexity of the victim's 'grand' production sets as 'fundamental'.[11] If one accepts the Starrett argument, then one must conclude that artificial markets do not solve the problem of inefficiency in the presence of detrimental externalities.

Pigou taxes and bounties as a remedy

Can this failure of the classical market mechanism be remedied by a Pigouvian tax? In principle, yes, but only to a limited extent, as will be illustrated by the working of a Pigou tax in an economy of type (B). Here the polluter producing y_i units of output would pay the tax ty_i, with the tax rate t (to be treated parametrically by the polluting firm) given by $t = G_{y_1}^2$, i.e. $t = \partial G^2 / \partial y_1$. The polluter will then be induced to reduce its level of output to the point where the first-order necessary condition (2.4) is satisfied. But as is well known (and was pointed out by Pigou himself in 1912, although not in the context of externality taxes), first-order conditions may well not be sufficient to guarantee optimality. Starrett (1972, pp. 194–5) gives an example[12] where there are three Pigouvian equilibria, but only one is efficient.

So what is good about Pigou taxes? They have two points in their favor. First, when the victim's own (conditional) production possibility sets are convex (which is not inconsistent with the presence of Starrett non-convexities), there does exist a Pigouvian equilibrium at every aggregate

---

[11] A critique of Starrett's argument is found in Otani and Sicilian (1977).

[12] In Starrett's example (1972, pp. 194–96), the production functions are $y_1 = a_1 x_1$ and $y_2 = a_2 x_2 / (1 + y_1)$, so the own sets are convex (conditional constant returns to scale).

production-efficient allocation.[13] This contrasts with the situation in an artificial commodities economy, where due to Starrett non-convexities there would be no equilibrium. This result may be viewed as an analogue of the Second Welfare Theorem. Second, analogous to the First Welfare Theorem, there is a narrower class of situations in which a Pigouvian equilibrium allocation is in fact Pareto optimal.

In an economy of type (B), consider the feasible transformation set T, i.e., the set of commodity points (y_1, y_2) that are feasible, given the two firms' technologies (input requirement functions) and the available input resources. This set, as illustrated in Baumol and Oates (1988, p. 114, fig 8.2 and p. 128, fig 8.7), can be convex even in the presence of externalities, although it can also be non-convex when the externality effect is sufficiently strong.

It turns out that when (1) the transformation set T is convex, (2) the two firms' own production sets are also convex, and (3) the consumer's preferences are representable by a concave function $u(y_1, y_2)$, then Pigou equilibrium allocations will exist and will necessarily be Pareto optimal. Again, this proposition is compatible with the presence of Starrett non-convexities. (This proposition reflects research in progress and might ultimately have to be refined or corrected. It is stated for a very simple economy, but I believe it to have more general validity.)[14]

Although of much more limited scope, this proposition is the counterpart of what could be inferred in the absence of externalities about 'natural' competitive allocations from the First Welfare Theorem, together with classical theorems on the existence of competitive equilibria.

The sad dilemma

But what if the feasible transformation set is not convex? We know that there are examples of non-optimal Pigou equilibria for such situations and, according to Starrett, artificial markets may have no equilibria. The question is whether there is some other remedy that does not sacrifice decentralization.

That the answer is negative is suggested by a result of Calsamiglia, who considered an economy with one convex consumer and one non-convex firm, with no externalities. He showed that if the efficient boundary of the firm is smooth, has negative slope, but is convex to the origin (so the transformation set is not convex), then there does not exist any decentralized mechanism that guarantees the absence of non-optimal equilibria. An

---

[13] This proposition was proved, in considerable generality, both in Starrett (1972) and in Baumol and Bradford (1972), although in slightly different forms.
[14] See Proposition 2 in Hurwicz (1999) p. 238.—SB

analogous impossibility proposition appears to hold for a type (B) economy with two firms and an externality. (Again, this proposition represents research in progress.)

In fact, perhaps somewhat surprisingly, the problem would not be cured even if the two firms, the polluter and the victim, merged; the transformation set would remain non-convex, and so a Calsarniglia-type impossibility theorem for economies with externalities would still apply!

If the impossibility result for economies with externalities is correct, it follows that we are between the rock and the hard place: in the presence of externalities yielding non-convex transformation sets, nothing will guarantee both existence and optimality. We may, therefore, have to resign ourselves to mechanisms that sacrifice one or other of our two desiderata (universal existence and optimality of equilibria). If so, Pigou taxes may deserve reconsideration in this apparently unavoidably second-best world.

Other microeconomic limitations

The microeconomic approach has several serious limitations. First, it does not adequately represent the process by which equilibrium is determined by alternative mechanisms, such as Walrasian perfect competition, various types of auctions, and bargaining and negotiations. In contrast, game-theoretic models explicitly represent alternative equilibrating mechanisms.

Second, transaction costs are not included in the traditional microeconomic model, and are difficult to incorporate. Coase, Posner, and others have argued that the main reason for studying economies without transaction costs is to show that it is the transaction costs that account for institutional arrangements. But, as indicated above, their argument is too strong because *income effects can help to explain differences in institutional arrangements, even when no transaction costs are present*. Nevertheless, there is little doubt that transaction costs (in the broad sense, including uncertainty and other phenomena not found in many traditional models) are important factors in explaining institutional phenomena. As we shall see below, game-theoretic models provide a very natural framework for including transactions costs and looking more at institutions than markets. Even when the hypotheses of the classical theorems are satisfied, there is a serious, and well-known, difficulty: the individualized markets are likely to be so 'thin' that the assumption of price-taking behavior, essential to the concept of perfectly competitive equilibrium, is implausible.

Furthermore, the problem of *excludability* must be faced in treating public goods as commodities. When it is costly or impossible to exclude users of a (beneficial) public good who are unwilling to pay, the 'seller' of the good is in effect forced to sell at an unacceptably low price. Similarly, for detrimental externalities, the victim may be unable to avoid exposure to, say, smoke or acid rain. Yet 'buyers' of smoke should not be forced to absorb it; they should 'buy' it only if the negative price (i.e. compensation) is right. Technological factors may account for such involuntary transactions, but typically they have institutional aspects, such as the liability for damage caused by smoke. We shall illustrate the liability problem using an example in the spirit of Coase.

Institutional Arrangements as Game Rules

A game theory framework[15] can be used to analyze the incentive aspects of alternative institutions. For example, the 'tragedy of the commons' can be modeled as a game. The pessimistic model represents the problem as corresponding to a Prisoners' Dilemma. But, some basis for optimism may be found by modeling the situation as a supergame, an infinite repetition of the one-shot Prisoners' Dilemma, in which a player's strategy is defined for the infinite sequence of time points, and the move at time t may be based on (partial or complete) knowledge of the preceding moves up to and including time $t-1$. However, it follows from the so-called Folk Theorems that supergames can have bad as well as good equilibria. Alternative institutional arrangements that result in positive outcomes—definitely not a tragedy!— have been explored by Ostrom (1993).

Distinguishing games from mechanisms ('game-forms')

Informally, if a social process is a 'game', then institutions are the rules governing the play of the game.[16,17] The analysis of one-move games has been important in the development of game theory, but many—perhaps most— social phenomena are best modeled by multi-move games. The rules of a multi-move game, such as chess or poker, can be specified[18] in a natural way in three parts:

---

[15] What are called noncooperative games are the main object of interest here. But one should keep in mind that, despite terminology, cooperative behavior can be modeled within the framework of such games.

[16] For a different interpretation of the relationship between institutions and games, refer to Schotter (1981, 1986).

[17] More precisely, we later define an institution as a *class* of rules governing a class of related games.

[18] This specification corresponds to the so-called extensive-form game, rather than the normal (or strategic) form, which is discussed below.

(1) the set of players;[19]

(2) the specification of moves (permissible, obligatory, or optional) at any given stage of the game, given its prior history; and

(3) the outcomes, or consequences of the totality of choices made by the players, (who wins, what or how much is won, etc.).

We shall call this specification an *extensive game-form*.[20] The extensive game-form describes the game 'according to Hoyle'. For expository purposes, it can be presented graphically in the form of a game-form tree.[21]

Instead of indicating the permissible moves at all stages of the game, as in (2), permissible *strategies* that define moves could be prescribed. In a sense, a multi-move game is thus converted into a one-move game, in which the single move is to choose a complete strategy. Together with the set of players (1), and the *outcome function* (3) prescribing the consequences of the various strategy choices, this specification will be called the *normal game-form*.

For expository purposes we often focus on the case of two players, each with only a finite set of available strategies. The normal game-form is then presented as a two-way table, with (say) rows corresponding to the first player's strategies, and columns to the second player's. The cell in the i-th row and j-th column then contains a description of the outcome occurring when the first actor uses his or her i-th strategy and the second his or her j-th strategy.

Formally, the *normal game-form* is defined as follows. Denote by $N = \{1, \ldots, n\}$ the set of players, by S^i the i-th player's permissible strategy domain, by S the Cartesian product[22] $S^1 \times \cdots \times S^n$ (called the *joint strategy domain*), and by Z the set of possible outcomes. Then the outcome function, denoted h, associates a specific element of the outcome space Z, say z, with each possible

---

[19] In modeling social institutions, the rules defining players are important. Humans without decision-making rights (e.g., children or prisoners in certain contexts) are not viewed as players. On the other hand, institutional entities (e.g., governments) having legal status of persons can be players.

[20] In the economic literature a game-form (whether in extensive or normal form) is often called a *mechanism*.

[21] The extensive game-form tree differs from the game tree seen in textbooks as *a* representation of a game in extensive form: in the latter, the terminal nodes represent numerical utilities, while in the extensive game-form tree, the terminal nodes represent (physical) outcomes, rather than the utilities of those outcomes.

[22] As an example, suppose that there are two players, that S^1 consists of the two strategies a_1 and a_2 available to player 1, while S^2 consists of the three strategies b_1, b_2, and b_3 available to player 2. Then the joint strategy domain consists of six ordered pairs of strategies: (a_1, b_1), (a_1, b_2), (a_1, b_3), (a_2, b_1), (a_2, b_2), and (a_2, b_3), i.e., all possible combinations of strategic choices by the two players. Despite the terminology, the players are assumed to make their strategy choices independently, not jointly. We have not listed mixed strategies.

n-tuple of strategies, say $(s_1, \ldots, s_n)$, chosen by the players, where s_1 is in $S^1, \ldots, s_n$ is in S^n. Thus, in customary functional notation, $h: S \to Z$, i.e.

$$z = h(s_1, \ldots, s_n).$$

In turn, the normal game-form is formally defined as the triple (N, S, h), although often the set of players is understood and we suppress N, thinking of the normal game-form as the pair (S, h). Design issues have to do with specification of h.

What is informally called the 'game' of chess, say, is usually a reference to 'the rules according to Hoyle', i.e. the (extensive) game-form. But the formal meaning of the term 'game' in the game theory literature is different; we adopt the game theorists' definition even though it is not in agreement with everyday usage. The distinction between 'game-form' and 'game' (as in game theory) is very important in the analysis of institutions.

We shall first illustrate the distinction in the context of normal game-forms. As seen above, the *normal game-form* is the triple (N, S, h) where h, the outcome function, has domain S, the players' joint strategy set, and range Z, the (physical) outcome space. The game-theory concept of a game also involves the joint strategy set S, but instead of the outcome function h, it specifies n so-called payoff functions, $\pi^1, \ldots, \pi^n$. Each of these functions has domain S and range $\mathbb{R}$, the set of all real numbers. Formally, therefore, a normal game is specified as $(N, S, \pi^1, \ldots, \pi^n)$, with $\pi^i: S \to \mathbb{R}$ for every $i = 1, \ldots, n$. The interpretation is that $\pi^i(s_1, \ldots, s_n)$ represents the (numerical) utility derived by player i from the outcome occurring as the result of the players' strategy choices $s_1, \ldots, s_n$.

This interpretation makes it easy to see the relationship between the payoff functions defining the game and the outcome function defining the game-form. One need only note that the domain of a player's utility function is the outcome space Z, i.e. the i-th the player's utility function is $u^i : Z \to \mathbb{R}$. If the strategy n-tuple is $s_1, \ldots, s_n$, the outcome is $z = h(s_1, \ldots, s_n)$, and the utility is $u^i(z)$. But, since z is the outcome generated by the choices $(s_1, \ldots, s_n)$, the numerical utility $u^i(z)$ must equal the payoff $\pi^i(s_1, \ldots, s_n)$ associated with the strategy choices $(s_1, \ldots, s_n)$. It follows that

$$\pi^i(s_1, \ldots, s_n) = u^i(h(s_1, \ldots, s_n)),$$

or that π^i is the composition of u^i with h,

$$\pi^i = u^i \circ h,$$

and is indistinguishable from the i-th component of the outcome function.

There is a special class of situations in which the distinction between game and game-form has often been blurred. Suppose that the outcome consists of an allocation of money amounts, say $m_1, \ldots, m_n$, to the n selfish players, so that $h(s_1, \ldots, s_n) = (m_1, \ldots, m_n) = Z \in \mathbb{R}^n$. Suppose further that each player's utility function is linear in money, and is normalized so that $u^i(z) = u^i(m_1, \ldots, m_n) = m_i$. Then $\pi^i(s_1, \ldots, s_n) = h^i(s_1, \ldots, s_n)$ where $h^i(s)$ is the i-th component of $h(s)$.

A similar relation between game and game-form exists for extensive games. An extensive game is usually modeled as a tree, with numerical (utility) payoffs indicated at the terminal nodes. An extensive game-form is also represented by a tree, but the information associated with terminal notes indicates the corresponding (physical) outcome rather than the utility payoff.

Example: Auctioning a common resource

As an illustration of interest in resource economics, consider the problem of allocating a scarce resource, such as rights to a radio frequency, to one of n agents. Denote by $v^i > 0$ the monetary value of the resource to the i-th agent. Suppose the method of allocation is a sealed-bid auction.

A sealed-bid auction may be considered a one-move game in which agent i's strategy is its bid, s^i. When bids are admissible if and only if they are positive, agent i's strategy domain is $S^i = \mathbb{R}_{++}$, the set of all positive numbers. For the individual player i, an outcome is an ordered pair, $z^i = (x^i, y^i)$, where x^i is the change in i's money holdings and y^i is the change in i's holdings of the resource being auctioned. Hence, if i is unsuccessful in the auction, $z^i = (0,0)$, while if i succeeds, $z^i = (-p, 1)$, where $x^i = p$ is the price paid and $y^i = 1$ indicates that the resource has been acquired by i. An element z of the outcome space is an n-tuple $z = (z^1, \ldots, z^n)$, and the outcome to agent i is written $z^i = h^i(s)$. To simplify matters, we assume for the moment the absence of ties, and denote the highest bidder by i^*, and the runner-up by i^{**}.

What exactly is the outcome function? It depends on the type of auction as specified by the rules. For example, in the usual 'English' auction, $z^i = h^i(s) = (-s^i, 1)$ for $i = i^*$, while $z^j = h^j(s) = (0,0)$ for any $j \neq i^*$. In words, the highest bidder pays his or her bid, so $p = s^{i^*}$ and receives the resource, while every other agent pays nothing and, of course, receives nothing.

Because this type of auction suffers from the danger of misrepresentation, an ingenious alternative, the second-price (Vickrey) auction, has been proposed. Here the strategy domains are the same and the highest bidder still gets the resource, but the price paid equals the second highest bid, $p = s^{i^{**}}$, rather than the highest. So here $h^{i^*} = (-s^{i^{**}}, 1)$, while, just as in the English auction, $z^j = (0,0)$ for all $j \neq i^*$.

Contrary to common belief, perhaps, second-price auctions do not always produce truthful or efficient equilibria when proceeds are distributed among the bidders (see Cramton et al., 1987, and Hurwicz and Walker, 1990).

Institutions as game-forms and families of game-forms

Different institutional arrangements correspond to different game-forms. When we speak of institutional reform, we are thinking of changing the rules of the game, i.e. the game-form. But, assuming preferences remain constant, changes in the game-form will result in changed payoff functions, and therefore a different game.

The literature contains much information on game-forms and their limitations. Interpreting institutional changes as changes in game-forms enables us to apply existing results in the theory of mechanisms to study institutions.[23] Identifying institutions with game-forms[24] ignores the more common meaning of institution.[25] In many contexts, an 'institution' is an entity such as a state, the office of an ombudsman office (as distinct from the ombudsman's person), a church, a legislative body, a government agency, or a university. An institution can indicate an artificial person or player, as distinct from what are often called institutional arrangements that correspond to the rules of the game. The creation of an international body (as at Rio de Janeiro or Montreal) to deal with an environmental issue (such as biodiversity or ozone depletion) introduces both a new artificial player and a change in the rules of the game.

The term 'institutional framework' encompasses both meanings of 'institution', i.e. both institutional arrangements (game-forms) and artificial players (institutional entities).[26] Even though the game formalization may not be present or obvious, much analysis in the social sciences—especially economics and political science—is devoted to the examination of alternative

[23] Schotter (1981, 1986, 1989) advocates an alternative view, interpreting institutional arrangements as the solutions of (super)games, rather than the rules governing them. I believe (see Hurwicz, 1996), that these two seemingly incompatible interpretations can be reconciled within a somewhat broader framework.

[24] Or, more appropriately as *families* of game-forms, as I have argued (Hurwicz, 1996). For instance, when we speak of the institution of marriage, we refer to arrangements that vary across cultures and times, although with many elements in common. Since each variant has different 'rules of the game', it would be represented by a different game-form. Thus the umbrella concept of marriage corresponds to a whole family of game-forms, rather than just one game-form.

[25] Corresponding to what I call the second type (or meaning) of institution, North speaks of an organization, but I feel this term is too narrow, as it does not encompass institutional entities with a one-person incumbent such as the (institution of the) president's office.

[26] We may not want to consider all artificial (legal) persons as institutional entities. For instance, a partnership of a few individuals may be an artificial person, but viewing it as an institutional entity might not be useful. I have not given sufficient thought to this distinction, but perhaps it has something to do with the nature of the mission of the institutional entity, or whether outsiders are bound by its decisions.

institutional frameworks. Such studies may operate in two ways. They may take as given a certain institutional framework, say a type of market economy or parliamentary democracy. Or they may start with a problem or objective and seek to identify an institutional framework to solve the problem or accomplish the objective. The latter approach, in which the institutional framework is viewed as a variable or unknown, is often termed *design*.

Implementation via Nash equilibria

An important variant of the design approach is the so-called theory of *implementation*.[27] For an implementation problem, mechanisms are sought that would result in outcomes satisfying desiderata that might be applied to game-forms, such as Pareto optimality and fairness in allocations.

The outcomes associated with a mechanism (S, h) depend on several factors: the characteristics of the players or agents (their preferences, technologies, initial resources, etc.), the strategies they choose, and the structure of equilibria. Often, it is hypothesized that the outcome will be a Nash equilibrium of the game defined by the game-form (S, h) and the prevailing preferences (represented by utility functions $u^1(\cdot), \ldots,$ and $u^n(\cdot)$), together with feasibility-determining factors such as endowments and technologies. Another outcome hypothesis is dominance equilibrium, and there are many others.

We shall refer to preferences and feasibility-determining factors as 'data'.[28] A goal correspondence is a relation specifying the set of acceptable outcomes given the data. Formally, then, a correspondence F (a 'set-valued function') has as domain a class E of data that could conceivably occur, and maps it into the set of outcomes. Thus, for given data $e \in E$, the correspondence F specifies a set $F(e)$ in the outcome space, Z.[29] For instance, if the desideratum is fairness (however defined), then $F(e)$ would be the set of outcomes that are fair when the prevailing data are e.

With this formalization, the (Maskin) notion of implementation can be stated simply. A mechanism (S, h) implements the goal correspondence F over the class of E of conceivably occurring data (or 'economic environments') if, for every e in E, (1) the game defined by (S, h) and the preferences

---

27 This term was introduced by Maskin (1977), but, as discussed in Hurwicz (1996), its meaning is somewhat different from common usage.

28 We use this term in part because, in the context of institutional design, preferences and feasibility are taken as given, and in part because the term used elsewhere in the literature is 'environment' (i.e. economic environment—not the quality of air, water, etc.), which would be confusing in a book using the term to refer to ambient physical factors.

29 In the literature, F is often called a 'social choice rule', but I feel that this terminology is confusing because it suggests the rules of the game rather than the objective of design. I prefer to call F the 'goal correspondence'.

implied by e has at least one Nash equilibrium strategy n-tuple s^*, and (2) if s^* is a Nash equilibrium when e prevails, then the outcome $h(s^*)$ is F-acceptable, i.e., the outcome $z^* = h(s^*)$ belongs to $F(e)$. For instance, if F represents fairness, then the condition is that any Nash equilibrium outcome be fair. Analogously, one can define implementability in terms of solution concepts other than Nash equilibrium, such as dominance equilibrium or Nash equilibrium refinements.

It is of interest whether, ignoring enforceability and enforcement costs, it is possible to design mechanisms implementing a given set of desiderata over a specified class of economic environments. Maskin's contribution (1977) has been to provide necessary[30] and sufficient conditions for the implementability of goal correspondences, and, furthermore, to propose a general procedure for constructing implementing mechanisms, that is, mechanisms whose Nash equilibria satisfy the goal desiderata.

Not surprisingly, the problem of implementability is central to many issues of public policy. In economies having small numbers of agents, or detrimental externalities, or increasing returns, the perfect competition mechanism (in its standard formulation) does not Nash-implement the Pareto optimality desideratum. Similarly, the Lindahl mechanism[31] in economies with public goods does not implement Pareto optimality because of the free-rider problem. This poses the question of whether with incentive problems it is possible

---

[30] In Maskin's mechanisms, each player's generic strategy element is of the form $(R^1, \ldots, R^n)$, a profile of all players' preference relations. If it is known only that these relations have certain qualitative properties, such as convexity or continuity, then they are infinite-dimensional unless they are also required to belong to some finite-parameter family, such as Cobb-Douglas or quadratic. Maskin's necessary condition is that the goal correspondence have the property he calls monotonicity. More recently, it has been shown (Moore and Repullo, 1988; Palfrey and Srivastava, 1991) that if the Nash equilibrium postulate is replaced by one of its 'refinements' (subgame perfect or undominated Nash), a much broader class of goal correspondences becomes implementable, but apparently at the cost of even larger strategy spaces.

In this context, we mean by 'impossibility of institutional implementation' the impossibility of so doing with a finite-dimensional message space and a finite number of equations to be verified. In such a situation, it would take an infinitely long time to verify whether a given allocation is, for example, Pareto optimal. It is interesting to note that these negative results follow directly from informational considerations and do not involve game theory. (Maskin's notion of implementation does not impose the finiteness requirement.)

[31] Although these mechanisms produce Lindahl allocations as Nash equilibrium outcomes, the rules of the game are not the Lindahl rules. A similar situation exists with regard to mechanisms Nash-implementing Walrasian equilibria. Schmeidler's mechanism implementing the Walrasian correspondence in a pure exchange economy has only the traders as players, and the same is true of many other Nash implementation mechanisms for economic environments. An alternative approach uses the popular 'Walrasian auctioneer' as a player endowed with a payoff function equal, say, to $-\sum_k d_k^2$, where d_k is aggregate excess demand for the k-th good. The auctioneer's strategy variable is, of course, the price vector. Note that, by the definition of Nash equilibrium, traders will treat prices parametrically. In the standard microeconomic version of the auctioneer's operations, feasibility out of equilibrium is not assured, and may well be absent. For this reason, game-theoretic models such as Schmeidler's, with or without auctioneer, often require some form of 'rationing' to guarantee balance when the economy is out of equilibrium.

to design mechanisms to implement Pareto optimality, or other desiderata such as fairness, in various 'non-classical' economies.

In some cases, research has provided affirmative answers. But when the concept of implementation does not take into account the costs and feasibility of information transfer and enforcement, a positive answer may be of little practical value. The concept of implementability therefore should be strengthened to what I have called 'genuine implementability' by including in desiderata information and enforcement costs as well as the feasibility of information processing; consistency with other social values may also be included in genuine implementation.

These practical problems are briefly discussed in Section 4, below, where it is noted that in some economies (for instance, non-convex economies or those with an infinite time horizon) there are no Nash-implementing mechanisms. But for some convex economies with finite horizons, mechanisms have been designed using finite-dimensional messge spaces. The breakthrough contributions were Groves and Ledyard (1977) for Pareto optimal allocations in economies with public goods, and Schmeidler (1982) for Walrasian allocations in economies with private goods. Mechanisms have also been designed for Nash-implementation of Lindahl allocations; see Hurwicz (1979a, b) and Walker (1981).

Informational Aspects of Economics

Genuine implementation issues for policy or institutional reform may be classified under one of two headings, incentives or information. The incentive issue raised by Samuelson and others was that the Lindahl solution for resource allocation in an economy with public goods would provide participants with an incentive to misrepresent their marginal rates of substitution in order to reduce their share of support.[32] This situation has both incentive and informational problems. Because government in a large economy cannot practically observe individual behavior, preferences can be misrepresented.

Informational issues play a central role in economic analysis. The famous critique of socialism by Hayek (1935) and Mises (1932), for instance, was based on the claim that socialist systems, lacking market mechanisms, are *informationally* infeasible. Lange's (1936, 1937) response was that the informational requirements of the Lange-Lerner version of market socialism are essentially no different from those of a capitalist market economy. But more relevant to this volume are the informational issues associated with

[32] An important step toward integration of the informational and incentive aspects of mechanisms is taken in Reichelstein and Reiter (1988).

alternative mechanisms proposed to solve problems due to externalities, public goods, or the commons.

Informational efficiency of the Walrasian process

Not all results obtained in the study of decentralized processes lead to pessimistic conclusions. One that may be considered positive is that the Walrasian mechanism for private goods is informationally efficient in that it uses a message space of essentially minimal dimension. A similar theorem holds for the Lindahl mechanism for economies with public goods.

Informational aspects of externalities

As an illustration, let us look again at a particular externality problem, an economy with a unilateral detrimental externality such as smoke pollution. For a system of Pigouvian taxes (or subsidies), some authors have stressed problems associated with informational requirements, because these taxes must be calculated at an efficient allocation which requires full information about the economy (see Starrett, 1972, p. 195; Baumol and Oates, 1988, pp. 180–1). The burden of such information requirements reflects mainly the centralized nature of the procedures by which the taxes are assumed to be determined.

An alternative is the use of personalized commodity prices, à la Lindahl, Foley, and Arrow for the case of public goods, but here for public 'bads'. Instead of centrally computed taxes, the relevant price parameters could be obtained through an informationally decentralized process in which the computational burden is distributed among the participants, thus reducing the requirement for central collection of private data. (If personalized prices had to be obtained centrally, rather than through a process, the informational burden would be similar. Parametric treatment of prices by agents would be part of the definition of this process.)

When equilibria exist, iterative processes such as tâtonnement may fail to converge to an equilibrium. Furthermore, the informational requirements for a dynamic process can exceed that for a static situation (Reiter, 1979; Baumol and Oates, 1988, p. 161).

Intuitively, it seems clear that certain information must be available for *any* mechanism to have outcomes guaranteed to be optimal. Thus if it could be proved that the information essential for the Pigouvian process is also necessary for any mechanism guaranteeing optimality in the presence of externalities, one could conclude that only second best solutions are possible.

But is it possible to prove that certain information is necessary to *any* mechanism guaranteeing optimality? The answer is affirmative, as the following elementary example illustrates (see Hurwicz, 1972b, especially Example A, p. 312). A desired commodity, Y, is produced by two producers, 1 and 2. The optimum is defined as maximum aggregate output of the two producers. Producer 1 is a polluter, and producer 2 is the pollutee. Producer i's activity level is denoted a_i, and output level y_i. Their technologies are

$$y_1 = \alpha_1 a_1 + \gamma_1 a_2 - (1/2)a_1^2$$
$$y_2 = \alpha_2 a_2 - (1/2)a_2^2$$

The term $\gamma_1 a_2$ represents the externality, with $\gamma_1 < 0$ if the externality, like pollution, is detrimental.

Clearly, the optimal activity levels are $a_1^* = \alpha_1$, $a_2^* = \alpha_2 + \gamma_1$. If there were no externality ($\gamma_1 = 0$), knowledge of both α_1 and α_2 would suffice to determine optimal activity levels. But suppose the value of γ_1 is not known. Then it is not possible to optimize, for if it were, a fixed value of a_2, say a_2^* would be optimal regardless of the value of γ_1. If c' and c'' are distinct values of γ_1, we would have $a_2^* = \alpha_2 + c'$ and $a_2^* = \alpha_2 + c''$, a contradiction. Thus, a mechanism without information about γ_1, could not guarantee optimality.[33] As Hurwicz (1972b) shows, every informationally decentralized mechanism satisfying certain continuity conditions must have a message space of dimension at least three, corresponding to knowledge of the three technology parameters and, in particular, of the externality γ_2 (marginal damage) parameter.[34]

In the preceding example, determination of the minimum dimension of the message space (hence the minimum information) to ensure optimality is very simple. More sophisticated techniques are required in general, however, and in particular in economies with non-convexities and infinite horizons.

---

[33] T. Marschak (see Hurwicz, 1972b, pp. 317–18) provides an analogous proof for a more general class of situations.

[34] Here, a mechanism is interpreted as verifying whether an economy is at a stationary point of an *adjustment process*. An adjustment process involves an exchange of messages among all n participants, described by a system of difference equations

$$m^i(t+1) - m^i(t) = g(m(t); e), \quad i = 1, \ldots, n, \quad t = 0, \ldots,$$

where $m(t) = (m^1(t), \ldots, m^1(t), \ldots, m^n(t))$, e^j is the *characteristic* of the j-th participant, and $e = (e^1, \ldots, e^j, \ldots, e^n)$ is the *(economic) environment*. (If j is a consumer, e^j is defined by j's preferences, consumption set, and endowments; if j is a producer, by j's production possibilities.) An adjustment process is called *informationally decentralized* if, for each i, g^1 is independent of any e^j, $j \neq 1$. (In the literature, the latter property is sometimes called 'privacy-preserving', and the term 'informationally decentralized' reserved for processes satisfying additional requirements.) A *stationary value* $m^* = (m^{*1}, \ldots, m^{n*})$ of the process is defined by $g^i(m^*; e) = 0$, $i = 1, \ldots, n$.

A *verification scenario* for an informationally decentralized process is a procedure in which each participant, i, knowing its equilibrium function g^i and its characteristic e^i is informed of a 'candidate for equilibrium', say m^0, and proceeds to verify whether the relation $g^i(m^0; e^i) = 0$ is satisfied. (Since the process is assumed informationally decentralized, we write $g^i(m^0; e^i)$ instead of $g^i(m^0; e)$.)

Non-convexities

Calsamiglia (1977) showed that, when there are non-convexities (of either consumption or production), it may be the case that no mechanism with a finite-dimensional message space can guarantee optimality for any rea sonably broad class of economic environments (i.e., preferences and technologies). All price mechanisms proposed for non-convex situations, such as marginal cost pricing or Pigouvian taxes, rely on finite-dimensional message spaces. (The dimension is determined by the number of commodities and economic agents.) If the Calsamiglia argument applies to the economic environments postulated in the usual analysis of economies with externalities, it would follow that the proposed price and tax mechanisms would not work even if all information concerning the marginal entities were available. Even more serious, no finite decentralized mechanism would work either. On the other hand, a mechanism with an infinite message space would not be feasible in practice, as it would not permit even static verification in a finite time.

This impossibility result has implications for (Maskin) implementability. The reason is that under assumptions of differentiability, the conditions defining Nash equilibrium can be interpreted as stationarity conditions for an informationally decentralized process.[35] Hence impossibility results for informationally decentralized adjustment processes imply the corresponding impossibilities for (Maskin-) Nash implementation. Consequently, first best optima (although technically feasible) may be institutionally unattainable.

Infinite time horizons

A similar situation exists in economies with an infinite time horizon. Here, too, it has been shown (Hurwicz and Weinberger, 1990) that in some cases, no finite system of equations is sufficient to guarantee that decisions made at a given time will not violate the requirements of optimality. As noted in 4.3, this implies that Nash implementation of first best optimality is institutionally impossible. This finding is obviously relevant to issues such as conservation, and more generally to issues of intergenerational efficiency,[36]

---

[35] Consider the i-th player's strategy s_t as its message, and define an adjustment ('gradient') process by $s_i(t+1) - s_i(t) = \partial \pi^i / \partial S_i, i = 1, \ldots, n$, where $\pi^i(s_1, \ldots, s_n)$ is the i-th player's payoff function. At a stationary point, we then have $\partial \pi^i / \partial s_i = 0, i = 1, \ldots, n$; these conditions are all necessary for an interior Nash equilibrium. (In implementation, we have $\pi^i = u^i \circ h$.)

[36] The efficiency criterion used by Hurwicz and Weinberger (1990) is the discounted sum of future utilities, i.e., $\sum_t \delta^t u(c_t)$, with t ranging from 0 to ∞. (Here, c_1 is the consumption at time t, and d the discount coefficient.) On the production side, the model assumes 'overlapping generations', *à la* Malinvaud. Bala et al. (1992) show that this difficulty does not arise under a less demanding efficiency criterion.

because—as in non-convex economies—it may force the acceptance of second best solutions.

Incomplete information and the interpretation of Nash equilibria

A different informational issue arising in the context of Nash equilibria should also be mentioned. By definition, $S^* = (S_1^*, \ldots, S_n^*)$ is a Nash equilibrium for the game defined by payoff functions $\pi^1, \ldots, \pi^n$ and strategy domains $S^1, \ldots, S^n$ if and only if, for each i, s^* maximizes $\pi^i(s_i, s_{-i}^*)$ with respect to s_i in S^i, where s_{-i}^* denotes the $(n-1)$-tuple obtained by deleting the i-th component of s^*. Hence to verify whether a candidate n-tuple s^0 of strategies is a Nash equilibrium it is sufficient for each player to know his or her own payoff function and the strategies used by other players; it is not necessary for player i to know the other players' payoff functions $\pi^i, j \neq i$.

However, there is a widespread, indeed dominant, view that the hypothesis that players would choose to adopt their Nash equilibrium strategies (at least when the Nash equilibrium is unique) is plausible only if each player knows all the payoff functions, since each player can then calculate the equilibrium, and (assuming it is unique) count on others doing so as well. A situation in which all payoff functions are known to all players is one of *complete information*. Otherwise, we are said to be dealing with incomplete information, in which Bayesian procedures are required.

In the context of implementation, the i-th payoff function π^i is the composition of the outcome function h with the i-th utility function u^i. The outcome function, part of the rules of the game (i.e., part of the game-form), is assumed known to all players. But if $j \neq i$, i cannot know j's payoff function π^j, unless i also knows j's utility function; see Roberts (1987, p. 185) for an example.

In economics applications, we typically do not wish to assume such knowledge. This creates a dilemma. My own (minority!) opinion is that complete information is not required to justify use of Nash equilibrium. There are alternative, less demanding justifications that require only that each player know his or her own utility function and be able to observe other players' strategies (sometimes in aggregated form). The gradient process mentioned above may be viewed as an 'adaptive' or learning model that justifies the Nash equilibrium as a stationary point.

Concluding Remarks

Early mechanism design literature focused on informational issues, in particular issues arising in the context of social planning. Models emphasized information flows and the informational burdens of attaining efficiency, such as the size of the message space. Subsequently, attention turned to the role of incentives, and game models became the tool of choice.

At the same time, traditional microeconomic approaches have continued to be useful to clarify both the efficiency and distributional features of the economic systems under consideration. This chapter explored design issues for economic mechanisms and institutions, with particular attention to relevance for environmental problems and resource management. A microeconomic and welfare-economic framework was applied to examine externality issues—such as the 'Coase' Theorem, Pigouvian taxes (or subsidies), and personalized prices—with regard to possibility and impossibility theorems and implications for institutional design.

Many issues remain unexplored, and there are undoubtedly many opportunities for creativity in designing mechanisms to address the limitations of policies that have been proposed and analyzed so far. Reluctantly, it must be recognized that there are situations such as non-convexities and infinite time horizons for which we may have to reconcile ourselves to second best solutions. In such situations, the known limitations of proposed policy mechanisms may not be a sufficient basis for rejection!

References

Arrow, K. (1969) The organization of economic activity: Issues pertinent to the choice of market versus nonmarket allocation, in *The Analysis and Evaluation of Public Expenditure: The PPB System* (Compendium of papers submitted to the Subcommittee on Economy in Government of the Joint Economic Committee, 91st Congress, 1st Session), US Government Printing Office, 47–64. Reprinted 1970 in *Public Expenditure and Policy Analysis*, ed. R. Haveman and J. Margolis, 59–73. Chicago, IL: Markham.

Bala, V., M. Majumdar, and T. Mitra (1992) Decentralized evolutionary mechanisms for intertemporal economies: A possibility result, in *Decentralization and Infinite Horizon Economies*, ed. M. Majumdar, 152–80. Boulder, CO: Westview Press.

Baumol, W. and D. Bradford (1972) Detrimental externalities and non-convexity of the production set, *Economica*, 39(1): 160–76.

Baumol, W. and W. Oates (1988) *The Theory of Environmental Policy*, 2nd ed. Cambridge, MA: Cambridge University Press.

Blad, M. and H. Keiding (1990) *Microeconomics*. Amsterdam: North-Holland.

Calsamiglia, X. (1975) On the possibility of informational decentralization in non-convex economies, Ph.D. thesis, University of Minnesota.

Calsamiglia, X. (1977) Decentralized resource allocation and increasing returns, *Journal of Economic Theory*, 14(2): 263–83.

Chipman, J. and G. Tian (2012) Detrimental externalities, pollution rights, and the 'Coase theorem', *Economic Theory*, 49(2): 309–27.

Coase, R. (1960) The problem of social cost, *Journal of Law and Economics*, 3(1): 1–44.

Cramton, P., R. Gibbons, and P. Klemperer. (1987) Dissolving a partnership efficiently, *Econometrica*, 55(3): 615–32.

Eggertsson, T. (1990) *Economic Behavior and Institutions*. Cambridge, MA: Cambridge University Press.

Foley, D. (1970) Lindahl's solution and the core of an economy with public goods, *Econometrica*, 38(1): 66–72.

Groves, T., and J. Ledyard (1977) Optimal allocation of public goods: A solution to the 'free rider' problem, *Econometrica*, 45(4): 783–809.

Haddock, D. and M. Spiegel (1984) Property rules, liability rules, and inalienability: One view of the Edgeworth Box, in *Papers presented at the first meeting of the European Association for Law and Economics*, ed. G. Skogh, 97: 47–75. Lund, Sweden: Nationalekonomiska Institutionen.

Hayek, F. (1935) *Collectivist Economic Planning*. London: Routledge.

Hurwicz, L. (1972a) On informationally decentralized systems, in *Decision and Organization*, ed. C. McGuire and R. Radner, 297–336. Amsterdam: North-Holland.

Hurwicz, L. (1972b) Organizational structures for joint decision-making: A designer's point of view, in *Interorganizational decision-making*, ed. M. Tuite, R. Chisholm, and M. Radnor, 37–44. Chicago, IL: Aldine Publishing Co.

Hurwicz, L. (1979a) Outcome functions yielding Walrasian and Lindahl allocations at Nash equilibrium points, *Review of Economic Studies*, 46(2): 217–25.

Hurwicz, L. (1979b) Balanced outcome functions yielding Walrasian and Lindahl allocations at Nash equilibrium points for two or more agents, in *General Equilibrium, Growth and Trade*, ed. J. Green and J. Scheinkman, 125–37. New York, NY: Academic Press.

Hurwicz, L. (1995) What is the Coase Theorem?, *Japan and the World Economy*, 7(1): 49–74.

Hurwicz, L. (1996) Institutions as families of game forms, *The Japanese Economic Review*, 47(2): 113–32.

Hurwicz, L. (1999) Revisiting externalities, *Journal of Public Economic Theory*, 1(2): 225–45.

Hurwicz, L. and M. Walker (1990). On the generic nonoptimality of dominant strategy allocation mechanisms: A general theorem that includes pure exchange economies, *Econometrica*, 58(3): 683–704.

Hurwicz, L. and H. Weinberger (1990) A necessary condition for decentralization and an application to intertemporal allocation, *Journal of Economic Theory*, 15(2): 313–45.

Lange, O. (1936) On the economic theory of socialism, Part One, *Review of Economic Studies*, 4(1): 53–71.

Lange, O. (1937) On the economic theory of socialism, Part Two, *Review of Economic Studies*, 4(2): 123–42.

Malinvaud, E. (1972) *Lectures on Macroeconomic Theory*. Amsterdam: North-Holland.

Mas-Colell, A., M. Whinston, and J. Green (1995). *Microeconomic Theory*. New York, NY: Oxford University Press.

Maskin, E. (1977) Nash equilibrium and welfare optimality, mimeo. Published as Maskin, E. (1999) Nash equilibrium and welfare optimality, *Review of Economic Studies*, 66(1): 23–38.

Milleron, J.-C. (1972). Theory of value with public goods: A survey article, *Journal of Economic Theory*, 5(3): 419–77.

Mises, L. (1932) *Die Gemeinwirtschaft: Untersuchungen über den Sozialismus*, zweite auflage. Jena, Germany: Verlag von Gustav Fischer.

Moore, J. and R. Repullo (1988) Subgame perfect implementation, *Econometrica*, 56(5): 1191–1220.

Ostrom, E. (1993) Institutional arrangements and the commons dilemma, in *Rethinking Institutional Analysis and Development: Issues, Alternatives, and Choices*, ed. V. Ostrom, D. Feeny, and H. Pith, 101–39. San Francisco, CA: ICS Press.

Otani, Y. and J. Sicilian (1977) Externalities and problems of nonconvexity and overhead costs in welfare economics, *Journal of Economic Theory*, 14(2): 239–51.

Palfrey, T. and S. Srivastava (1991) Nash implementation using undominated strategies, *Econometrica*, 59(2): 479–501.

Pigou, A. (1912) *Wealth and Welfare*. London: Macmillan.

Reichelstein, S. and S. Reiter (1988) Game forms with minimal message spaces, *Econometrica*, 56(3): 661–92.

Reiter, S. (1979) There is no adjustment process with 2-dimensional message space for counterexamples, mimeo, Northwestern University.

Roberts, J. (1987) Lindahl equilibrium, in *The New Palgrave: General Equilibrium*, ed. J. Eatwell, M. Milgate, and P. Newman, 181–86. New York, NY: W.W. Norton.

Schmeidler, D. (1980) Walrasian analysis via strategic outcome functions, *Econometrica*, 48(7): 1585–94.

Schotter, A. (1981) *The Economic Theory of Social Institutions*. Cambridge, MA: Cambridge University Press.

Schotter, A. (1986) The evolution of rules, in *Economics as a Process*, ed. R. Langlois, 117–34. Cambridge, MA: Cambridge University Press.

Schotter, A. (1989) Comment (on Market and Institutions by Siro Lombardini), in *Economic Institutions in a Dynamic Society*, ed. T. Shiraishi and S. Tsuru, 50–55. New York, NY: Macmillan.

Starrett, D. (1972) Fundamental nonconvexities in the theory of externalities, *Journal of Economic Theory*, 4(2): 180–99.

Walker, M. (1981) A simple incentive compatible scheme for attaining Lindahl allocations, *Econometrica*, 49(1): 65–71.

18

But Who Will Guard the Guardians?

Contrary to what one might have guessed, in posing the famous question,[1] Juvenal was not concerned with affairs of state or politics, but rather trying to convince a friend that marriage is folly, women are not to be trusted, and keeping them locked under guard is not a solution—because the guards could not be trusted either.

But half a millennium or so earlier, Plato[2] did raise a closely related issue in discussing standards of behavior appropriate for the guardians of the city-state, the best of whom were to be chosen as rulers, thus in the context of ideal structure of governance. Socrates, referring to an earlier statement[3] that "drunkenness is most unbefitting guardians," says: "From intoxication we said that they must abstain. For a guardian is surely the last person in the world to whom it is allowable to get drunk and not know where on earth he is." To which Glaucon, Socrates' interlocutor, replies: "Yes, it would be absurd[4] that a guardian should need a guard." Instead of Juvenal's later pessimism, indeed cynicism, Plato—through Glaucon—expresses the optimistic view that one should be able to trust the city's guardians and rulers to behave properly; that they should require oversight is an absurdity.

Even a casual perusal of daily newspapers should be sufficient to convince us that there is nothing absurd about the present day 'guardians'—leaders

Leonid Hurwicz delivered a homonymous lecture on the occasion of receiving the Bank of Sweden Prize in Economic Sciences in Memory of Alfred Nobel on December 8, 2007. An edited version of his Nobel lecture appeared in *American Economic Review*, 2008, 98(3): 577–85. This version is ten years older, dated May 13, 1998. It is reproduced with edits indicated in square brackets.

[1] "Sed quis custodiet ipsos custodes?" in Liber secundus, Satura VI, 325, lines 347–48, p. 385 in Juvenal (1895).

[2] Book III, XII, 403E, volume I, p. 264 (Greek) and p. 265 (English) in volume I of Plato (1930).

[3] Ibid., pp. 246–47, no. 398E.

[4] In B. Jowett's translation, Plato (1908), "ridiculous" replaces "absurd." (Jowett's rendering seems better because the etymology of the Greek word used by Glaucon appears to be 'laughable'—as is that of 'ridiculous.') But the recent Plato (1992) translation by A.D. Lindsay again uses "absurd."

But Who Will Guard the Guardians? In: *The Collected Papers of Leonid Hurwicz Volume 1.*
Edited by Samiran Banerjee, Oxford University Press. © Oxford University Press 2022.
DOI: 10.1093/oso/9780199313280.003.0018

and officials of political, economic, and social entities—needing, and indeed getting, a great deal of oversight.[5] The question is rather as to the extent oversight is, or even can be, effective. The publicly expressed attitudes toward government, law enforcement, and union and corporate leadership are often more reminiscent of Juvenal than Plato.

The problem is obviously of central importance for political science, but why should it be of interest to economists, and, in particular, to theorists? And if there are good reasons for interest, how should we go about analyzing the problem? It is to these questions that the present essay is devoted.

An answer to these questions lies in the increased importance being attributed to the role of institutions[6] in influencing economic phenomena, and it hinges on the role of implementation (in particular, prevalence of the rule of law and its enforcement) as an essential ingredient in the functioning of institutions.[7]

The economic importance of institutions, stressed at least as far back as the nineteenth-century German Historical School, is not, I believe, controversial. Some of the most basic contemporary policy issues involve choice of institutions: markets versus central planning, the scope and structure of social insurance (unemployment, old age, health), 'property rights' as solutions to problems posed by externalities, world free trade, and the degree of economic integration of independent nations are obvious examples. The question is rather whether the role of institutions can be captured by appropriate analytical tools and incorporated into economic models, so as to become an integral part of the theoretical edifice. Metaphorically, whether institutions can be introduced into models as variables, even as unknowns, rather than as fixed parts of the landscape (as is, for instance, perfect competition in so many mainstream models). It is only when such models are available that we can face the issue of incorporating implementation devices, with their limitations and potentials.

Much economic analysis is based on the perfectly competitive model. Implicitly, at least, this model (or, more precisely, its applicability) requires

---

[5] Without explicitly mentioning the classical precedents, the *Wall Street Journal* of May 8, 1998 (pages B1–B2), carries a story under the headline "Guardians may need someone to watch over them." It speaks of court-appointed guardians and conservators who dishonestly dissipate their wards' assets, and of the difficulties the courts have in exercising their oversight responsibilities. In turn, watchdog groups and legislative task forces try to improve the performance of the judicial branch.

[6] In the sense of institutional arrangements ('rules of the game') rather than entities such as various types of organizations ('artificial players').

[7] Ostrom et al. (1992) point out that emphasis on the importance of enforcement is found in Hobbes, although they disagree with his stress on the need for an external enforcing authority (the sovereign). They stress on intra-group mutual enforcement. Schotter (1981, p. 11) makes self-policing or external policing authority an integral part of the definition of a social institution. He recognizes the possibility of intra-group enforcement through a supergame model (p. 165, note 8).

strong assumptions concerning the information available to 'agents' (individuals, firms, etc.) engag[ing] in economic activity, as well as the existence of implementation mechanisms such as the enforcement of contracts and absence of collusion. Similarly, conclusions concerning the effects of alternative forms of taxation, subsidies, or social insurance depend in an essential way on implementation mechanisms supplying information concerning obligations and entitlements, entities facilitating financial flows, as well as enforcement of payments or disclosure of relevant information. I think it may be fair to say that until recently in economic model building (as distinct from obiter dicta), much more attention has been paid to informational requirements (and uncertainty when precise information is not available) than to problems of implementation. Yet if implementation is impossible or prohibitively costly, even the most attractive mechanism remains a utopia.

Progress relevant to the issues being raised here occurred in the 1960s and 1970s in connection with the study of informationally decentralized and game-modeled mechanisms.

Message Exchange (Non-Game-Theoretic) Processes

Taking as a point of departure the assumption[8] that information is dispersed among participants in the economic process, a process is defined as *informationally decentralized* when each economic unit (consumer, firm, etc.) only has information about itself (its preferences, technology, or resources), but not about the characteristics of other units. The process then requires an exchange of signals (called *messages*) to attain objectives such as efficiency of the system as a whole. Once the amount of information carried by the signals has been quantified,[9] it makes sense to speak of the informational requirements of the process if objectives are to be attained in a specified environment. In rigorously formulated models, it has, for instance, been possible to prove that in the presence of increasing returns to scale, no finite-dimensional message space is adequate to guarantee efficiency (in the sense of Pareto optimality) of the equilibrium outcomes of any informationally

---

[8] Recognized already in the 1920s in the context of debates about the feasibility of socialism by Lange, Hayek, and von Mises, but especially stressed by Hayek (1945).

[9] When messages are vectors (n-tuples of numbers), the dimensionality of the messages provides such quantification. Specifically, the informational requirements of the processes are measured by the dimension of the message space (e.g., the sum of dimensionalities of the messages produced by the various participants), a concept analogous to the capacity of a communication channel. See Hurwicz (1977), Calsamiglia (1977).

decentralized process.[10] A similar result has been obtained for economies with detrimental externalities such as pollution.

These 'impossibility' results apply not to a particular mechanism or institutional structure but to all mechanisms qualifying as informationally decentralized. They tell us that even *if one assumes that the participants will be truthful and will abide by whatever the rules of the process prescribe*, no rules can guarantee the attainment of the desired objectives (e.g., efficiency). Such results must be viewed as specifying limitations on implementability due to the dispersion of information even in the presence of perfect enforcement. Thus enforceability of rules is not always an issue.

But, of course, in this essay, we are primarily interested [in] institutions where one cannot assume that participants will always be truthful. Is it possible to design processes that would give the participants [incentives] to be truthful? This question was raised by Samuelson in the mid-1950s in his classic articles on public goods, and in particular on the so-called Lindahl solution, [in which individuals pay for a specified supply of the public good according to their marginal willingness to pay]. He pointed out that for the Lindahl mechanism to work properly, one has to rely on the participants' truthful revelation of their preferences which, however, they would find advantageous to misrepresent [by understating their interest in the public good]. Hence, the Lindahl solution did not take care of the classic free rider problem. But Samuelson went on to make a stronger claim: he further stated that the same problem would arise with any other decentralized mechanism [in allocating public goods]. Could these two claims be formalized and rigorously justified?

Game-Theoretic Framework

A natural framework for such analysis turned out to be the theory of noncooperative games formulated by Nash, and the equilibrium concept now named after him [in which no player gains by changing only his or her own strategy unilaterally]. The economic process could be viewed as a noncooperative game[11] in which the strategy of each participant was

---

10 In the jargon of the field, Pareto optimality cannot be 'realized' by a decentralized ('privacy-preserving') process with a finite-dimensional message space. In addition to informational decentralization, these results presuppose certain mathematical regularity properties of the process rules. These properties involve a strengthening of continuity and are usually referred to as 'smoothness'. (Lipschitz-continuity is an example.)

11 In this essay we confine ourselves to non-cooperative games in normal form, although in some contexts extensive form would have been more appropriate. This is so, in particular, because rules of a game typically specify which moves (rather than strategies) are prohibited. (However, prohibitions may be aimed at strategies; this seems to be the case in antitrust law.)

a statement (not necessarily truthful) about his/her preferences, and the participant's utility of the outcome (defined in Samuelson's analysis by the Lindahl formula) as the 'payoff'. Samuelson's first claim could then be formalized as the proposition that truthful revelation of preferences is not a Nash equilibrium in the Lindahl game.[12] That is, when results (level of public goods and the required individual contributions) are calculated according to the Lindahl formula based on the participants own statements about their preferences, and given that all participants other than the i-th participant are being truthful, it would be in the general to i's advantage (yield higher utility) to misrepresent his/her preferences. Not surprisingly, thus formalized, Samuelson's first claim turned out to be correct: truth was not a Nash equilibrium.

But Samuelson's second, more general (impossibility) claim, was more difficult to deal with for two reasons. To analyze the claim, one had to answer two questions: first, how broad a class of mechanism would qualify as decentralized, and, second, what types of the system's performance are viewed as desirable. As to the latter, primary attention was paid to efficiency (Pareto optimality). As to the former, a significant broadening of perspective was provided by Groves and Ledyard (1977) who introduced an element of message exchange processes (previously used in non-game-theoretic models) into the Nash-type model and admitted as strategies any signals ('messages'), not necessarily just revelations of one's own preferences. I.e., they moved *beyond* the narrow class of *revelation games* characteristic of earlier work. They showed that this generalization enabled them to construct a (non-revelation) model yielding Pareto optimal (though not Lindahl) Nash equilibrium outcomes in economies with three or more participants. Later [in Hurwicz (1979a, 1979b, 1997)], it was shown that even Lindahl outcomes could be obtained as a Nash equilibrium of a suitably designed non-revelation game. If one regards this broader (not necessarily revelation) class of mechanisms as decentralized, Samuelson's second (impossibility) claim cannot be accepted. Hence optimism replaces pessimism.

Are Nash Equilibria Self-Enforcing?

But what about the implementability of mechanisms such as those (mentioned above) designed by Groves and Ledyard or Hurwicz? Is there a problem of enforcement? In fact, one occasionally hears the claim that there can be no enforcement problem with Nash equilibria because (allegedly) Nash

---

[12] See Hurwicz (1972) and Ledyard and Roberts (1974) [or Groves and Ledyard (1987) pp. 65–8].

equilibria are self-enforcing. Suppose, for instance, that $(s_1^*, \ldots, s_n^*)$ is the n-tuple of Nash equilibrium strategies in some game (where n is the number of players). By definition, this means that for any player i, a unilateral departure from his/her equilibrium strategy s_i^* to an alternative strategy s_i cannot increase i's payoff. Hence, once equilibrium is established, there is no incentive for unilateral departure, and [because] collusions are infeasible in a non-cooperative game, [there is] no need for an enforcement mechanism.

But this argument has two implicit assumptions. One is that the only strategies that player i would consider as alternatives to s_i^* are members of the admissible strategy domain, say S^i, prescribed by the mechanism governing the system, what we may call the 'legal' strategies; i.e., that any alternative strategy s_i belongs to S^i. But player i may, in fact, have available to him/her some 'illegal' strategies, those that are physically feasible but not in the admissible domain $[S^i]$, that are more advantageous to player i given that everybody else is behaving legally. Hence, the above argument has the implicit assumption that there are no illegal feasible strategies or, at least, none that might be advantageous.

The other assumption implicit in the argument that Nash equilibria are self-implementing is somewhat less obvious. A player's strategic calculations are based on the structure of the payoff function, which in turn depends on the physical outcomes produced by the mechanisms given the strategic choices made by players. These outcomes may involve delivery of goods or payments by various participants. Typically, there must exist some machinery (involving not only enforcement but also information processing and financial procedures) ensuring that the specified outcomes will in fact be produced. An assumption underlying the above claim of implementability of Nash equilibria is that such machinery is in place and in effective operation.

Formalizing Rules of a Game as Game-Forms (Mechanisms)

It will be helpful at this point to formalize the concept of a mechanism and its relation to the non-cooperative game (in normal form) defined by it. A game Γ in normal form for n players is defined by their admissible strategy domains S^i and payoff functions $\pi^i, i = 1, \ldots, n$.[13] We write $\pi = (\pi^1, \ldots, \pi^n)$, and formally define the game as $\Gamma = (S, \pi)$.

A mechanism shares with the game the strategy domains, but differs in that it involves an outcome function, say $h : S \to Z$, where Z is the space of conceivable outcomes (resource allocations in economic models, candidate

---

13 A payoff function is a numerical-valued function whose domain is the set of admissible n-tuples of strategies, i.e., the joint strategy domain, defined as the Cartesian product of the individual domains, $S = S^1 \times \ldots \times S^n$. So $\pi^i : S \to R$, where R represents the real numbers.

lists in voting models). Assume further that each player i has a utility function $u^i : Z \to R$, associating a real [number] with any conceivable outcome.[14] Then the i-th player's payoff function is obtained as the composition of the i-th utility function with the outcome function. I.e., for any s in S, and any i,

$$\pi^i(s) = u^i(h(s)).$$

In special cases, $h(s) = (h^1(s), \ldots, h^n(s))$, where $h^i(s)$ may represent the monetary payment to player i, and (1) the i-th utility function depends only on the i-th payment of which it is (2) a linear function. After a normalization, this can be written as $u^i(h^i(s)) = h^i(s)$, hence $\pi^i(s) = h^i(s)$, so that in such special cases the i-th payoff function can be identified with the i-th component of the outcome function. But in general, when (1) and (2) may not both hold, this identification does not hold.[15] In any case, it is important conceptually to distinguish outcome functions from payoff functions, because typically we consider preferences (hence utility functions) as given data (part of the 'environment'), while outcome functions, as well as strategy domains may be subject to the designer's choice, say as institutional reforms.

Indeed, in a model devoted to the analysis of institutional arrangements, it is essential to separate that which belongs to the data ('environment')—thus preferences, endowments, and technologies—from that which is subject to human manipulation, in our model the strategy domain S and the outcome function h. It is natural to refer to the pair (S, h) as the *rules of a game* since the domain S defines the class of legal moves (strategies), and the outcome function h their consequences. In game theory jargon, the pair (S, h) is called a *game-form*; in economics, a *mechanism*. The mechanism is not affected by changes in preferences, but the payoff functions are. The game-form can be changed directly by legislation or other human actions; the payoff functions only indirectly through changes in the game-form.

To make sense of the need for enforcement, one must admit the possibility of behavior that violates the rules of the game. In a typical game, the admissible strategy domains do not cover all behaviors that are physically (or psychologically) feasible. In card games, for instance, certain types of signaling are physically possible, but prohibited by rules of the game.[16]

---

[14] It would be more realistic to define the utility function on a subset of the outcome space and our analysis would be in no way affected, but we make the more extreme assumption to avoid notational complications.

[15] For example, when the mechanism represents a system of voting for the country's president, the outcome function cannot be split into components. But even when individual monetary payments are involved, the non-linearity of utility functions, typical in situations involving risk, would invalidate the identification.

[16] E.g., in bridge, the individual strategy domain S^i does not include kicking your partner under the table.

As indicated above, one reason why enforcement may be needed is that actions not included in the admissible domain may be advantageous for some players. After all, that is why it may be desirable, or even necessary, to guard the guardians! But, again as indicated above, in applications the effectiveness of the outcome function may also require either enforcement or other implementation apparatus (informational, financial, etc.).

To formalize, we introduce into the player's domain of choice strategies that are prohibited by the rules of the game. We refer to such strategies as *illegal*, while those that are permitted by the rules are called *legal*. To represent the actual choices facing players we take the radical step of introducing the set of all feasible actions (the *true strategy domain*), to be denoted by S', and correspondingly the *true outcome function* $h' : S' \to Z$, representing the consequences of any combination of strategy choices, whether legal or not. That is, we consider the participants to be playing the '*true game*' whose true game-form is the pair (S', h') and the i-th payoff function is $\pi'^i = u^i(h'(s))$. Here s is the n-tuple of strategies whose any component may be legal or illegal. We shall denote the true game whose rules are (S', h') by Γ', while the legal game governed by the legal strategy domain (S, h) is denoted by Γ. To simplify matters, we shall provisionally[17] assume that all legal strategies of a given mechanism (S, h) are feasible, i.e., that S is a subset of S', and that the two outcome functions coincide when only legal strategies are used. Also, it will be assumed that S' is a Cartesian product of individual feasible domains, S'^j. Denoting the feasible strategies of player i by S'^i, we then have $S' = S'^1 \times \ldots \times S'^m$, with any n-tuple of individually feasible strategies (i.e., elements of S'^i, $i = 1, \ldots, n$) being feasible. Furthermore, each S'^i is a disjoint union of the legal strategy set S^i with the illegal strategy set denoted by $\tilde{S}^i$.[18]

We are thus in the presence of two games, the true Γ' and the legal game Γ. Although it is the legal game Γ we want the participants to play, they are in fact playing the true game Γ'.

Successful Enforcement and Implementation

This framework makes it possible to formalize the notions of enforcement and implementation. To say that the *legal game rules are being successfully enforced* means that the outcomes of the true game that allow the use of illegal

---

[17] As pointed out below, an institutional structure may be necessary to ensure that in fact $h = h'$ when all players use legal strategies.

[18] Certain game models imply that $S = S'$, i.e., that all feasible strategies are included in S. Thus in the Prisoners' Dilemma game, the prisoners' two ('legal') choices are sometimes stated as 'to denounce' or 'not to denounce'. Since other aspects of behavior are assumed not to affect the outcome (or at least not to be relevant), in effect the (exhaustive!) class of legal behaviors is coextensive with that of feasible behaviors.

strategies is less attractive than that of legal strategies. A strong formulation of successful enforcement might require that every illegal strategy is dominated by some legal strategy for every player. I.e., that for every i, every $(n-1)$-tuple s_{-i} of strategies of players other than i, and every illegal strategy s_i in $\tilde{S}^i$ available to player i, there exists a preferable alternative legal strategy s^i in S^i, so that[19]

$$u^i(h'(\hat{s}^i, s_{-i}) > u^i(h'(s_i, s_{-i}).$$

However, this may be asking too much: if everyone else is acting illegally, a player may not find it possible to remain law-abiding. It seems, therefore, more reasonable to adopt a somewhat *weaker concept of successful enforcement* of the rules of a given mechanism (S, h), namely, to require that (1) the only Nash equilibria of the true game Γ' are n-tuples of strategies that are legal for the given mechanism (i.e., using strategies from S only); (2) that these Nash equilibria of Γ' are also Nash equilibria of the game Γ defined by the given mechanism,[20] and (3) that the set of Nash equilibria of the true game Γ' be non-empty.

[Regarding *implementation*],[21] consider what is involved in making effective an institution such as social security. The desired mechanism—say as defined by legislation[22]—specifies the class of persons receiving payments in relation to previous income and other variables. It may also specify the sources of funding. There is a need to formulate a *modus operandi*, verify whether specific applicants are entitled to receive payments and, if so, at what level, and how to collect the required funds. Typically, special agencies are created to accomplish such tasks, both informational and related to enforcement. It is the complex of such activities and arrangements that I think of as the effort to implement the legislation. Implementation is successful if the equilibrium

---

[19] 'Weak' domination would permit the replacement of some—but not all—of these strict inequalities by weak inequalities (i.e., by $\geq$) for certain choices of s_{-i}. I.e., in some situations, player i would be no worse but no better by staying within the law.

[20] Or, at least, that such relations hold for the components of Nash equilibrium outcomes corresponding to behavior subject to enforcement attempt.

[21] The concept of implementation used in the present essay, perhaps closer to common usage, is different from that introduced by Maskin (1977) and used in much of the subsequent literature. Maskin's implementation concept involves a relationship between Nash equilibrium outcomes of a given mechanism and an optimality criterion ('social choice rule'); it implicitly assumes that no player will use strategies outside of those permitted by the game-form. My concept involves activities designed to make the given game-form effective—in particular to discourage use of prohibited strategies and to make the assumed outcome function a reality. For my concept of implementation, it is the desired game-form Γ that is being implemented, although, of course, when successful, such implementation contributes to the realization of the optimality criterion. Thus the concept of implementation used in this essay involves the relationship of two games—the true game and the desired game, rather than the desired game and the optimality criterion.

[22] In this essay, I simplify the discussion by identifying legislated rules with a specific mechanism. But in practice, legislation tends to be rather vague on many specifics, often qualitative rather than quantitative. This can be formalized by considering legislated institutional arrangements as classes of game-forms rather than specific game-forms (see Hurwicz 1996).

outcomes correspond to those of the desired game, i.e., those envisaged by the legislation.[23]

Expressed in this framework, a reason why Nash equilibria are not self-enforcing is that, in the absence of enforcement, a Nash equilibrium only makes it unprofitable to move to alternative strategies in S^i but not necessarily to those in $\tilde{S}^i$. I.e., the fact that a strategy n-tuple s is a Nash equilibrium for game Γ, does not in general imply that every illegal strategy is dominated by a component of s.

A reason why Nash equilibria cannot be considered self-implementing is that the assumption of effectiveness of the outcome function h hides the need for institutional arrangements typically required to accomplish this. Thus, even if all players behave legally, the assumption that $h = h'$ requires implementing actions. It is insufficient merely to postulate the desired outcome function h.

Back to Juvenal

Let us now come back to the initial problem, the need for guarding the guardians. Juvenal's cynical question suggests either that there is no way to guard the guardians, hence it is impossible to enforce the wives' desired behavior, or that, in addition to having 'guardians of the first order' (those guarding the wives), one must also have 'guardians of the second order' to guard the guardians of the first order. But then, if those are also subject to corruption, guardians of the third order are also necessary, and so on. This conjures the image of an infinite regress of guardians, with the guardian of order $k + 1$ needed to guard the guardian of order k, $k = 2, 3, \ldots$ *ad infinitum*. Since an infinity of guardians is not usually available, this seems to preclude enforcement!

Why do we care about Juvenal's (or rather the husband's) problem? Mainly because some view it as a parable for the proposition that enforcement is in principle impossible due to the prospect of infinite regress of corrupt guardians. 'Casual empiricism' suggests that the pessimism of this proposition is not always justified. We know of many situations where rules are

---

23 In the context of most mechanisms that are considered in the literature, the above definition must be further qualified. The reason is that enforcement (or any implementation) requires the use of resources. If the desired model does not take this into account, it typically asks for efficiency relative to total resource endowment of the economy ('gross efficiency'). But this is infeasible when resources needed for implementation are subtracted. At best one can hope for efficiency relative to resources net of those diverted for implementation ('net efficiency'). Hence even if implementation is successful, it can only provide equilibria that are net-efficient and hence, formally, not the gross-efficient equilibria considered in the desired mechanism.

substantially (if not perfectly[24]) implemented and/or enforced. But many factors are in the picture determining whether implementation of rules is possible.

First, and perhaps least important, there may exist methods of implementation that depend on purely *physical or mechanical* factors that do not require human guardians. Examples: devices used by some parking lots that result in cutting tires of those who use unauthorized exits or entrances; punishments involving the placing of a culprit on an isolated island without a boat, and too far to swim ashore.

Second, somewhere at a finite end in the chain of guardians, there may be guardians (individual or collective) who are in sympathy with the rules (game-form) that makes certain behavior illegal, e.g., whose ethical standards rule out corrupt behavior, and who have the ability (through power, financial assets, personal charisma, or status combined with a population's respect for it), as well as the inclination to act so as to discourage improper behavior of the guardians of lower order. In some of my writings [(e.g., Hurwicz 1993)], I have referred to such individuals or groups as *intervenors*.

In such a situation, the rule is likely to be successfully enforced. Well-functioning societies try to choose judges and rulers from among such individuals.[25] Juvenal's pessimistic question suggests an infinite regress of needed guardians, hence non-existence of intervenors. Glaucon's comment, on the other hand, assumes self-control on the part of Plato's guardians, who in effect qualify as intervenors. Thus in terms of their views, Juvenal and Plato are at opposite ends of the spectrum.

But we do not have to rely on the presence of intervenors. There are other structures conducive to successful enforcement. Consider, for example, a rule of law that is designed to protect citizens from harmful or dangerous behavior of certain individuals. Suppose that those charged with enforcement of the law (first-order guardians) are corrupt or otherwise ineffective, and so are their supervisors (second-order guardians). If the latter are holders of elective office, citizens (voters) may be viewed as third-order guardians (as well as being guarded by first-order guardians). They have both an incentive and the power to intervene by throwing the supervisors out of office. This gives the supervisors an incentive to make sure that first-order guardians discharge their duties properly. Effective enforcement is the result.

---

[24] A more realistic model of performance would allow for imperfections. This could be accomplished by postulating a random choice of enforcement attempts when rule-breaking is known or suspected and recognizing that only a fraction of enforcement attempts is likely to be successful.

[25] Some years ago, we heard of a city where corruption spread from the police to local judges. It was stopped by a sting operation [instigated] by a higher level uncorrupted judiciary group.

A similar situation [arises], in principle, if the elective guardians are those of any (finite) order k. Graphically, the situation may be represented as a *closed circle*, with the voters being given two numbers (0 and $k+1$), and so that the guardian of order m (with $m = 1, 2, \ldots, k+1$) 'guards' the guardian of order $m-1$. Thus everyone is a guardian but also guarded. The voters as 'guardians' of top guardians is an essential aspect of democracy. This type of structure is also closely related to (but not identical with) the notion of separation of powers.[26]

The circular model can be applied in Juvenal's satire, where, by hypothesis, the husband himself is unable to monitor either the wife's or her immediate (first-order) guardian's behavior. But, in principle, it is conceivable that a second-order guardian might be found who could effectively supervise the first-order guardian's discharge of his duties and be so beholden to the husband that he would in effect make sure the immediate guardian does discharge his duties. This would close the circle.[27]

On the other hand, suppose that such a person of second (or higher order) does not exist. Then the husband's objective is not implementable. In this there is no paradox. It reminds us that, depending on circumstances, implementation may or may not be possible.

When implementation is possible, it can be modeled in terms of the relationship of the true game to the desired mechanism (or game). It is important to note that the equilibria of the true game depend on what is feasible and the actual consequences, and on the preferences (sometimes called attitudes or values) of the players. Thus, for instance, an intervenor must have preferences that rule out his/her own illegal behavior (especially corruption) and harbor a dislike for others' illegal behavior (at least of the relevant type); these factors would affect the intervenor's utility function. On the other hand, he/she must have powers, assets, or charisma enabling him/her to influence others in the desired direction; these features come under strategies available to the intervenor and the consequences of their use, hence are contained in the true game-form. Depending on the participants in the game (i.e., composition of the society) and their preferences/values, a given desired mechanism may or may not be implementable within that society. The history of experience with prohibition, [namely, that it was never effectively enforced], may be an illustration for the negative case. Clearly, implementability depends on the nature of the object or goal of

---

[26] Ostrom et al. (1992) stress the possibility of mutual enforcement within a group (analogous to the circular example), as opposed to the need for enforcing authorities external to the group, with theoretical models as well as empirical examples involving the allocation of common pool resources. It seems clear that such intra-group enforcement is likely to be effective in certain classes of situations but not all.

[27] More generally, it might take a chain of k such guardians.

implementation, and attitudes toward the likely outcomes of successful implementation.

What are our conclusions? Juvenal to the contrary, enforcement (or, more generally, implementation) is not always impossible. But even when it is possible to construct a (theoretical) mechanism 'M implementing' (i.e., implementing in Maskin's sense)[28] an optimality criterion, it could still be the case that 'genuine implementation' (the concept used in this essay) is infeasible (or too costly in required resources if the criterion ignores the costs of implementation).[29] Furthermore, even when 'genuine implementation' is feasible and not prohibitively costly, it may require institutional arrangements not evident from the appearance of the mechanism M-implementing the optimality criterion.

Nevertheless, it is my opinion, tinged with a dose of self-interest, that research aimed at discovering mechanisms M-implementing various optimality criteria is important and deserves encouragement. Where such implementation turns out impossible, this should serve as (negative) guidance to reformers, and the problem of 'genuine implementation' does not arise. When we do discover M-implementing mechanisms, we must still investigate the problem of 'genuine implementation' (including enforcement where relevant), but at at least we have an idea of what might be worth (genuinely) implementing.

References

Calsamiglia, X. (1977) Decentralized resource allocation and increasing returns, *Journal of Economic Theory*, 14(2): 263–83.

Groves, T., and J. Ledyard (1977) Optimal allocation of public goods: A solution to the 'free rider' problem, *Econometrica*, 45(4): 783–809.

Groves, T., and J. Ledyard (1987) Incentive compatibility since 1972, in *Information, Incentives, and Economics Mechanisms*, ed. T. Groves, R. Radner, and S. Reiter, 48–111. Minneapolis, MN: University of Minnesota Press.

Hayek, F. (1945) The use of knowledge in society, *American Economic Review*, 35(4): 519–30.

Hurwicz, L. (1972) On informationally decentralized systems, in *Decision and Organization*, ed. C. McGuire and R. Radner, 297–336. Amsterdam: North-Holland.

---

[28] A game-form weakly implements an optimality criterion (social choice rule) for a class of environments in Maskin's sense if, for every admissible environment, all its Nash equilibrium outcomes are optimal in terms of that criterion, and the set of equilibria is non-empty. Full implementability in Maskin's sense requires that every optimal outcome be an equilibrium outcome.

[29] Since equilibria of the true game depend on preferences, this includes political infeasibility (due, for instance, to high costs, value conflicts, or other factors).

Hurwicz, L. (1977) On the dimensional requirements of informationally decentralized Paretosatisfactory processes, in *Studies in Resource Allocation Processes*, ed. K. Arrow and L. Hurwicz, 413–24. Cambridge, MA: Cambridge University Press.

Hurwicz, L. (1979a) Outcome functions yielding Walrasian and Lindahl allocations at Nash equilibrium points, *Review of Economic Studies*, 46(2): 217–25.

Hurwicz, L. (1979b) Balanced outcome functions yielding Walrasian and Lindahl allocations at Nash equilibrium points for two or more agents, in *General Equilibrium, Growth and Trade*, ed. J. Green and J. Scheinkman, 125–37. New York, NY: Academic Press.

Hurwicz, L. (1993) Implementation and enforcement, in *Political Economy, Institutions, Competition, and Representation*, ed. W. Barnett, M. Heinrich, and N. Schofield, 51–59. Cambridge, MA: Cambridge University Press.

Hurwicz, L. (1996) Institutions as families of game forms, *The Japanese Economic Review*, 47(2): 113–32.

Hurwicz, L. (1997) Feasible balanced outcome functions yielding constrained Walrasian and Lindahl allocations at Nash equilibrium points in economies with two agents when the designer knows the feasible set, mimeo. (Presented at the Pennsylvania State University Decentralization Conference, University Park, PA.)

Juvenal (1895) *D. Junii Juvenalis Saturarum libri V*, Mit erklärenden Anmerkungen von Ludwig Friedlaender, Erster Band. Leipzig: Verlag von S. Hirzel.

Ledyard, J. and J. Roberts (1974) On the incentive problem with public goods, Discussion Paper 116, Center for Mathematical Studies in Economics and Management Science, Northwestern University.

Maskin, E. (1977) Nash equilibrium and welfare optimality, mimeo. Published as Maskin, E. (1999) Nash equilibrium and welfare optimality, *Review of Economic Studies*, 66: 23–38.

Ostrom, E., J. Walker, and R. Gardner (1992) Covenants with and without a sword: Self-governance is possible, *American Political Science Review*, 86(2): 404–17.

Plato (1908) *The Republic*, trans. B. Jowett (3rd ed., reprinted 1928). Oxford: Clarendon Press.

Plato (1930) *The Republic* [ΠΟΛΙΤΕΙΑ], trans. P. Shorey. New York, NY: G. P. Putnam's Sons.

Plato (1992) *The Republic*, trans. A. Lindsay. London: Everyman's Library.

Schotter, A. (1981) *The Economic Theory of Social Institutions*. Cambridge, MA: Cambridge University Press.

19

Fundamental Theory of Institutions:
A Lecture in Honor of Leo Hurwicz

Roger B. Myerson

Abstract   We follow Hurwicz in considering fundamental questions about social institutions. Hurwicz's concept of incentive compatibility may help clarify old debates about socialism, where such questions arose. Moral hazard models show disadvantages of socialism, while adverse selection models may delimit its advantages. We review Hurwicz's general theory of how institutions can be enforced in larger games, suggesting curb sets as an alternative enforcement theory that admits focal point effects. Finally, we consider specific problems of leadership and trust in establishing sovereign political institutions, where high officials can be deterred from abuse of power only by promises of large future rewards, which a leader must be credibly committed to fulfill.

> The economic problem of society is not merely a problem of how to allocate 'given' resources ... It is rather a problem of how to secure the best use of resources known to any of the members of society, for ends whose relative importance only these individuals know ... it is a problem of the utilization of knowledge not given to anyone in its totality. This character of the fundamental problem has, I am afraid, been rather obscured than illuminated by many of the recent refinements of economic theory, particularly by many of the uses made of mathematics.
>
> F. A. Hayek, "The Use of Knowledge in Society" (1945)

The Hurwicz Lecture, presented at the North American Meetings of the Econometric Society, at the University of Minnesota, on June 22, 2006, is reprinted from *Review of Economic Design*, 2009, 13(1–2): 59–75.

Recognizing the Need for a Fundamental Theory of Institutions

In the early twentieth century, economic theorists from left and right (Barone 1908; Lange 1938; Mises 1920; Hayek 1935) argued whether socialist reform of economic institutions was possible without loss of economic efficiency. The inconclusive nature of their debate showed that the existing framework of economic analysis was not adequate to formalize the justifications for the strongly held convictions on each side of this vital argument. To allow analytical comparison of fundamentally different forms of economic organization, a new and more general theoretical framework was needed. In an influential paper, Hayek (1945) argued that a key to this new economic theory should be the recognition that economic institutions of all kinds must serve an essential function of communicating widely dispersed information about the desires and the resources of different individuals in society. From this perspective, different economic institutions should be compared as mechanisms for communication.

Hayek also alleged that the mathematical economists of his day were particularly guilty of overlooking the importance of communication in market systems. But questions about fundamental social reforms require fundamental social theory, and in a search for new fundamental theories, the abstract generality of mathematics should be particularly helpful. So the failure that Hayek perceived should not have been attributed to mathematical modeling per se, but it was evidence of a need for fundamentally new mathematical models. Among the mathematical economists who accepted this challenge from Hayek, Leo Hurwicz has long been the leader.

Over many years and decades, Leo Hurwicz has worked to show how mathematical economic models can provide a general framework for analyzing different economic institutions, like those of capitalism and socialism, as mechanisms for coordinating the individuals of society. Hurwicz (1973) noted that, in late nineteenth-century economics, the institutionalists were economists who avoided analytical modeling. Today, all this has changed, since Leo Hurwicz set the standard for mathematical economists to study institutions as coordination mechanisms.

The pivotal moment occurred when Hurwicz (1972) introduced the concept of incentive compatibility. In doing so, he took a long step beyond Hayek in advancing our ability to analyze the fundamental problems of institutions. From that point on, as Makowski and Ostroy (1993) have observed, "the issue of incentives surfaced forcefully, as if a pair of blinders had been removed." By learning to think more deeply about the nature of incentives in institutions, we have gained better insights into important social problems and policy debates. But as Hurwicz (1998) has observed, there are still basic questions in the theory of institutions that we need to understand better.

As one of many followers in this tradition, I feel privileged to have this opportunity of presenting a Hurwicz lecture. In this lecture, I want to take a broad perspective on the state of these questions and what we have learned about them. First, I will re-examine how modern analysis of incentive constraints can help us to see what was missing in the old socialist debates. Then I will follow Hurwicz (1998) in proposing an abstract general model of how institutions are defined and enforced in a broader social environment. Finally, I will consider more specific models of incentive problems in establishing the fundamental political institutions of a society. Throughout, I will suggest a shift away from Hayek's focus on communication. Although we should recognize the universal significance of informational (adverse-selection) incentive problems in all social systems, I will suggest that strategic (moral-hazard) incentive problems may be even more important for understanding the foundations of social institutions.

An Old Debate and a New Theoretical Framework

In a polemic against naive dreams of a socialist paradise, Mises (1920) argued that prices from a competitive market equilibrium are necessary for efficient allocation of resources. Countering this argument, Barone (1908) and Lange (1938) saw no reason why socialist managers could not be coordinated equally well by value indexes set by a socialist Ministry of Planning. Mises (1920) and Hayek (1935) expressed great skepticism about the feasibility of such central economic planning without free competitive prices, but their argument on this point remained informal, focusing largely on the intractable complexity of the resource allocation problem. It is hard to be persuasive with such arguments of intractability. After all, if the economy is too complex for our analysis, then how can we be sure that a competitive market will find an efficient solution, or that a socialist planner will not find one? For a convincing argument, they needed a simple economic model in which socialism (suitably defined) could be proven to be less efficient than capitalism.

Of course, the later twentieth century provided much evidence of capitalist economic success and socialist economic failure, but a theorist should not give up a good question simply because there seems to be evidence to answer it empirically. If our theories do not give an adequate answer, then we must continue working to develop theories that can, because one can always propose new institutional structures that do not exactly match those for which we have data. If we have no general theory about why socialism should fail, then we have no way to say that greater success could not be achieved by

301

some new kind of socialism that is different from the socialist systems that have been tried in the past.

Economic theorists today have a strong sense of what was missing from the old debates. The old economists could model resource constraints, but not incentive constraints. Hayek and others made verbal arguments that show a basic awareness of incentive problems, but their arguments remained rhetoric without tight logical support in the absence of any general theoretical framework for analysis of incentives.

In particular, Samuelson (1954) argued that no feasible mechanism could guarantee an efficient allocation of public goods, because asking a person to pay for public goods according to his benefit creates an incentive for him to misrepresent his benefit. This remark seemed consistent with the general view that efficiency is found only in competitive private-good markets. But in trying to formalize this argument, Hurwicz (1972) found that the same incentive problems arise in the allocation of private goods, once we drop the assumptions required for perfect competition. He showed that, with finitely many individuals, no incentive-compatible mechanism can guarantee a Pareto-efficient allocation that is at least as good as autarky for all combinations of individual preferences in a broad class. Thus, the concept of incentive-compatibility was introduced.

The concept of incentive-compatibility developed rapidly after Hurwicz introduced it (Myerson 1982). We have come to understand that there are really two kinds of incentive constraints in the general social coordination problem: *informational incentive constraints* that formalize *adverse-selection* problems of gathering decentralized information, and *strategic incentive constraints* that formalize *moral-hazard* problems of controlling decentralized activity. As Hayek (1945) emphasized, economic plans must make use of decentralized information that different individuals have about their resources and desires. An individual could not be expected to honestly reveal private information that would be used against his interests, and such adverse-selection problems are formalized in economic models by informational incentive constraints. But economic plans must be implemented by decentralized actions of many different individuals, and there is a problem of getting individuals to accept appropriate guidance and direction when they have conflicting strategic incentives. An individual could not be expected to obediently refrain from opportunistic behavior that would be more rewarding to him, and such moral-hazard problems are formalized in economic models by strategic incentive constraints.

So, although the old socialist debates took place at a time when formal economic models only took account of resource constraints, we have now expanded the scope of economic analysis to take account of informational and strategic incentive constraints. If there was any validity to the intuitive arguments of Hayek and Mises, we should now be much better able to formulate them analytically in our new incentivist framework. Thus, we should ask, what is the simplest model in which we can support Mises's and Hayek's conclusions about socialism's failure?

Mises (1920) saw the essential problem arising in socialist allocation of capital, because state ownership of means of production implies the lack of any capital market. Such questions about mechanisms for allocating capital are a topic of corporate finance. Jean Tirole's *Theory of Corporate Finance* (2006) is full of models applying mechanism design to corporate finance, and we may naturally look to these models for insights into the old debate on socialism. Tirole has many models with many different features, but they are generally based on two simple models: one of moral hazard (Sect. 3.2), one of adverse selection (Sect. 6.2). Each model describes a simple world which we can transform by socialist reforms, and we can see how the efficiency of capital allocation is affected. The result may tell us something about what is truly fundamental in our models.

Advantages of Socialism in a Simple Adverse-Selection Model

In Tirole's (2006, section 6.2) basic adverse-selection model, a manager has private information about the probability of success for a unique investment opportunity. The basic parameters of the model are $(I, A, R, p_H, p_L, \eta)$. Here I denotes the capital investment cost required for a new project. The parameter A denotes the value of assets that the manager can pledge to forfeit if the project fails. The parameter R denotes the returns from the project if it succeeds, but the returns will be 0 if the project fails. The probability of success depends on the manager's type. If the manager's type is high then the project's probability of success in the project is p_H; but if the manager's type is low then the project's probability of success is p_L, where $p_L < p_H$. The manager knows his own type, but it is uncertain to anyone else, and the manager can lie about his type. Let η denote the probability of the manager being the high type. For simplicity here, let us assume risk neutrality and no discounting of future returns (zero interest rate). We assume that

$$p_H R > I > p_L R \quad \text{and} \quad I > A,$$

so that the project is worthwhile only if the manager's type is high, but the manager does not have enough wealth to undertake the project himself.

Under socialism, there is no problem getting the manager to reveal type honestly, because he is willing to report his type honestly when we just pay him a flat wage no matter what he reports. If we want to give him strict incentives to guide social decision-making about the project, the state could pay the manager $\varepsilon(R - I)$ if the project succeeds, but make him pay εI if the project fails. For any $\varepsilon > 0$, this payment plan would give the manager a positive incentive to recommend the project only when its expected social profit is positive. Feasibility requires $\varepsilon I < A$, but for any endowment size $A > 0$, this liquidity constraint can be satisfied when $\varepsilon > 0$ is sufficiently small.

This example is interesting for Tirole (2006) because he is assuming that competition among investors in the financial market always lets the manager borrow at an interest rate such that investors get expected profit equal to zero given their information about the manager. With access to such competitive lenders, low-type managers would want to imitate high-type managers to get their favorable terms of credit. But under socialism, the monopolistic state lender can fully exploit the high-type manager, and then the low type would not want to borrow at all. So we find that socialism may actually have an advantage here, because socialism can flatten the manager's incentives to eliminate his temptation to lie about his chances of success (for other advantages and disadvantages of a monopolistic supply of credit, see Dewatripont and Maskin 1993).

Disadvantages of Socialism in a Simple Moral-Hazard Model

In Tirole's (2006, section 3.2) basic moral-hazard model, the probability of success depends on the manager's actions (instead of the manager's hidden type). Most of the parameters here (I, A, R, p_H, p_L, B) are as in the previous model: the parameter I denotes the capital investment cost required for a new project, A denotes the value of assets that the manager can pledge to forfeit if the project fails, and R denotes the returns from the project if it succeeds, but the returns will be 0 if the project fails. Now p_H is the probability of success if the manager behaves appropriately, but p_L is the probability of success if the manager misbehaves, where $p_L < p_H$, and B denotes the value of private benefits that the manager gets by misbehaving. We assume that

$$p_H R > I > p_L R + B, \quad \text{and} \quad I > A,$$

so that the project is worthwhile only if the manager behaves appropriately, but the manager cannot undertake the project alone.

As individuals should have only modest wealth under an egalitarian socialist system, let us suppose that the manager's assets are bounded by the inequality

$$A < Bp_H / (p_H - p_L).$$

In a social investment plan, let w denote the wage that will be paid to the manager if the project succeeds. Then a feasible plan must satisfy

$$p_H w - (1 - p_H)A \geq 0,$$
$$p_H w - (1 - p_H)A \geq B + p_L w - (1 - p_L)A.$$

Here the first constraint is a participation constraint, that the manager should not expect to lose by participating in the project. (We are assuming that the social investment I includes a payment to the manager for the opportunity cost of his time in managing the project.) The second constraint is a strategic incentive constraint, that the manager should not expect better rewards from opportunistic misbehavior. The expected social profit, to be maximized, is

$$Y = p_H (R - w) + (1 - p_H) A - I.$$

The participation constraint implies $w \geq A/p_H - A$, and the moral-hazard constraint implies $w \geq B/(p_H - p_L) - A$. So with our modest-wealth assumption, the lowest feasible wage is

$$w = B/(p_H - p_L) - A,$$

which yields expected social profit

$$Y = p_H R + A - Bp_H/(p_H - p_L) - I.$$

(Because the manager is risk neutral, we could not increase Y by adding payments to the manager when the project fails.) Thus, the manager must be allowed to get a moral-hazard rent that has expected value

$$p_H w - (1 - p_H)A = Bp_H/(p_H - p_L) - A.$$

Notice that the expected social profit Y is strictly increasing in the manager's collateral A.

Now let us add the possibility that managers can be punished, and let x denote the punishment cost inflicted on manager if the project fails. Then a feasible mechanism (w, x) must satisfy the participation constraint

$$p_H w - (1 - p_H)(A + x) \geq 0,$$

and the strategic incentive constraint

$$p_H w - (1 - p_H)(A + x) \geq B + p_L w - (1 - p_L)(A + x).$$

The punishment x is not assumed to yield any social value to anyone else. So expected social profit is still

$$Y = p_H(R - w) + (1 - p_H)A - I.$$

The participation and incentive constraints now imply

$$w \geq (A + x)(1/p_H - 1) \text{ and } w \geq B/(p_H - p_L) - (A + x).$$

With modest endowments $A < Bp_H/(p_H - p_L)$, the wage cost is minimized by the punishment

$$x = Bp_H/(p_H - p_L) - A,$$

which allows the wage

$$w = B(1 - p_H)/(p_H - p_L)$$

and so yields the expected social profit

$$Y = p_H R + (1 - p_H)[A - Bp_H/(p_H - p_L)] - I.$$

Thus, punishment of failures can improve social profit. But increasing the manager's private collateral A still helps, even when punishment is allowed.

On the other hand, if there are rich agents who have assets A greater than $Bp_H/(p_H - p_L)$ then we could achieve the ideal social profit $Y = p_H R - I$, by letting the project be managed by such a rich agent for the wage $w = A(1 - p_H)/p_H$ to be paid if the project succeeds, but taking his collateral A if the project fails, with no further punishment ($x = 0$). This wage makes the participation constraint binding ($p_H w - (1 - p_H)A = 0$) and satisfies the moral-hazard constraint with $w + A \geq B/(p_H - p_L)$.

So there are two obvious ways for socialist reformers to achieve full efficiency here. First, they could allow some individuals to hold more wealth, up to $Bp_H/(p_H - p_L)$. Perhaps such favored people could be heroes of the socialist revolution (or of the Norman conquest). Second, they could drop the participation constraint and force people to become managers without compensation for punishment risks. Perhaps such disfavored people might be prisoners or enemies of the state. But either way, socialism looks rather less appealing from the perspective of this moral-hazard model, as it forces us to admit either inequality or coercion or productive inefficiency into our imagined socialist paradise. Indeed, our simple model does not do badly as a source of theoretical insights into the flaws of Soviet communism, and it formalizes some of Hayek's informal intuitive arguments: "To assume that it is possible to create conditions of full competition without making those who are responsible for the decisions pay for their mistakes seems to be pure illusion" (Hayek 1935, p. 237).

Comparing Moral Hazard and Adverse Selection

The comparison of these two models suggests that, when we probe the logical foundations of social institutions, moral-hazard problems may be more fundamental than adverse-selection problems. The problems of motivating hidden actions can explain why efficient institutions give individuals property rights, as owners of property are better motivated to maintain it. But property rights give people different vested interests, which can make it more difficult to motivate them to share their private information with each other. Thus, adverse selection might not be so problematic if there were no moral hazard. Socialism differs from capitalism in allowing less property rights for individuals, but moral hazard provides a fundamental economic rationale for some property rights that must apply even under socialism. So adverse-selection problems can be important under socialism, just as under capitalism.

For example, take Tirole's basic moral-hazard model with no punishment ($x = 0$), but now let us add a small probability ε that the manager is a bad type who cannot do better than the p_L probability of success (and cannot get the benefit B). With small collateral $A < p_L B/(p_H - p_L)$, such a bad manager would imitate the good type, to enjoy the positive expected benefits $(p_L B/(p_H - p_L)) - A$ from getting his project financed. So in the presence of moral hazard, the socialist system loses its ability to trivially solve informational adverse-selection problems.

On the other hand, if the uncertainty in the basic adverse-selection model were about the required investment amount I (instead of the success probability p), the socialist planner would have to allow informational rents to low-I type managers. But nobody would even try to take these rents away if the manager were a capitalist entrepreneur.

More generally, even if incentive analysis of other adverse-selection models does not reveal actual disadvantages of socialism, it can help to show that the supposed advantages of socialism may be less than its advocates would have suggested when they failed to recognize the possibility of opportunistic misrepresentations under systems other than capitalism. Analysis of mechanism design with informational incentive constraints has taught us that individuals with unique private information may have to be allowed informational rents in an efficient mechanism. But mechanism design as a conceptual framework can fit capitalist or socialist institutions, and so it can help us to see that the manager of a socialist monopoly who has private information about production costs (and can divert unaudited profits) may extract informational rents that look essentially like the profits of a monopoly in capitalism. Conversely, a capitalist monopoly's profits could be regulated away if its costs were publicly known, and it may be the monopolist's private information about costs that enables him to fend off such regulation. Thus, mechanism design teaches us that having multiple independent sources of supply may be just as important under socialism as under capitalism, which traditional market models could not show. Soviet planning may have suffered from failing to recognize such benefits of informational decentralization.

General Theory of Institutions Enforced in Larger Games

In recent work, Hurwicz (1998) has focused on questions of how institutions are constructed and how institutional rules are enforced (see also Schotter 1981). Here strategic incentive constraints are at the heart of the problem, so we can focus on games in strategic form where N is the set of players, C_i denotes the set of strategies of player i, and $U_i(c)$ denotes the utility payoff to player i from strategy profile c in $C = \prod_{j \in N} C_j$.

To a game theorist, an institutional reform means changing the structure of the game that people play in the institution. So it is common for game theorists to think that institutions are games. But Hurwicz (1998) observes that what we normally mean by institutions (or institutional arrangements) typically does not include the specification of individuals' preferences (nor does it typically include the beliefs that we specify in Bayesian games). So an institution for Hurwicz is more properly to be identified with a *game-form* of Gibbard (1973), specifying only the set of players N, the sets of strategies C_i for each player i, and an outcome function $\Theta : C \to Y$ that defines how outcomes in some set Y would depend on the players' strategies. Such game-forms are mechanisms in Hurwicz's sense. To analyze such a game-form or mechanism, however, we must specify each player i's preferences for outcomes by a utility function $u_i : Y \to \mathbb{R}$ on the outcome set Y. With these outcome-based utility functions, we can then define the strategy-based utility functions $U_i(c) = u_i(\Theta(c))$ that complete the structure of the strategic-form game which corresponds to the institution once preferences are given.

When we ask how an institution is established, we must embed it somehow in a larger game. For example, when two people play a game of chess, typically each of them is physically able to grab the other's king at any time, but is deterred from chess-illegal moves by the damage such behavior could do to one's reputation in the larger game of life. So the chess game seems supported by some kind of reputational equilibrium in a larger more fundamental game. But saying "games are equilibria of larger games" cannot be right, because if chess were embedded as an equilibrium in the game of life, then that equilibrium would specify each player's strategy in the chess game itself.

Hurwicz (1998) explains that, if our *legal game* $G = (N, (C_i)_{i \in N}, (U_i)_{i \in N})$ is embedded in some true game H, the structural relationship must be that $H = (N, (D_i)_{i \in N}, (U_i)_{i \in N})$ has larger strategy spaces

$$D_i \supset C_i \quad \forall_i \in N$$

and has utility functions that extend those of the legal game G to the larger domain $D = \prod_{j \in N} D_j$. Hurwicz (1998) then suggests that a strong formulation of successful enforcement could require that, for each player i, each illegal strategy outside C_i should be dominated by some legal strategy in C_i, so that a player's best responses always take him into the legal game, even if others deviate.

Hurwicz (1998) remarks, however, that a normally law-abiding player might not want to remain law-abiding when others are acting illegally, and so a weaker concept of enforcement may be appropriate. Thus, I would suggest that the definition of institutional enforcement should be weakened, to say that G is enforceable in H when

$$\forall i \in N, \ \forall c_i \in \prod_{j \in N \setminus \{i\}} C_j, \ \forall d_i \in D_i \setminus C_i, \ \exists c_i \in C_i$$

such that

$$U_i(c_{-i}, c_i) > U_i(c_{-i}, d_i),$$

so that each player's optimal actions are in his legal strategy set when all others' actions are expected to be in their legal sets. That is, G is enforceable when its strategy sets form a *curb set* (curb sets are closed under rational behavior) in H, as defined by Basu and Weibull (1991).

This weaker definition of enforceability can admit a great multiplicity of enforceable institutions for a given environment, because a big true game H can contain many different minimal curb sets. This multiplicity may seem an annoying indeterminacy to theorists who believe in economic determinism. But I would argue that the right mathematical model of institutions should admit such a multiplicity of solutions, because real institutions are manifestly determined by cultural norms and traditional concepts of legitimacy, which would have no scope for effect if the economic structure of the true game H admitted only one dominant solution.

For example, legal rules of a political constitution that are written on a piece of parchment in a museum may be enforced in a true game that involves millions of people on a large land-mass. What would prevent anyone from writing another set of rules (on a bigger piece of parchment) and acting according to them instead? Under any political constitution, such an act should be punished as sedition or treason by others who accept the given constitutional rules. But although treason never prospers, the definition of what is treason depends on an arbitrary social consensus. We all understand that a broad failure to agree about constitutional rules and authority can create an anarchy in which everyone suffers. So the social process of identifying what are the constitutional rules of politics and who are the legitimate leaders of our society has the basic structure of a coordination game with multiple equilibria, where the outcome must depend on culture and tradition through Schelling's (1960) focal-point effect.

The essential role of the focal-point effect in the foundations of our basic political institutions has been emphasized by Hardin (1989) and Myerson (2004, 2008). The new theoretical point here is that Schelling's focal-point effect can be extended to questions of selecting among multiple curb sets, just as among multiple equilibria. Once everyone understands that everybody else will be restricting themselves to strategies in one particular constitutional curb set, it becomes rational for each individual to stay in his or her respective portion of this curb set.

Although people may be symmetric in the true game H, this symmetry can be broken in the curb set G. Indeed, the enforcement of a constitutional curb set may depend crucially on a small group of specially designated individuals (called law-enforcement officials) whose curb-set strategies stipulate that they would punish any deviator who violated constitutional restrictions.

Moral Hazard and Privilege in Sovereign Political Institutions

The preceding model of how institutions are enforced in larger games is very abstract. To move from broad abstractions to practical specifics, we need to think more carefully about the officials who are the guardians of our institutions, as Hurwicz (1998) has emphasized. Let me follow him now in examining the basic question of who guards these guardians, that is, who forces the enforcers to enforce our laws.

Consider again the problem of enforcing the fundamental political institution of a nation, such as the Constitution of the United States. A constitution can be effective only when there are agents who expect to be rewarded for implementing its rules. In particular, it must designate officials who are expected to prosecute sedition and other violations of the constitution, so as to deter the rest of the population from such illegal moves. But what makes these officials do their official function? Of course, a problem of getting people to do what they are supposed to do is what we call a moral-hazard problem. So the basic problem of getting government officials to enforce constitutional rules is a moral-hazard agency problem in the upper levels of government.

Such an agency model has been analyzed by Becker and Stigler (1974). They recognized that powerful officials have regular opportunities to profit from abuse of power, and that such abuse of power can be difficult for others to detect. For abuse of power to be deterred, the official must expect to do better by acting to enforce the rules correctly, and so must expect substantial rewards that would be forfeited if evidence of abuse of power were discovered. Assuming risk-neutrality, the magnitude of these rewards must be at least the potential profit that the official could earn from abuse of power divided by the probability that such abuse of power would be discovered. So when temptations are large and the probability of detection is small, powerful officials may need to be very well rewarded. Thus, we should expect the leaders of fundamental political institutions to be a very well-rewarded elite, highly motivated by the need to preserve their privileges, as Michels (1915) observed even of socialist political parties.

So our concept of a constitution is incomplete if we ignore the essential role of those who expect to enjoy the privileges of high office under the constitution and are therefore well motivated to act to sustain it. From a purely structuralist perspective, it might seem that a political constitution could be fully defined by specifying (1) a set of political offices, (2) the powers, privileges, and responsibilities of these offices, and (3) the procedures for selecting future holders of these offices. But to fully characterize a political constitution as a self-enforcing dynamic system, embedded in a true game where people are symmetric, one must also specify (4) the privileged individuals who actually hold these offices at some initial time (or who expect to be on the short list of serious candidates for these offices in the first elections). In this sense, the specific identity of the small privileged group who are called 'Founding Fathers' of the American Republic may be considered an essential component of the American Constitution, as essential as the words written on an old parchment in Philadelphia.

If moral-hazard opportunities imply that responsible officials must be well rewarded, then people should be willing to pay for promotion to such offices. In Becker and Stigler (1974) theory, an efficient organization would pass the cost of an official's incentive rewards back to the official ex ante, by charging a fee for promotion to the office. In effect, a candidate for office would be asked to post a bond, which would be returned to the official on retirement if there is no evidence of malfeasance. Such a plan appears to be a simple efficient solution to the fundamental agency problem of government. But it creates a new moral-hazard problem at the highest level, because it implies that the leader who controls appointments to high offices will have an incentive to convict officials of malfeasance and resell their offices. The whole scheme depends on the promise that high officials will be appropriately judged, so that they can expect to be rewarded for correct service and punished for abuse of power, but there may be no neutral party to make such judgments. An official must always be worried that others in the power structure would be tempted to convict him of malfeasance and sell his position to someone else.

Thus, the organizational problem of metering rewards, which Alchian and Demsetz (1972) considered for economic producers, arises even more forcefully for political organizations. Indeed, the terms of the problem may be sharpened in the political context, where there can be no question of looking to some higher court for adjudication of contractual relationships.

Hurwicz (1998) recognized that the guardian officials of a sovereign political institution must in some sense be organized into a circle of mutual monitoring and judgment, where the actions of each individual are monitored and judged by others in the circle. But when an individual i is called to monitor the actions of some individual j in such a circle, the monitored actions may include j's monitoring of yet other individuals, which further broadens the scope of activity that individual i must be prepared to observe. So some collective aspect of the fundamental adjudication process seems unavoidable. Within a ruling political faction that admits no higher court of appeal, membership in the faction may require an individual to keep manifestly informed about the general status of other members, perhaps formally by attending regular factional meetings, or informally by staying current in a factional network of gossip.

So the survival of a political institution must depend on its being led by some faction or core group of powerful officials who share a basic trust in each others' judgments. In effect, the members of this group may form a court where they each have a right to be tried before any punishment or loss of privilege. In such a court, evidence of malfeasance against any of them would be commonly heard, so that all members of the group should be able to evaluate whether resulting judgment was reached appropriately. The collective sanction against wrongful judgments in this court could be that the members of this ruling faction would lose trust in each other, so that they would all switch to an equilibrium where each opportunistically abuses his individual power. We may assume that, in a competitive world, a faction would not long hold political power over a large society if members of the faction could not solve free-rider problems in collective actions to defend their power against challenges from other potential factions (Myerson 2008). With this assumption, any one member of a ruling faction could feel protected by the expectation that her colleagues could not mistreat her without risking a general loss of mutual trust within the faction, which would jeopardize all of their privileged positions.

Leadership and Moral Hazard at the Center

To be more specific about how such factions are formed, we must recognize the role of leaders as entrepreneurs of institutions. Throughout history, governments have been formed by political leaders whose path to power began by gathering a trusted group of active supporters. When a faction has been organized in this way, privileges of membership in the faction are allocated by the leader. Then the circle of monitoring can be closed by a simple factional rule that the leader should never remove a member's privileges without a process of judgment that is collectively witnessed by other members of the faction. Indeed, rulers throughout history have generally maintained courts or councils, where high officials and others close to the ruler were regularly gathered, and where the ruler's treatment of any courtier could be witnessed and scrutinized by other courtiers. Thus, each individual courtier could feel confident of getting appropriate rewards from the leader, because of the leader's need to maintain a general reputation for appropriately rewarding all courtiers, who are the primary agents of his power.

Popular books on leadership have filled shelves in bookstores, but their descriptions of leadership are often focused on leadership as visionary strategic decision-making (Maxwell 2002). Of course, when people need to coordinate, they may look to a leader for strategic decisions about whether to attack at dawn, or at noon, or not at all. But when we ask what is really the essential function of a leader, I would suggest that the role of strategic planner may be generally less important than the role of honest monitor and reliable paymaster that Alchian and Demsetz (1972) identified. A leader makes a group into an effective team by his reputation for actively monitoring the contributions of individuals in the group and appropriately rewarding their efforts. Such a reputation with a group of supporters, small enough to be individually monitored but large enough to achieve competitive success by their collective actions, is the essential asset that defines a leader. If a leader loses this reputation for appropriately rewarding the members of his group, then the leader must be replaced or the group will lose its ability to compete with other teams that have better leadership.

313

This idea dates back at least to Xenophon, whose 'Education of Cyrus' (c. 360 BCE) depicts a great leader who establishes a great empire by cultivating a reputation for honestly and generously rewarding captains who serve well in battle. While other leaders think that their power depends on the assets in their treasury, Cyrus understands that his power really depends on his credit with his captains, so that it can be better to pay out generously than to keep anything for himself. In another paper (Myerson 2008), I have analyzed a similar model of the foundations of the state by leaders whose ability to hold power depends on their reputation for reliably rewarding the captains who support them against their rivals in contests for power.

An economic entrepreneur must be able to credibly promise future payments both to the investors who supplied his initial capitalization and to the managers whose moral-hazard opportunities require promises of large future rewards. Similarly, a political leader must be able to credibly promise future rewards both to the supporters or captains whose efforts put him in power and to the high officials or governors through whom his power is exercised.

To further probe the difficulties of maintaining a reputation for appropriately rewarding agents in political institutions, let me describe one more model of moral hazard by high government officials, an extension of the Becker-Stigler model that I have recently analyzed (Myerson 2015). In this model we consider a high official, whom we may call a governor, in a state that is ruled by a single leader or monarch. At any time, the governor can behave well (govern appropriately), or misbehave (govern corruptly), or openly rebel. The leader cannot directly observe whether a governor is behaving or misbehaving, but he can observe any costly crises that occur in the governor's province. Crises occur as a Poisson process with a low expected rate α when governor behaves, but a high expected rate β when the governor misbehaves, where $\beta > \alpha$. Misbehavior also gives the governor a flow of additional hidden benefits that are worth γ per unit time. The governor observes any crisis in her province shortly before the leader does, but she can be called to court for a brief visit during which rebellion is impossible. Let D denote the expected payoff to the governor when she rebels (which is observable to the leader). Crises and rebellions are very costly for the leader, so he wants his governors to always behave well, that is, to never misbehave or rebel. Each individual is risk neutral and has discount rate δ.

To be deterred from rebellion, a governor must always expect rewards that are worth at least D. Candidates for governor can be asked to pay something for promotion to the office, but any candidate's ability to pay is limited by her wealth, which we denote by A. We assume that a governor's potential gains from rebellion are greater than the private wealth of any candidate for office, so $A < D$. On the other hand, the leader may feel tempted to free himself of his debts to a governor, by sacking the governor, and such moral hazard at the top is essential to the problem of political leadership. To admit it into our model as simply as possible, we assume an upper bound H on the debt that the leader can be trusted to owe a governor. These parameters $(\alpha, \beta, \gamma, \delta, A, D, H)$ characterize our model.

To minimize the leader's expected cost of paying governors, the optimal incentive plan (derived in Myerson 2015) can be characterized at any time by the expected present discounted value of all future rewards to the incumbent governor, which we may call the governor's credit. To deter hidden misbehavior, any crisis in the province must cause the governor's credit to decrease by a penalty that has expected value

$$\tau = \gamma/(\beta - \alpha).$$

Normally, the sanction for a crisis should be to reduce the governor's credit by this amount τ. But the governor would rebel if her credit ever went below D after a crisis, and so the governor's credit beforehand must never be less than $D + \tau$. So if a crisis occurs when the governor's credit U is less than $D + 2\tau$, then the governor should be called to the leader's court for a trial, where the outcome is either to reinstate the governor at the credit $D + \tau$ with probability $(U - \tau)/(D + \tau)$, or else to dismiss the governor (who thereafter gets 0) and instead appoint a new governor at the minimum feasible credit level $D + \tau$.

Thus, the need to deter both hidden misbehavior and open rebellion requires the leader to make randomized decisions about whether to dismiss or forgive a governor after a crisis. But the leader is not indifferent in such situations, because dismissing the incumbent governor would create an opportunity to resell the office to a new governor for the payment $A > 0$. So the process of deciding a governor's fate in such a situation must be actively monitored by others, because otherwise the leader's ex post incentive would always be to dismiss the governor. That is, the leader needs to institutionalize a formal trial procedure where others (whose trust he needs to maintain) can observe that he has given the governor an appropriate chance of reinstatement before any dismissal.

The expected discounted value of the leader's cost, at any point in time, is equal to the credit U that he owes to the current governor, plus the expected discounted value of the leader's net cost of promises to other governors who will be promoted into the position after dismissals in the future ($D + \tau - A$ at each promotion). So the optimal plan for the leader should minimize the expected frequency of future dismissals, which can be achieved by keeping governors as far as possible from the low credit range (below $D + 2\tau$) where dismissals occur. Thus, in the optimal incentive plan, a governor should be paid only in credit, not in cash, until the credit bound H is reached. To keep promises to a governor, her credit should increase between crises at the rate $U' = \delta U + \alpha \tau$ until it reaches the bound H on what the leader can be trusted to owe. When the credit owed equals H, the governor should be paid $\delta H + \alpha \tau$ until the next crisis causes her credit to drop to $H - \tau$. In this solution, increasing the trust bound H would strictly decrease the leader's expected discounted cost, as assessed ex ante when a new governor is first appointed. But with very high H, the leader will ultimately incur large expensive debts to governors who become entrenched in their offices.

That is, even when the leader has the same discount rate as the high officials of his government, the need to deter them from abuse of power creates a motivation for the leader to become a debtor to these officials. Of course this conclusion is just an extension of the results of Becker and Stigler's (1974) analysis. Our extended model has been designed only to show how problematic this debt relationship can be, because (to deter corruption) the leader must sometimes actually dismiss officials without paying them their promised rewards, but the circumstances of these dismissals cannot be simply predictable (to avoid rebellions) and so can be verified only by actively monitoring the judgment process, during which the leader's natural incentive is actually to dismiss rather than reinstate (because he can resell the office).

Thus, someone needs to actively monitor the leader's judgments of his high officials and constrain him to act according to an optimal random rule. But who can have such power over the leader of a sovereign political institution? The other high officials on whom his regime depends have such power, because they would rationally misbehave or rebel if they lost trust in the leader's promises of future rewards. (In particular, the leader's problem of deterring misbehavior and rebellion would become infeasible if the amount H that they trust him to owe ever became less than $D + \tau$.) So a sovereign political leader needs a court or council where high officials witness his appropriate treatment of other high officials. Such high councils of government seem universal in political systems. In them, the chief guardian's reputation for rewarding his supporters is collectively guarded by his chief supporters.

Thus, in our fundamental theory of institutions, we should recognize that political institutions are established by political leaders, and political leaders need active supporters. Like a banker, a leader's promises of future credit must be trusted and valued as rewards for current service. The leader's relationship of trust with his inner circle of high officials and supporters requires that they must act collectively to monitor and verify his judgments against any of them. Such a relationship of trust with a group of supporters, small enough for the leader to personally monitor but large enough to effectively control the larger institutions of government, is a political leader's most valuable asset. Furthermore, the members of this group must share a sense of identity, in that each must be confident that the leader's wrongly punishing any one of them could cause all others to lose trust in the leader.

So the establishment of fundamental institutions by political leaders may ultimately rely on a sense of identity among members of a group that is small enough to gather in a court of common judgment to hear a case against any one of them. From this perspective, we can make sense of cases throughout history where powerful political forces have been led by small groups of people who are connected by narrower forms of identity, such as family relationships, or old school ties, or bonds of personal loyalty to their leader, even though these personal connections may seem to have no intrinsic relationship with anyone's position on great questions of national policy. Like the nineteenth-century socialists, we may dream of great utopian social reforms, but we should understand that the institutions of any such brave new world would be built on narrower factional foundations, organized by political leaders whose first imperative is to maintain their reputation for rewarding loyal supporters.

References

Alchian, A., and H. Demsetz (1972) Production, information costs, and economic organization, *American Economic Review*, 62(5): 777–95.

Barone. E. (1908) The ministry of production in the collectivist state, in *Collectivist Economic Planning* ed. F. Hayek (1935), 245–90. London: Routledge.

Basu, K., and J. Weibull (1991) Strategy subsets closed under rational behavior, *Economics Letters*, 36(2): 141–46.

Becker, G., and G. Stigler (1974) Law enforcement, malfeasance, and compensation of enforcers, *Journal of Legal Studies* 3(1): 1–18.

Dewatripont, M., and E. Maskin (1993) Centralization of credit and long-term investment, in *Market Socialism*, ed. P. Bardhan and J. Roemer, 169–74. Oxford: Oxford University Press.

Gibbard, A. (1973) Manipulation of voting schemes: a general result, *Econometrica* 41(4): 587–601.

Hardin, R. (1989) Why a constitution, in *The Federalist Papers and the New Institutionalism*, ed. B. Grofman and D. Wittman, 100–20. New York, NY: Agathon Press.

Hayek, F. (1935) The present state of the debate, in *Collectivist Economic Planning*, ed. F. Hayek, 201–43. London: Routledge.

Hayek, F. (1945) The use of knowledge in society, *American Economic Review*, 35(4): 519–30.

Hurwicz, L. (1972) On informationally decentralized systems, in *Decision and Organization*, ed. C. McGuire and R. Radner, 297–336. Amsterdam: North-Holland.

Hurwicz, L. (1973) The design of mechanisms for resource allocations, *American Economic Review* 63(2): 1–30.

Hurwicz, L. (1998) But who will guard the guardians?, University of Minnesota mimeo, and Chapter 18, this volume. A version published in *American Economic Review* 2008, 98(3): 577–85.

Lange, O. (1938) On the economic theory of socialism, in *On the Economic Theory of Socialism*, ed. B. Lippincott, 55–143. Minneapolis, MN: University of Minnesota Press.

Maxwell, J. (2002) *Leadership 101*. Nashville, TN: Thomas Nelson, Inc.

Makowski, L., and J. Ostroy (1993) General equilibrium and market socialism: Clarifying the logic of competitive markets, in *Market Socialism*, ed. P. Bardhan and J. Roemer, 69–88. Oxford: Oxford University Press.

Michels, R. (1915) *Political Parties: A Sociological Study of Oligarchic Tendencies in Modern Democracy*. New York, NY: Hearst.

Mises, L. (1920) Economic calculation in the socialist commonwealth, in *Collectivist Economic Planning*, ed. F. Hayek (1935), 87–130. London: Routledge.

Myerson, R. (1982) Optimal coordination mechanisms in generalized principal-agent problems, *Journal of Mathematical Economics*, 10(1): 67–81.

Myerson, R. (2004) Justice, institutions, and multiple equilibria, *Chicago Journal of International Law*, 5(1): 91–107.

Myerson, R. (2015) Moral hazard in high office and the dynamics of aristocracy, University of Chicago working paper. http://home.uchicago.edu/~rmyerson/research/power.pdf

Myerson, R. (2008) The autocrat's credibility problem and foundations of the constitutional state, *American Political Science Review*, 102(1): 125–39.

Samuelson, P. (1954) The pure theory of public expenditure, *Review of Economic Statistics*, 36(4): 387–89.

Schelling, T. (1960) *Strategy of Conflict*. Cambridge, MA: Harvard University Press.

Schotter, A. (1981) *The Economic Theory of Social Institutions*. Cambridge, MA: Cambridge University Press.

Tirole, J. (2006) *Theory of Corporate Finance*. Princeton, NJ: Princeton University Press.

Xenophon (2001) *The Education of Cyrus*, translated by W. Ambler. Ithaca, NY: Cornell University.

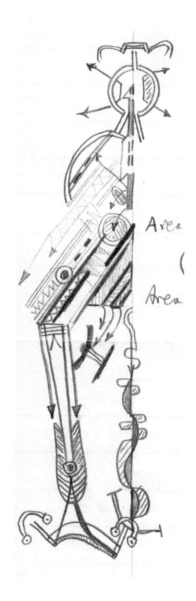

Area

Area

Part III
Other Essays

This section presents a miscellany of mostly shorter writings that are still of interest to the lay reader. Chapter 20 looks at solutions to environmental pollution through the lens of mechanism design. In the guise of a review of the classic 1944 book *Theory of Games and Economic Behavior* by John von Neumann and Oskar Morgenstern, Chapter 21 presents a lucid introduction to game theory. Chapter 22 is a shorter review of the 1947 second edition of the same book. Chapter 23 is a look at the state of game theory from the vantage of 1953, in the aftermath of John Nash's seminal papers from 1950 and 1951. Chapter 24 is an article on decision-making under uncertainty that was published in *Scientific American*. Chapter 25 is Leo's humorous review of his friend Gerard Debreu's 1959 classic book, *Theory of Value*, followed by an exchange of correspondence between them in a postscript. Finally, Chapter 26 is short proposal submitted to the Minnesota Democratic-Farm-Labor party to ensure that minority groups have adequate representation of their views.

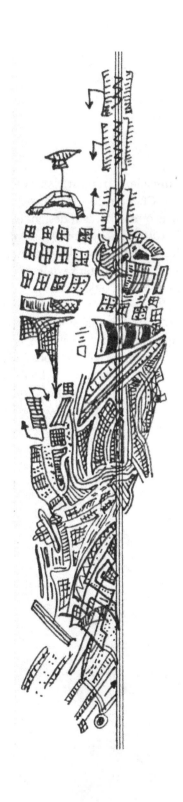

20

Environmental Issues: Economic Perspectives

Let me start by acknowledging my indebtedness to Professors Sandra Archibald, Zbigniew Bochniarz, and Richard Bolan for stimulating my interest in these issues, for formulating questions to be addressed, and for laying foundations, both empirical and analytical, for answers.

My own special interest is in analyzing institutional solutions, especially decentralized mechanisms, for problems posed by recent increases in environmental pollution, as well as by threats to biodiversity and exhaustion of natural resources. The policy objective is often described as sustainable development.

In my remarks I shall be focusing more narrowly on issues of environmental pollution, classified by economists under the rubric of detrimental externalities. By definition, detrimental externalities are activities damaging others that are not discouraged (i.e., not economically penalized) by 'natural' market forces. In particular, these market forces fail to decrease costs or decrease revenues of a polluter, even though they cause economic damage to other firms or individuals. In many cases, the level of damage can be brought down by actions whose cost is below the value of damages these actions prevent.

In such cases, the economy as a whole will benefit if incentives can be created that encourage pollution abatement. Since neither complete laissez-faire nor exhortations provide such incentives, some form of social intervention seems unavoidable. Another reason for intervention may be the view that fairness require victims of pollution to be compensated, especially when the polluter benefits financially from pollution-producing activities.

Reprinted from *Periphery: Journal of Polish Affairs*, 2000/01, (6/7): 81–85. This paper was presented at the 2000 conference 'Poland and East Central Europe after Ten Years of Transition' organized by the Center for Nations in Transition at the Hubert H. Humphrey Institute of Public Affairs in cooperation with the Polish American Cultural Institute of Minnesota.

Environmental Issues: Economic Perspectives In: *The Collected Papers of Leonid Hurwicz Volume 1.* Edited by Samiran Banerjee, Oxford University Press. © Oxford University Press 2022. DOI: 10.1093/oso/9780199313280.003.0020

It is natural, especially in the latter type of situation, to advocate the 'polluter pays' principle. However, it may be the case that avoidance actions by victims are less costly than abatement by the polluter. For instance, airport noise pollution damaging nearby residents might be difficult or very costly to avoid, and if there are only a few affected by the noise, relocation—subject to suitable compensation—might be a cheaper solution. However, in my view, this is not the typical situation with major environmental pollution problems of our era. in important cases, such as chemical pollution of ground or water, the entities (organization or firms) responsible for damage may no longer exist or may be financially unable to remove contamination and provide compensations.

In what follows, I concentrate on the design of institutions, more specifically decentralized mechanisms, for giving polluters incentives for minimizing external damage down to the level where additional abatement effort would be more costly than its benefit.

It has often been asserted (on the basis of the so-called Coase Theorem)[1] that, were it not for transaction costs (e.g., legal expenses of suing for damages), the level of abatement (hence also of pollution) would be independent of whether the polluter is liable for damage inflicted on the victim.

There is little, if any, disagreement, that the presence of significant transaction costs is likely to invalidate the Coase Theorem claim. But what about its validity when transaction costs are assumed to be absent? The argument[2] for the Coase Theorem goes roughly as follows.[3]

(a) If *damage exceeds the cost of abatement* and (i) the polluter *is* liable, he/she will have an incentive to invest in abatement. But if (ii) the polluter is *not* liable while damage exceeds abatement costs, the (potential) victim will have an incentive to compensate the polluter for abatement costs. Consequently, the resulting level of abatement (hence also of pollution) when the polluter is not liable will be the same as when he/she is.

On the other hand, if (b) *abatement costs exceed pollution damage*, (i) the polluter, *if liable*, will choose to pay damages rather than invest in abatement, and (ii) if the polluter is not liable, the victim will be better off to sustain damage than to finance abatement. Hence, in this case again, the outcome with regard to abatement (hence the pollution level) will be the same regardless of the polluter's liability status. It is convenient to have a term for this lack of impact of liability status on abatement/pollution outcomes: we shall call this phenomenon *invariance*.

---

[1] I shall sometimes refer to this proposition as the Coase Invariance Theorem, to distinguish it from other propositions that are also so labeled in the literature.

[2] The argument, as presented here, ignores the possibility that the level of damage might be influenced by the victim's behavior.

[3] See Coase (1960).

Of course, the preceding (Coase) invariance argument does not imply that liability status makes no difference on outcomes other than abatement/ pollution. Clearly, whether damage exceeds abatement cost or vice versa, the polluter, when not liable is financially better off (and the victim worse off) than when subject to liability. But, according to the invariance argument, while admittedly *financial* outcomes are affected by the polluter's liability status, the resulting *pollution* and *abatement* levels are not. It might appear, therefore, that *on environmental grounds* alone (as distinct from distributional or fairness considerations), there is no case for or against making polluters liable.[4]

Careful analysis shows that this, somewhat paradoxical, conclusion is based on the implicit assumption known in the economist's jargon as *absence of income effects*. An economic agent's behavior is said to be free of income effects if his/her demand for (or supply of) goods is independent of wealth or income and only depends on the various goods' relative prices. When income effects are absent, if one party is enriched while another becomes poorer, the competitive market processes would leave the equilibrium level of the goods (but not money) unchanged. Essentially, that is what leads to Coasian invariance.[5]

Modern economics, however, does not usually postulate absence of income effects.[6] Indeed, they are regarded as important factors in the determination of demand or supply. When these effects are admitted, shifts in wealth or income do result in different demand behavior, and the polluter's liability status (or pollution taxes) turns out to make a difference in the equilibrium levels of pollution and abatement.[7] In fact, under standard assumptions on individual preferences (e.g., preferences represented by Cobb-Douglas utility functions[8]) there is less pollution at equilibrium when 'polluter pays', than when he/she does not. Thus the Coasian invariance no longer holds. The analysis yields conclusions consistent with the common intuition that placing the financial burden on the polluter leads to lessening of pollution. This is more than a mere technicality. In policy choice contexts, the Coase Invariance Theorem is used to deny the need for, or usefulness of, intervention, at least on environmental grounds. But there may be a case for intervention when the presence of income effects implies differential effects determined by where the financial burdens are placed.

[4] Provided transaction costs are disregarded.

[5] Instead of basing the argument on competitive processes, one can reach the invariance conclusion by postulating that the equilibrium is efficient (in the sense of Pareto optimality).

[6] Although textbook examples using quasi-linear utility functions do. Income effects are sometimes implicitly assumed away in simplified expositions of cost-benefit analysis when demand functions are identified with marginal utility functions.

[7] See Hurwicz (1995).

[8] Thus implying the presence of positive income effects (goods being 'normal' rather than 'inferior'). See Hurwicz (1995, p. 63, esp. fig. 3) for details.

When intervention seems appropriate, economists typically favor 'indirect' policy instruments such as taxes and/or subsidies over administrative or judicial methods.[9] The classical proposal is due to Pigou.[10] For detrimental externalities, it involves a tax proportional to (or, more generally, an increasing function of) the pollution generating activity, usually based either on output or polluting input (e.g., 'dirty' fuel). The objective is to create an incentive for the polluter either to undertake direct abatement (e.g., scrubbers) or curtail the level of higher-polluting operations (perhaps replacing them with lower polluting technologies) to the point where the marginal benefit equals marginal social cost, the latter defined as the sum of the offender's private (variable) costs of production[11] plus the marginal damage due to pollution. The theory is such that a tax, when imposed at an appropriate level, would induce polluters to to undertake abatement to a socially optimal level. Furthermore, the revenue produced by such a tax could be used to compensate the victims of the remaining pollution. Typically, the 'socially optimal' level of pollution would be above zero and so would cause damage to victims.[12]

Objections have been raised against the Pigou taxation approach. One important criticism has been that the appropriate level of a Pigou tax rate requires information concerning marginal costs and benefits at the desired optimum point, while the decision concerning the tax rate is to be made when the actual level may be far from optimal, i.e., when the values of the marginal variables may be quite different from those at the hypothetical optimal levels. A partial remedy might be to use iterative (successive approximation, trial-and-error) methods. But these, in turn, are open to two types of objections. First, there may exist multiple Pigou equilibria, i.e., different resource allocations at which the Pigouvian marginal equalities are satisfied, but some of those allocations may fail to be socially efficient.[13] An iteration, if it converged at all, might converge to a non-optimal resource allocation. Second, even if all Pigouvian equilbrium allocations are efficient, an iterative process may fail to converge.

Recent research throws light on the first point, the possibility of inefficient Pigou equilibria.[14] It turns out that this possibility may or may not be present depending on the relative intensity of damages produced by the pollution,

---

[9] A 'mixed' approach with both administrative and market aspects is that of tradable pollution permits (see comments below).

[10] See Pigou (1912).

[11] E.g., marginal costs of (variable) inputs.

[12] To avoid giving the victim an incentive to increase compensation through behavior raising damage levels, the theory suggests so-called lump-sum compensation payments. Their feasibility has often been questioned.

[13] I.e., they may not be Pareto optimal. See Baumol and Oates (1988) and Starrett (1988).

[14] See Hurwicz (1999).

for instance on the partial derivative of some measure of victim's damage with respect to the level of activity of the polluter. An instructive example was provided by Baumol and Bradford (1972) where the technology of the two firms (polluter = firm 1 and victim = firm 2) is represented by the input requirements (respectively x_1 and x_2 of the same input commodity used by the two firms) as functions of the respective output levels of the two commodities they produce (respectively, y_1 and y_2). These inputs are given by the equations

$$x_1 = \frac{1}{2}y_1^2 \quad \text{and} \quad x_2 = \frac{1}{2}y_2^2 + ky_1y_2.$$

The cross-product term ky_1y_2 in the second equation represents the increment in the input requirements of the victim firm in producing y_2 units of its output when the polluter firm is producing y_1 units of its output. The coefficient k is positive, since pollution is detrimental, hence—given its output level—the victim's input requirement rise as pollution (assumed proportional to the polluter's output) intensifies.

It turns out that, assuming concave utility functions, all Pigou equilbria will be efficient (i.e., Pareto optimal) if the coefficient does not exceed 1. But when $k > 1$, the possibility of inefficient Pigou equilibria cannot be ruled out. This is so because the transformation set[15] T is convex if and only if $k \leq 1$. When the constraint set (here T) is convex and the maximands (here the utility functions) are concave, first-order conditions are sufficent for maximization and this, in turn, implies efficiency (Pareto optimality).[16]

The Baumol-Bradford example illustrates the important fact that the possibility of inefficient Pigou equilibria in the presence of detrimental externalities depends on the severity of the externality's impact and not just on the mere presence of an externality.

Thus when an externality is not too severe (i.e., when $k \leq 1$), the first objection against the Pigou tax approach loses its punch: if the economy with Pigouvian taxes and a 'mild' detrimental externality (e.g., $k \leq 1$) converges to an equilibrium, one need not fear inefficiency. (Multiple equilibria may still be present, but if so they will all be efficient.)

The problem raised by the second objection is more serious. I am not familiar with studies of the dynamics of Pigouvian economies for 'mild'

---

[15] Given the total amount $x > 0$ of the input available, the transformation set is defined as

$$T = \{(y_1, y_2): 12y_1^2 + \frac{1}{2}y_2^2 + ky_1y_2 \leq x, \ (y_1, y_2) \geq 0\},$$

i.e., the set of possible output combinations given the available total input.
[16] See Arrow and Enthoven (1961) and the remark there referring to Uzawa.

equilibria, but I would not be surprised to find that, in general, they do not guarantee global stability. That is, there may be situations where the system, governed by some form of tâtonnement, fails to converge to any equilibrium. But this phenomenon would not be special to Pigouvian taxes or even to detrimental externalities: there are well-known examples (e.g., Scarf (1960)) of convergence failures in a classical economy without externalities.

Still, even 'mild' externalities pose problems more difficult than those arising in classical economies free of externalities. That is in particular the case, because in many situations an externality involves two specific firms, hence we are in a case of 'small numbers' where the assumption that agents will treat prices parametrically (rather than strategically) is not very plausible.

As for the case of 'severe' externalities (e.g., $k > 1$), the situation is somewhat analogous to that arising in the absence of externalities but where firms have technologies characterized by increasing returns to scale. In both cases it has been shown[17] that, in general, infinite-dimensional message spaces may have to be used to assure efficient outcomes in economies governed by decentralized mechanisms, hence in particular by forms of market mechanisms. It is not clear whether this implies in practice that some second-best solutions are unavoidable.

The link between 'severe' detrimental externalities and increasing returns to scale is particularly striking when we consider the question whether mergers can be viewed as a solution for such 'severe' externalities. If, say, the upstream firm A pollutes river water for the downstream firm B, isn't merger (hence 'internalization') a solution? It is of course true that if the two firms merge, formally the externality disappears. But suppose the respective technologies are represented by the Baumol-Bradford example, with 'severe' $k > 1$. Then the above-mentioned transformation set T becomes a cross-section of the merged firm's production possibility set. Hence this firm is characterized by increasing returns to scale, in fact a 'natural monopoly'. What the merger has accomplished is to replace a situation where competitive equilibrium would be non-optimal by a situation where competitive equilibrium is (even theoretically) impossible, and quite possibly resulting in monopolistic inefficient equilibrium.

Somewhat similar issues have been raised[18] in connection with concepts (e.g., Arrow's (1970)) involving what I call the 'commodification' of externalities. For instance, let pollution by smoke traveling from agent A to agent B serve as example. In the absence of rules prohibiting or penalizing such pollution, A can 'send to B' as much smoke as he/she desires. But if law treats

---

[17] See Calsamiglia (1977) and Hurwicz (1997, 1999).
[18] Provided preferences were not locally satiated. (But even if there were instances of local satiation, as least weak Pareto optimality would prevail.)

smoke as a commodity, *A* has no right to 'sell' it to *B* except with the latter's consent, hence only at a (presumably negative) price acceptable to *B*. Clearly, not all forms of pollution can be treated as commodities, but we shall ignore this difficulty. If all externalities were commodified, the list of commodities in the 'reformed' economy would be much longer but, by definition there would no longer be any externalities.

If one could postulate a competitive equilibrium in the 'reformed' economy, the resulting resource allocation would (by the First Fundamental Theorem of Welfare Economics) be Pareto optimal. However, the 'if' condition of the preceding statement may be difficult to satisfy, for two reasons. First, we may again encounter the phenomenon of small numbers in many markets of the new economy and hence agents might be unlikely to treat prices parametrically (i.e., to act as price-takers), as required in a competitive equilibrium. Secondly, as pointed out[19] by Starrett, detrimental externalities present in the 'unreformed' economy might reappear as non-convexity of production sets in the 'reformed' economy, which in turn might make the existence of competitive equilibrium (even theoretically) impossible.

Given the problems arising with the various approaches so far tried, it seems highly desirable to explore the techniques of mechanism design, specifically those involving implementation in Nash equilibria. A beginning has been made by Varian (1992 esp. ch. 24, section 24.3, pp. 436–38, 1994, 1995) although still in a rather limited class of externality situations.

As for actual practice, an important example of a compromise solution may be that of tradable pollution permits. It is a 'mixed' mechanism in that it involves an administrative allocation procedure for the permit allocation, but when trading is permitted it tends to minimize the aggregate cost of abatement. On the other hand, unlike the Pigou tax system, the tradable permit mechanism does not have inherent characteristics to equate at the margin the aggregate social costs of abatement with the corresponding aggregate benefits. Proposals to apply such systems on an international scale have encountered resistance on grounds other than efficiency.

In countries in transition (perhaps everywhere!) compromise solutions are inevitable. The conference heard from Professors Bochniarz and Bolan of a number of innovative designs used in Poland, in particular soft loans, subsidies combined with putting abatement programs on solid financial basis by earmarking and other devices. To what extent the subjective aspects of decision-making can be regarded as early iterations in the direction of what the decision-makers know to be efficient (or, at least, more efficient) solutions

---

[19] Actually, Starrett (1972) argues that detrimental externalities *unavoidably* create what he calls fundamental non-convexities in the 'reformed' economy, and that these non-convexities make competitive equilibria impossible. But even if one does not accept the unavoidability view (see Boyd and Conley (1977) and Otani and Sicilian (1977)), a category of non-convexity phenomena has, in my view, considerable plausibility (see Hurwicz (1999)).

is difficult to judge. But there seems no question that these early steps have already brought about significant improvements.

References

Arrow, K. (1969) The organization of economic activity: Issues pertinent to the choice of market versus nonmarket allocation, in *The Analysis and Evaluation of Public Expenditure: The PPB System* (Compendium of papers submitted to the Subcommittee on Economy in Government of the Joint Economic Committee, 91st Congress, 1st Session), US Government Printing Office, 47–64. Reprinted 1970 in *Public Expenditure and Policy Analysis*, ed. R. Haveman and J. Margolis, 59–73. Chicago, IL: Markham.

Arrow, K. and A. Enthoven (1961) Quasi-concave programming, *Econometrica*, 29(4): 779–800.

Baumol, W. and D. Bradford (1972) Detrimental externalities and non-convexity of the production set, *Economica*, 39(1): 160–76.

Baumol, W. and W. Oates (1988) *The Theory of Environmental Policy*, 2nd ed. Cambridge, MA: Cambridge University Press.

Boyd III, J. and J. Conley (1997) Fundamental nonconvexities in Arrovian markets and a Coasian solution to the problem of externalities, *Journal of Economic Theory*, 72(2): 388–407.

Calsamiglia, X. (1977) Decentralized resource allocation and increasing returns, *Journal of Economic Theory*, 14(2): 263–83.

Coase, R. (1960) The problem of social cost, *Journal of Law and Economics*, 3(1): 1–44.

Hurwicz, L. (1995) What is the Coase Theorem?, *Japan and the World Economy*, 7(1): 49–74.

Hurwicz, L. (1997) A sequence of functions for the uniqueness property in the impossibility proof for externalities between firms, mimeo. Presented at the Decentralization Conference, University of Minneapolis, April 1998.

Hurwicz, L. (1998) Revisiting externalities, *Journal of Public Economic Theory*, 1(2): 225–45.

Pigou, A. (1912) *Wealth and Welfare*. London: Macmillan.

Scarf, H. (1960) Some examples of global instability of competitive equilibrium, *International Economic Review*, 1(3): 157–72.

Starrett, D. (1972) Fundamental nonconvexities in the theory of externalities, *Journal of Economic Theory*, 4(2): 180–99.

Starrett, D. (1988) *Foundations of Public Economics*, Cambridge, MA: Cambridge University Press.

Varian, H. (1922) *Microeconomic Analysis*, third edition. New York, NY: W.W. Norton.

Varian, H. (1994) A solution to the problem of externalities when agents are well-informed, *American Economic Review*, 84(5): 1278–93.

Varian, H. (1995) Coase, competition, and compensation, *Japan and the World Economy*, 7(1): 13–27.

21

The Theory of Economic Behavior

Had it merely called to our attention the existence and exact nature of certain fundamental gaps in economic theory, the *Theory of Games and Economic Behavior* by von Neumann and Morgenstern (1944) would have been a book of outstanding importance. But it does more than that. It is essentially constructive: where existing theory is considered to be inadequate, the authors put in its place a highly novel analytical apparatus designed to cope with the problem.

It would be doing the authors an injustice to say that theirs is a contribution to economics only. The scope of the book is much broader. The techniques applied by the authors in tackling economic problems are of sufficient generality to be valid in political science, sociology, or even military strategy. The applicability to games proper (chess and poker) is obvious from the title. Moreover, the book is of considerable interest from a purely mathematical point of view. This review, however, is in the main confined to the purely economic aspects of the *Theory of Games and Economic Behavior*.

To a considerable extent this review is of an expository[1] nature. This seems justified by the importance of the book, its use of new and unfamiliar concepts and its very length which some may find a serious obstacle.

The existence of the gap which the book attempts to fill has been known to the economic theorists at least since Cournot's work on duopoly, although even now many do not seem to realize its seriousness. There is no adequate solution of the problem of defining 'rational economic behavior' on the part of an individual when the very rationality of his actions depends on the probable behavior of other individuals: in the case of oligopoly, other sellers. Cournot and many after him have attempted to sidetrack the difficulty by

Reprinted from *American Economic Review*, 1945, 35(5): 909–25.

[1] The exposition is mostly carried out by means of comparatively simple numerical examples. This involves loss of generality and rigor, but it may be hoped that it will make the presentation more accessible.

The Theory of Economic Behavior In: *The Collected Papers of Leonid Hurwicz Volume 1.*
Edited by Samiran Banerjee, Oxford University Press. © Oxford University Press 2022.
DOI: 10.1093/oso/9780199313280.003.0021

assuming that every individual has a definite idea as to what others will do under given conditions. Depending on the nature of this expected behavior of other individuals, we have the special, well-known solutions of Bertrand and Cournot, as well as the more general Bowley concept of the 'conjectural variation.'[2] Thus, the individual's 'rational behavior' is determinate *if* the pattern of behavior of 'others' can be assumed a priori known. But the behavior of "others" cannot be known a priori if the 'others' too are to behave rationally! Thus a logical impasse is reached.

The way, or at least *a* way,[3] out of this difficulty had been pointed out by one of the authors, von Neumann (1928), over a decade ago. It lies in the rejection of a narrowly interpreted maximization principle as synonymous with rational behavior. Not that maximization (of utility[4] or profits) would not be desirable if it were feasible, but there can be no true maximization when only one of the several factors which decide the outcome (of, say, oligopolistic competition) is controlled by the given individual.

Consider, for instance, a duopolistic situation[5] where each one of the duopolists A and B is *trying* to maximize his profits. A's profits will depend not only on his behavior ('strategy') but on B's strategy as well. Thus, *if* A could control (directly or indirectly) the strategy to be adopted by B, he would select a strategy for himself and one for B so as to maximize his own profits. But he cannot select B's strategy. Therefore, he can in no way make sure that by a proper choice of his own strategy his profits will actually be unconditionally maximized.

It might seem that in such a situation there is no possibility of defining rational behavior on the part of the two duopolists. But it is here that the novel solution proposed by the authors comes in. An example will illustrate this.

Suppose each of the duopolists has three possible strategies at his disposal.[6] Denote the strategies open to duopolist A by A_1, A_2, and A_3, and those open to duopolist B by B_1, B_2, and B_3. The profit made by A, to be denoted

2 More recent investigations have led to the idea of a kinked demand curve. This, however, is a special—though very interesting—case of the conjectural variation.

3 *Cf.* reference to von Stackelberg in footnote 16 and some of the work quoted by von Stackelberg (1932).

4 A side-issue of considerable interest discussed in the *Theory of Games* is that of measurability of the utility function. The authors need measurability in order to be able to set up tables of the type to be presented later in the case where utility rather than profit is being maximized. The proof of measurability is not given; however, an article giving the proof is promised for the near future and it seems advisable to postpone comment until the proof appears. But it should be emphasized that the validity of the core of the *Theory of Games* is by no means dependent on measurability or transferability of the utilities and those who feel strongly on the subject would perhaps do best to substitute 'profits' for 'utility' in most of the book in order to avoid judging the achievements of the *Theory of Games* from the point of view of an unessential assumption.

5 It is assumed that the buyers' behavior may be regarded as known.

6 Actually the number of strategies could be very high, perhaps infinite.

A's Profits

B's choice of strategies

		B_1	B_2	B_3
	A_1	a_{11}	a_{12}	a_{13}
	A_2	a_{21}	a_{22}	a_{23}
	A_3	a_{31}	a_{32}	a_{33}

A's choice of strategies

Table 1*a*

B's Profits

B's choice of strategies

		B_1	B_2	B_3
	A_1	b_{11}	b_{12}	b_{13}
	A_2	b_{21}	b_{22}	b_{23}
	A_3	b_{31}	b_{32}	b_{33}

A's choice of strategies

Table 1*b*

by a, obviously is determined by the choices of strategy made by the two duopolists. This dependence will be indicated by subscripts attached to a, with the first subscript referring to A's strategy and the second subscript to that of B; thus, e.g., a_{13} is the profit which will be made by A if he chooses strategy A_1, while B chooses the strategy B_3. Similarly, b_{13} would denote the profits by B under the same circumstances. The possible outcomes of the 'duopolistic competition' are represented in Tables 1*a* and 1*b*.

Table 1*a* shows the profits A will make depending on his own and B's choice of strategies. The first row corresponds to the choice of A_1, etc.; columns correspond to B's strategies. Table 1*b* gives analogous information regarding B's profits.

In order to show how A and B will make decisions concerning strategies we shall avail ourselves of a numerical example given in Tables 2*a* and 2*b*.

Now let us watch A's thinking processes as he considers his choice of strategy. First of all, he will notice that by choosing strategy A_3 he will be sure that his profits cannot go down below 5, while either of the remaining

A's Profits

B's choice of strategies

		B_1	B_2	B_3
	A_1	2	8	1
	A_2	4	3	9
	A_3	5	6	7

A's choice of strategies

Table 2*a*

B's Profits

B's choice of strategies

		B_1	B_2	B_3
	A_1	11	2	20
	A_2	9	15	3
	A_3	8	7	6

A's choice of strategies

Table 2*b*

alternatives would expose him to the danger of going down to 3 or even to 1. But there is another reason for his choosing A_3. Suppose there is a danger of a 'leak': B might learn what A's decision is before he makes his own. Had A chosen, say, A_1, B—if he knew about this—would obviously choose B_3 so as to maximize his own profits; this would leave A with a profit of only 1. Had A chosen A_2, B would respond by selecting B_2, which again would leave A with a profit below 5 which he could be sure of getting if he chose A_3.

One might perhaps argue whether A's choice of A_3 under such circumstances is the only way of defining rational behavior, but it certainly is *a* way of accomplishing this and, as will be seen later, a very fruitful one. The reader will verify without difficulty that similar reasoning on B's part will make him choose B_1 as the optimal strategy. Thus, the outcome of the duopolistic competition is determinate and can be described as follows: A will choose A_3, and B will choose B_1, A's profit will be 5, B's 8.

An interesting property of this solution is that neither duopolist would be inclined to alter his decision, even if he were able to do so, after he found out what the other man's strategy was.

To see this, suppose B has found out that A's decision was in favor of strategy A_3. Looking at the third row of Table 2b, he will immediately see that in no case could he do better than by choosing B_1, which gives him the highest profit consistent with A's choice of A_3. The solution arrived at is of a very stable nature, independent of finding out the other man's strategy.

But the above example is artificial in several important respects. For one thing, it ignores the possibility of a 'collusion' or, to use a more neutral term, coalition between A and B. In our solution, yielding the strategy combination (A_3, B_1), the joint profits of the two duopolists amount to 13; they could do better than that by acting together. By agreeing to choose the strategies A_1 and B_3 respectively, they would bring their joint profits up to 21; this sum could then be so divided that both would be better off than under the previous solution.

A major achievement of the *Theory of Games* is the analysis of the conditions and nature of coalition formation. How that is done will be shown below. But, for the moment, let us eliminate the problem of coalitions by considering a case which is somewhat special but nevertheless of great theoretical interest: the case of *constant sum* profits. An example of such a case is given in Tables 3a and 3b.

Table 3a is identical with Table 2a. But figures in Table 3b have been selected in such a manner that the joint profits of the two duopolists always amount to the same (10), no matter what strategies have been chosen. In such a case, A's gain is B's loss and vice versa. Hence, it is intuitively obvious (although the authors take great pains to show it rigorously) that no coalition will be formed.

A's Profits
B's choice of strategies

	B_1	B_2	B_3
A_1	2	8	1
A_2	4	3	9
A_3	5	6	7

A's choice of strategies

Table 3a

B's Profits
B's choice of strategies

	B_1	B_2	B_3
A_1	8	2	9
A_2	6	7	1
A_3	5	4	3

A's choice of strategies

Table 3b

The solution can again be obtained by reasoning used in the previous case and it will again turn out to be (A_3, B_1) with the respective profits 5 and 5 adding up to 10. What was said above about stability of solution and absence of advantage in finding the opponent[7] out still applies.

There is, however, an element of artificiality in the example chosen that is responsible for the determinateness of the solution. To see this it will suffice to interchange 5 and 6 in Table 3a. The changed situation is portrayed in Table 4 which gives A's profits for different choices of strategies.[8]

A's Profits
B's choice of strategies

	B_1	B_2	B_3
A_1	2	8	1
A_2	4	3	9
A_3	6	5	7

A's choice of strategies

Table 4

There is no solution now which would possess the kind of stability found in the earlier example. For suppose A again chooses A_3; then if B should find that

---

[7] In this case the interests of the two duopolists are diametrically opposed and the term 'opponents' is fully justified; in the previous example it would not have been.

[8] The table for B's profits is omitted because of the constant sum assumption. Clearly, in the constant sum case, B may be regarded as minimizing A's profits since this implies maximization of his own.

out, he would obviously 'play' B_2 which gives him the highest possible profit consistent with A_3. But then A_3 would no longer be A's optimum strategy: he could do much better by choosing A_1; but if he does so, B's optimum strategy is B_3, not B_2, etc. There is no solution which would not give at least one of the opponents an incentive to change his decision if he found the other man out! There is no stability.[9]

What is it in the construction of the table that insured determinateness in the case of Table 3 and made it impossible in Table 4? The answer is that Table 3 has a *saddle point* ('minimax') while Table 4 does not.

The saddle point has the following two properties: it is the highest of all the row minima and at the same time it is lowest of the column maxima. Thus, in Table 3*a* the row minima are respectively 1, 3, and 5, the last one being highest among them (*Maximum Minimorum*); on the other hand, the column maxima are respectively 5, 8, and 9 with 5 as the lowest (*Minimum Maximorum*). Hence the combination (A_3, B_1) yields both the highest row minimum and the lowest column maximum, and, therefore, constitutes a saddle point. It is easy to see that Table 4 does *not* possess a saddle point. Here 5 is still the *Maximum Minimorum*, but the *Minimum Maximorum* is given by 6; the two do not coincide, and it is the absence of the saddle point that makes for indeterminateness in Table 4.

Why is the existence of a unique saddle point necessary (as well as sufficient) to insure the determinateness of the solution? The answer is inherent in the reasoning used in connection with the earlier examples: if A chooses his strategy so as to be protected in case of any leakage of information concerning his decision, he will choose the strategy whose row in the table has the highest minimum value, i.e., the row corresponding to the *Maximum minimorum*—A_3 in case of Table 4—for then he is sure he will not get less than 5, even if B should learn of this decision. B, following the same principle, will choose the column (i.e., strategy) corresponding to the *Minimum maximorum*—B_1 in Table 4—thus making sure he will get at least 4, even if the information does leak out.

In this fashion both duopolists are sure of a certain minimum of profit— 5 and 4, respectively. But this adds up to only 9. The residual—1—is still to be allocated and this allocation depends on outguessing the opponent. It is this residual that provides an explanation, as well as a measure, of the extent of indeterminacy. Its presence will not surprise economists familiar with this type of phenomenon from the theory of bilateral monopoly. But there are cases when this residual does equal zero, that is, when the *Minimum*

---

[9] There is, however, a certain amount of determinateness, at least in the negative sense, since certain strategy combinations are excluded: e.g. (A_2, B_1); A would never choose A_2 if he knew B had chosen B_1, and vice versa.

maximorum equals the *Maximum minimorum,* which (by definition) implies the existence of the saddle point and complete determinacy.

At this stage the authors of the *Theory of Games* had to make a choice. They could have accepted the fact that saddle points do not always exist so that a certain amount of indeterminacy would, in general, be present. They preferred, however, to get rid of the indeterminacy by a highly ingenious modification of the process which leads to the choice of appropriate strategy.

So far our picture of the duopolist making a decision on strategy was that of a man reasoning out which of the several possible courses of action is most favorable ('pure strategy'). We now change this picture and put in his hands a set of dice which he will throw to determine the strategy to be chosen. Thus, an element of chance is introduced into decision-making ('mixed strategy').[10] But not everything is left to chance. The duopolist *A* must in advance formulate a rule as to what results of the throw—assume that just one die is thrown—would make him choose a given strategy. In order to illustrate this we shall use a table that is somewhat simpler, even if less interesting than those used previously. In this new table (Table 5),[11] each duopolist has only two strategies at his disposal.

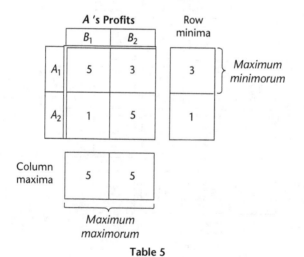

Table 5

An example of a rule A might adopt would be:
If the result of the throw is 1 or 2, choose A_1;
if the result of the throw is 3, 4, 5, or 6, choose A_2.

---

[10] The authors' justification for introducing 'mixed strategies' is that leaving one's decision to chance is an effective way of preventing 'leakage' of information since the individual making the decision does not himself know which strategy he will choose.
[11] In Table 5 there is no saddle point.

If this rule were followed, the probability that A will choose A_1 is 1/3, that of his choosing A_2 is 2/3. If a different rule had been decided upon (say, one of choosing A_1 whenever the result of the throw is 1, 2, or 3), the probability of choosing A_1 would have been 1/2. Let us call the fraction giving the probability of choosing A_1 A's *chance coefficient*; in the two examples, A's chance coefficients were 1/3 and 1/2 respectively.[12]

As a special case the value of the chance coefficient might be zero (meaning, that is, definitely choosing strategy A_2) or one (meaning that A is definitely choosing strategy A_1); thus in a sense 'pure strategies' may be regarded as a special case of mixed strategies. However, this last statement is subject to rather important qualifications which are of a complex nature and will not be given here.

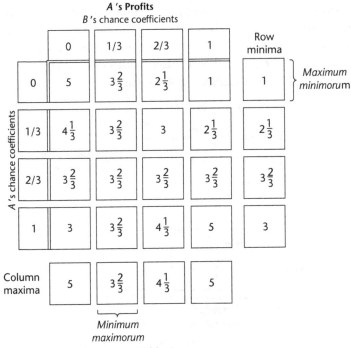

Table 6

Now instead of choosing one of the available strategies the duopolist A must choose the optimal (in a sense not yet defined) chance coefficient. How is the choice of the chance coefficient made? The answer lies in constructing

[12] Since the probability of choosing A_2 is always equal to one minus that of choosing A_1, specification of the probability of choosing A_1 is sufficient to describe a given rule. However, when the number of available strategies exceeds two, there are several such chance coefficients to be specified.

a table which differs in two important respects from those used earlier. Table 6 provides an example. Each row in the table now corresponds to a possible value of A's chance coefficient; similarly, columns correspond to possible values of B's chance coefficient. Since the chance coefficient may assume any value between zero and one (including the latter two values), the table is to be regarded merely as a 'sample'. This is indicated by spaces between rows and between columns.

The numbers entered in the table are the average values (mathematical expectations) corresponding to the choice of chance coefficients indicated by the row and column.[13] (One should mention that Table 6 is only an expository device: the actual procedures used in the book are algebraic and much simpler computationally.)

If we now assume with the authors that each duopolist is trying to maximize the mathematical expectation of his profits (Table 6) rather than the profits themselves (Table 5), it might seem that the original source of difficulty remains if a saddle point does not happen to exist. But the mixed strategies were not introduced in vain! It is shown (the theorem was originally proved by von Neumann in 1928) that in the table of mathematical expectations (like Table 6) a saddle point *must* exist; the problem is always determinate.[14]

The reader who may have viewed the introduction of dice into the decisionmaking process with a certain amount of suspicion will probably agree that this is a rather spectacular result. Contrary to the initial impression,

---

[13] To see this we shall show how, e.g., we have obtained the value in the second row and third column of Table 6 (viz., 3). We construct an auxiliary table valid only for this particular combination of chance coefficients (A's 1/3, B's 2/3).

B's chance coefficients		B's strategies	
		B_1	B_2
A's chance coefficients		2/3	1/3
A_1	1/3	5	3
A_2	2/3	1	5

Mathematical Expectation for 2nd row, 3rd column in Table 6:
1/3 x 2/3 x 5 + 1/3 x 1/3 x 3 + 2/3 x 2/3 x 1 + 2/3 x 1/3 x 5 = 27/9 = 3

This table differs from Table 5 only by the omission of row maxima and column minima and by the insertion of the probabilities of choosing the available strategies corresponding to the second row third column of Table 6. The computation of the mathematical expectation is indicated above.

[14] In Table 6 the saddle point is in the third row second column; it is to be stressed that Table 5 has no saddle point.

it *is* possible to render the problem determinate. But there is a price to be paid: acceptance of mixed strategies, assumption that only the mathematical expectation of profit (not its variance, for instance) matters, seem to be necessary. Many an economist will consider the price too high. Moreover, one might question the need for introducing determinateness into a problem of this nature. Perhaps we should consider as the 'solution' the interval of indeterminacy given by the two critical points: the *Minimum maximorum* and *Maximum minimorum*.

As indicated earlier in this review, one should not ignore, in general, the possibility of a collusion. This is especially evident when more complex economic situations are considered.

We might, for instance, have a situation where there are two sellers facing two buyers. Here a 'coalition' of buyers, as well as one of sellers, may be formed. But it is also conceivable that a buyer would bribe a seller into some sort of cooperation against the other two participants. Several other combinations of this type can easily be found.

When only *two* persons enter the picture, as in the case of duopoly (where the role of buyers was ignored), it was seen that a coalition would not be formed if the sum of the two persons' profits remained constant. But when the number of participants is *three* or more, subcoalitions can profitably be formed even if the sum of all participants' profits is constant; in the above four-person example it might pay the sellers to combine against the buyers even if (or, perhaps, especially if) the profits of all four always add to the same amount.

Hence, the formation of coalitions may be adequately treated without abandoning the highly convenient constant-sum assumption. In fact, when the sum is known to be non-constant, it is possible to introduce (conceptually) an additional fictitious participant who, by definition, loses what all the real participants gain and vice versa. In this fashion a non-constant sum situation involving, say, three persons may be considered as a special case of a constant-sum four-person situation. This is an additional justification for confining most of the discussion (both in the book and in the review) to the constant-sum case despite the fact that economic problems are as a rule of the non-constant sum variety.

We shall now proceed to study the simplest constant-sum case which admits coalition formation, that involving three participants. The technique of analysis presented earlier in the two-person case is no longer adequate. The number of possibilities increases rapidly. Each of the participants may be acting independently; or else, one of the three possible two-person coalitions (*A* and *B* vs. *C*, *A* and *C* vs. *B*, *B* and *C* vs. *A*) may be formed. Were it not for the constant-sum restriction, there would be the additional possibility of the coalition comprising all three participants.

Here again we realize the novel character of the authors' approach to the problem. In most[15] of traditional economic theory the formation—or absence—of specific coalitions is *postulated*. Thus, for instance, we discuss the economics of a cartel without rigorously investigating the necessary and sufficient conditions for its formation. Moreover, we tend to exclude a priori such phenomena as collusion between buyers and sellers even if these phenomena are known to occur in practice. The *Theory of Games,* though seemingly more abstract than economic theory known to us, approaches reality much more closely on points of this nature. A complete solution to the problems of economic theory requires an answer to the question of coalition formation, bribery, collusion, etc. This answer is now provided, even though it is of a somewhat formal nature in the more complex cases; and even though it does not always give sufficient insight into the actual workings of the market.

Let us now return to the case of three participants. Suppose two of them are sellers, one a buyer. Traditional theory would tell us the quantity sold by each seller and the price. But we know that in the process of bargaining one of the sellers might bribe the other one into staying out of the competition. Hence the seller who refrained from market operations would make a profit; on the other hand, the nominal profit made by the man who did make the sale would exceed (by the amount of bribe) the actual gain made.

It is convenient, therefore, to introduce the concept of *gain*: the bribed man's gain is the amount of the bribe, the seller's gain is the profit made on a sale minus the bribe, etc. A given distribution of gains among the participants is called an *imputation*. The imputation is not a number: it is a set of numbers. For instance, if the gains of the participants in a given situation were (g_A, g_B, g_C), it is the set of these three g's that is called the imputation. The imputation summarizes the outcome of the economic process. In any given situation there are a great many possible imputations. Therefore, one of the chief objectives of economic theory is that of finding those among all the possible imputations which will actually be observed under rational behavior.

---

[15] In von Stackelberg (1932), he does point out (p. 89) that "the competitors [duopolists] must somehow unite; they must...supplement the economic mechanics, which in this case is inadequate, by economic politics". But no rigorous theory is developed for such situations (although an outline of possible developments is given). This is where the *Theory of Games* has made real progress.

Table 7

I. If A acts alone, he can get	5
If B acts alone, he can get	7
If C acts alone, he can get	10
II. If A and B from a coalition, they can get	15
If A and C from a coalition, they can get	18
If B and C from a coalition, they can get	20
III. If A, B and C act together, they can get	25

Table 8

	A	B	C
#1	6.5	8.3	10.2
#2	5.0	9.5	10.5
#3	4.0	10.0	11.0

In a situation such as that described (three participants, constant-sum) each man will start by asking himself how much he could get acting independently, even if the worst should happen and the other two formed a coalition against him. He can determine this by treating the situation as a two-person case (the opposing coalition regarded as one person) and finding the relevant *Maximum minimorum*, or the saddle point, if that point does exist; the saddle point would, of course, exist if 'mixed strategies' are used. Next, the participant will consider the possibility of forming a coalition with one of the other two men. Now comes the crucial question: under what conditions might such a coalition be formed?

Before discussing this in detail, let us summarize, in Table 7, all the relevant information. Among the many possible imputations, let us now consider the three given in Table 8.

It will be noted that under imputation #1, B and C are each better off than if they had been acting individually: they get respectively 8.3 and 10.2 instead of 7 and 10. Hence, there is an incentive for B and C to form a coalition since without such a coalition imputation #1 would not be possible. But once the coalition is formed, they can do better than under #1; viz., under #2, where each gets more (9.5 and 10.5 instead of 8.3 and 10.2, respectively). In such a case we say that imputation #2 *dominates* imputation #1. It might seem that #3, in turn, dominates #2 since it promises still more to both B and C. But it promises too much: the sum of B's and C's gains under #3 is 21, which is more than their coalition could get (cf. Table 7)! Thus #3 is ruled out as unrealistic and cannot be said to dominate any other imputation.

Domination is an exceptionally interesting type of relation. For one thing, it is not transitive: we may have an imputation i_1 dominating the imputation i_2 and i_2 dominating i_3, without thereby implying that i_1 dominates i_3; in

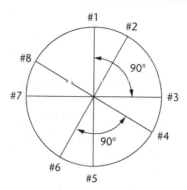

Fig. 1.

fact, i_1 might be dominated by i_3.[16] Moreover, it is easy to construct examples of, say, two imputations, neither of which dominates the other one.[17]

To get a geometric picture of this somewhat unusual situation one may turn to Figure 1, where points on the circle represent different possible imputations. (The reader must be cautioned that this is merely a geometrical analogy, though a helpful one.) Let us now say that point #1 dominates point #2 if #2 is less than 90° (clockwise) from #1. It is easy to see in Figure 1 that #1 dominates #2 and #2 dominates #3, but in spite of that, #1 does not dominate #3.

This geometrical picture will help define the very fundamental concept of a *solution.*

Consider the points (imputations) #1, 3, 5, and 7 in Figure 1. None of them dominates any other since any two are either *exactly* or more than 90° apart. But any other point on the circle is dominated by at least (in this case: exactly) one of them: all points between #1 and #3 are dominated by #1, etc. There is no point on the circle which is not dominated by one of the above four points. Now we *define* a solution as a set of points (imputations) with two properties: (1) no element of the set dominates any other element of the set, and (2) any point outside the set must be dominated by at least one element within the set.

---

[16] I.e., domination may be a *cyclic* relation. For instance, consider the following three imputations in the above problem: #1 and #2 as in Table 8, and #4, where

	A	B	C
#4	6.0	7.0	12.0

Here #2 (as shown before) dominates #1 (for the coalition B, C), #4 dominates #2 (for coalition A, C), but at the same tune #1 dominates #4 (for the coalition A, B): the cycle is completed.

[17] For instance, #2 and #3 in Table 8.

We have seen that the points #1, 3, 5, 7 do have both of these properties; hence, the four points together form a solution. It is important to see that none of the individual points by itself can be regarded as a solution. In fact, if we tried to leave out any one of the four points of the set, the remaining three would no longer form a solution; for instance, if #1 were left out, the points between #1 and #3 are not dominated by any of the points #3, 5, 7. This violates the second property required of a solution and the three points by themselves are not a solution. On the other hand, if a fifth point were added to #1, 3, 5, 7, the resulting five element set would not form a solution either; suppose #2 is the fifth point chosen: we note that #2 is dominated by #1 and it also dominates #3. Thus, the first property of a solution is absent.

Contrary to what would be one's intuitive guess, an element of the solution may be dominated by points outside the solution: #1 is dominated by #8, etc.

There can easily be more than one solution. The reader should have no trouble verifying the fact that #2, 4, 6, 8 also form a solution, and it is clear that infinitely many other solutions exist.

Does there always exist at least one solution? So far this question remains unanswered. Among the cases examined by the authors none has been found without at least one solution. But it has not yet been proved that there must always be a solution. To see the theoretical possibility of a case without a solution we shall redefine slightly our concept of domination (cf. Fig. 2): #1 dominates #2 if the angle between them (measured clockwise) does not exceed 180°.

Hence, in Figure 2 point #1 dominates #3, but not #4, etc. It can now be shown that in this case *no* solution exists. For suppose there is one; then we may, without loss of generality, choose #1 as one of its points. Clearly, #1 by itself does not constitute a solution, for there are points on the circle (e.g., #4) not dominated by #1; thus the solution must have at least two points. But any

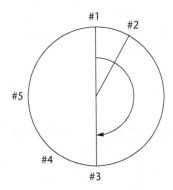

Fig. 2.

other point on the circle either is dominated by #1 (e.g., #2), or it dominates #1 (e.g., #4), or both (#3), which contradicts the first requirement for the elements of a solution. Hence there is no solution consisting of two points either. A fortiori, there are no solutions containing more than two points. Hence we have been able to construct an example without a solution. But whether this type of situation could arise in economics (or in games, for that matter) is still an open question.

Now for the economic interpretation of the concept of solution. Within the solution there is no reason for switching from one imputation to another since they do not dominate each other. Moreover, there is never a good reason for going outside a given solution: any imputation outside the solution can be 'discredited' by an imputation within the solution which dominates the one outside. But, as we have seen, the reverse is also usually true: imputations within the solution may be dominated by those outside. If we are to assume that the latter consideration is ignored, the given solution acquires an institutional, if not accidental, character. According to the authors, a solution may be equivalent to what one would call the 'standards of behavior' which are accepted by a given community.

The multiplicity of solutions can then be considered as corresponding to alternative institutional setups; for a given institutional framework only one solution would be relevant. But even then a large number of possibilities remains since, in general, a solution contains more than one imputation. More indeterminacy yet would be present if we had refrained from introducing mixed strategies.

It would be surprising, therefore, if in their applications von Neumann and Morgenstern should get no more than the classical results without discovering imputations hitherto neglected or ignored. And there are some rather interesting 'unorthodox' results pointed out, especially in the last chapter of the book.

In one case, at least, the authors' claim to generality exceeding that of economic theory is not altogether justified in view of the more recent literature. That is the case of what essentially corresponds to bilateral monopoly (p. 564, proposition 61:C). The authors obtain (by using their newly developed methods) a certain interval of indeterminacy for the price; this interval is wider than that indicated by Böhm-Bawerk, because (as the authors themselves point out) of the dropping of Böhm-Bawerk's assumption of a unique price. But this assumption has been abandoned, to give only one example, in the theories of consumer's surplus, with analogous extension of the price interval.

It will stand repeating, however, that the *Theory of Games* does offer a greater generality of approach than could be attained otherwise. The existence of 'discriminatory' solutions, discovered by purely analytical methods, is an instance of this. Also, the possibility of accounting for various types of deals and collusions mentioned earlier in connection with the three-person and four-person cases go far beyond results usually obtained by customarily used methods and techniques of economic theory.

The potentialities of von Neumann's and Morgenstern's new approach seem tremendous and may, one hopes, lead to revamping, and enriching in realism, a good deal of economic theory. But to a large extent they are only potentialities: results are still largely a matter of future developments.

The difficulties encountered in handling, even by the more powerful mathematical methods, the situations involving more than three persons are quite formidable. Even the problems of monopoly and monopsony are beyond reach at the present stage of investigation. The same is true of perfect competition, though it may turn out that the latter is not a 'legitimate' solution since it excludes the formation of coalitions which may dominate the competitive imputations. A good deal of light has been thrown on the problem of oligopoly, but there again the results are far from the degree of concreteness desired by the economic theorist.

The reviewer therefore regards as somewhat regrettable some of the statements made in the initial chapter of the book attacking (rather indiscriminately) the analytical techniques at present used by the economic theorists. True enough, the deficiencies of economic theory pointed out in the *Theory of Games* are very real; nothing would be more welcome than a model giving the general properties of a system with, say, *m* sellers and *n* buyers, so that monopoly, duopoly, or perfect competition could simply be treated as special cases of the general analysis. Unfortunately, however, such a model is not yet in sight. In its absence less satisfactory, but still highly useful, models have been and no doubt will continue to be used by economic theorists. One can hardly afford to ignore the social need for the results of economic theory even if the best is rather crude. The fact that the theory of economic fluctuations has been studied as much as it has is not a proof of "how much the attendant difficulties have been underestimated" (p. 5). Rather it shows that economics cannot afford the luxury of developing in the theoretically most 'logical' manner when the need for the results is as strong as it happens to be in the case of the ups and downs of the employment level!

Nor is it quite certain, though of course conceivable, that, when a rigorous theory developed along the lines suggested by von Neumann and Morgenstern is available, the results obtained in the important problems will be sufficiently remote from those obtained with the help of the current (admittedly imperfect) tools to justify some of the harsher accusations to be found in the opening chapter of the book. It must not be forgotten, for instance, that, while theoretical derivation of coalitions to be formed is of great value, we do have empirical knowledge which can be used as a substitute (again imperfect) for theory. For example, cartel formation may be so clearly 'in the cards' in a given situation that the economic theorist will simply include it as one of his assumptions while von Neumann and Morgenstern would (at least in principle) be able to *prove* the formation of the cartel without making it an additional (and logically unnecessary) assumption.

The authors criticize applications of the mathematical methods to economics in a way which might almost, in spite of protests to the contrary, mislead some readers into thinking that von Neumann and Morgenstern are not aware of the amount of recent progress in many fields of economic theory due largely to the use of mathematical tools. They also seem to ignore the fact that economics developed in literary form is, implicitly, based on the mathematical techniques which the authors criticize. (Thus it is not the methods of mathematical economics they are really questioning, but rather those elements of economic theory which literary and mathematical economics have in common.) While it is true that even mathematical treatment is not always sufficiently rigorous, it is as a rule more so than the corresponding literary form, even though the latter is not infrequently more realistic in important respects.

There is little doubt in the reviewer's mind that nothing could have been further from the authors' intentions than to give aid and comfort to the opponents of rigorous thinking in economics or to increase their complacency. Yet such may be the effect of some of the vague criticisms contained in the first chapter; they hardly seem worthy of the constructive achievements of the rest of the book.

Economists will probably be surprised to find so few references to more recent economic writings. One might almost form the impression that economics is synonymous with Böhm-Bawerk plus Pareto. Neither the nineteenth-century pioneers (such as Cournot) nor the writers of the last few decades (Chamberlin, Joan Robinson, Frisch, Stackelberg) are even alluded to. But, perhaps, the authors are entitled to claim exemption from the task of relating their work to that of their predecessors by virtue of the tremendous amount of constructive effort they put into their opus. One cannot but admire the audacity of vision, the perseverance in details, and the depth of thought displayed on almost every page of the book.

The exposition is remarkably lucid and fascinating, no matter how involved the argument happens to be. The authors made an effort to avoid the assumption that the reader is familiar with any but the more elementary parts of mathematics; more refined tools are forged 'on the spot' whenever needed.

One should also mention, though this transcends the scope of the review, that in the realm of strategic games proper (chess, poker) the results obtained are more specific than some of the economic applications. Those interested in the nature of determinacy of chess, in the theory of 'bluffing' in poker, or in the proper strategy for Sherlock Holmes in his famous encounter with Professor Moriarty will enjoy reading the sections of the book which have no direct bearing on economics. The reader's views on optimum military or diplomatic strategies are also likely to be affected.

Thus, the reading of the book is a treat as well as a stage in one's intellectual development. The great majority of economists should be able to go through the book even if the going is slow at times; it is well worth the effort. The appearance of a book of the caliber of the *Theory of Games* is indeed a rare event.

References

von Neumann, J. (1928) Zur Theorie der Gesellschaftsspiele, *Mathematische Annalen*, 100(1): 295–320.

von Neumann, J. and O. Morgenstern (1944) *Theory of Games and Economic Behavior*. Princeton, NJ: Princeton University Press.

von Stackelberg, H. (1932) *Grundlagen einer reinen Kostentheorie*. Vienna: Julius Springer.

22

Book Review: *The Theory of Games and Economic Behavior*

The Theory of Games and Economic Behavior by John von Neumann and Oskar Morgenstern (1947), second edition. Princeton: Princeton University Press, Pp. xviii, 641. $10.00.

This review is devoted to the second edition of a book which from its first appearance was acknowledged to be a major contribution in the field of theory of rational behavior. As is pointed out in the Preface, "the second edition differs from the first in some minor respects only". The main change is the addition of a proof (of 'measurability' of utility) omitted in the first edition.

The book's objective is to solve the problem of rational behavior in a very general type of situation.

It is, therefore, not surprising that its results are of relevance in many fields of knowledge, among them economics and statistical inference. In both economics and statistics the problem of rational behavior is a fundamental one. Thus one of the classical problems treated by the economic theory is that of profit maximization by a firm. The firm is assumed to be maximizing its net profit which is a function of prices of the product, materials used, etc., as well as the quantities used and produced. In the simplest case prices are taken as given; more generally they are assumed to be functions (known to the firm) of the quantities sold and purchased. But assuming this function to be known presupposes the knowledge of behavior of other firms. This procedure has for a long time been regarded as highly unsatisfactory; it is analogous to elaborating the theory of rational behavior of a poker player on the assumption that he knows the strategy of the other players!

Reprinted from *The Annals of Mathematical Statistics*, 1948, 19(3): 436–37.

Book Review: The Theory of Games and Economic Behavior In: *The Collected Papers of Leonid Hurwicz Volume 1*. Edited by Samiran Banerjee, Oxford University Press.

It is the type of situation in which not only the behavior of various individuals but even their strategies, are interdependent, that is treated by von Neumann and Morgenstern. The essence of their solutions is to base the optimal strategy on the minimax principle. As applied to a game, the principle requires that one should choose a strategy which minimizes the maximum loss that could be inflicted by the opponent.

The minimax principle, when applied by both players need not, in general, lead to a stable solution. To ensure the existence of such a solution the authors are led to the postulate that the choice of strategies be made through a random process. The minimax to be found is that of the mathematical expectation of the loss in the game. The latter postulate is of a restrictive nature[1] since it implies that the game is played for numerical ('measurable') stakes and that the second and higher moments of the probability distribution of the losses are immaterial. This restriction, however, has permitted the authors to go deeper in other directions. Given the great complexity of the problem, even in its restricted version, the authors' decision can hardly be criticized. One could only wish that similar considerations had made the authors more tolerant towards other work in the field of economics than is shown in some sections of the book.

The readers of the *Annals* will be particularly interested in the connection between the *Theory of Games* and the theory of statistical inference. As has been pointed out by Abraham Wald (1945) the problem faced by the statistician is somewhat similar to that of a player in a game of strategy. The theory of statistical inference may be viewed as a theory of rational behavior of the statistician. His 'strategy' consists in adopting an optimal test or estimate, more generally an optimal decision function. This optimal decision function must be chosen without the knowledge of the 'a priori' distribution of the population parameters. Wald's basic postulate of minimization of maximum risk is equivalent to regarding the statistician as a player in a game of strategy, with 'Nature' as the other player. The optimal decision function is chosen in a way which (as shown by Wald) is equivalent to assuming the 'least favorable' a priori distribution of the parameters. As Wald says, "we cannot say that Nature wants to maximize [the statistician's risk]. However, if the statistician is completely ignorant as to Nature's choice, it is perhaps not unreasonable to base the theory of a proper choice of [the decision function] on the assumption that Nature wants to maximize (the statistician's risk)". It may be noted, however, that statistical inference, as seen by Wald, is a relatively simple game since it involves only two players and is of the zero-sum variety.

---

[1] See Marschak (1946).

The admiring and enthusiastic reception given to the book's first edition would make any further general appraisal somewhat anticlimactic. Suffice it to say that a good deal of valuable work has already been stimulated by the *Theory of Games*, both in the field of social sciences and in mathematics.

References

Marschak, J. (1946) Neumann's and Morgenstern's new approach to static economics, *Journal of Political Economy*, 54(2): 97–115.

Wald, A. (1945) Statistical decision functions which minimize the maximum risk, *Annals of Mathematics*, 46(2): 265–80.

23

What Has Happened to the Theory of Games

Since the publication in 1944 of the first edition of the by now classic *Theory of Games and Economic Behavior* by von Neumann and Morgenstern, there has been a minor flood of contributions to the various aspects of the theory of games and its applications; a recent book by McKinsey (1952) provides a systematic treatment of some of the developments, while a collective volume edited by Kuhn and Tucker (1950) indicates some of the directions of research in this field. Other valuable contributions, scattered in many journals, are too numerous to be listed or even referred to in this brief survey, but it may be helpful to mention that McKinsey (1952) and Kuhn and Tucker (1950) contain very comprehensive bibliographies.

The theory of games thus has an undisputed fascination for, and a stimulating effect on, workers in many fields, ranging from (comparatively) pure mathematics to applied social sciences. There is a natural curiosity as to the directions in which the theory of games and its application have been developing; one also wishes to know which of the developments have found widespread agreement as against those which still are controversial. The limited scope and non-technical nature of the present exposition can do little more than give a very sketchy indication of the nature of these developments.

The problems of the theory of games are characterized by the presence of two types of issues: the nature of individual behavior in situations involving (non-probabilistic) uncertainty; and the interactions in the behavior of individuals when everyone's action may affect the well-being of others. Since both of these present difficulties of their own, we shall start by discussing problems in which only issues of the first type are present.

Reprinted from *American Economic Review*, 1953, 43(2): 398–405.

Individual Behavior under Uncertainty

There is no doubt that this type of problem is of great importance to the economist (e.g., in the study of investment decisions) and has been receiving in recent years an increasing amount of attention. One might question, however, the relationship of this problem to the theory of games. The answer is twofold. First, the problem of individual decision-making under uncertainty is an essential ingredient of most or all game-theoretic problems and hence, at the very least, has a very close conceptual link with the theory of games. Second, certain tools of the two-person theory of games have been found to be extremely useful in attacking even the one-person uncertainty type of problem. A brief discussion concerning the latter point seems in order.

It may be recalled that one class of two-person games has turned out to be of particular interest; viz., the constant-sum games where the (algebraic) sum of the gains of the two players does not depend on the way either of the players has played but always equals a certain fixed number.[1] For a given player, each strategy is characterized by the different (positive or negative) gains ('payoffs') he would obtain depending on the strategy chosen by the opponent.[2] The solution proposed by von Neumann and Morgenstern makes each player choose that strategy for which the minimal gain is at least as high as, and possibly higher than, the minimal gain guaranteed by any alternative strategy. Thus the player is maximizing the minimum pay off, or 'playing the maximin'.[3] An interesting feature of maximizing the minimum expected gains is that it may lead to a 'mixed' (i.e., randomized) strategy as superior to any 'pure' (non-randomized) strategy.

Now the same principle (in its minimax form) had been suggested and applied to an important class of statistical problems by Abraham Wald (1939, esp. p. 305).[4] Since there might be two or more minimax strategies not identical in their effects (but guaranteeing the same minimal risk), Wald combined the minimax principle with that of admissibility: to be optimal, a strategy (say s) must be admissible; i.e., there must not exist another strategy which promises sometimes a better, and never a worse, outcome than s.

---

[1] This number is often chosen to be zero and the game is then called zero-sum.

[2] To be precise we should substitute expected or long-run average gains for gains, since chance factors may be present.

[3] Because of a customary formulation in terms of minimizing maximal loss or risk rather than maximizing minimal gains this principle is usually referred to as the 'minimax' principle.

[4] The possibility of applying the minimax principle in statistical problems was mentioned previously in a contribution by Neyman and Pearson (1933). Von Neumann's (1928) initial publication in the field of game theory antedates Wald (1939) and Neyman and Pearson, but the present writer is not aware of any influence it might have had on Neyman and Pearson or Wald, or, for that matter, of any influence that Neyman and Pearson might have had on Wald.

Following the appearance of von Neumann and Morgenstern (1944), Wald (1945) reformulated the statistician's problem as one of playing a zero-sum game 'against nature', the nature representing the unknown properties of the universe from which the statistician draws his samples. Given this formulation, as well as the nature of the von Neumann-Morgenstern solution for two-person constant-sum games, it was again natural for the statistician to minimax, so that the 'game language' was not inconsistent with his earlier concept of optimality. However, the new language made it possible to pool the results obtained in two previously separate fields (game theory and statistics), with considerable gain for both.

The economic models involving decision-making under non-probabilistic uncertainty are very closely related to those appearing in the problem of statistical decision-making, hence here again the game language has attained considerable vogue.[5]

It should be noted, however, that recent discussions concerning behavior under uncertainty have led to a formulation of 'optimal' behavior which is broader than the maximin principle. Among examples of alternatives to the maximin (minimax) principle one may mention the principle (formulated by L. J. Savage) of minimaxing the regret rather than the loss (or the disutility), the maximax principle of maximizing the maximal (rather than the minimal, as in maximin) expected gain (suggested by F. Modigliani), and the principle of maximizing some weighted average of the maximal and minimal expected gains (suggested by the present writer); all of these are to be interpreted as combined with the condition of admissibility defined above.

None of these uncertainty behavior principles commands universal acceptance, since they all exhibit certain unsatisfactory properties. Just to what extent that is inevitable is not yet completely known. In the opinion of the present writer, one should not expect unanimous acceptance of some particular one among these principles, since it seems reasonable that some individuals might, say, find the regret principle a natural one, while others would feel inclined to maximax. In any case, however, if an individual is to have any consistent behavior pattern in non-probabilistic uncertainty situations, he must (implicitly or explicitly) follow some uncertainty behavior principle, whether it be minimax or something else.

---

[5] An example of a problem of this type treated by game-theory methods: the question of an optimal amount of insurance to be carried [in Morrison (1950)]. Among ideas inspired by the game analogy is that of using randomized strategies as policy tools in situations where it is desired to achieve a certain measure of unpredictability without permitting arbitrary action (e.g., in open market operations by stabilization agencies). Cf. Hurwicz (1951, p. 418). The problem of how best to aggregate economic variables yields another example of the application of game-theoretic (or uncertainty decision-making) methods (Hurwicz (1952)).

Many-Person Situations

Where two or more persons participate, we find, in general, that the problem of how an individual should act in a situation of uncertainty is still very much present, but that a rather peculiar type of uncertainty arises in an attempt to anticipate the others' behavior. The problem of oligopoly is a classical illustration of this type of situation in economics. Von Neumann and Morgenstern further enriched the problem by considering the possibility of coalitions, threats, and compensations (the latter appearing very naturally in modern welfare economics), regarding these phenomena as unknowns rather than data. The concept of a solution (a set of mutually undominated imputations)[6] offered by von Neumann and Morgenstern for the general case involving an arbitrary number of participants and a wealth of possibilities of communication among players has not found universal acceptance.

Under the circumstances it was natural that a simpler class of game situations, viz., that free of intercommunication among players ('non-cooperative'), should be attacked separately; this was done by Nash (1950, 1951).

Games wiithout Communication

In order to appreciate the nature of Nash's proposed solution, it is desirable to return for a moment to the two-person constant-sum case. It was mentioned earlier that the von Neumann-Morgenstern solution in this case makes the two players use their respective minimax strategies. Hence the solution has the valuable property of postulating that each of the players is following a (fairly acceptable) criterion of behavior under uncertainty. A fundamental result, however, of the theory of games shows that (under appropriate assumptions) the two minimax strategies 'meet' at a 'saddle-point', the important implication being that when one of the players uses his minimax strategy, the other player cannot do any better than to use his minimax strategy. Thus if the two players, after having decided on their respective minimax strategies, revealed the choice, neither would have an incentive to change his strategy, provided that the other player was expected to stick to his (minimax) strategy. Consequently, the saddle-point enjoys a certain

---

6 Since the exposition of the general concept of solution would exceed the scope of this paper, the reader is referred to Sec. 30.1.1 of von Neumann and Morgenstern (1944) for the relevant definition and to Marschak (1946) for an exposition against the background of a three-person barter problem.

equilibrium property: there is a tendency to stay at the saddle-point once it has been reached. This combination of the two advantageous properties of the maximin strategies, viz., 'rationality' of the players' behavior (in the sense of their following an uncertainty behavior principle) and the resulting equilibrium, is probably a good part of the reason for the favor which the saddle-point (minimax) solution of the constant-sum two-person game has generally enjoyed.

That (minimax) rationality and (saddle-point) equilibrium can be attained simultaneously is a special feature of the constant-sum two-person games. As soon as the game is two-person variable-sum or it involves more than two persons one must, in general, sacrifice at least one of these two features. Nash's solution favors the equilibrium as against the rationality feature of the solution. In fact, his solution is defined in terms of the equilibrium property. For the sake of simplifying the exposition, we shall give the Nash definition for the case of a two-person game only. Let A and B be the two players and denote by a a strategy of the player A while b represents a strategy of the player B. The pair (a, b) of the two players' strategies is a Nash equilibrium point if the following is true: given that A plays a, B cannot do better than play b, while at the same time, given that B plays b, A cannot do better than play a.

It may be noted that if the game happens to be of the constant-sum type, the Nash definition yields the same saddle-point solution that is implied by the von Neumann-Morgenstern solution concept (i.e., it corresponds to both players maximining). A constant-sum game is, of course, 'naturally' non-cooperative. It has been pointed out by Arrow and others that the Nash solution, when applied to the classical oligopoly problem (the mineral water example, for instance), essentially corresponds to the so-called 'Cournot solution.' It should be noted, however, that since the Nash definition avoids the reaction curve approach, it is immune to the Stackelberg objection: when all oligopolists but one follow the Cournot reaction curve behavior pattern, the one who does not can profit thereby; but if each of the oligopolists sticks to his Nash strategy, then (by definition) the remaining one could not possibly profit by abandoning his Nash strategy.

The present writer's inclination is to question the advisability of seeking solutions possessing the required equilibrium properties but sacrificing the rationality of behavior. To see the disadvantage of the equilibrium approach, one only has to visualize an individual who is inclined to follow the maximin principle when faced by uncertainty situations. Such an individual (let us call him A) would be disinclined to count on the likelihood of his opponent B adopting (or retaining) his Nash strategy, since he (A) might suffer considerable losses were B (for whatever reasons) to follow some strategy other than that corresponding to the Nash equilibrium point.

One might, therefore, argue that in a two-person (or many-person) game without communication (Nash's non-cooperative game) each player should simply follow his usual uncertainty behavior-principle (whether it be maximin, maximax, or anything else), subject to taking into account such information as he believes to have about his opponent's probable behavior. Thus it would seem safe to assume that the other player will not use a strategy which is inadmissible. This need not be true in a game with communication! The simplest solution then would be obtained by assuming that (after the elimination of all inadmissible strategies) each player selects his maximin strategy. The simplicity of the maximin (minimax) principle is mainly due to the fact that its nature has been explored much more thoroughly than that of most alternatives. Of course, this would not, in general, result in a Nash equilibrium point. However, the situation obtained would be one of equilibrium nature if the players are genuinely attached to the uncertainty behavior principle being followed.[7]

It should be stressed that even if the Nash model is inadequate as a basis for a realistic description of what people actually do, and even if one would regard it unwise to advise an individual player to follow his Nash strategy, there is an important area in which the Nash model and solution concepts appear to be tools of great usefulness, both for descriptive and expository purposes. The area meant here is that of the allocative properties of the market mechanism. Thus a position of the market variables (outputs, inputs, consumption levels, prices) attained when every agent in the market finds his utility (profits) maximized, provided he assumes the variables (or reaction patterns) controlled by other agents to be fixed, is clearly a Nash equilibrium point. The basic results concerning the optimal properties of the market mechanism can roughly be summarized in the proposition that in a properly defined market economy, a point is one of Nash equilibrium whenever it is Pareto optimal and vice versa.[8]

It may be remarked that some of the controversies in the game theory field result from the lack of distinction between the descriptive as against normative character of a theoretical model; we note that there is a third category of usefulness, viz., as a tool, which includes the utilization of a model for the purpose of setting up an organizational structure. Another source of difficulties, of relevance with regard to models claimed to be realistic, is vagueness as to observational implications of a given solution concept.

---

[7] One might note that on the latter assumption a Nash equilibrium point would lack the equilibrium property!

[8] A situation is defined as Pareto optimal if there is no way of raising anyone's utility without lowering that of someone else. For a game formulation of the allocative process, see Koopmans (1951).

Games with Communication

In this field there is perhaps most still to be accomplished; in view of its complexity, this is hardly surprising. While there are some attempts at the application of the proposed solution concepts to economic and other situations, the lack of confidence in the solution concept itself has a tendency to undermine the interest in the applications.[9]

Among attempts known to the present writer to seek an approach different from the solution of von Neuman and Morgenstern (1944), two deserve mention. One (Vickrey, 1952) appears to be relatively close to the formulation of von Neuman and Morgenstern, differing from the latter in that it imposes an additional requirement that the solution be, in a certain sense, self-policing. Another, due to Nash (1951, p. 295), is based on the idea of fitting the cooperative game into the general scheme of a non-cooperative game; this is to be achieved by introducing such elements as the bargaining process, as well as compensations, etc., explicitly into the game, instead of leaving them on the outside as appears to be the case in von Neuman and Morgenstern (1944).[10] With only very sketchy information available at this time, one must refrain from passing judgment on the chances of success of these proposals in terms of providing a workable and reasonably realistic tool for treating the multiperson games with communication.

Even if the case involving communication cannot yet be handled in a satisfactory manner, game theory (together with recent developments in the science of information and communication, including cybernetics) is to be credited for the increased attention being paid to information and communication aspects of social situations.[11] In the field of economics there is a class of problems very likely to profit greatly from increased emphasis on the information-processing aspects of the economy. Among problems of this class is that of the optimal size of the firm, as well as the more general one of optimal (internal) economic structure of an economic unit, especially with regard to the location of the limiting line between market structure (characteristic of interfirm relationships) and the administrative structure (characterizing—typically, but not without exceptions—the intrafirm relationships). An interesting special case is that of conditions under which a

---

[9] Some contributions in this area are to appear shortly in the Econometrica [possibly a reference to Nash (1953) and Mayberry, Nash, and Shubik (1953)—SB] and in vol. 2 of Kuhn and Tucker (1950), but are not available to the present writer at this time. Among papers of interest in this context one may mention Nash (1950) and Shubik (1952).

[10] Once it is known how to reduce cooperative to non-cooperative games, there is still freedom with regard to which theory of non-cooperative games is to be applied to the reduced games.

[11] See Shubik (1952) for an example related to certain problems of economic theory.

firm is likely to wish to introduce the pricing mechanism as a method of internal allocation of resources.

In a broader perspective, there is reason to hope that the development of an analytic approach to problems of economic structure (whether along the lines just indicated or in some other fashion) will tend to wipe out the traditional division between the theorists and the institutionalists. Recent developments in fields such as the theory of organization seem to add further justification to this hope.

While the present paper is in no way a systematic appraisal of the impact of game theory and related developments on economics, the writer does wish to express his opinion on one aspect of the manner in which economics has profited from the developments in the field of game theory. Even where the theory of games does not provide satisfactory answers, it has contributed to a more lucid, rigorous, and natural formulation of many problems. In many cases, it has led to the use of mathematical tools not involving calculus and often very close to intuitive thinking, thus creating the possibility of exploiting both the mathematical and common-sense (literary) type of talent available. A further development, which would seem at least partly due to the influence of game theory (as well as to that of statistical decision theory) is a trend toward axiomatic formulation of economic theory, with the consequent increase in rigor and greater transparency in the relationships between assumptions made and conclusions reached.

In the present writer's mind there is little doubt with regard to both the value of what the game theory (with its 'relatives') has accomplished, and the length of the road that still remains to be traversed.

References

Hurwicz, L. (1951) Comment on 'Business Cycle Analysis and Public Policy' by Arthur Smithies, in *Conference on Business Cycles*, 416–20. New York, NY: National Bureau of Economic Research.

Hurwicz, L. (1952) Aggregation in macroeconomic models, *Econometrica*, 20(3): 489–90.

Koopmans, T. (1951) Analysis of production as an efficient combination of activities, in *Activity Analysis of Production and Allocation*, ed. T. Koopmans, 33–97. New York, NY: Wiley.

Kuhn, H. and A. Tucker (1950) *Contribution to the Theory of Games*. Princeton, NJ: Princeton University Press.

Marschak, J. (1946) Neumann's and Morgenstern's new approach to static economics, *Journal of Political Economy*, 54(2): 97–115.

Mayberry, J., J. Nash, and M. Shubik (1953) A comparison of treatments of a duopoly situation, *Econometrica*, 21(1): 141–54.

McKinsey, J. (1952) *Introduction to the Theory of Games*. New York, NY: McGraw-Hill.

Morrison, A. (1950) *Consumer's Choice in Insurance*. Ph.D. thesis, Iowa State College.

Nash, J. (1950) Equilibrium points in *n*-person games, *Proceedings of National Academy of Science*, 36(1): 48–49.

Nash, J. (1950) The bargaining problem, *Econometrica*, 18(2): 155–62.

Nash, J. (1951) Non-cooperative games, *Annals of Mathematics*, 54(2): 286–95.

Nash, J. (1953) Two-person cooperative games, *Econometrica*, 21(1): 128–40.

von Neumann, J. (1928) Zur Theorie der Gesellschaftsspiele, *Mathematische Annalen*, 100(1): 295–320.

von Neumann, J. and O. Morgenstern (1944) *Theory of Games and Economic Behavior*. Second ed. (1947). Princeton, NJ: Princeton University Press.

Neyman, S. and E. Pearson (1933) The testing of statistical hypotheses in relation to probabilities a priori, *Mathematical Proceedings of the Cambridge Philosophical Society*, 29(4): 492–510.

Shubik, M. (1952) A business cycle model with organized labor considered, *Econometrica*, 20(2): 284–94.

Shubik, M. (1952) Information, theories of competition, and the theory of games, *Journal of Political Economy*, 60(2): 145–50.

Vickrey, W. (1952) Self-policing solutions in the theory of games, presented at the Econometric Society meetings in Chicago, December 1952. (Early versions privately circulated in 1949.) Published as Vickrey, W. (1959) Self-policing properties of certain imputation sets, in *Contributions to the Theory of Games*, vol. 4, ed. H. Kuhn and A. Tucker, 213–46. Princeton, NJ: Princeton University Press.

Wald, A. (1939) Contributions to the theory of statistical estimation and testing hypotheses, *Annals of Mathematical Statistics*, 10(4): 299–326.

Wald, A. (1945) Statistical decision functions which minimize the maximum risk, *Annals of Mathematics*, 46(2): 265–80.

Wald, A. (1950) *Statistical Decision Functions*. New York, NY: John Wiley and Sons.

24

Game Theory and Decisions

We are often forced to make decisions without complete information as to the consequences of the possible alternative actions. Such is the case, for instance, when an individual must decide in May whether to take his vacation in July or in August, when a nation must decide on the size of its defense program though uncertain about other nations' intentions, when a scientist must decide on a plan for an experiment. Uncertainty is present in many decision problems, big and little, routine and unusual.

Some problems involving uncertainty can be treated scientifically by means of the mathematics of probability. The modern sciences of genetics and physics are largely based on probability theory. But what of the innumerable kinds of situations in which the probabilities cannot be computed? Think, for instance, of Columbus' problem when his crew demanded that he turn back. Could he have evaluated the probability of finding land to the west before food and water gave out?

Within the last few years mathematicians have begun to develop a systematic theory of 'rational' decision-making in problems involving such uncertainties. Like the probability theory, originally developed in the seventeenth century from studies of simple games of chance (e.g., dice), the new theory has grown out of studies of a 'laboratory model'—in this case certain simple games of strategy against a thinking opponent (e.g., chess and poker).

John von Neumann constructed the theory of games in the 1920s (earlier, the mathematician Émile Borel had also had some ideas on the subject), but the subject did not achieve prominence until the publication in 1944 of the now classic *Theory of Games and Economic Behavior* by von Neumann and the economist Oskar Morgenstern. The theory then 'caught on', and there has been a multitude of studies and papers developing it in a great many directions.

Reprinted from *Scientific American*, 1955, 192(2): 78–83.

Game Theory and Decisions In: *The Collected Papers of Leonid Hurwicz Volume 1.*
Edited by Samiran Banerjee, Oxford University Press. © Oxford University Press 2022.
DOI: 10.1093/oso/9780199313280.003.0024

The theory of games and the theory of decision-making met on the territory of statistical inference. It had occurred to Abraham Wald, one of the founders of modern statistics, that statistical inference could be thought of as a game played against nature by the statistician attempting to uncover its secrets. Wald's principle of 'minimizing the maximum risk,' indeed, turned out to be equivalent to a principle of choosing a strategy in a game.

Game theory is so complex and heavily mathematical that it cannot be presented in a comprehensive fashion in one article. But many of us are not so much interested in the details of the theory as in its underlying logic, and of that one can get a rough idea from some simplified examples.

Among games of strategy, it is convenient to distinguish between games of pure chance and what we shall call games with strategic uncertainty. In a game of pure chance (e.g., dice) whether a player wins or loses, and how much, depends only on his own choices and on luck. In a game with strategic uncertainty (e.g., poker) he must think about an additional factor: What will the other fellow do? Our main interest is in games involving strategic uncertainty, but we shall find them easier to understand if we first devote some attention to how one might apply general principles of 'rational' conduct to games of pure chance.

Suppose that I am invited to place a bet on the outcome of a simultaneous throw of two dice: I will be paid $10 if two aces (single dots) show, otherwise I shall have to pay $1. Should I accept the bet? To answer, we start by doing a little computing. On the average a double ace will appear once in 36 throws. Hence I can expect that in 36 throws I shall win $10 once and lose $1 35 times. The 'mathematical expectation' would be a loss of $25, about 69 cents per throw. If all I cared about was the mathematical odds, I would obviously refuse to bet on such terms, since my expectation when not playing is zero—which is better than minus 69 cents! In fact, if I cared only about the mathematical expectation, I would insist that if I am to pay $1 whenever I lose, I ought to be paid at least $35 when the two aces come up; for only then would I be, in terms of my expectation, no worse off than if I refrained from betting.

But we know that people do make bets on a roulette wheel or in a lottery where their expectation is negative, i.e., where, on the average, they must expect to lose. Of course, one could say that this only shows how irrational they are. Yet simple examples will show that a reasonable person will sometimes refuse a bet with a positive expectation and accept one with a negative expectation.

Imagine, for instance, a rich man who has walked far from his house, is tired and plans to take a bus home. The bus fare is 20 cents and it so happens he has only 20 cents in his pocket. At this point someone offers him the following bet: A coin will be tossed; if heads come up, he will be paid $1, if tails come up, he will have to pay 20 cents. In other words, he is offered five to one on what should be an even money bet. Yet we can be pretty sure that the rich man would not be lured into the game, for winning a dollar would mean very little to him, but having to walk home would be a darned nuisance.

Thus the amount of money one can expect to win or lose per throw is not all that matters. What does matter is the amount of satisfaction (or discomfort) associated with the possible outcome of a gamble. If one is willing to measure satisfaction in numerical units, there is a way to explain the rich man's decision in mathematical terms. Suppose that walking home would mean to him a loss of five units of satisfaction while winning a dollar would mean a gain of only three units of satisfaction. In units of satisfaction rather than in dollars his expectation on each toss of the coin would be negative.

On the other hand, the expectation in terms of satisfaction units may be positive when that in terms of dollars is negative. Imagine that it costs $2 to buy a ticket in a lottery where there is one chance in a million of winning a million dollars. Since one would have to bet $2 a million times in order to win a million dollars once, on the average, the expectation here is minus one million dollars, or minus $1 per drawing. But to a person with drab prospects in life the gain of one million dollars might mean, say, 10 million units of satisfaction as against only four units being lost when $2 is paid out. For such an individual the outcome in a million drawings, in *satisfaction units*, would be 10 million minus four times one million, which amounts to an expectation of gain of one and a half units per drawing.

Is it meaningful to speak of satisfaction units? Isn't satisfaction an inner psychological phenomenon that defies numerical measurement? It turns out that such measurement is possible if one is willing to postulate that the individual will always try to make his decision so as to maximize the expectation. Of course we have to construct a satisfaction scale, but, as in measuring temperature, we are free to select the zero point and the unit arbitrarily. Suppose, for instance, that I locate the zero of my scale at my present money holdings and decide that a $10 gain would mean one positive satisfaction unit. Imagine, further, that I am offered $10 for a correct call on the toss of a coin at various odds and that I am unwilling to bet $8, eager to bet $4 and more or less indifferent as to betting $7 against the $10. Assuming that my behavior is consistent with choosing the course of action leading to highest expectations, it must be that to me a loss of $8 means losing more than one unit of satisfaction, a loss of $4 means losing less than one unit of satisfaction and a loss of $7 is just about equivalent to one unit of satisfaction. Thus my satisfaction scale can be constructed by experimental methods.

In what follows the numbers in our examples can be interpreted as units of satisfaction. But readers who feel some reluctance to indulge in satisfaction measurement may prefer to think of the units as dollars.

The idea of computing expectations in terms of satisfaction units dates back at least to Daniel Bernoulli, who in the first half of the eighteenth century formulated a concept which he called the 'moral expectation.' Now the computation, with the new approach via maximizing expectations, has been put on a rigorous theoretical basis by the recent work of von Neumann and Morgenstern, Jacob Marschak, Milton Friedman, L. J. Savage, and others, while Frederick Mosteller and others have done some interesting experiments.

Let us proceed to games possessing strategic uncertainty. If you knew the chances of the other fellow's playing one way or another in a poker game, you could determine the best strategy simply by computing expectations as in a game of chance. But in most social games peeking is frowned upon. It is precisely this lack of knowledge as to the opponent's probable strategy that gives poker its additional element of uncertainty and makes it so exciting.

In order to get a better picture of the problem, we shall consider an artificially simple game. Jones plays against Smith. Jones is to choose one of the three letters A, B, or C; Smith, one of the four Roman numerals I, II, III, or IV. Each writes his choice on a slip of paper and then the choices are compared. A payment is made according to the table below. The figure zero means that neither pays; a positive number means that Smith pays that amount to Jones; a negative number, that Jones pays Smith. Thus if Jones chooses A and Smith chooses II, for example, Smith pays Jones $100.

		Smith's choice			
		I	II	III	IV
	A	−200	100	300	−2
Jones's choice	B	0	−1,000	1,000	0
	C	1	2	3	4

Let us put ourselves in Jones's shoes and see how he might make his choice. If he peeked and knew what Smith had chosen, the answer would be simple; for instance, if he knew Smith had selected II, he would choose A, because C would get him only $2 and if he chose B, he would have to pay Smith $1,000. Suppose that Jones happens to know only that Smith has eliminated III and IV and the chances are even as between I and II. If he played A, his expectation would then be minus 50 (dividing minus 200 plus 100 by 2); if he played B, it would be minus 500 (0 minus 1,000 divided by 2); if he played

C, the expectation would be $1\frac{1}{2}$ (1 plus 2 divided by 2). Thus in terms of the expectation, C is the best choice.

But ordinarily Jones will have no such information. Nonetheless there are principles which can guide his play; we shall present a few of them. The first is 'the principle of insufficient reason,' associated with the names of the mathematicians Thomas Bayes and Pierre-Simon de Laplace. This principle would require that Jones behave as if Smith were equally likely to make any of his four choices. He would compute his expectations on that basis, and would find that if he chose A his expectation would be 49.5, for B it would be 0 and for C it would be 2.5, Thus A would be the best choice.

If Jones is an optimist, he might make his choice on the basis of another principle we shall call 'visualize the best.' In that case he would choose B, because it offers the opportunity for the largest pay-off ($1,000).

On the other hand, Jones may be a conservative man, even a pessimist. It would then be natural for him to follow the 'visualize the worst' principle, named by mathematicians 'minimax,' because it amounts to minimizing the maximum possible loss—the principle suggested, as we have seen, by Wald.

Jones would then choose C, for while it affords no possibility of a large gain, its 'worst' is a gain of 1.

Similar computations on Smith's behalf would show that the principle of insufficient reason and the 'visualize the best' principle lead to the choice of II, while 'visualize the worst' favors I. We should note that under no principle would it make sense for Smith to choose IV, because I is superior to IV if Jones chooses A or C and just as good as IV if Jones's choice is B. In the jargon of the decision theory, IV is 'inadmissible.' Similar comparison shows that III also is inadmissible. Thus the principle of insufficient reason, postulating that all four of Smith's choices are equally likely, is actually ruled out for Jones; he knows that Smith will never play III or IV.

Suppose that Smith knows Jones to be of the 'visualize the best' school. He can collect $1,000 from Jones by playing II, anticipating that Jones will play B according to the optimistic principle. On the other hand, if Jones gets wind of this reasoning by Smith, he may switch to A and win $100. Thus a stable pattern of behavior is not likely to be established.

But things are strikingly different when both players visualize the worst, so that Jones plays C and Smith plays I. In this case it makes no difference whether the two players know each other's strategy; they can still do no better than play C and I, respectively. In other words, the 'visualize the worst' principle apparently is spy-proof—if either Player had hired a spy to find out the other's strategy, he would have wasted his money.

Now it is easy to construct a game (see table on the next page) in which this principle seemingly is not spy-proof. For instance, suppose we give each player only two choices—the first two choices of the preceding game, with the same pay-off schedule. In the new game if both players visualize the worst Jones will choose A and Smith I. But now if Jones knows that Smith is operating on this principle, he will switch to B, because he would lose $200 by playing A and break even by playing B. Certainly Smith has good reason to guard against espionage.

		Smith's choice	
		I	II
Jones's choice	A	−200	100
	B	0	−1,000

So it seems that the 'visualize the worst' policy is not always spy-proof after all. But at this point one of the most ingenious ideas of the theory of games enters the stage. The idea is to let chance play a role in the choice of strategy, that is, to use a randomized or 'mixed' strategy.

Suppose that Jones marks A on 10 slips of paper and B on three slips, then mixes them up very thoroughly and proceeds to draw blindly to determine his play. What is his expectation? On the average he will play A 10 times and B 3 times in 13 games. If Smith were to play I all the time, Jones would lose 200 units 10 times and break even 3 times, thus losing 2,000. If Smith were to play II all the time, in 13 games Jones would, on the average, gain 100 units 10 times and lose 1,000 units 3 times; the total net loss again would be 2,000. Were Smith to alternate between I and II, whether according to a system or at random, Jones's expectation would still be minus 2,000 for 13 games. Thus his randomized strategy would yield the same result no matter what Smith did—and the result would be better than the worst he could expect (a loss of 200 per game) if he played A all the time, which, on the 'visualize the worst' principle, is the best of the 'pure' (non-randomized) strategies.

This example shows that a mixed strategy may be better than the best pure strategy. It does not, of course, imply that any strategy using random choices has this property. The fact that the slips were marked A and B in the ratio 10 to 3 was of crucial importance. Had there been 5 As and 5 Bs to draw from, for instance, the outcome would have been inferior to playing 'pure' A. It can be shown by algebraic computation that the 10-to-3 ratio yields the optimal strategy for Jones.

Let us now recall that what started us on the investigation of the mixed strategies was the fact that Smith's best 'pure' strategy, namely I, was not spy-proof. With mixed strategies in the picture, has the situation changed? To answer the question we must first find Smith's optimal strategy, which turns out, like Jones's, to be of the mixed variety; in his case he must play I and II in the ratio 11 to 2. On the assumption that Jones plays A, this mixture gives Smith the expectation of a gain of 2,000 units in 13 games (11 times 200 plus 2 times minus 100). And his expectation is exactly the same if he assumes that Jones will play B; Smith then wins 1,000 twice and breaks even 11 times for a total gain of 2,000 in 13 games. Indeed, it would make no difference if Jones were to alternate, in any manner whatsoever, between A and B. Thus Smith's strategy is spy-proof in the sense that it would not help Jones to know that Smith was playing I and II in the ratio 11 to 2; Jones could still do no better than play 10 As to 3 Bs.

The preceding example illustrates a general phenomenon discovered and proved by von Neumann: in 'zero-sum' two-person games (i.e., in games where the amount lost by one player equals the amount gained by the other) the 'visualize the worst' principle is spy-proof provided mixed strategies are not disregarded.

Let us go back to Columbus and see whether the theory of games would have helped him in his dilemma, or at least how it might have formulated the problem for him. We start by setting up in table form Columbus' two possible choices (to turn back or keep going), the uncertain factual alternatives (that land was near or not near) and the probable consequences of Columbus' decisions in either case.

		Actual location of land	
		Land near	No land near
Columbus' decision	Turn back	Probable later disappointment	Life saved
	Keep going	Prospect of glory	Prospect of death

Now as an experimental approach, suppose we assign very hypothetical and preliminary values in satisfaction units to the various consequences (see table below). That is to say, let us assume that Columbus, attempting to envisage how disappointed he would feel if he later learned that he had turned back on the verge of discovering land, appraises this disappointment as a loss of 50 satisfaction units; that he values the saving of life by turning back from a hopeless quest as a gain of 20 satisfaction units, and so on.

		Actual location of land	
		Land near	No land near
Columbus' decision	Turn back	−50	20
	Keep going	100	−1,000

Let us also make one further assumption: that Columbus feels he can make some kind of estimate as to the probability of land being near. If he supposed that the chances of land being near were 3 to 1, he would compute the expectation of 'satisfaction' (actually dissatisfaction!) from turning back as follows: 3 times minus 50 added to 1 times 20 and the sum divided by 4—i.e., minus 32.5. In other words, if he turns back, the net expectation is a loss of 32.5 satisfaction units. On the other hand, if he keeps going, the expectation is a loss of 175 satisfaction units (3 times 100 added to 1 times minus 1,000 and the sum divided by 4). Since the expectation of loss in going on is so much greater than that in turning back, Columbus' decision would be: better turn back. On the basis of the satisfaction values we have postulated, it would have taken a probability of 9 to 1 that land was near to induce Columbus to keep going.

Would he actually have insisted on such high odds in favor of success? If not, it must be that the satisfaction units we have assigned to the various possible consequences are unrealistic; perhaps we have overvalued Columbus' fear of death and undervalued his eagerness for the prize of discovery. We may therefore construct another table of values which might be considered more realistic (see below). On this new basis, a probability of 3 to 1 that land was near would have been sufficient to make Columbus decide to keep going.

		Actual location of land	
		Land near	No land near
Columbus' decision	Turn back	−1,000	20
	Keep going	500	−500

But what if he had no idea as to the chances of land being near? The theory of games and decision-making would still have offered him several means of calculating his expectations. He might have followed the principle of insufficient reason, the strategy of 'visualize the best' or the strategy of 'visualize the worst.' On the basis of the satisfaction figures in our last table Columbus would have found it worthwhile to keep going no matter which of these principles he applied. But on the basis of the first figures he would have turned back unless he belonged to the 'visualize the best' school—which may not be too unrealistic an assumption.

It may seem strange that principles for making decisions should be served cafeteria style—take your choice. Is there not some way of proving that only one of these principles is truly rational? A great deal of thought has been devoted to this problem, mainly via attempts to find logical flaws or paradoxes which would eliminate one or another of the principles from consideration. For instance, it has been argued that nature, being presumably non-malicious and not out to inflict maximum loss on its 'opponents' (investigators), might well use an 'inadmissible' strategy though a smart player would not. Also, some argue that there is no need for spy-proofing against nature, and this raises doubts as to whether a principle leading to the use of randomized strategies is reasonable. In defense of the rationality of randomized decision-making, one is tempted to recall Rabelais's Judge Bridlegoose, who decided lawsuits by the throw of dice and was known for his wisdom and fairness until his failing eyesight made him commit errors in reading the spots. (Less facetious arguments in favor of randomized decision-making also are available!)

The development of methods for rational decision-making where uncertainties exist certainly has a long way to go. The field is still rife with differences of opinion. Nevertheless, it is highly instructive to study the tools we have, and particularly to notice how often the various principles, despite the difference of their underlying assumptions, all lead to very similar if not identical conclusions as to the best decision to take in a given situation.

25

Book Review: *The Theory of Value*

The Theory of Value: An Axiomatic Analysis of Economic Equilibrium by Gerard Debreu (1959), Cowles Foundation for Research in Economics Monograph 17. New York: Wiley. Pp. ix, 114. $4.75.

The main theme of this uniquely structured piece of work is competitive equilibrium in its static aspects. Of the seven chapters, Chapter 5 deals with the existence, Chapter 6 with the optimality properties, of such an equilibrium. Chapter 7 may be viewed as a sample of the technique of applying the abstract results to situations (here, uncertainty) not covered by the more narrow interpretations of the concept of a commodity. The conventional interpretations of the concept, including their possible differentiation as to time, place, etc., together with the corresponding price concepts, including interests rates, are provided in Chapter 2. Chapters 3 and 4 are devoted respectively to production and consumption, with complete concentration on those phenomena which are of direct relevance for the problems of the existence and optimality of the competitive equilibrium. Chapter 1 provides the mathematical background for the remainder of the book.

   The interest of the economic theorist in the rigorous analysis of the competitive equilibrium, pioneered by Walras and Pareto, has had its ups and downs during recent decades. The thirties, although marked by focus on phenomena difficult to fit into the framework of the perfectly competitive model (monopolistic competition, involuntary unemployment), also witnessed a renewed interest in the logical structure of the classical model (if only for comparison with the Keynesian), and, quite independently, the first application (by Abraham Wald)[1] of rigorous modern mathematics to the problem of existence of the competitive equilibrium.

Reprinted from *American Economic Review*, 1961, 51(3): 414–17.

[1] See Wald (1936).—SB

Book Review: The Theory of Value In: *The Collected Papers of Leonid Hurwicz Volume 1.* Edited by Samiran Banerjee, Oxford University Press. © Oxford University Press 2022. DOI: 10.1093/oso/9780199313280.003.0025

In the decade following the second world war the problem of existence was attacked afresh and the use of powerful mathematical techniques has led to results of impressive generality. Without undertaking the dangerous task of apportioning historical merit to the various outstanding contributors (among them McKenzie, Gale, Nikaido, and Uzawa) it is proper to note the crucial role played by the Arrow-Debreu (1954) paper (and a series of papers published by Debreu between 1951 and 1956. The existence theorem given by Debreu in the monograph [(1) in section 5.7, pp. 83–84] corresponds very closely to Theorem I of the 1954 Arrow-Debreu paper. Except for telegraphically compressed comments in the Notes (pp. 88–89), no attempt is made to present the most powerful results already available at the time the book was written. This is due to the author's stated policy of minimizing the cost of erecting the required axiomatic structure.

The chapter on optimality contains two results: on the optimality of the equilibria, and on the 'reachability' (static) of optima through the competitive equilibria section (6.3, p. 94 and 6.4, p. 95, respectively); the formulation is very close to that of Debreu's 1954 paper on the subject which in turn is a lineal descendant of the basic paper by Arrow (1950),[2] with the work of Lange, Koopmans, Allais, and Debreu also in the background. Here again the results presented are not as general as those contained in the author's own earlier work.

This renunciation of generality, added to the monograph's other self-imposed limitations (e.g., exclusion of monopoly, dynamics, external [dis]economies, indivisibilities), points up the author's chief objective: the construction of a rigorous, self-contained axiomatic structure leading to certain basic propositions of economic theory.

In order to accomplish this, a sharp distinction is drawn throughout between parts of the formal structure and their interpretation. Thus, after seven and a half pages devoted to the discussion of commodities and prices (which, by the standards of this monograph, is an extreme in talkativeness), the following is a complete formal summary: "The number l of commodities is a positive integer. An action a of an agent is a point of R^l, the commodity space. A price system p is a point of R^l. The value of an action a relative to a price system p is the inner product $p \cdot a$." And then the author adds: "All that precedes this statement is irrelevant for the logical development of the theory" (p. 35).

To attain the logical rigor, all of the economist's terms of discourse are systematically defined with the help of the mathematical vocabulary introduced in Chapter 1. Thus production is described in terms of certain subsets

---

2 Most probably, this is a reference to an earlier version of Arrow (1951).—SB

of a finite-dimensional Euclidean space (interpretation: feasible production sets, commodity space), consumption in terms of certain sets (interpretation: consumption possible aside from budget limitations) and binary relations (interpretation: preferences).

In turn, the mathematical vocabulary is introduced in a manner that uses relatively few primitive terms (e.g., set) and (taking for granted the machinery of logic) defines other terms (e.g., cone) in terms of the earlier ones. One's first reaction may be that the author should have referred his readers to standard texts in mathematics, rather than resorted to such complete coverage. Actually, had he attempted this, he would not have saved many of the twenty-four pages devoted to the exposition of mathematics, given his determination to state explicitly every one of the notational and terminological conventions and all the mathematical theorems used in the remainder of the work. Thanks to this procedure we are not in doubt as to the notational distinction between the empty set and the origin; similarly, while the term 'preordering' may seem strange or unnatural, its consistent use and the availability of a formal definition in Chapter 1 eliminates ambiguity from the assumptions on preferences in Chapter 4.

One should be clear, of course, that most of present-day mathematical economics work is done in a similar spirit of rigor and completeness, but Debreu's *Theory of Value* is unique in its uncompromising devotion to maintaining the clarity and rigor of the axiomatic structure even at the expense of other objectives. One detects the influence of the contemporary classic exposition of modern mathematics in the *Éléments de Mathématique* whose authorship is officially ascribed to the non-existent Bourbaki. It may not be out of place, therefore, to point out that the existence of Gerard Debreu as a flesh and blood individual is firmly established, although without the benefit of the axiomatic method.

That Debreu should have succeeded in his methodological objective gives his book significance that transcends the particular competitive equilibrium theorems on which he has concentrated. But there is a heavy price to be paid for this success. As modern communication theory teaches, there is value in redundance; its absence from the monograph (especially in proofs of theorems) makes for extremely difficult reading of crucial sections, and the occasional effort at motivating the proof (e.g., the last two paragraphs of Section 5.6) seems to presuppose a degree of insight that would make the explanations given almost superfluous.

While brevity of terms is a virtue, and the use of new terms minimizes the danger of confusion due to the reader's (possibly inaccurate) preconceptions, one feels that it would have been reasonably safe to mention that "equilibrium of the private ownership economy" (p. 79) corresponds to 'competitive equilibrium' as used by most authors, or that 'optimality' of Chapter 6 is the familiar 'Pareto-optimality.'

The didactic value of the monograph would have been increased immeasurably, had the author provided some examples in the crucial Chapters 5 and 6. It would have been nice to have a model in which, for instance, all the assumptions of the main existence theorem are satisfied and the equilibrium prices and quantities exhibited. But, more important, one's understanding of the problem would have been greatly deepened by examples lacking equilibrium due to the failure of one or another of the assumptions. If, as I hope, there is to be a second edition of this monograph (and I realize that this suggestion alone is enough to make an author into a mortal enemy), a provision of such examples would be a boon to those among us who do not merit Debreu's flattering estimate of our skill in 'making up our own', and I feel certain that even Bourbaki would not disapprove.

Any feelings of unhappiness one may have with regard to the deliberate austerity and exclusions that characterize Debreu's *Theory of Value* are of minor significance as against the usefulness and beauty of the high-precision instrument it contains. It would not surprise me if it turned out to be one of the few classics produced in our period.

References

Arrow, K. (1951) An extension of the basic theorems of classical welfare economics, in *Proceedings of the Second Berkeley Symposium on Mathematical Statistics and Probability*, ed. J. Neyman, 507–32. Berkeley, CA: University of California Press.

Bourbaki, N. (1939) *Éléments de Mathématique*. Paris: Hermann.

Debreu, G. (1954) Valuation equilibrium and Pareto optimum, *Proceedings of the National Academy of the Sciences*, 40(7): 588–92.

Arrow, K. and G. Debreu (1954) Existence of an equilibrium for a competitive economy, *Econometrica*, 22(3): 265–90.

Wald, A. (1936) Über einige Gleichungssysteme der mathematischen Ökonomie, *Zeitschrift für Nationalökonomie*, 7(5): 637–70, translated as Wald, A. (1951) On some systems of equations of mathematical economics, *Econometrica*, 19(4): 368–403.

Editor's Postscript

On March 13, 1961, Hurwicz wrote a letter to Debreu:

Dear Gerard:

Every few years (which, for me, means 'frequently') I am forced to write a letter asking for an explanation that a competent mathematician could answer by himself. I hope you don't feel too annoyed.

After a page and half of technical questions regarding Debreu's assumptions and seeking clarification on a couple of papers, the letter ends with:

Please give my best regards to your family. I still shudder (as you must have at the time) when I think of the terrible stories with which your guests (but I myself especially) attempted to ruin what, nevertheless, turned out to be a most delectable evening at your home.

Yours,
Leo

Attached to Hurwicz's letter is a reply from December 1, 1961, which suggests that perhaps Debreu did not respond to his set of questions:

Dear Leo:

You probably gave up long ago any hope of seeing my discussion paper on quasi-equilibria. I am therefore delighted to surprise you with the news that it was mailed to you yesterday. [...]

If CFDP[3] 130 does not answer all your questions of last winter, you must prod me without mercy.

This is my first letter to you since I read your review of monograph 17. I must therefore reassure you that you have not made me into a mortal enemy.

Cordially yours,
Gerard

---

[3] Cowles Foundation Discussion Paper.—SB

26

A Voting System Reform Proposal
to Provide for Minority Representation

That the limited vote should have been adopted for a considerable number of uses in this country and several others, where true representation was desired, is a good example of men's astonishing laziness in these matters of voting. If a twentieth part of the thought that has been devoted to advertising patent medicines during the last century had been put on voting, which is the very basis of modern governments, such a makeshift as the limited vote would scarcely have been used anywhere. Yet often, because of the unwillingness of most people to consider anything very different from what they were accustomed to, the limited vote has been the best that could be got.

C. G. Hoag and G. H. Hallett, Jr. (1926)

The motivation for this proposal stems from the observed bitterness that is engendered by the present system of electing district and state convention delegates from the various wards under the prevailing 'winner take all' system. When a division develops, as, for instance, Keith-Rolvaag in 1966, the Vietnam issue in 1968, or Naftalin-Roe a few years earlier, there are typically two slates and the losers feel shut out from party activities even if they have been loyal and effective leaders or workers for many years. This may happen even if in a given ward the prevailing side has only 51% of the caucus votes. As a result, large groups become strongly disaffected just at the time when elections come. Consequently, the DFL is seriously weakened. Similar resentment develops in connection with the election of national convention

Mimeo dated April 18, 1969, presented to the Minnesota DFL (Democratic-Farmer-Labor Party) Constitutional Reform Committee, courtesy the David M. Rubenstein Rare Book and Manuscript Library, Duke University. The proposal formed the basis of the 'walking subcaucus' system that was adopted to elect delegates in proportion to their support, with the idea of protecting the rights of minority groups to elect delegates representing their interests. Details of the walking subcaucus system can be found at https://en.wikipedia.org/wiki/Walking_subcaucus. The quote is from the 1926 book, *Proportional Representation* by Hoag and Hallett, published by Macmillan, New York.

delegates, whether from the congressional districts or at large (by the state convention).

The remedy, in my view, is to change to a system that would tend to provide minority representation in the ward delegations to the state and district conventions, as well as in the delegations from districts and at large to the national convention. However, I recognize that the problem of electing national convention delegates has special ramifications and should be handled separately. In what follows, therefore, I shall deal exclusively with elections of state and district delegates from wards (or counties).[1]

In designing a voting system one must recognize the need for a fair representation for different points of view, but also the danger of excessive fragmentation of the party into smaller splinter groups. Furthermore, one must bear in mind the practical difficulties of handling complex vote counting procedures under the pressures of a typical caucus night and often by inexperienced persons. For both of these reasons it is difficult to advocate the system that gives the closest approach to proportional representation, namely the so-called Hare system ('single transferable vote') in which each voter indicates his order of preference among as many candidates as are to be elected.

Since the dividing lines and issues change from year to year one must also rule out systems based on 'list' voting. In fact, there may sometimes be several complete slates, while at other times only separate names are place[d] in nomination.

Under these circumstances two methods of protecting minority representation deserve particular consideration: *cumulative* voting and *limited* voting.

Under *cumulative voting*, each voter has as many votes as there are delegates to be elected and he can distribute these as he wishes. For instance, if eight delegates are to be elected from the ward, each voter has the choice of giving eight votes to one candidate, or one vote to each of the candidates, or five votes to Smith and three to Jones.[2]

Under the *limited vote* system, each voter has fewer votes than the number of candidates to be elected. For instance, the rule could be that each voter can vote for a number of names that is approximately 75% of the delegates to be elected.[3] For instance, if eight are to be elected, he could vote for up to six names. In such a situation, if the ward had two well-organized factions, one

---

[1] The principles of reform would be the same for a reform of the model of electing the national delegates from districts or at large.

[2] This could be accomplished either by writing on the ballot 'Smith 5, Jones 3' or by writing 'Smith, Smith, Smith, Smith, Smith, Jones, Jones, Jones'. In either case counting ballots is no more difficult than under the present system.

[3] Some other percentage figure could be chosen, say 67%. However, since the minority may have anywhere between 49% and 1%, it seems reasonable to give it a chance of electing, on the average, 25% of the delegates.

could assume that each would field six candidates; the majority faction would then elect all of its six candidates, the minority two. This would admittedly result in either over- or under-representation for the minority, depending on whether it had less or more than 25% of the votes, but such discrepancies might cancel out on the average, at present the minority is always under-represented, with average under-representation of 25%.

Of course, if there are only as many candidates as positions to be filled, they are declared elected and there is no problem. But it is true that even a very small minority would get representation under the limited vote system; if desired, this could be avoided by specifying that a candidate must have at least 10% of the vote to be elected. However, I would not advocate such a restriction.[4]

It should also be realized that if the majority faction is large enough and extremely well-disciplined, it can split into subgroups and so capture all positions. For instance, if there were three delegates to be elected and each voter was given two votes, the majority could capture all three delegateships if it had over 60% of the votes and was sufficiently organized to split into three subgroups each of which would be instructed to vote for specified two candidates. However, the probability of such a high level of discipline among Minnesota's DFLers seems small. In any case, the system would still be more favorable to minorities than the present one.

The limited voting system would also work well to provide a fair representation for different points of view in the absence of any organized slates. On the other hand, if there were three slates, the smallest of the three would still tend to remain unrepresented. Those who are concerned about excessive fragmentation may regard this as an advantage.

As between the limited and the cumulative vote, I lean toward the limited vote, but I would choose either in preference to the present 'winner take all' system.

Since 75% will not always be a whole number, one would have to use closest possible approximations. The following table shows how this might be done:

Number of delegates to be elected	Maximum number of candidates a voter can vote for
3	2
4	3
5	4
6	4 or 5
7	5
8	6
9	7
10	7 or 8

[4] In this case the appropriate percentage would be 70% and each voter would list his secondary choices as well.

381

27

Publications of Leonid Hurwicz

Books

[1] *Studies in Linear and Non-Linear Programming*, ed. Kenneth J. Arrow, Leonid Hurwicz, and Hirofumi Uzawa. Stanford University Press, 1958. Translated into Russian by E. G. Goldstein, Foreign Literature Publisher, 1962.

[2] *Preferences, Utility, and Demand*, ed. John S. Chipman, Leonid Hurwicz, Marcel K. Richter, and Hugo Sonnenschein, Harcourt Brace Jovanovich, Inc., 1971.

[3] *Patents, Invention, and Economic Change.* by Jacob Schmookler, ed. Zvi Griliches and Leonid Hurwicz. Harvard University Press, 1972.

[4] *Studies in Resource Allocation Processes*, ed. Kenneth J. Arrow and Leonid Hurwicz. Cambridge University Press, 1977.

[5] *Social Goals and Social Organization: A Volume in Memory of Elisha Pazner*, ed. Leonid Hurwicz, David Schmeidler, and Hugo Sonnenschein. Cambridge University Press, 1985.

[6] *Designing Economic Mechanisms*, Leonid Hurwicz and Stanley Reiter. Cambridge University Press, 2006.

Articles

1940s

[1943a] Review of *The Analysis of Economic Time Series* by Harold T. Davis, *American Economic Review*, 33(2): 399–401.

[1943b] Review of *A Significance Test for Time Series and Other Ordered Observations* by W. Allen Wallis and Geoffrey H. Moore, *American Economic Review*, 33(2): 401–402.

[1944] Stochastic models of economic fluctuations, *Econometrica*, 12(2): 114–24. Reprinted in *The Probability Approach to Simultaneous Equations*, ed. Omar Hamouda and J. C. R. Rowley (1997), pp. 118–28. Lyme, NH: Elgar. Also in *Landmark Papers in Economic Fluctuations, Economic Policy and Related Subjects*, ed. Lawrence R. Klein (2001), pp. 331–41. Lyme, NH: Elgar.

[1945a] Forecasting post war demand: Discussion, *Econometrica*, 13(1): 55.

[1945b] Aspects of the theory of economic fluctuations, (abstract), *Econometrica*, 13(1): 79.

[1945c] The theory of economic behavior, *American Economic Review*, 35(5): 909–25. Reprinted in *Readings in Price Theory*, ed. Kenneth Boulding and George Stigler (1952), 505–26. Chicago, IL: Irwin; *The World of Mathematics, Volume 2*, ed. James R. Newman (1956), 1267–83. New York, NY: Simon and Schuster; and in the 60th anniversary edition of *Theory of Games and Economic Behavior*, by John von Neumann and Oskar Morgenstern (2004), 646–64. Princeton, NJ: Princeton University Press. Chapter 21 this volume.

[1946a] Theory of the Firm and Investment, *Econometrica*, 14(2): 109–36. Reprinted in *Landmark Papers in Economic Fluctuations, Economic Policy and Related Subjects*, ed. Lawrence R. Klein (2001), 342–69. Lyme, NH: Elgar.

[1946b] Sampling Aspects of Structural Estimation and Prediction I: Model and Definitions, (abstract) *Econometrica*, 14(2): 167–70.

[1946c] Review of *Time Series Analysis* by Lewis Maverick, *Journal of the American Statistical Association*, 41(234): 254–55.

[1947a] Estimation of economic relationships and multivariate regressions, (abstract) *Econometrica*, 15(2): 160.

[1947b] Business cycles and secular stagnation, (abstract), *Econometrica*, 15(2): 168–69.

[1947c] Some problems arising in estimating economic relations, *Econometrica*, 15(3): 236–40.

[1947d] Review of *Measuring Business Cycles* by Arthur F. Burns and Wesley C. Mitchell, *Journal of the American Statistical Association*, 42(239): 461–67.

[1948a] Book review of *The Theory of Games and Economic Behavior*, by John von Neumann and Oskar Morgenstern, *Annals of Mathematical Statistics*, 19(3): 436–37. Chapter 22 this volume.

[1948b] Errors and Shocks in Economic Relationships (with T. W. Anderson), (abstract), *Econometrica*, 16(1): 36–37; and (1949) 17(Supplement): 23–25, and in *Bulletin of the International Statistical Institute*, 31(5): 23–25.

[1949] Linear programming and general theory of optimal behavior, (abstract), *Econometrica*, 17(2): 161–62.

1950s

[1950a] Generalization of the concept of identification, in *Statistical Inference in Dynamic Economic Models*, ed. Tjalling Koopmans, 245–57. New York, NY: John Wiley.

[1950b] Prediction and least squares, ibid., 266–300.

[1950c] Variable parameters in stochastic processes: Trend and seasonality, ibid., 329–44.

[1950d] Least-squares bias in time series, ibid., 365–83.

[1950e] Systems with nonadditive disturbances, ibid., 410–18.

[1950f] Some implications of electronic thinking organisms, *Current Economic Comment*, 12(2): 3–6.

[1950g] A theory of stabilizing business fluctuations, (abstract), *Econometrica*, 18(3): 278–79.

[1950h] Survey of econometrics, *Bulletin de l'Institut International de Statistique*, 32(2): 125–31.

[1951a] Theory of economic organization, (abstract), *Econometrica*, 19(1): 54.

[1951b] Comment on 'Business cycle analysis and public policy' by Arthur Smithies, in *Conference on Business Cycles*, 416–20. New York, NY: National Bureau of Economic Research.

[1951c] Some specification problems and applications to econometric models, (abstract), *Econometrica*, 19(3): 343–44.

[1952a] Dynamic aspects of achieving optimal allocation of resources (with Kenneth J. Arrow), (abstract), *Econometrica*, 20(1): 86–87.

[1952b] Aggregation in macroeconomic models, (abstract), *Econometrica*, 20(3): 489–90.

[1953] What has happened to the theory of games? *American Economic Review*, 43(2): 398–405. Reprinted in *The Foundations of Game Theory, Volume 1*, ed. Mary Ann Dimand and Robert W. Dimand (1997), 401–408. Lyme, NH: Elgar. Chapter 23 this volume.

[1954] A test of a proposition in the theory of choice (with Papandreou, Andreas G., Owen H. Sauerlender, Oswald H. Brownlee, and William Franklin), (abstract), *Econometrica*, September 1954, 23(3): 333–34; published as [1957d].

[1955a] Game theory and decisions, *Scientific American*, 192(2): 78–83. Translated into Italian as La teoria dei giochi e le decisioni, *L'Industria* 2: 261–68. Chapter 24 this volume.

[1955b] Decentralized resource allocation, (abstract), *Econometrica*, 23(3): 342–43.

[1955c] Input-output analysis and economic structure: A review article, *American Economic Review*, 45(4): 626–36. Correction: 45(5): 945.

[1956a] Reduction of constrained maxima to saddle-point problems (with Kenneth J. Arrow) in *Proceedings of the Third Berkeley Symposium on Mathematical Statistics and Probability*, ed. Jerzy Neyman, 1–20. Berkeley, CA: University of California Press. Reprinted in [4], 154–77.

[1956b] Programming in linear spaces, (abstract), *Econometrica*, 24(2): 208.

[1957a] Gradient methods for constrained maxima (with Kenneth J. Arrow), *Operations Research*, 5(2): 258–65. Reprinted in [4], 146–53.

[1957b] Resource allocation as a dynamic process, (abstract), *Econometrica*, 25(2): 352–53.

[1957c] External diseconomies and the possibility of decentralization, (abstract), *Econometrica*, 25(4): 599–600. Longer version published as [1971a].

[1957d] *A Test of a Stochastic Theory of Choice* (with Papandreou, Andreas G., Owen H. Sauerlender, Oswald H. Brownlee, and William Franklin). Berkeley, CA: University of California Publications in Economics, 16(1), 18p.

[1958a] Programming in linear spaces, in [1], 38–102.

[1958b] A note on the Lagrangian saddle-points (with Hirofumi Uzawa), in [1], 103–13.

[1958c] Gradient method for concave programming, I: Local results, (with Kenneth J. Arrow) in [1]: 117–26.

[1958d] Gradient method for concave programming, III: Further global results and applications to resource allocation (with Kenneth J. Arrow), in [1], pp. 133–45.

[1958e] On the stability of the competitive equilibrium I (with Kenneth J. Arrow), *Econometrica*, 26(4): 522–52. Reprinted in [4], 199–228; in *Microeconomics: Theoretical and Applied, Volume 3*, ed. Robert Kuenne (1991), 213–43. Lyme, NH: Elgar; and in *General Equilibrium Theory, Volume 1*, ed. Gerard Debreu (1996), 64–94. Lyme, NH: Elgar.

[1958f] On the stability of the competitive equilibrium II (with Kenneth J. Arrow and H. D. Block), *Econometrica*, 27(1): 82–109. Reprinted in [4], 228–55; and in *General Equilibrium Theory, Volume 1*, ed. Gerard Debreu (1996), 95–122. Lyme, NH: Elgar.

[1959] Review of *The Investment Decision: An Empirical Study* by John R. Meyer and Edwin Kuh, *American Economic Review*, 49(1): 152–69.

1960s

[1960a] Optimality and informational efficiency in resource allocation processes, in *Mathematical Methods in the Social Sciences*, ed. Kenneth J. Arrow, Samuel Karlin, and Patrick Suppes, 27–46. Palo Alto: Stanford University Press. Reprinted in *Readings in Welfare Economics*, ed. Kenneth J. Arrow and Tibor Scitovsky, 61–80. Chicago, IL: Irwin; and in [4], 393–412.

[1960b] Competitive stability under weak gross substitutability: The 'Euclidean distance' approach (with Kenneth J. Arrow), *International Economic Review*, 1(1): 38–49. Reprinted in [4], pp. 265–75; and in *Critical Ideas in Economics, Volume 2*, ed. Donald A. Walker, 181–92. Lyme, NH: Elgar.

[1960c] Some remarks on the equilibria of economic systems (with Kenneth J. Arrow), *Econometrica*, 28(3): 640–46. Reprinted in [4], 258–64.

[1960d] Decentralization and computation in resource allocation (with Kenneth J. Arrow), in *Essays in Economics and Econometrics*, ed. Ralph W. Pfouts, 34–104. Chapel Hill, NC: University of North Carolina Press. Reprinted in [4], 41–95.

[1960e] Stability of the gradient process in *n*-person games (with Kenneth J. Arrow), *Journal of the Society for Industrial and Applied Mathematics*, 8(2): 280–94. Reprinted in [4], 296–310.

[1960f] Conditions for economic efficiency of centralized and decentralized structures, in *Value and Plan: Economic Calculation and Organization in Eastern Europe*, ed. Gregory Grossman, 162–83. Berkeley, CA: University of California Press.

[1961a] Constraint qualifications in maximization problems (with Kenneth J. Arrow and Hirofumi Uzawa), *Naval Research Logistics Quarterly*, 8(2): 175–91. Reprinted in [4], 96–112.

[1961b] Book review of *Theory of Value* by Gerard Debreu, *American Economic Review*, 51(2): 414–17. Chapter 25 this volume.

[1962a] On the structural form of interdependent systems, in *Logic, Methodology, and Philosophy of Science*, ed. Ernest Nagel, Patrick Suppes, and Alfred Tarski, 232–39. Palo Alto, CA: Stanford University Press.

[1962b] Competitive stability under weak gross substitutability: Non-linear price adjustment and adaptive expectations (with Kenneth J. Arrow), *International*

Economic Review, 3(2): 233–55. Reprinted in [4], 275–95; and in *Critical Ideas in Economics, Volume 2*, ed. Donald A. Walker, 193–215. Lyme, NH: Elgar.

[1962c] Basic mathematical and statistical considerations in the study of rhythms and near-rhythms, *Annals of the New York Academy of Sciences*, 98(4): 851–57.

[1962d] Discussion: Analytic framework for measuring social costs, *Journal of Farm Economics*, 44(5): 574–79.

[1963] Mathematics in economics: Language and instrument, in *Mathematics and the Social Sciences: A Symposium*, ed. James Charlesworth, 1–11. Philadelphia, PA: American Academy of Political and Social Science.

[1967] Programming involving infinitely many variables and constraints, in *Activity Analysis in the Theory of Growth and Planning*, ed. Edmond Malinvaud and M. O. L. Bacharach, 142–49. New York, NY: St. Martin's Press.

[1969] On the concept and possibility of informational decentralization, *American Economic Review*, 59(2): 513–24. Chapter 7 this volume.

1970s

[1970] Economics: Nobel Prize awarded to Samuelson of MIT, *Science*, New Series 170(3959): 720–21.

[1971a] Centralization and decentralization in economic processes, in *Comparison of Economic Systems: Theoretical and Methodological Approaches*, ed. A. Eckstein, 79–102. Berkeley, CA: University of California Press. Reprinted in *Jahrbuch der Wirtschaft Osteuropas, Band 3*, 1972, 87–113. Chapter 8 this volume.

[1971b] On the problem of integrability of demand functions, in [3], 174–214.

[1971c] On the integrability of demand functions (with Hirofumi Uzawa), in [3], 114–48.

[1971d] Revealed preference without demand continuity assumptions (with Marcel K. Richter), in [3], 59–76.

[1972a] On informationally decentralized systems, in *Decision and Organization: A Volume in Honor of J. Marschak*, ed. Roy Radner and Bernard McGuire, 297–336. Amsterdam: North-Holland; second edition, University of Minnesota Press, 1986, 297–336. Reprinted in [4], 425–59.

[1972b] Introduction (with Zvi Griliches), in [3], xi–xii.

[1972c] Organizational structures for joint decision-making: A designer's point of view, in *Interorganizational decision-making*, ed. Matthew Tuite, Roger Chisholm, and Michael Radnor, 37–44. Chicago, IL: Aldine Publishing Co.

[1972d] On an optimality criterion for decision-making under ignorance (with Kenneth J. Arrow), in *Uncertainty and Expectations in Economics*, ed. Charles Carter and J. L. Ford, 1–11. Oxford: Blackwell. Reprinted in [4], 463–71.

[1973a] The design of resource allocation mechanisms (Richard T. Ely Lecture), *American Economic Review*, 63(2): 1–30. Reprinted in *Frontiers of Quantitative Economics*, ed. Michael D. Intriligator and David A. Kendrick, 3–42. Amsterdam: North-Holland. Reprinted in [4], 3–37. Chapter 9 this volume.

[1973b] On the boundedness of the feasible set without convexity assumptions (with Stanley Reiter), *International Economic Review*, 14(3): 580–86.

[1975a] A stochastic decentralized resource allocation process, part I (with Roy Radner and Stanley Reiter), *Econometrica*, 43(2): 187–221.

[1975b] A stochastic decentralized resource allocation process, part II (with Roy Radner and Stanley Reiter), *Econometrica*, 43(3): 363–93.

[1977a] On the dimensional requirements of informationally decentralized Pareto-satisfactory processes, in [4], 413–24.

[1977b] Convexity of asymptotic, average production possibility sets (with Hirofumi Uzawa), in [4], 185–95.

[1977c] On the stability of competitive equilibrium II: A postscript (with Arrow, Kenneth J.), in [4], 255–58.

[1977d:] Perspectives on economics, in *Perspectives on Economic Education: Proceedings from the National Conference on Needed Research and Development in Precollege Economic Education*, ed. D. R. Wentworth, W. Lee Hansen, and Sharryl H. Hawke, 21–40. New York, NY: Joint Council on Economic Education. Reprinted in *Essays in Contemporary Fields in Economics: Essays in Honor of Emanuel T. Weiler*, ed. George Horwich and James P. Quirk (1981), 290–310. West Lafayette, IN: Purdue University Press.

[1978a] Construction of outcome functions guaranteeing existence and Pareto optimality of Nash equilibria (with David Schmeidler), *Econometrica*, 46(6): 1447–74.

[1978b] Incentive structures maximizing residual gain under incomplete information (with Leonard Shapiro), *Bell Journal of Economics*, 9(1): 180–91. (A more complete version in Minnesota CER Paper #83, April 1977, 69p.)

[1978c] On informational requirements for non-wasteful resource allocation systems, in *Mathematical Models in Economics: Papers and Proceedings of a U.S.-U.S.S.R. Seminar Moscow*, ed. Sydney Shulman, 2–60. New York, NY: National Bureau of Economic Research. Reprinted with additional material as [1985d].

[1979a] On the interaction between information and incentives in organizations, in *Communication and Control in Society*, ed. Klaus Krippendorff, 123–47. London: Gordon and Breach Science Publishers. Chapter 10 this volume.

[1979b] An integrability condition, with application to utility theory and thermodynamics (with Marcel K. Richter), *Journal of Mathematical Economics*, 6(1): 7–14.

[1979c] Ville axioms and consumer theory (with Marcel K. Richter), *Econometrica*, 47(3): 603–19.

[1979d] Outcome functions yielding Walrasian and Lindahl allocations at Nash equilibrium points, *Review of Economic Studies*, 46(2): 217–25.

[1979e] On allocations attainable through Nash equilibria, *Journal of Economic Theory*, 21(1): 140–65. Reprinted in *Aggregation and Revelation of Preferences*, ed. Jean-Jacques Laffont, 397–419. Amsterdam: North-Holland.

[1979f] Socialism and incentives: Developing a framework, *Journal of Comparative Economics*, 3(3): 207–16.

[1979g] Balanced outcome functions yielding Walrasian and Lindahl allocations at Nash equilibrium points for two or more agents, in *General Equilibrium, Growth, and Trade: Essays in Honor of Lionel McKenzie*, ed. Jerry Green and José Scheinkman, 126–36. San Diego, CA: Academic Press.

1980s

[1980a] Discussion of Lucas' 'Equilibrium in a pure currency economy', in *Models of Monetary Economics*, ed. Neil Wallace and John Kareken, 147–55. Minneapolis, MN: Federal Reserve Bank of Minneapolis.

[1980b] Appendix A: Structural models in *Forecasting the Impact of Legislation On Courts*, ed. Samuel Krislov and Keith Boyum, 109–24. Washington, DC: National Academy Press.

[1981a] Commentary on H. G. Johnson's 'Networks of economists: the role in international monetary reforms' and L. R. Klein's 'Project LINK: Policy implications for the world economy', in *Knowledge and Power in a Global Society*, ed. William M. Evan, 127–30. Beverly Hills, CA: Sage Publications.

[1981b] On incentive problems in the design of non-wasteful resource allocation systems, in *Studies in Economic Theory and Practice: Essays in Honor of Edward Lipinski*, ed. by Nina Assorodobraj-Kula, et al., 93–106. Amsterdam: North-Holland.

[1983] Economic issues in the utilization of knowledge, in *The Optimum Utilization of Knowledge: Making Knowledge Serve Human Betterment*, ed. Kenneth Boulding and Lawrence Senesh, 281–94. Boulder, CO: Westview Press. Reprinted in *Dimensions of Rural Development in India: T. K. Lakshman Commemoration Volume*, ed. P. R. Brahmananda, B. K. Narayan, and A. Kalappa (1987), 1–17. Bombay: Himalaya Publishing House.

[1984] Economic planning and the knowledge problem: A comment, *The Cato Journal*, 4(2): 419–25. Reprinted in *Critical Assessments of Contemporary Economists, Volume 4*, ed. John Wood and Ronald Woods (1991), 83–88. Abingdon-on-Thames: Routledge.

[1985a] Incentive aspects of decentralization, in *Handbook of Mathematical Economics, Volume 3*, ed. Kenneth J. Arrow and Michael Intriligator, 1441–82. Amsterdam: North-Holland.

[1985b] Discrete allocation mechanisms: Dimensional requirements for resource-allocation mechanisms when desired outcomes are unbounded (with Thomas Marschak), *Journal of Complexity*, 1(2): 264–303.

[1985c] Social goals and social organization: A perspective, in [5], 1–16.

[1985d] Information and incentives in designing non-wasteful resource allocation system, in *Issues in Contemporary Microeconomics and Welfare*, ed. George Feiwel, 125–68. New York, NY: Macmillan.

[1986a] On informational decentralization and efficiency in resource allocation mechanisms, in *Studies in Mathematical Economics*, ed. Stanley Reiter, 238–350. Washington, DC: The Mathematical Association of America.

[1986b] On the stability of the tâtonnement approach to competitive equilibrium, in *Models of Economic Dynamics: Lecture Notes in Economics and Mathematical Systems Volume 264*, ed. Hugo F. Sonnenschein, 45–48. Berlin: Springer.

[1986c] On the implementation of social choice rules in irrational societies, in *Social Choice and Public decision-making: Essays in Honor of Kenneth Arrow, Volume 1*, ed. Walter Heller, Ross Starr, and David Starrett, 75–96. Cambridge, MA: Cambridge University Press.

[1987a] Arrow and the ascent of modern economic theory: Oral history III: An Interview, in *Arrow and the Ascent of Modern Economic Theory*, ed. George Feiwel, 258–92. New York, NY: New York University Press.

[1987b] Partners in crime: An interview, in *Arrow and the Foundations of the Theory of Economic Policy*, ed. George Feiwel, 663–65. New York, NY: New York University Press.

[1987c] Inventing new institutions: The design perspective, *American Journal of Agricultural Economics*, 69(2): 395–402. Reprinted in *The Foundations of the New Institutional Economics*, ed. Claude Menard (2004), 219–26. Lyme, NH: Elgar.

[1987d] On the demand generated by a smooth and concavifiable preference ordering (with James Jordan and Yakar Kannai), *Journal of Mathematical Economics*, 16(2): 169–89.

[1987e] Koopmans, Tjalling Charles (1910–85) (with Carl F. Christ), in *The New Palgrave: A Dictionary of Economics*, ed. John Eatwell, Murray Milgate, and Peter Newman, 62–67. New York, NY: Macmillan; 2nd ed., ed. Steven N. Durlauf and Lawrence E. Blume, Palgrave Macmillan, 2008 (online).

[1988a] Approximating a function by choosing a covering of its domain and *k* points from its range (with Thomas Marschak), *Journal of Complexity*, 4(2): 137–74.

[1988b] Optimal intertemporal allocation mechanisms and decentralization of decisions (with Mukul Majumdar), *Journal of Economic Theory*, 45(2): 228–61. Reprinted in *Decentralization in Infinite Horizon Economies*, ed. Mukul Majumdar, 12–45. Boulder, CO: Westview Press.

[1989a] Effects of entry on profits under monopolistic competition, in *The Economics of Imperfect Competition and Employment: Joan Robinson and Beyond*, ed. George R. Feiwel, 305–64. New York, NY: New York University Press.

[1989b] Mechanisms and institutions, in *Economic Institutions in a Dynamic Society: Search for a New Frontier*, ed. Takashi Shiraishi and Shigeto Tsuru, 87–104. New York, NY: St. Martin's Press.

1990s

[1990a] Different approaches to the economic analysis of institutions: Concluding comments, *Journal of Institutional and Theoretical Economics*, 146(1): 233–35. Reprinted in *The New Institutional Economics*, ed. Eirik G. Furubotn and Rudolf Richter (1991), 363–65. Tübingen: Mohr (Siebeck).

[1990b] On the generic non-optimality of dominant-strategy allocation mechanisms: A general theorem that includes pure exchange economies (with Mark Walker), *Econometrica*, 58(3): 683–704.

[1990c] A necessary condition for decentralization and an application to intertemporal allocation (with Hans Weinberger), *Journal of Economic Theory*, 51(2): 313–45. Reprinted in *Decentralization in Infinite Horizon Economies*, ed. Mukul Majumdar (1992), 119–51. Boulder, CO: Westview Press.

[1991a] Iterative planning procedures with a finite memory (with William Thomson), in *Theoretical Foundations of Development Planning, Volume 2*, ed. S. Bhagwan Dahiya, 109–25. New Delhi: Concept Publishing.

[1991b] The price mechanism, decentralization, and incentives, *Journal of Asian Economics*, 2(2): 185–99.

[1992a] Some issues in the transformation of ownership institutions in Poland: Comment, *Journal of Institutional and Theoretical Economics*, 148(1): 66–68.

[1992h] Problems of institutional analysis, in *Global Climate Change: Social and Economic Research Issues*, ed. Marian Rice, Joel Snow, and Harold Jacobson, 95–100. Chicago, IL: Midwest Consortium for International Security Studies and Argonne National Laboratory.

[1993a] Toward a framework for analyzing institutions and institutional change, in *Markets and Democracy: Participation, Accountability, and Efficiency*, ed. Samuel Bowles, Herbert Gintis, and Bo Gustafsson, 51–67. Cambridge, MA: Cambridge University Press. Chapter 13 this volume.

[1993b] Implementation and enforcement in institutional modeling, in *Political Economy: Institutions, Competition, and Representation*, ed. William A. Barnett, Melvin J. Hinich, and Norman J. Schofield, 51–59. Cambridge, MA: Cambridge University Press.

[1994a] Economic design, adjustment processes, mechanisms, and institutions, *Economic Design*, 1(1): 1–14. Chapter 14 this volume.

[1994b] Institutional change and the theory of mechanism design, *Academia Economic Papers*, 22(2): 1–27. Chapter 15 this volume.

[1995a] Feasible Nash implementation of social choice rules when the designer does not know endowments or production sets (with Eric Maskin and Andrew P. Postlewaite), in *The Economics of Informational Decentralization: Complexity, Efficiency and Stability; Essays in Honor of Stanley Reiter*, ed. John O. Ledyard, 367–433. Dordrecht: Kluwer Academic Publishers.

[1995b] Cores, almost competitive prices, and the approximate optimality of Walrasian allocations in discrete spaces, in *Nonlinear and Convex Analysis in Economic Theory*, ed. Toru Maruyama and Wataru Takahashi, 79–99. Berlin: Springer. Also (in Japanese translation) in Mita, *Journal of Economics*, 88(1): 86–105.

[1995c] What is the Coase theorem? *Japan and the World Economy*, 7(1): 49–74.

[1995d] Social absorption capability and economic development, in *Social Capability and Long-Term Economic Growth*, ed. Bon Ho Koo and Dwight H. Perkins, 123–41. New York, NY: St. Martin's Press.

[1996a] Beyond perfect competition, in *Education for Transition to Market Economy in Countries of Central and Eastern Europe: Conference Proceedings, Warsaw, June 29–30, 1995*, ed. Krzysztof Cichocki and Paul Marer, 191–201. Warsaw: Polish Fulbright Alumni Association.

[1996b] Institutions as families of game forms, *The Japanese Economic Review*, 47(2): 113–32. Reprinted in *The Foundations of the New Institutional Economics*, ed. Claude Menard (2004), 248–67. Lyme, NH: Elgar. Chapter 16 this volume.

[1998a] Issues in the design of mechanisms and institutions, in *Designing Institutions for Environmental and Resource Management*, ed. Edna T. Loehman and D. Marc Kilgour, 29–56. Lyme, NH: Elgar. Chapter 17 this volume.

[1998b] Harold Hotelling and the Neoclassical dream: A comment, in *Economics and Methodology: Crossing Boundaries*, ed. Roger Backhouse, Daniel Hausman, Uskali Mäki, and Andrea Salanti, 398–416. New York, NY: St. Martin's Press.

[1998c] Modelling institutional change, in *Economic Transformation and Integration: Problems, Arguments, Proposals*, ed. Roman Kulikowski, Zbigniew Nahorski, and Jan W. Owsinski. Systems Research Institute, Polish Academy of Sciences.

[1999a] Revisiting externalities, *Journal of Public Economic Theory*, 1(2): 225–45.

[1999b] Designing mechanisms, in particular for electoral systems: The majoritarian compromise (with Murat Sertel), in *Contemporary Economic Issues: Proceedings of the Eleventh World Congress and the International Economic Association, Tunis, Volume 4*, ed. Murat Sertel, 69–88. New York, NY: St. Martin's Press.

2000s

[2001a] Environmental Issues: Economic Perspectives, *Periphery*, 6/7: 81–85. Chapter 20 this volume.

[2001b] Transversals, systems of distinct representatives, mechanism design and matching (with Stanley Reiter), *Review of Economic Design*, 6(2): 289–304. Reprinted in *Markets, Games, and Organizations: Essays in Honor of Roy Radner*, ed. Tatsuro Ichiishi and Thomas Marschak, 163–78. Berlin: Springer, 2003.

[2003a] Mechanism design without games, in *Advances in Economic Design*, ed. Murat Sertel and Semih Koray, 429–37. Berlin: Springer. Chapter 11 this volume.

[2003b] Finite allocation mechanisms: Approximate Walrasian versus approximate direct revelation (with Thomas Marschak), *Economic Theory*, 21(2–3): 545–72.

[2003c] Comparing finite mechanisms (with Thomas Marschak), *Economic Theory*, 21(4): 783–841.

[2003d] Implicit functions and diffeomorphisms without C^1 (with Marcel K. Richter), in *Advances in Mathematical Economics, 5*, ed. Shigeo Kusuoka and Toru Maruyama, 65–96. Tokyo: Springer.

[2003e:] Optimization and Lagrange multipliers: Non-C^1 constraints and 'minimal' constraint qualifications (with Marcel K. Richter), in *Advances in Mathematical Economics, 5*, ed. Shigeo Kusuoka and Toru Maruyama, 97–151. Tokyo: Springer.

[2004] The informational efficiency of finite price mechanisms (with Thomas Marschak), in *Assets, Beliefs, and Equilibria in Economic Dynamics: Essays in Honor of Mordecai Kurz*, ed. Charalambos Aliprantis et al., 413–60. Berlin: Springer.

[2006] Implementation with unknown endowments in a two-trader pure exchange economy, in *Advances in Mathematical Economics, 8*, ed. Shigeo Kusuoka and Toru Maruyama, 257–71. Tokyo: Springer.

[2008] But who will guard the guardians?, *American Economic Review*, 98(3): 577–85; also in Le Prix Nobel (2007, 2008), 280–91.

Index